# Gap Years for Grown Ups

# Gap Years for Grown Ups

SUSAN GRIFFITH

Distributed in the USA by
The Globe Pequot Press, Guilford, Connecticut

VACATION WORK PUBLICATIONS

Published by Vacation Work, 9 Park End Street, Oxford
www.vacationwork.co.uk

*Gap Years for Grown-Ups*
**by Susan Griffith**

First edition 2004
Second edition 2006



ISBN 13: 978 1 85458 351 2
ISBN 10: 1 85458 351 4



Cover design by mccdesign ltd

Typeset by Guy Hobbs

Illustrations by John Taylor

Printed and bound in Italy by Legoprint SpA, Trento

# Contents

While every effort has been made to ensure that the information contained in this book was accurate at the time of going to press, some details are bound to change within the lifetime of this edition. If you do take a gap year or come across something which might be of interest to readers of the next edition, please write to Susan Griffith at Vacation-Work, 9 Park End Street, Oxford OX1 1HJ or e-mail her at susan@vacationwork.co.uk. Substantial contributions will be rewarded with a free copy of the next edition or any other Vacation-Work title (see inside back cover).

# PREFACE

As an enthusiastic traveller, I vividly remember my 26th birthday as a low point. Transalpino, for those too young to remember, offered at that time student and youth discounts on European rail travel to anyone under 26. For me, turning 26 marked the end of carefree youth as symbolised by the overnight doubling of rail fares. This of course was in the era before £37 no-frills flights to Berlin and Barcelona were accessible to everyone aged two to ninety-nine.

That dreaded watershed has been eroded in many other ways too. It may not yet be routine for ordinary people in their late twenties or in their middle years to disappear from their homes and jobs for extended periods, but the numbers are dramatically increasing. No longer is it the unique privilege of the young and of students to be able to contemplate taking time off to travel in search of adventure. The idea of leaving it all behind, of temporarily shedding responsibilities at home and at work, has become so mainstream that in recent months it has been championed in the online publication lawcareers.net, an American personal finance magazine and Saga magazine. A whole new market has suddenly materialised among those not in the first flush of youth for extended adventures and a chance to contribute something worthwhile abroad. Furthermore more and more firms are introducing a sabbatical policy.

Several decades ago, a commonplace vision of the future was one of vast quantities of leisure time. I am not sure what happened to that dream, but it certainly hasn't come true for the majority of us in hot pursuit of our careers. Rather than liberating us from the servitude of the office, the new technology seems to have enslaved us even further so that we are expected to be within email reach of the boss wherever we are. The answer to this patently unhealthy state of affairs is to absent ourselves properly for a life-enriching period of time.

The rising popularity among professionals and freelancers of taking three, six or twelve months out to travel, volunteer or study has prompted a corresponding increase in the number of programmes and schemes offered by specialist companies. These target not only the school leaver but the grown-up gapper as well. The path leading to exciting and memorable gap year experiences whether teaching in Mongolia, enjoying the café life of Melbourne or doing conservation in Mexico may be smoother than you think.

This book aims to canvas the possibilities as comprehensively as possible, and covers a wealth of both mainstream and obscure options. Enterprising and energetic grown-ups from all walks of life are beginning to realise that the opportunity to take time out is open to them, whether to join a project in some exotic part of the world, to enhance their CVs through improving a foreign language, or simply to see the world through fresh eyes.

In addition to providing practical and realistic advice about where and how to spend your gap year, these 352 pages aim to spark the imagination of anyone trying to decide whether or not to take time out.

**Susan Griffith**
**Cambridge**
**August 2006**

# ACKNOWLEDGMENTS

This second edition of Gap Years for Grown-ups owes a substantial debt to all the kind folk (some of them personal friends) who have told me how they finally came to bite the bullet and head off into the unknown. I never get tired of meeting and hearing from those intrepid (and sometimes not-so-intrepid) grown-ups who have set the workaday world to one side long enough to explore places and test dreams.

This new revised edition would not have been possible without the help and inspiration of grown-ups from all walks of life including a lorry driver and a Conservative party worker, all of whom have generously shared their information. Their insights and experiences have been enthusiastically received and have been distilled into the pages that follow. I won't list all the scores of people here who are included in the next section called Dramatis Personae and whose stories are quoted throughout the book. Special thanks are owed to Till Bruckner who has been writing to me since before he was a grown-up, and also to Phil Bond, Chrissie Ellison, Susanna Mann and Till Wahnbaeck.

I am also grateful to the many directors and PR staff of the specialist year out organisations who patiently rooted round in their client files to put me in touch with grown-ups who have had some amazing experiences on their various gap years.

The photographs for the colour section have been supplied by MondoChallenge of Malsor House, Gayton Road, Milton Malsor, Northampton NN7 3AB (☎01604-858225; www.mondochallenge.org). MondoChallenge is a UK based non-profit organisation, sending volunteers to work on teaching and business development in Africa, Asia and South America. The average age of a MondoChallenge volunteer is 29 years, while 50% are non-UK based and couples/families are welcome.

Mondo Challenge

*Foundation*

International development

# DRAMATIS PERSONAE

All of these individuals, couples and families have generously shared their memories, insights and pearls of travelling and volunteering wisdom since the first edition of this book was published in 2004. Turn to the Personal Case Histories at the end of the book for more detailed accounts from some of these and other enterprising grown-ups.

**Andrew Allright** was working in the market risk division of a bank when he took advantage of its sabbatical scheme. He negotiated 13 weeks of unpaid leave and signed up with MondoChallenge to work at a school in Kalimpong, Northern India, where every day was spent in view in the foothills of the Himalaya teaching the children.

**Lucy Bailey** found herself at age 31 with a broken heart looking for a way to make herself feel good about life again. Travel had worked in the past so she signed up with The Leap to spend four months in Kenya, divided between working at an eco-lodge and at a wildlife park resort.

**Mark Bernhardt** had completed his two years as a Newly Qualified Teacher in Hampshire and was free to arrange a year off before getting a permanent post as a sports science teacher. With his keen interest in sport and fitness the programmes of Gapsport appealed to him so he spent five months coaching basketball in a suburb of Accra, Ghana. He even wrote a coaching manual to be used throughout Ghanaian schools.

**Jenna Bonistalli's** mother had given her a gift after her graduation from NYU to be spent on the trip of her choice. At first she planned to blow the money on an African safari but then she began to think she would rather spend it on something that would benefit humanity as well as herself. So she spent six months volunteering in India, first at a school in the Himalayas and later working for an NGO (found after a search on the Internet) that organises health and education outreach to a number of villages in rural Rajasthan.

**Jake Brumby** heard from a friend about the volunteer programme of the Orangutan Foundation and thought it sounded fantastic. Since he wanted to spend some of his six-month gap travelling in Australia and New Zealand, a conservation project in Borneo was just the ticket. Although he did not negotiate a sabbatical with the website development company that employed him, they took him back as soon as he got back.

**Gillian Drake** was looking for a way of breaking out of the daily routines that get in the way of life, after 24 'glorious and varied' years in the same job. She decided to spend ten weeks teaching English to children and adults in Sri Lanka through i-to-i. To her surprise she found that taking three months out was far easier both practically and emotionally than she expected.

**Cheryl Drewitz** is a paramedic working in Ontario who volunteered with the US organisation Cosmic Volunteers at a rural clinic in Machakos, Kenya. Although many agencies have medical programmes for nurses and doctors, she had to search hard for a placement suitable for someone like her interested in different ways of practising medicine.

**Jen Dyer** wanted to find out more about careers in the humanitarian and development sector so took up an unpaid internship at the Oxfam office in Oxford. The months she spent there persuaded her to pursue a Masters degree at Manchester Uni in Environment and Development.

**Paul Egan** is a 48 year old retail manager who did an 11-week snowboarding instructor course in the Canadian Rockies last year with Nonstop Ski.

**Stuart Everard** was assigned by Challenges Worldwide to work in Ecuador helping deploy internet services in schools. He did not expect that working in a developing country, for an organisation with a lower quality of management, would improve his professional skills, but found that it did.

**Debra Fuccio** from California has taken a series of gap years in Europe, Taiwan, Argentina and most recently Guatemala to improve her Spanish, go trekking and see the sights.

**Patricia Gott** had owned and managed a roller skating rink in the US for 24 years before selling her business in August of 2005 and signing up as a volunteer with Cross-Cultural Solutions. After helping local women in Moshi Municipality, Tanzania, make the most of their batik business, she concluded that Americans are glutted with riches but have poverty of the soul.

**Eva Hagen** from Sweden was semi-retired when she signed up for a conservation/farming project on a homestead in Australia, having harboured a life-long dream to live and work there.

**Jo Hanbury** had been number-crunching for too long and decided to join a VentureCo expedition to Patagonia with a group of like-minded stress-fleeing strangers. She learned some Spanish in Peru, spent a month in the Andes on a reforestation project and some did serious trekking. Three months turned out not to be enough so she carried on travelling solo to Australia and China.

**Peter and Debra Hardy** from Okehampton had toyed for years with the idea of doing voluntary work abroad but it was not until their children were safely installed in universities that they took the leap. Peter negotiated some weeks off from the veterinary practice where he worked as a manager while Debra had just qualified as a nurse and not yet started her job. They took a weekend TEFL course in preparation for their placements in Surin in western Thailand and both enjoyed the teaching and travelling far more than expected.

**Marjorie Harris** resigned as headteacher of a girls' school in Surrey and followed in her son's footsteps by enlisting with Teaching & Projects Abroad. In her case she volunteered in Peru, Bolivia and later Argentina, working with teachers and at orphanages.

**Bryan Havenhand** had been publishing work and travel books for many years in Australia and in 2005 decided to take his own advice by moving with his wife and teenage daughter to Siem Reap in Cambodia for a year.

**Bradwell Jackson** gave up his job as a youth counsellor in the United States to work and travel the world at whim. His first foray was to Mexico where he found a teaching job and a host family with minimal effort. At the time of writing he was in England planning to go on to France for the summer in the hope of finding more teaching work.

**Paul Jones** had already given up an IT job in his native Australia and found paid work in the Netherlands and then England. He then heard about the charity Volunteer Africa through whom he joined a volunteer project in a remote part of Tanzania. After coming back to the UK to earn more money, he is off this summer to work at a summer camp in Russia.

**Caroline Kippen** decided to take a gap year in the depths of winter when life had lost its savour and she was overcome with job dissatisfacton. She went on a two-month round-the-world trip and then volunteered for an HIV/AIDS education programme in Africa through SPW where she now works as their Recruiting and Marketing Co-ordinator.

**Paul Kirk** accepted voluntary redundancy from his post as associate dean, rented out his house and took up several placements through *MondoChallenge* in Sri Lanka, India and Tanzania.

**Peter Larter** from Australia was born in Africa and had always had an urge to give something back to that continent by participating in a development project. A supportive CEO provided him with the opportunity to take a break to volunteer in Tanzania. Although the fees were expensive he soon realised that the biggest contribution was the money donated to the project rather than his labour and was quite happy with that arrangement.

**Nick Leader** is a semi-retired college administrator in his late 60s who piloted a volunteer scheme at a township school in Cape Town at the behest of the new sending agency People & Places. Although he concluded that volunteers go out as idealists and come back as realists, he still felt his contribution had been worthwhile.

**Tara Leaver** had wanted to take a round the world tour for several years, but it had never seemed the right time. A six-week placement with *Teaching & Projects Abroad* in a Mexican school the previous summer gave her the taste for a year out, and an inheritance gave her the wherewithal. Her employer (at a Montessori nursery) and all her friends and family were very supportive, knowing what a significant step this was since Tara had suffered from depression for many years. At last report in 2006 she was on a building project in Costa Rica, only six weeks into her year-long gap year.

**David MacKintosh** had been working at a frenetic pace for the Conservative Party in the run-up to the 2005 General Election and had accrued so much holiday time that he was prompted to think of something out of the ordinary to do with it. With hardly any time to research and anticipate his trip, he turned to

MondoChallenge who arranged for him to teach at the Lotus Academy near Darjeeling. He was so impressed with the set-up that on his return he helped set up a school sponsorship scheme for the area.

**Susanna Mann** had come to the end of a freelance marketing contract and wanted to go travelling, but with a purpose. She decided to go back to her favourite country, India, where she had first landed in Calcutta aged 18, and donate her time and talents to an NGO-run business development project in West Bengal.

**Ed McFadd** had moved north of San Diego after retiring as a school teacher and school principal on is sixtieth birthday and marrying a lovely woman two days later. He then had the leisure to pursue a long dormant interest in the French language and France. He signed up on a full-time language course in the nearest French-speaking place, Montreal and is now planning to spend six months in France in 2008.

**Stephanie Metcalfe** spent the winter of 2005/2006 in Helsinki because her husband's employer had given him the chance to work abroad. Initially she arranged a sabbatical from her job as a social worker but when the stay in Finland was extended, she resigned. She worked as a live-out nanny for two young dual heritage children (American father, Finnish mother).

**Giselle Minoli** is a fine jewelry designer in New York and a writer working on a memoir about her parents. She has always wanted to visit her father's native Italy with an in-depth knowledge of his language and dreams of standing in the exact spot in Florence from which in 1932 he made the pen and drawing that hangs in her living room. In 2006 she enrolled in an Italian language course at the Università per Stranieri in Siena.

**David Moncur** chose the redundancy package from his employer in publishing rather than relocate to Sweden (November 2005). He relished the prospect of taking up to one year off to travel, pursue interests and explore the possibilities of becoming a freelance consultant in his area of expertise. He spent much of the winter travelling and visiting friends in New Zealand and Australia and is yet to decide whether his redundancy money will stretch to another trip to Asia or Latin America in the autumn.

**Jen Moon** is an energetic single mother who was determined to keep a promise to herself to do something really memorable for her fortieth birthday. She arranged to travel round-the-world for four months with her two young daughters Lisa and Sarah. By the time the family returned home to Northeast England (Easter 2006), Jen felt a huge sense of achievement and therefore more at peace with herself. She now runs a website www.grownupgapyear.co.uk.

**Anne Morris** from the US may be near retirement age, but she still considers herself a free spirit and gave up a small business designing ponchos (called Grandcaper) to move to Prague two years ago and obtain a TEFL Certificate from TEFL Worldwide. She looks forward to becoming a 'gypsy wanderer', living and working in interesting parts of the world such as China and the United Emirates. She just wishes she'd made this discovery much earlier in life.

**Neil Munro** had emerged from a family trauma battered and bruised and in need of a dramatic change of scene. Through Travellers Worldwide, he spent months at a game park in Zimbabwe learning patiently how to bond with lion cubs, something he never thought that he would be doing at age 66.

**Richard Nimmo** originally planned an escape from the pressures of work for three or four months but this stretched into 16 months. He volunteered on the Marine Conservation programme in Madagascar run by Blue Ventures for whom he now works full-time in London.

**Clodagh O'Brien** from Ireland had been living in London for some years working in science journalism when he decided he needed a break to decide what his next step would be personally and professionally. He travelled extensively in Southeast Asia and included a stint as a volunteer working with orangutans in a remote rainforest in Borneo.

**Paddy Pringle** was 28 when he took a break from his job as an economic development consultant to volunteer in Africa. Through the mediating agency 2Way Development he found an appropriate placement at an NGO called FUGA in Uganda. The longer he was there, the more he realised that progress had to be measured by the little steps forward rather than aiming for the lofty, if naïve, ambitions he had had when he arrived.

**Alefiya Rajkotwala** found out about her employer Accenture's partnership with VSO and spent nine months working in the field of education in Rwanda.

**Diane Ralph** participated in Cross-Cultural Solutions' Russia programme with her nephew, as part of a six-month break to celebrate her 50th birthday. She volunteered in an orphanage and a home for the elderly, both in Yaroslavl.

**Debbie Risborough** was coming up to 40 and enjoying her job in accountancy with a small friendly firm. Yet she was bored and restless enough to ignore her nerves and her mother's misgivings, and to take off to see the world for 14 months. She took advantage of volunteering opportunities in many of the countries to which she travelled, including India, Australia, Fiji, South Africa, Argentina and Canada. Within ten days of returning to the UK, she had landed a job with an NGO working in the Sudan where she met a man she married not long after and whose baby she was expecting at the time of writing.

**Marcelle Salerno** was laid off after two decades working in the insurance industry in the United States and decided to live off savings and investments for up to five years and to divide that time among the five continents. She has come to the conclusion that paying to volunteer in exotic places like the Seychelles or African game parks is an economic way to experience these marvellous places.

**Barbara Schick** is an Austrian freelance photographer who followed her husband when he was posted to Brazil. She had a wonderful time extending her portfolio and volunteering through the charity Iko Poran (see entry) with a Rio NGO which uses film projects to help deprived children from the *favelas.*

**Jackie Smith** and her husband Peter Greig had been working for many years and were keen to take six months out to get some perspective on their work and family choices for the future. They spent just under half their time volunteering through MondoChallenge in India and the rest travelling in India, Nepal and Vietnam. The trip has made Jackie want to focus more on a contribution to society rather than simply consuming her way through life.

**David Storey** is a 30 year old HGV driver who began to feel guilty that all his lorry-driving colleagues on the continent spoke to him in English. He signed up with CESA for a three-month French language course in Bordeaux.

**Siamak Tannazi** was 29 when she decided to apply to her boss at BT for a six-month break, partly in response to the tragedy of the Tsunami which she felt would draw potential volunteers away from unaffected areas in India and elsewhere. With the help of Changing Worlds, she arranged to teach at a village school in Kerala India for three months and travelled for the rest.

**Mark Tanner** is a serial career-gapper who tries to take off one year in three from his job in Wellington New Zealand. When he was in Canada, he worked as a market research co-ordinator for an online nanny agency in Vancouver and then cycled solo 8,000km across the country in winter. More recently he spent six months teaching English in Khartoum, learning a little Arabic and familiarising himself with the culture, as good preparation for completing the first unbroken paddle from the source of the Blue Nile in Ethiopia to the mouth at Rosetta in Egypt.

**Davide Tassi** from Italy began to find the corporate world in which he worked falling short of his ideals and ambitions, so funded himself to spend a year in Latin America. He divided the time between assisting with a business development project in Ecuador and volunteering with 6 to 12 years olds at the National Circus School in Rio through Iko Poran.

**Till Wahnbaeck**, a 34 year old from Switzerland, used the first edition of this book when preparing for his leave of absence from Proctor & Gamble in 2005 to work on an HIV/AIDS business project near Arusha, Tanzania. He described his experience as a 'Mini-MBA in Applied Entrepreneurship.'

**Allan Westray** and his wife were comfortably off after Allan sold his wine-importing company, and decided to travel and volunteer in India.

**Lindsay Whitlock** with husband Nick and two children took a thrilling year off to travel round the world, all recorded on their website www.thewhitlocks.org.uk.

**Rachael Wood** from Kent took a large chunk of time out to travel and was converted to the concept. She now works as marketing manager for the company Gap Year for Grown Ups.

**Sylvia Wright** was a Council youth worker in her early 30s who, once she had cleared her debts left over from university, decided to fulfil her ambition to travel the world as an itinerant volunteer for ten months.

# Introduction

The rise and rise of the gap year has become one of the travel sensations of the past decade. Now that the concept is firmly embedded in the consciousness of school leavers, grown-ups are beginning to catch on too. Statistics in this area are fiendishly difficult to establish but, according to research published by the market analyst Mintel in 2005 in a report called 'Denture Venturers and Career Gappers,' there are almost as many British pre-retirement gappers as pre-university gappers. It has been consistently estimated that 200,000 people take gap years and this figure has been steadily rising.

An article in *The Times* (June 2005) reinforces this by identifying the biggest trend in travel as the number of '28-40 year old career breakers who are opting out of the rat race in search of a better work-life balance.' A staggering 40% of the population under 35 in full-time employment claim that they have considered trading a high-pressured life for a simpler and better quality of life, which very often includes travel, adventure and volunteering. Just as adults and young people have swapped the teacher/learner roles when it comes to using new technologies, so the 18 year olds have introduced to an older generation the notion that taking time away can cure all sorts of ills, primarily stress and burn-out – just as likely to be suffered by a teacher, IT contract worker or accountant as by a pre-university student examined within an inch of his or her life.

The concept of a break is central to the natural world. We spend a third of our lives sleeping at night to rejuvenate ourselves for the day. Why then should it be considered self-indulgent or lazy to take a chunk of time out of our working lives to pursue a different agenda? When work becomes onerous, stressful or dull and begins to swamp other interests, it might be time to reclaim our lives by taking a break.

**GAP YEARS FOR GROWN UPS**

A gap year can embrace anything from a period of rest and relaxation to an opportunity for reassessing goals and reconnecting with our real values. For some it is simply a case of itchy feet; for others it is a chance to test an alternative vocation or spend time with loved ones. Taking stock periodically allows us to look beyond the details to the bigger picture. The individuals who have shared their experiences during the research for this book each illustrates how liberating and important a gap year can be.

The gap year between leaving school and attending higher education is now a well-established transition between childhood dependence and adult maturity. A new trend is for the parents of these teenagers and their contemporaries to follow suit. A desire to trek in distant mountain ranges, volunteer in an African village, take a cookery course in Italy is not unique to youth.

In response to the sometimes overwhelming demands of our jobs and the news that we may be expected to work until well past the current retirement age, the notion of a career break is becoming more attractive. One more week dealing with a broken photocopier or waking in the night with your head spinning with office tasks and politics may force your hand. Setting a boundary between the personal and the professional is essential for maintaining good mental health.

The stories in this book establish that taking a gap year can be a choice for everyone, not just people with authority and wealth nor those who want to drop out. Now that institutions like National Health Trusts, large supermarket chains and multinational companies recognise the value of breaks for their employees, they are establishing the principle that time out from work is more than just an eccentric and nostalgic hankering for freedom from responsibility. The idea is gradually gaining legitimacy in the corporate world. Government too is pushing the concept of a work-life balance so that family life will not be sacrificed on the altar of Mammon. When people step back and do the calculations, they often conclude that the balance needs to be shifted a little bit more in favour of life.

Gap years have nearly become part of the zeitgeist, the spirit of the age we live in. Every week it is possible to find references in the media to adventurous grown-ups taking off as individuals, couples or families. A prime illustration of this was the airing on BBC2 in 2005 of a mainstream observational documentary *Grown-up Gappers* which featured eight individuals who had temporarily packed in their everyday lives to explore the world. (The BBC maintains some general information on the subject on its website www.bbc.co.uk/holiday/tv_and_radio/grown_up_gappers.) As the number of people who are pioneering this choice increases and in a society where the span of working life is stretching well beyond forty years, taking breaks may eventually become routine.

Trawling the Internet will lead you to the 'blogs' of any number of heroes and eccentrics who have thrown over safe secure jobs to do something fresh and inspiring. For example the Fleming family whose 'Family Tale of a Global Adventure' can be read at www.rfleming.net/aboutus.htm completed a round-the-world trip a few years ago. The media has shown huge interest in the phenomenon of older people kicking over the traces. For example *The Times* published the first instalment by the Tims family ('The Rats Can Race Without Us,' June 2006) as they prepared to set off on their adventurous travels in Africa and beyond with their children aged four, six and eight.

The *Independent* published an article called 'Gap Years for All' with the sub-

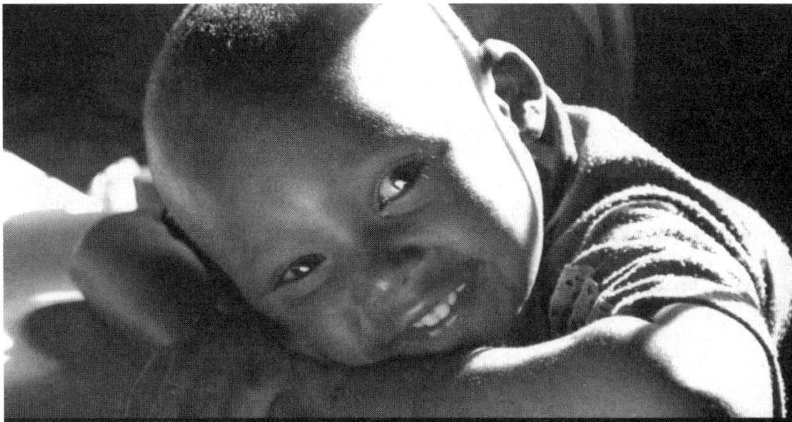

head 'Gap years are too important to be the sole preserve of the young'. An online BBC debate on the topic 'Are gap years a waste of time?' attracted a number of adults who waxed enthusiastic: one wrote 'My wife and I decided to take two years out to travel, read and hang out, which was the best, mostliberating 24 months we've ever had. We're better people – mentally, physically and socially. Gap years are the best thing anyone could do.' At the other end of the spectrum the mass market women's magazine *Win & Go* was recently looking for career gappers to help with a feature on gap years for its magazine full of 'true life holiday stories'.

A large expanse of time can be the ideal opportunity to stretch yourself or to act on a long-held ambition whether it be to navigate the Amazon, help to rescue orangutans in Borneo or perform music. Big dreams and long-range goals give people something to aim for, and the bigger the dreams, the more the dreamer achieves. Striving for different experiences is a way of feeling that we have done something with our lives and it could be something as simple as exploring the Pyramids or Tibet. This trend also complements another recent travel phenomenon, the growing interest in ethical or responsible travel.

One of the most ardent advocates of pursuing a dream has been the journalist Matthew Parris. Having turned 50, he felt stuck in a rut and in need of a change so he went to live on the bleak and remote Kerguelen Island close to Antarctica for four months, which he had hoped to visit once in his lifetime since first finding it on a map as a boy. His articles in *The Times* chronicle how he gradually adjusted to the loss of all that was familiar. Writing of his decision to go, he summed up the common fantasy of escape that many feel at some point in their lives:

> *Everybody, every busy man or woman, must have experienced the urge to drop everything. In moments of fatigue, moments when either the workload or the routine – the sameness of things – get on top of us, who has not offered a silent prayer: 'Beam me up. Pluck me out. Whisk me away. Sweep me off my feet.' Each has an impossible dream about how we might abdicate. For some it would be holy orders in a monastery beneath Mount Sinai; for some, the ascent of Everest, the Foreign Legion or a new life sketching wild flowers on the Isles of Scilly. And for others it might be a glorious slide into as many of the seven deadly sins as it proved possible to embrace.*

But a gap year shouldn't be viewed purely as an escape. There's a larger purpose too, which some view as an almost spiritual search for meaning beyond material satisfaction. In the developed world, work has undoubtedly brought great material comforts and technological progress has also suppressed the threat of hunger and mitigated the worst effects of disease. But you may find that you have to look elsewhere for happiness. Some of us have become too fixated on economics and money to be able to gauge the value of experiences.

Try not to view a gap year as a self-indulgence, but simply a period to regain your balance. More ambitiously, it can be a rite of passage like learning to swim again, that moment in childhood of heading out of your depth in the water to learn that instead of sinking, you float.

Some accounts of taking time out resemble mythological journeys of self-discovery. **Deborah Howell** eloquently captures the awe-inspiring benefits of a personal odyssey:

*In terms of what I actually 'did' during my year out, the answer is everything! I visited monuments and art galleries. I climbed glaciers and went white water rafting. I met hill tribe people and holy men. I swam with dolphins and sharks. I spent an entire day trying to send a parcel in India. I lay on beaches and sailed around desert islands. I climbed pyramids and temples and was awed by the giant Ayers Rock. I panned for opals in an underground Australian town and was offered and declined the chance to get involved in smuggling. I walked away from Las Vegas a winner and flew through the Grand Canyon. I sang karaoke with the locals in China and listened to the voice of Peter Ustinov guide me round the Forbidden City. I played with children in the Vietnamese jungle amidst the ruins of shot down helicopters. I slept in palaces and in squalid, depressing places. I sat on buses and trains for hours and relaxed on deserted white sandy beaches. I snorkelled with exotic fish and found a scorpion snuggled in my shorts! I missed friends and family and met some wonderful people. I fell in love with some countries and cultures and hated others. Like I say, I did everything.*

# Taking the Plunge

## What is a Gap Year?

In the first place a gap year need not be literally twelve months long. Mini gaps lasting a couple of months can be invigorating and bring with them all the benefits extolled throughout this book. But the expression 'gap quarter-year' is unlikely to catch on (just as a new coinage 'quarter-life crisis' is unlikely to achieve common currency).

The term Gap Year must remain a loose one but, essentially, it means changing the regular pattern of your working life over a period that is longer than just a regular holiday. A short gap 'year' might last six weeks, though the premise of this book is that you will have three, six or twelve months of freedom from professional obligations, a miraculous period of time in which to pursue dreams and create memories.

In academia and the teaching profession, the notion of a sabbatical is established by tradition. A sabbatical leave of absence from duties allows a teacher or lecturer to recharge, refresh their knowledge of a subject, conduct original research or join an exchange programme. Whereas sabbaticals are earned with loyal service and are normally paid, gap years or career breaks tend to be thought of as self-granted and unpaid. But sabbaticals are a version of gap years and the expression 'career sabbatical' is often used by companies that permit them. In business the concept of an earned break is becoming more common as an incentive for staying on with the same employer. Typically, after a fixed period of time, the employee is allowed to take up to a specified number of weeks off, normally without pay but without loss of benefits like pension contributions. Where there is no formal policy of granting career breaks, employees are negotiating unpaid gap years on a discretionary basis, a concept which is gaining wider acceptance.

For example at the Nationwide Building Society, employees may apply for up to six months unpaid sabbatical while tax and auditing firm Deloitte offers its loyal employees the possibility of up to two years unpaid leave. Other firms stipulate that time off must be used for personal development; for example Avis has introduced such a sabbatical scheme and makes £250 awards available for deserving employees. A gap year may take place as a pause from a specific job to which you fully intend to return. Alternatively it can encompass leaving one job to further your education or take the opportunity to experience an extended period of travel before returning home to look for new employment. In either case your professional life is put on hold.

Going abroad is not an essential component since career breaks at home are perfectly feasible. For some it might simply mean stepping off the treadmill or whatever metaphor you wish to use, to slow down or spend more time with children, immerse yourself in a hobby or do full-time voluntary work. You don't need to leave the country to take a challenging journey. A gap year is more disruptive than a holiday, but that is precisely its appeal. It demands a level of radical change in your normal routine.

A gap year provides a chance to re-connect with former interests and old friends or to acquire new interests and new friends beyond the boundaries of work. Emotionally, your activities during a break may reawaken old loves, introduce new interests and act to inspire your efforts back in the workplace.

**A gap year involves six stages:**

- *The Dream* – This might be associated with a specific ambition (e.g. to see the world) or just a longing to get out of your present circumstances
- *The Determination* – Achieving the confidence to go ahead and do it
- *Persuading the Boss (or delegating your business)* – Employers are increasingly aware that it is in their interests to grant unpaid leave
- *The Practicalities* – Organising your life, partner, family, mortgage, finances and so on must be given careful consideration
- *The Break Itself* – What you can do with a stint away from work
- *Re-entry* – What differences can a gap year make when it comes to an end?

## PURSUING A DREAM

Grown-up gap years are for people who don't want to end up saying 'I could have' or 'I should have' instead of 'I did.' The decision is never easy. Some experience 'Road to Damascus' revelation when suddenly they feel a compulsion to pursue a specific dream or escape an unsatisfactory situation. Others take years of toying with the idea, taking a few tentative steps before they finally discover the wherewithal to carry through the idea. While pursuing a career in the city, 30-something Roz Savage claims to have imagined two possible obituaries for herself: the safe and dull one and the risky and daring one, which is why she found herself giving up her career and in 2006 rowing across the Atlantic by herself.

There seems to be no end to the original and energetic ways found by working people of all ages to spend two or four, six or twelve scintillating months. Once you have squared taking a break from work, either by sorting something out with your employer or working out the financial implications if you are self-employed, it all gets much easier. After you have explained to your friends and family that you have decided to take a chunk of time off work (they will either be envious or disapproving) and once you have booked your flight, enrolled in a course, contacted some voluntary organisations, put a specific project in motion or embarked on whatever you want to do with your gap year, the rest seems to look after itself.

## Is a Gap Year Right for Me?

Anyone who has uttered the words, 'How I'd love to be a …' or 'I'd give anything to see…' is a possible candidate for achieving their dream on a career break. People sometimes hide behind an assumption that something they dream of doing is impossible because of the pressures of work and home life. While airing your fantasies, your family or friends might be tempted to say, 'Why don't you just go ahead and do it?' – whatever it is, such as write a play, build a harpsichord, renovate a bothy, climb Kilimanjaro with your children, work for Mother Teresa's charity in Calcutta, explore your genealogy.

Humphrey Walters, an international management training guru (www.humphreywalters.com), believes that the most important element is the simple decision to take a break:

> *Once you make a decision to take a sabbatical, to do something, you don't need to base it on an event or activity. If you wait for something to drop out of the woodwork, it won't happen and a lot of people do. People should simply take the plunge because the payoff is massive. The trick is to create the dream for yourself. Look for a dream. At the outset you don't need to know what it is.*

## Who Can Take a Gap Year?

Taking a year off is a luxury, a product of a wealthy society. If you suggested the concept to say a Nepali porter, Brazilian taxi driver or Polish farmer, they would think you were speaking Martian. But in the privileged west, people from many backgrounds, not just an elite few, have the freedom to exercise the choice to withdraw temporarily from work. This is a freedom that should be cherished and not squandered.

The thesis of this book is that ordinary people can entertain extraordinary ambitions and do extraordinary things. An eye-catching ad campaign was run by VSO (Voluntary Service Overseas) to persuade ordinary working people to consider a stint of voluntary work. A flyer read: 'The tanned, toned, blonde Australian Ironman Champion who normally hands out these flyers is in Liverpool helping to build a youth centre for disabled children.' Another one was displayed prominently on a truck: 'This truck should have been towed away but the driver is away in Peru rescuing llamas by four-wheel drive.' People on ordinary wages have managed to save enough money to fund trips to far corners of the world to do amazing things.

When you are wondering whether you are the right sort to take a break from work, do not imagine that your circumstances are peculiarly disadvantageous. We have come across:

- A school inspector who at age 55 took a four-month sabbatical in 2006 to work at an orphanage in Argentina.
- An American jewelry designer who went to Italy to perfect her English so that she could translate some family papers.
- Two parents and their 13 year old daughter who lived for a year in Siem Reap (near Angkor Wat) in Cambodia.
- A bored accountant who during her 14-month gap year volunteered in India and South Africa, joined a diving expedition in Fiji, taught in Argentina and travelled across Canada.
- A plumber who joined a scientific expedition in Malawi to mark his 50th birthday.
- A sales manager for a radio station who gave it up to join a marine conservation project in Madagascar.
- A self-employed tree surgeon from Northern Ireland who has worked as a staff volunteer on Raleigh International expeditions in Namibia, Borneo and Chile.
- A young teacher who coached basketball in Ghana.
- A single mother who took her two young daughters out of school to travel in Australia, New Zealand and the USA for four months.
- An Italian working for a multinational in London who volunteered with poor children in Rio at the national Circus School.
- A journalist who left her desk at the *Daily Telegraph* to travel the world solo (and report back to the paper).

## THE DETERMINATION TO REALISE YOUR DREAM

Deciding to take a period of time off work and then deciding how to spend it may not be as momentous as some other life decisions like choosing a life partner, having babies, choosing or changing careers, but it is as individual. It certainly takes guts and that is an essential ingredient in achieving a break from your career. The hardest step is summoning up the determination simply to get up and leave. No book or even trusted adviser can make the decision for you. All that outsiders can do is set out the possibilities and see if any of them takes your fancy enough to pursue. Do as much research as possible, let the ideas swill around in your head and see what floats up.

There is no doubt that it is far easier to stay on the funicular of employment that chugs along its tracks to the goal of retirement. After all, that is exactly what the majority of working people still do. For many people in work, the decision to treat oneself to a sabbatical is a difficult and complex one. The first question to ask yourself is: does the idea have a strong appeal? Do you get a buzz if you close your eyes and imagine yourself trekking through a Costa Rican rainforest or teaching in a Tanzanian village school or studying in an Italian language class? The next question is, do you have the energy to make the dream actual?

One of the most radical career breaks that could be imagined is described in David Grant's *The Seven Year Hitch* (Pocket Books, 2000; £7.99), the Preface of which provides a glimpse into the author's motivation for setting off from Scotland for China in a horse-drawn caravan with his wife and three young children:

> *The journey was a private venture, undertaken for no great cause or deserving charity. It did, however, have a purpose. We wanted to give our children a wide look at the world they will inherit, in the hope that experience of different places, peoples and cultures will enable them to become more understanding, caring, tolerant and wiser citizens of it than if they had simply slogged through the National Curriculum...As far as can be judged at this point, I think we have probably achieved it.*

David Grant's initial inspiration came from Apsley Cherry-Garrard's *The Worst Journey in the World*, the classic account of an Antarctic expedition in 1910-1913:

> *Exploration is the physical expression of the Intellectual Passion... Some will tell you that you are mad, and nearly all will say, 'What is the use?' For we are a nation of shopkeepers, and no shopkeeper will look at research which does not promise him a financial return within a year. And so you will sledge nearly alone, but those with whom you sledge will not be shopkeepers; that is worth a good deal.*

## Reasons to be Tempted

We all fantasise about taking extended time off from work. But acting on this fantasy is a daunting prospect. What are the practical implications for our careers, families and daily responsibilities? Much depends on the complexity of our lives and to what extent we rely on the structures and routines we have built to provide personal security, self-esteem, professional achievement and financial stability. Younger people in their late twenties and early thirties with fewer commitments are better placed to take an extended break. However, individuals in their forties and fifties will be more likely to have a degree of financial security and better professional qualifications, which may allow a smoother return to professional life.

Sometimes we just need to step back from work to put our lives in perspective or re-evaluate our goals, professional or otherwise. People sometimes feel that their lives have become too detached from simple pleasures and the rhythms of nature. Even if the gap year you choose does not specifically focus on the natural world, exposure to beautiful landscapes is often a by-product of travel and volunteering in distant lands, as **David MacKintosh** commented about his *MondoChallenge* placement teaching in Kalimpong in West Bengal:

> *I had gone from a bustling office (Conservative Party HQ), with people screaming of political scandal and urgent deadlines, to the calm tranquillity of the Himalayas with snow-topped Kanchenjunga in the background and no mobile reception for days!*

Perhaps you have simply become miserable in your job and want a complete change. Sometimes people are pushed into a career break against their wishes (and not just members of the acting profession). Economic recession or an employer's financial misfortunes may force a period of unemployment or under-employment. One of the most common reasons is to be with a partner or spouse who is living and working elsewhere. For example freelance photographer **Barbara Schick** followed her husband when he was posted to Brazil and had a wonderful time extending her portfolio and volunteering with *Iko Poran* with the Rio charity Nos do Cinema which works with children from the *favelas* (and was involved with the making of the film *City of God).*

At a deep level some people are dissatisfied with their lives, not necessarily because of their job but for reasons unrelated to work. Perhaps your relationship is foundering and it is time to break free for a while. Perhaps you are single and are longing for a shake-up in your social life. Perhaps your children have recently left home and you and your partner are looking for a new activity to fill the emptiness at home. Perhaps you have come into an inheritance on the death of a relative or found yourself with a windfall. Your personal circumstances may have altered for any number of reasons making it possible in practical terms for the first time to consider a break from work.

Provided you can delegate or shed your responsibilities (see chapter *Nuts and Bolts* for advice), ask yourself 'why shouldn't I take a gap year?' In all probability you have worked very hard and earned the right to step back temporarily from the demands of your job, to concentrate on yourself for a change. It's a period for establishing your values, for appreciating what you really value in your life.

## TRIGGERS AND MOTIVES

Most of us sail along on our normal work-a-day and domestic course more or less contentedly. But then something happens that throws us off-course and makes us wonder where the meaning lies in our ordinary routines. Why do we have to spend hours every day on crowded tube trains or in boring meetings or placating irate bosses? When was the last time we gasped with amazement at some new sight or laughed out loud at some absurdity?

Sometimes we have no choice in the matter. Women are lucky in this respect. Many have a career break thrust upon them when a baby is born. Few experiences in life so radically change daily routines as the birth of a child. Most new mothers stay away from work for their full entitlement of 26 weeks and many take extra unpaid maternity leave knowing that their jobs are guaranteed (see chapter *Taking the Family*).

People who are made redundant and are forced to take a career break are less lucky but even this can have a positive outcome. Understandably, people can be thrown into total consternation by redundancy but with luck and determination, this will only last 48 hours. If you have marketable skills, you may find that it will mark a liberation, as it does for many who treat themselves to an exciting break with their redundancy money and then come home to make their way as a freelancer, thereby achieving a more balanced lifestyle.

Sometimes there is an identifiable event or circumstance which prompts a desire to do something a bit mad. It is not unusual for career breaks to follow in the wake of a failed romance, as one 30 year old gapper described it: 'The main catalyst for going was that I had just had my heart well and truly trampled over and I felt that by far the best way was to go abroad to feel good about life once again'.

But often it is the culmination of a background urge long suppressed – to do something selfless, to pursue a sport, to swim with dolphins before you die, whatever it is. The worst thing about doing the same thing for years on end is how it makes time speed up. Because there is so little to delineate one day from another, the days all collapse in on one another and get compacted, as if by a computer programme trying to make more space. But if you do something completely different, suddenly each day and each week stretches to accommodate the range of new experiences.

The impulse to organise a gap year can come from many directions. You may find yourself thinking (obsessively) that if you don't grab the opportunity now you never will. You may have come to the realisation that you need de-stressing or simply been inspired by the travel tales of a sibling, friend or television presenter.

All those who *do* it rather than merely talk about it or dream about it arrive at a point of no psychological return. For **Polly Botsford**, a lawyer who had just turned thirty, there was an underlying conviction that *something* was needed to shake up her life. For her it felt a bit like the need to change her bedroom around or try a new hairdresser. She thinks that if she had been younger, she might have been satisfied with a change of job. But once you are entrenched in a career, you cannot nonchalantly walk out of one job and into another. So the solution is to have an extended holiday from your job, which is what she did when she went to work for a small charity in Cambodia.

## Burn-Out

No matter how glamorous and interesting a job may be, it usually has the capacity to lead to boredom or burn-out at some level. No matter how hard you work, you can sometimes never clear the backlog, which can lead to a feeling of defeat and profound weariness. And it is this problem which a gap year can address. American TV documentary-maker Holly Morris has a vivid expression for what she felt in a 9-5 job: '*rigor mortis of the soul*'. Her solution was to take a sabbatical in Sumatra to rethink her position. On her return she went half-time as an editor, spending the other half freelancing and working on an idea for a TV series about strong adventurous women around the world. She simply created a more flexible life for herself which allowed her to make a pilot programme in Cuba. She then sold it to PBS and went on to make a TV series called 'Adventure Divas'.

**At about the age of 50, Andy Morgan was feeling burned out as a general practitioner and was even toying with the idea of leaving the NHS:**
Although he was prepared to take some unpaid leave, he decided to apply for one of the research grants offered (rarely) by the National Health Service and was successful. On the application he had described as honestly as he could his reasons for wanting the time out and his targets for the year. He was interested in the use of videos to improve doctor-patient interaction and wanted to explore how video training can be used more extensively in medical training. On a more practical level, he wanted to master the skill of touch-typing. Administering a busy medical practice in Twickenham, one of the frustrations of his job was that he was a very slow typist. Although he had had several stabs at teaching himself, he hadn't made much progress and was determined to acquire this time-saving skill.

On a more personal level, he had been coping with grief. He had been widowed quite young and had much more recently lost the elder of two daughters when she was killed in a road accident on her gap year in Malawi. But life began to look up when he formed an attachment to an Australian woman and decided that he would like to spend his year out with her in Melbourne, which is what he did. In that time he learned to type, he ran successful workshops with Australian doctors in video training, he got married and has since become a father again.

Andy came back to England much more positive about practising medicine and in pursuing video training to help future doctors deal more sensitively with their patients. He feels that the NHS's investment in allowing him a year out was not wasted, not only because of the 30,000-word report he touch-typed for them but because he has decided to remain in the health service for the foreseeable future.

## Excess and Affluence

You have only to read a newspaper or watch the television news about the plight of earthquake victims or the AIDS crisis in Africa or the feelings of hopelessness among Palestinians, to realise the extent to which citizens of Britain, North America and other developed countries are extraordinarily privileged even to be able to contemplate a grown-up gap year. Such a concept would be entirely alien to the vast majority of the inhabitants of the globe for whom it is an unrelenting daily struggle to obtain basic necessities.

Undoubtedly many of us have never been better off or had more opportunities at our disposal. Some might even consider themselves members (reluctant or otherwise) of the 'have-it-all generation'. With apologies to Harold Bloom's famous study of poetry called 'The Anxiety of Influence', the anxiety of *affluence* is (fortunately) not uncommon in our culture. The disparity between what we have and what millions of others lack through no fault of their own can be overwhelming at times. It is an awareness of our amazing good fortune to be born when and where we have been that prompts some people to withdraw temporarily from the good life and try to bring good to others. Many people want to reverse the cash-rich, time-poor equation.

The acronym 'TIRED' referring to 'Thirty-something Independent Radical Educated Dropout' invented in 2003 may not have caught on but the phenomenon persists. At that time a marketing company identified a sizeable proportion of the population attracted to the idea of 'pro-tiring', a term invented to describe a withdrawing from normal professional life to explore alternatives. (If you are concerned that your friends and relations will be flummoxed when you tell them you are thinking of taking a gap year, think of the looks on their faces if you declared an intention to protire!)

It is no doubt the case that a disincentive to many people in taking a gap year is the loss of income (i.e. buying power) that will ensue, if only temporarily. Depending on your predisposition and background, you may find it easy or well-nigh impossible to come to the view that it is probably not essential for you to earn constantly.

## Sensory Overload

The choice of goods in the shops, programmes in the media, training courses and possible career paths, travel destinations, information on the Internet, all of these are almost infinite. Many people feel oppressed by the sheer quantity of choice available to us in the 21st century. Their impulse is to seek out a simpler life and one way of achieving this is to put one's job on hold for a while, put one's possessions in storage and remove oneself from the busy crowded world of the materialistic west.

Paradoxically, in the midst of all this profusion of possessions and experiences, we have less time to absorb and reflect on the experiences open to us and often lack the ability to turn them into something of quality. An extended period spent away from the workaday treadmill, with all that it implies – the ringing phone, the expectations, the routines – can help to make that possible.

## Depression and Trauma

Anyone who is truly depressed is unlikely to be able to summon the energy and initiative necessary to plan a constructive gap year. But many people who feel worn down by their jobs and lives contemplate alternatives that will rescue them from their gloomy state of mind. **Caroline Kippen** is one for whom this worked splendidly:

> *I decided to take a gap year because I was finding life quite disheartening and depressing! I made my decision in the depths of winter when the UK has to be one of the most depressing places to be. I guess I was suffering from a severe case of SAD and decided to pro-actively do something to change my situation. I was also dissatisfied with my job (in customer services for a mortgage endowment company) so decided that the best thing would be to take a break and then start a new career after that. I guess I went away to decide what I wanted to do next – I kind of had the idea of teaching because it is easy to fall into, but luckily my gap year led me away!*
>
> *Firstly, I went on a 2 month round the world trip and was a real tourist seeing places I has always wanted to see and having incredible fun – that has now all blended into one and I have difficulty distinguishing one place from the next. The other part was volunteering in Africa. I chose an organisation called SPW which runs health education programmes in Africa. Teaching about HIV/AIDS seemed so much more important than teaching maths. The rewards have been great. I have so many skills now and my life has meaning and order to it! The drawbacks are that I can never go into another mundane boring job because I will always compare it to my experience and it means that I have to constantly challenge myself in new ways – but maybe that isn't a bad thing!*

Traumatic events occurring in your own life, those close to you or even to strangers (as in natural disasters around the world) can lead to a sudden re-assessment of what is important. Two friends of one of our contributors (in her 50s) became seriously ill without ever having done anything in their lives apart from work, and she didn't want to be like them.

**Siamak Tannazi** was 29 when she decided to apply to her boss at BT for a six-month break, partly because she had been in a serious motorbike accident and then the Tsunami happened which made her think about all the charities in the Indian sub-continent dependent on foreign volunteers who would be redirected to Tsunami relief. **Neil Munro** (who tells his story at the end of the book) had suffered a serious betrayal by a brother which made Neil fall apart and feel the need to get out of Scotland. Any number of unexpected events can bring you up short and make stepping out of your routine seem a necessity.

## The Danger Age

An article entitled 'Quarter life crisis hits UK PLC' appeared in *The Times* not long ago arguing that 30 is the crunch age for wanting more purpose at work. As soon as they can clear their debts, young high fliers who feel caught in a career trap are deserting employers whom they believe to be intolerant of their wider life ambitions.

Alongside the pressures to become a property owner, society (often in the guise of a parent) seems to expect people who have been earning a salary for a few years to 'settle down', find a spouse and reproduce. This might engender panic that it is time to have your last fling with youth. You may therefore derive great pleasure in announcing to all and sundy that in fact you have decided to leave your job for a while to sail across the Atlantic, do marine conservation in the Philippines or ride your bicycle through Chile. That will teach them to pin their assumptions on you! On a more serious note, you will want to avoid causing unnecessary anxiety to ageing parents. However you cannot please all of the people all of the time and if a mother is anxious that her daughter has hit thirty without making her a grandmother, this is not a sufficient reason to stay on the straight and (very) narrow.

Although it is possible to have a gap year after parenthood (see the chapter *Taking the Family*), the commitment-free gap year is the paradigm. **Jennie Sanders** at age 26 took nine months off from her job with PricewaterhouseCoopers to do a Yachtmaster sailing course:

> *I will probably spend a lot of the years to come sitting at a desk. To be able to take some time out while I had no commitments such as a family or a mortgage meant that it was an ideal time to seize the opportunity. I wouldn't say that I came back 'a changed person' but it was a fantastic experience and all I have missed out on is a few months sitting in an office! There were other people on our course who had borrowed from friends, given up jobs completely, sold their businesses and left family at home to come on the course, and I don't think anyone regretted taking the time out to do something completely different.*

## Property Ladder Pressures

After starting a job, most people are happy to rent property for a few years. But soon the knowledge that hundreds of pounds a month are disappearing into a black hole begins to worry them. Family and friends suddenly seem to be in cahoots with the local estate agent to pressurise full-time earners into getting onto the property ladder at any cost. This pressure can be hard to resist, especially in an economic climate where house prices have risen astronomically so the longer you delay the more you will have to borrow. However at the time of writing, the Bank of England was predicting that the price of houses had just about peaked and that buyers should be aware that prices could fall over the next couple of years, which might prompt some first-time-buyers-to-be to delay the inevitable.

**Rob Evans** came late to the joys of travel but had greatly enjoyed a one-month backpacking trip round Peru with friends in his late 20s. So he began to toy with the idea of taking leave from work to travel. On the same day that his landlord had told him that he wanted to reclaim the flat, he attended a party to welcome back some other travellers he had met in South America and a couple of choices started to crystallise:

> *On one hand I could make my belated first step onto London's property ladder and scour the suburbs for a grotty flat. On the other I could blow the money I'd been saving for a deposit on doing the thing I'd been threatening and disappear to foreign climes for some time. Given that I was at a party with a large number of people who had been travelling themselves, there was probably only one way this decision was ever going to go.*

There will be time enough for locating a grotty flat in the suburbs.

## Freedom from Responsibilities

The last child goes off to university or to a job and all of a sudden, people in their 40s and 50s have a lot more freedom. As their children progressed through adolescence, they may have been taking their first tentative steps to rediscovering the joys of child-free travel: an anniversary weekend in Barcelona or Prague, a week in a country cottage in Ireland. But now parents are at liberty to plan something more ambitious without having to take any account of their children's propensity to travel sickness or their dislike of hotels without swimming pools or of remote villages with no nightlife.

This sudden lifting of parental obligations is often more keenly felt by mothers than fathers. Whether busy career women or not, mothers frequently bear the burden of anxiety on their children's behalf. Not that this vanishes once the children leave home for further education or employment, but many women find that for the first time in many years they have an urge to think about themselves and what they would like. This may not come easily at first and it may take time before they can dust off an old pre-motherhood dream or two. According to *AidCamps International* (a volunteer sending agency), the single biggest demographic group among their volunteers is women in their 50s.

While still headteacher of a girls' school in Surrey, **Marjorie Harris** found herself free of family responsibilities:

> *The last of my four children had just gone away to University, my husband was working away from home and I decided that I was interested in doing what my three other children had done. I was working long hours, and whilst still enjoying my job I felt that I was missing out on a real life. Plus my school was due to have an inspection, which was another reason to resign when I did, as I had already done one excellent inspection at the school.*

## Turning Fifty

Mid-life crises are a bit like failing eyesight and greying hair; they can strike at any point between the ages of about 40 and 60. But research for this book revealed that the half-century seems to act frequently as a prompt to appraising the direction and priorities of one's life. People coming up to 50 often begin to panic that they have embarked on the gentle slope to retirement. They want something to wake them up, in the hope that it will extend their lives.

Sometimes attending a school or college reunion can instantly reinforce your suspicion that doing the same thing for years on end is not good for you, and this realisation may catapult you into a frenzy of planning on how to make your life take a different course, if only temporarily. After 20 years as an insurance executive **Marcelle Salerno** signed up for various exotic volunteer roles including a dive project in the Seychelles and concludes, 'After all this, if nothing else, I'm more interesting at cocktail parties'. Similarly 43 year old **Gillian Drake** enjoyed the attention that her plan to spend ten weeks teaching in Sri Lanka through *i-to-i* attracted among her friends and acquaintances. She felt flattered when they told her how brave she was, while also feeling anxious at the prospect of her adventure.

Time stretches when you are doing something outside your routine, for example it always seems that you pack much more into a week's holiday than a week spent at home. You can test this hypothesis over two weekends. In the first, do the usual stuff: hoover the sitting room, go to the supermarket, read a magazine, maybe go to the pub, sleep in, read the Sunday paper, watch television. Then at 7.45 on Monday morning, ask yourself 'How long ago was Friday?' and the answer will be 'it seems no time at all'. The following weekend, leave work a little early to catch a train to Bradford/Wales/Brussels; check in to a B&B/pension/hostel and spend the weekend exploring the local buildings/landscapes/cafés/museums. Then ask yourself the same question at the same time on Monday morning and the answer is guaranteed to be different. The second weekend will inevitably be more memorable, more rewarding and 'longer'. The same applies even more forcefully to the decade between our 50th and 60th birthdays. A recent coinage 'denture venturers' for this age group might bring on a premature mid-life crisis in some. A less depressing label (at least for the parents) is "SKI-ers" (Spending the Kids' Inheritance).

**Paul Edmunds was 43 and working for the British Airports Authority in a variety of managerial roles at Gatwick Airport, a job he had for over 20 years:**
The idea of turning 50 without having done anything apart from work in one field frightened him, and a combination of work and personal reasons led him to consider a change in direction. In the course of his work in the BAA training department, he often used external consultants to put on workshops to help managers communicate more effectively and was impressed with their approach. These workshops often tried to provoke people into taking more responsibility for their actions and not to hide behind a corporate image. It led Paul to question his own priorities. He realised that for some time he had been finding himself profoundly at odds with the direction that aviation has been taking in the UK, particularly the decision to add more runways at Heathrow and Stansted which in his view would merely enable more yobs to take £60 flights to Ibiza to urinate on the beaches and generally cause offence.

After deciding to resign and take a gap year, he asked himself many times why it had taken him so long to cut the umbilical cord. He now feels that the world is a place full of possibilities. He had noticed a small ad in the *Sunday Times* looking for volunteers over 35 for the BBC documentary on 'Grown-up Gappers' and was selected to be the subject of one of eight programmes (aired in 2005). Although he had been considering backpacking around South America, a long-time dream of his, the programme makers urged him to consider Africa, which also appealed. Once he had decided, he investigated what he might do in his three-month trip and decided to travel around Ethiopia for a month to meet the

Rastafarian community, and on to Uganda to see the gorillas, then climb Mt Kilimanjaro in Tanzania and relax for a week in Zanzibar and finally join a voluntary project in Ghana through *Travellers Worldwide* (the West Sussex gap year agency) for five weeks. In consultation with Travellers and based on his interests, a placement was arranged teaching cricket at three schools on the outskirts of the capital Accra.

He enjoyed the Ghana placement enormously and felt that it was extremely beneficial to the children to experience the structured framework of a sport. As well as bringing them pleasure, it also taught them discipline. All the children seemed to take to the sport with great enthusiasm and skill. This is not to say that they weren't unruly and naughty at times but sport provided a constructive outlet for their exuberance. One of the highlights was taking them to a British Council-sponsored coaching day involving the Ghanaian national cricket team to instil pride in the young people and to provide them with role models. This was a wonderful occasion and if he had been staying in Ghana longer, he would have made enquiries of the British Council whether they might support him in setting up a cricket-training programme.

Even if you don't plump for such an elaborate trip to commemorate turning fifty, you might think of a gap year-cum-party. For her 50$^{th}$ Jakki from Yorkshire found herself between jobs (in management of a housing association) and decided to rent a large villa with swimming pool in Andalucia for an extended period to which she invited all her friends and family to spend time whenever they could. This seemed to be a good place to be when the invitation to attend the mammogram clinic dropped through her letter box at home and also meant that she couldn't succumb to the temptation of going to Glastonbury alongside all those other wrinkly professionals.

It is not unknown for spouses in middle life (generally the female of the species) to think longingly of packing their life partner off for a period of time. Usually the idea goes no further than giving hubby a copy of this book for Christmas (hint hint) so I will not be taking up a friend's suggestion that I write a book for disgruntled middle-aged couples called 'A Gap Year Apart'.

## Retirement

If a change is as good as a rest, then Ed McFadd and Eva Hagen have the right idea. As soon as they hit retirement, they left home to do something completely different: Ed went from California to Montreal in the dead of winter to take a French course after rediscovering his long dormant love of the language and **Eva Hagen** signed up for a conservation/farming project on a homestead in Australia, having harboured a life-long dream to live and work there.

With an increasing number of early retired people expressing an interest in volunteering abroad, some organisations have developed programmes specially for the older volunteer. One such is *MondoChallenge* which has established a division specially for those who have retired and are looking for something worthwhile and reasonably challenging to do with their time. MondoChallenge Managing Director, Anthony Lunch, feels that the growth of early retired volunteers is a positive trend for projects of the kind the organisation specialises in. 'We have always focused on career break people and older volunteers and our programmes include business development as well as a range of teaching projects. The senior age group, mainly over 50s, has a huge amount to offer, not least life experience. They have a wider variety of skills that can be put to use'.

One year before his planned retirement, **Paul Kirk** accepted voluntary redundancy from the university where he was an associate dean, and started planning his gap year. He rented out his house, applied to VSO (unsuccessfully) and then lined up several placements through *Mondo Challenge* in Sri Lanka, India and Tanzania. Between placements he came back to the UK and stayed with his children (in his words, 'nice pay-back!'). On his return from Sri Lanka in June 2006, he reflected on his year of volunteering:

> *The range of placements gave me the opportunity to experience very different cultures. In Tanzania I was able to teach topics in Biology which were very relevant to the African situation (e.g. about infectious diseases and their control including malaria, tuberculosis, and HIV) which was a rewarding experience and linked well with some of the work Mondo was doing with the local communities in supporting HIV/AIDS patients. In Sri Lanka there was a kind of innocence about the way of life in the community which was charming. In India I learned what life was like without electricity. The history, politics and religion were all absolutely fascinating with a significant legacy from Colonial Britain. The people were always appreciative of the work that I did. I have made many friends in the different communities that I shall always remember. There were so many highlights in each of the three places I worked. It was just fantastic to see children so keen to learn, so enthusiastic and so well behaved. The communities I worked in were all relatively poor but the people were wonderfully warm, welcoming, friendly and above all happy – especially in Sri Lanka and India. If you like, it was a practical demonstration of the saying that 'money doesn't buy happiness'.*

## Overcoming Reluctance

You will almost certainly be assailed by doubts at various points, both in the early stages when you are wondering whether or not to go for it, as well as at the moment that you show your boarding pass at the departure gate. In between, possibly at your farewell party in the pub, you will suffer some pre-departure blues as you contemplate leaving behind the comfortable routines of your working life. But these separation anxieties are usually much worse in anticipation than in retrospect.

No one can avoid confronting the question, 'What if it all goes horribly wrong?' In the research for this book, I couldn't find anyone who said that they wished they had avoided the hassle of taking off and stayed quietly at home – including those whose gap years included a bout of homesickness or malaria and a finished relationship. Mark Twain is often quoted in this context: 'Twenty years from now you will be more disappointed by the things you didn't do than by the ones you did. So throw off the bowlines. Sail away from the safe harbour. Catch the trade winds in your sails. Explore. Dream. Discover.'

Once the decision has been made, obstacles fall away or at least become manageable. This is usually the case, however daunting the prospect of taking an extended period off seemed at the outset and however many problems stood in the way.

**Four major obstacles to taking a gap year can be readily identified:**

- It never occurs to people. They do not think outside the box, a jargon term implying that the best employees are those who can look for solutions outside the normal parameters.
- Their spouse/partner is not enthusiastic.
- They worry that they will slip down the career ladder and when they return will have to start at the bottom again or won't find a job.
- They can't afford it; too many financial commitments.

Being in a relationship with someone who is not keen on joining you in your adventures can be an understandable disincentive. 'Telegamy' (a neologism for marriage over a distance) is invariably problematic over an extended period. It is impossible to generalise or even for the individuals involved to know what the right course of action should be. Frequent writing, e-mailing and phoning alleviates some of the anxiety. Compromise is one answer, for example to organise a break that might be shorter than otherwise or plan to rendezvous with your partner part way through the gap year. What most people hope is that their relationship will survive a serious separation which is what happened to **Paul Carroll** who had a wonderful six months with *VentureCo* and then travelled independently in South America:

> *Colleagues, friends and family were very supportive of my plan to go away as they felt I spent too much time working. In fact I had absolute encouragement from everyone except my girlfriend of four years, who was not interested in travelling. I had no choice but to split with my girlfriend to go on the trip that I so wanted. That was difficult, but in the end we are much stronger as a couple than before. Where previously I had not considered taking things further, I now see no barriers.*

But there is no guarantee of a fairy tale ending. **Andrea Martins** found herself having risen as high as she could in an international export firm in London and was keen to take a gap year, possibly in Peru or Russia, though ended up with a teaching placement in Mexico:

> *I had positive feedback about my plan from my family, friends and work colleagues. Everyone knew how much the idea of travelling had been burning on my mind for months if not years. Unfortunately, my boyfriend at the time was not so keen. Due to my gap year (amongst other problems) we have since split up. This wasn't part of the plan though.*

## Shaking out the Cobwebs

You don't have to hate your job to want a change. But we all become stale when we conform to the same routine day in day out. You can liven yourself up by small things, take an evening class in botanical drawing or Spanish, join a jazz club or a choir, become involved in Amnesty or any cause close to your heart, choose unusual destinations for your annual holidays. But these will not alter the fundamentals of your life.

When the home routines begin to pall and you find yourself craving a challenge or an opportunity to expose yourself to risk, it is time to give some thought to bringing about a change. As they say, you'll be a long time dead. Few books (with the notable exception of *Diary of a Nobody*) have been written to catalogue every-day working life. But hundreds have been written by people who have had adventures when away from their offices and factories. The titles of some of these evince how precious time away from routines can be, like Libby Purves's *One Summer's Grace* about sailing around the perimeter of the British Isles with her husband and two pre-school children.

## HOW WILL A BREAK AFFECT MY CAREER?

The principal concern about taking a gap year is its potential effects on your professional life. Getting out of the swim and losing touch understandably frightens a lot of people. It's indisputable that single people in their twenties will probably feel less wedded to their jobs and their employers than those in their forties with responsibilities at a more senior level, and certainly far less bound than individuals who have spent years building up their own businesses.

As a founder of his own successful business, Humphrey Walters is an eloquent advocate of sabbaticals for their value in the modern economy and is quick to refute the obvious doubts that will arise:

> *I thought if you slogged your guts out and became indispensable and then went away, your business would go down the drain or your career would suffer. That's absolute rubbish. Quite the reverse. If you do not keep yourself in a learning environment you get left behind because your ability to acquire knowledge is diminished massively. It's essential that everyone should take a break no more than half way through his or her career. It could be going back to university. Just engineer a break.*

The government's championing of lifelong learning is underpinned by an appreciation that the nature of work has become flexible and this meshes nicely with the idea of a gap year. In the modern economy, we are less tied to a career in one field or to employment with one company for the duration of our working lives. Just as the pre-university structured gap year has been endorsed by the Department for Education and Skills and by UCAS (Universities & Colleges Admissions Service), so too the establishment is gradually giving its seal of approval to the idea of grown-up gap years.

### Improving Career Prospects

Improving career prospects is not or should not be the major motivation for taking a gap year. The break should be self-fulfilling as a unique opportunity to step back and examine one's life and lifestyle and to enrich and broaden interests and experiences. But that does not prevent many people from deriving concrete career advantages of many kinds from their career breaks.

Onlookers may doubt the value of a break and may view it as merely a self-indulgent opportunity to ease off the pressure of working life. But that view should be resisted. A career break can be regarded as an empowering move in the contemporary workplace, a chance to use your own time to equip yourself with experiences and skills that complement your formal professional training. It can be interpreted positively by employers as a sign of self-sufficiency and initiative. Perhaps most valuably, it will at least illustrate to yourself that you are capable of managing your own time to suit your own ends and that work need not dominate your life to the exclusion of everything else.

Those who contemplate a break are often deterred by a fear of the professional risk. **Clare Southwell** was not among them. She is convinced that her gap year volunteering with *Raleigh International* gave a substantial boost to her career. She took time out from her job in marketing at the age of 28 to volunteer as an assistant project manager in Chile. She believes the experience had a huge impact on her professional development. Although she still works in marketing, she feels more at home working for her current employer than she did when she worked in a health club:

> *When I got back everyone was absolutely amazed by what we had achieved on the expedition. Changes in my confidence were noticeable. You really do feel that the world's your oyster and that you can go out there and do what you want to do. My simple advice to anyone contemplating a career break in order to volunteer overseas is, just do it!*

Demanding experiences outside the normal workplace will make a beneficial contribution to anyone's career, which can be particularly useful in cases where the individual is unsure about the next career step. Clare cites the experience of one friend who recruited for a large bank. He admitted that he would put former Raleigh International volunteers at the top of the pile because he knew that they would never be short of an impressive answer to the question, 'which difficult situations have you faced?'.

Even rather frivolous ways of spending a career break have proved professionally beneficial as in the case of Michael Tunison from Michigan:

> *Newspaper work was exactly what I thought I was leaving behind by globetrotting. I'd temporarily sacrificed (I believed) my career as a journalist. The last place I thought I'd be working was at a daily paper in Mexico. But things never work out as planned and before I knew it I was the managing editor's assistant and a month or so later the managing editor of the paper's weekend editions. How ironic. By taking a step my newspaper friends believed to be an irresponsible career move, I was soon years ahead of where I'd have been following the old safe route back home.*

## EMPLOYERS' ATTITUDES

Large companies are beginning to introduce formal schemes for all employees, some of which have grown naturally out of their maternity leave policy. For example the BBC has been operating a career break scheme for about 15 years; originally it was designed for staff with caring responsibilities, was extended to covering further education breaks and more recently expanded to cover travel. Marks and Spencer grants career breaks for up to nine months (unpaid); the John Lewis Partnership offers 26 weeks of paid leave after 25 years of service; Asda allows long-standing employees over 50 to take off three months unpaid (referred to as 'Benidorm Leave'); and even McDonald's gives four weeks paid leave after ten years of service.

A growing number of companies and government organisations offer career break schemes including Lloyds TSB, Tesco, American Express, Littlewoods, Prudential, BT and the NHS. Most companies who belong to Employers for

Work-Life Balance (www.employersforwork-lifebalance.org.uk/EfWLB_memb_old.htm) offer career breaks. These large and important employers have introduced formal schemes in response to a growing interest in the opportunity to travel, live overseas, gain further qualifications or simply have the time to step back from the pressures of work to re-evaluate the direction of one's life. Smaller companies can afford to be much more flexible and agree to sabbaticals on a case-by-case basis. One of the most attractive ones around is offered by the famous map and travel bookshop, Stanfords in Covent Garden, which keeps open jobs for staff who have worked there for at least one year while they travel for up to three months. When they get back they do a presentation to the rest of the staff about their experiences.

Breaks can range from several weeks to the five years of unpaid leave that the Foreign & Commonwealth Office offers to staff who can return to a job at the same level. Some companies may offer paid leave, but the crucial feature of a formal company scheme is that employment and pension rights are guaranteed. These examples demonstrate how attitudes among public and private employers are changing as recognition grows that career breaks can re-energise, encourage motivation, develop skills and reward loyalty.

The Post Office is an example of a large organisation that runs an enlightened and long-standing scheme. For more than 30 years it has allowed its workforce to take unpaid extended leave for up to three years. All employees are eligible to apply for the career break scheme provided they have at least two years service, a good performance record and a good absence and conduct record. Permission is granted by the line manager and pension contributions cease during the break. The Post Office's guidelines stress the importance of maintaining regular contact with the organisation and it makes a point of communicating developments in the company to the employee on a sabbatical. These employees are also required to work a minimum of two weeks every year of the break. The right to return to the former division or business unit on the former grade is guaranteed. Retraining is offered if the employee is given a different job.

## TAKING CHARGE OF YOUR CAREER

The substantial economic shift during the last two decades has seen a decline in the notion that a job could be held for life. Once individuals were offered a tight and reliable career structure. But few people can fail to have been touched by significant changes in employment.

It is possible that a new psychological contract is emerging in the workforce. Managing your own career has become important because your employer no longer looks after your interests as a matter of course. Downsizing is commonplace; final pension schemes are becoming a thing of the past. This new approach stresses the importance of self-motivation, personal responsibility and a willingness to take risks. Employment practices at the BBC illustrate this shift: where once it encouraged lifelong loyalty, employees are now hired on short-term contracts.

One consequence of this perceptible shift is that loyalty to one employer is frequently being replaced by economic opportunism in which employees with valuable skills are tempted to look for the highest bidder. It is common for an organisation to experience high rates of turnover among the workforce particularly in areas of high growth like IT and the Internet. Within the private sector, companies have had to become more creative in devising non-pecuniary rewards for staff they want to keep.

As a consequence of general professional uncertainty, there is a growing perception among individuals that they only live once and they want their lives to have greater value, hence the growing popularity of volunteering. The prediction is for the contemporary sabbatical to evolve and become an important perk among the list of benefits designed to attract and retain good staff. Companies in the future will need to offer more flexible employment packages. If you are still relatively young and without parental responsibilities, the gamble involved in leaving a job will obviously be less serious. Many employees will have worked hard for years to build up a position within a company and will not be prepared to risk sacrificing that. More junior employees may be able to accumulate holiday or overtime to create space for a short career break. For example people like paramedics who work shifts may be able to do back-to-back shifts or those on flexi-time may be in a position to save up more than four weeks holiday time at a stretch.

## Considerations for the Self-Employed

The sharp rise in the number of people working freelance from home, many in front of computer screens all day, means that more people than ever have the freedom to opt out of work at intervals. Every so often it dawns on a freelance worker that he or she has barely stepped outside the house for days at a stretch and he or she will think with longing of the cheerful swirl and hubbub of the outside world. That might be the time for a freelancer to step back and answer the question whether it is really necessary to earn X number of pounds or dollars 52 weeks a year.

The self-employed can make their own decisions about taking time out from work without recourse to a line manager but they may have clients who depend on them. In an ideal world, you could pass the business on to a reliable contact, but at least you should give plenty of warning to customers about your intention to withdraw temporarily. Experienced freelancers who are paid sporadically often become adept at careful budgeting. With luck, they might be able to work extra hard for a limited period in order to accumulate enough savings to fund a career break. The downside is that they have no guarantee of work and benefits when they return.

## Persuading the Boss

It is surprising how many forward-thinking companies are at least willing to consider granting a sabbatical to a valued worker. When you bite the bullet and finally ask to have a word with your boss, he or she will probably be quite relieved when you do not announce that you have accepted a better job offer elsewhere but merely want six months unpaid leave to broaden your horizons. You should give some careful thought to how you can put as positive a spin as possible on what you intend to do so that your employer will be persuaded that the gap year will benefit the company as much as it will you. **Siamak Tannazi's** request to her boss was mentioned earlier. Together with citing her personal reasons for wanting to volunteer in Kerala, she described why the timing of her requested break might be beneficial. It was at a time when BT was preparing for a radical network transformation and Tan (as she is known) wanted to take her break before the change really kicked in. She pointed out to her boss that the other members of her team were happy to provide cover and were willing to support her in her efforts. In the end her boss granted three months special leave and that turned out to be about right for her. It turned out that the pitch she made was more than empty rhetoric:

*As things in India are prone to change ALL the time, you automatically become accustomed to thinking on the spot and expecting the unexpected. For example, half way through the school term in India, I had to help choose the English teacher out of a selection of applicants in an interview. This task was laid upon me at two minutes notice. It was a situation that I don't have experience in or ever expected to be placed in, yet it seems to happen all the time whilst I was in India. This has helped me in BT, as I do actually try to look at the bigger picture when I'm working. So changes happening at the moment, especially with the 21CN process, don't unsettle me as much as they did before I left for India.*

Of course it is much easier to arrange a sabbatical from some jobs than others. The word sabbatical means literally one in seven and a break (roughly) every seven terms or seven years is built into academic life. Sabbaticals are routinely granted in higher education to allow lecturers to pursue their research, which is as important a part of their job as teaching.

In most branches of the Civil Service, career breaks of up to five years are offered to established employees, especially if they can argue that a break will enhance their ability to contribute in the workplace. **Vicky Waite** was an established civil servant who had been working at the Cabinet Office for four years. Although she found her job challenging and interesting, she was nagged by a suspicion that something was missing. Her department was flexible about giving unpaid leave and at age 32 Vicky decided to go to Mongolia to work in an orphanage. Doing voluntary work was viewed favourably by her bosses as potentially broadening her skills and competencies, which would benefit them in the long run.

*I had always wanted to travel and do voluntary work, but had never had the opportunity. It just seemed like the ideal time and I very much wanted to go to Mongolia as I was fascinated by the nomadic culture. My three-month break in Ulaan Baatar, Mongolia, was arranged through Teaching and Projects Abroad. I spent a month in a state orphanage for 0-3 year olds, a couple of weeks in a private kindergarten for 4-7 year olds, and a month running an after-school English class in another state orphanage for 7-17 year olds.*

*Working with the very young children in the orphanage turned out to be much more rewarding than I expected. Building up relationships with individual children and offering time that the staff did not have was highly rewarding. For example, I looked after quite a sickly one-year-old child who had been born premature and as a result was very slow to develop. I took him outside into the sunshine every day and encouraged him to explore and play. By the time I left he was nearly crawling and reaching to grasp toys, which he had never done before. I went back to visit the orphanage a month after I'd left, and his face lit up when he saw me. I felt very glad that I'd given him some happiness in what was quite a deprived environment. He died a few weeks later of diarrhoea – he just was not strong enough to fight it. I felt desperately sad for him as his short life had been very harsh, but pleased that I'd given him some precious moments of play and one-to-one attention. I often wonder what will become of other children whose lives I touched. I would hope to take maybe a year off at some point in the future, and anticipate that it will be fairly easy to negotiate another career break.*

One of the leading placement agencies, *Madventurer,* has created a specialist website www.careerbreaker.com to put forward the arguments for taking an adult gap year. As they rightly point out, big companies spend thousands on team building exercises and leadership courses for middle managers which in many cases are aiming for the same things as a gap year project. The potential benefits of a volunteer expedition include recharged batteries, new skills outside your traditional skills set, improvement of communication and teamwork skills, a new found respect for community values, an appreciation for what privileges we often take for granted, incentives to progress your career and an enhanced CV:

*No longer does a gap on a CV suggest to an employer that they took time out to 'find themselves'. Increasingly nowadays, employers encourage people to take time out, recognising the importance of motivating key staff and encouraging creativity in the work place. As businesses become globally focussed, an understanding of cultures different from our own is considered a huge asset. Not only that, you become interesting. How many interviews are conducted which the candidates can barely be distinguished from one another? Everybody looks the same, everybody has the same qualifications and everybody has the same experience. How many built an orphanage, taught in a school in Africa or climbed a mountain? Employers are looking for evidence of experience beyond the workplace, for the ability to be innovative and creative. The recruiter will remember Ms X because she got a double first from Cambridge, Mr Y because he came up with the plan that saved his former company millions, but you'll be the one who climbed Mt Kilimanjaro. Which one would you be more interested in talking to?*

**Wendy Burridge** considers herself to be lucky in life with a fantastic job insuring art collections. She feels that we in the west have so much that we take for granted like fantastic health schemes and job opportunities, and yet there are people across the world that can't even begin to imagine living such a life. With gathering determination she decided she wanted to give something back. The next step was to persuade her employers to allow her to join a *Madventurer* project in Uganda helping AIDS orphans:

*At work I am part of a small team of six so negotiating nine weeks off work for sabbatical leave was rather tricky. I wanted to spend six weeks on the project site and take a further three weeks exploring Uganda, however with work pressures and trying to distribute my accounts this was simply impossible. Relentless in my desire to join the project, I negotiated six weeks, giving me 24 hours from landing back in the UK before stepping back into the office.*

Having had to fight with her boss to take a mini-sabbatical, Wendy was promoted on her return. She was also grateful for the support she got from her employer when fundraising since they allowed her the use of office stationery and equipment for her letter-writing campaign.

Everybody's circumstances are different. Many people reading this will feel discouraged, assuming that their present employer would not be prepared to consider granting leave of absence. For example in manufacturing, banking and industry generally, many companies have been down-sizing and would grab at the chance to get rid of one more employee if they stepped out of the usual groove.

Companies like Shell, Accenture and PricewaterhouseCoopers are among the companies that have entered into a scheme with Voluntary Service Overseas (VSO) to send skilled volunteers with financial, management and IT skills, to the developing world. Instead of the usual VSO two-year commitment expected of individual volunteers, these corporate employees will be seconded for shorter periods of between six and twelve months. Similarly, VSO has also established a Public Sector Partnership Scheme along similar lines to the Business Scheme for public sector employees (see the chapter on Volunteering for more about VSO).

Perhaps your employer has instituted similar opportunities for its workforce. If not, how can you persuade your employer to keep the job open for you? Are you sufficiently confident of your skills and experience to walk away from a job if an employer refuses to grant a sabbatical? Dismissal is seldom the tragedy that it might have been considered a generation or two ago. Of course your employer might surprise you and allow you to take a break. If they don't, maybe they were the wrong kind of employer for you in the first place.

Your chances of success when asking an employer for leave are greater if your contribution is highly valued or is in some way difficult to replace. Timing can be critical here, though again success is not guaranteed, as **Paul Carroll** found out:

> *I started by challenging the two-week maximum single holiday period permitted without CEO approval in the software testing company where I had been working. Upon completion of a major new project for our largest client, I requested a one-month holiday for trekking around the Himalayas. This was rejected. I then did the same six months later upon completion of the second phase for this client. Again this was rejected. The third time was four months later and the CEO personally took me aside to explain that if he agreed to my request, others would want a month or more. Although two of the three directors feel flexibility is needed, the CEO (who is responsible to the investors) doesn't believe the company can risk key members being away for longer than a fortnight at a time.*

So Paul had to reconsider his options, and decided to quit altogether. This left him with six months to join a *VentureCo* expedition and to travel independently round South America. On his return his old employer offered him a consultancy role but he has chosen to change his lifestyle considerably, exchanging the work-hard, play-hard London lifestyle for a more relaxed travelling consultant's job based near the Peak District. Although he still works quite hard, he now feels he is mobile, in control of his career and a lot happier with life in general because he is able to achieve his personal goals outside the working week.

Some companies offer the possibility of sabbaticals in the recruitment process, but may not want to advertise it to current staff. In other organisations a formal policy may actually be in place but is little known or quietly neglected for fear of encouraging a flood of applicants at the same time.

Check with the personnel department to see whether your company or organisation has established a specific policy on sabbaticals. Even if your employer doesn't have a formal policy, employees should make a case for an unpaid break and its value to the company in the long run. The process should be advantageous to each party. Emphasise the skills you will acquire in an activity outside the boundaries of your normal job. Your departure may give a colleague the opportunity to learn new skills too.

The more often the subject is discussed with the personnel department, the better the chance that a career break will become part of the employment culture within the organisation, something that Humphrey Walters would be very keen to see:

> *Any company worth its salt would not stop you if you came with a proposal or project to realise a dream; otherwise employees would just leave anyway. Nowadays managing directors require energy, passion and commitment. They won't get that if employees are just slogging their guts out. Eventually, they will lose the manager and have the disruption anyway.*

## Taking the Initiative

In all but a handful of cases, it is necessary to be proactive about making a grown-up gap year happen. Imagination and determination will be required so you must be strongly committed to the idea before setting out.

**Ceri Evans,** a senior Sexual Health Counsellor in the NHS, happened to spot a pamphlet in the human resources office about a scheme which allowed staff with at least two years service to take up to two years unpaid leave. The policy had not been advertised nor were applications actively encouraged. It seems that it was primarily intended for staff who needed to travel or care for sick relatives. It included the proviso that paid work was not allowed during the break. She later learned that a colleague's application to the scheme had previously been declined because she had wanted to study at university. Undeterred, Ceri decided to use her initiative to make her plan viable.

Ceri had decided to take a complete break from her work in the HIV field but needed to make the case that she wanted to go to Spain to study treatments there. In reality it was not very practical because she didn't speak Spanish and her primary concern was to spend a year in Barcelona living with her partner who was working there.

As the manager of her department, Ceri needed to persuade her boss that her absence wouldn't be too disruptive and so she took the initiative to find a replacement within the Trust. She found a colleague working in another clinic who wanted the experience afforded by her absence and who wouldn't require an extra salary. She also reassured her employers that she fully intended to resume her job on return, being conscious that there was a prevailing anxiety about losing trained staff. However be cautious about making promises you suspect you may not be able to keep. Dishonesty and maltreatment of employers will only engender distrust of employees who come after you with a request for a chance to take time away from work.

**CAREER BREAK CHECKLISTS**

Working Families is a UK-based campaigning organisation working towards a healthy work-life balance. It publishes a fact sheet entitled 'Breaks from Work' which can be read online (http://workingfamilies.org.uk/asp/family_zone/factsheets/Breaks_from_Work.doc). Its guidance on the subject of negotiating a career break includes some of the following.

**Negotiating a Break**
If you want to negotiate leave with an employer without a formal sabbatical scheme consider the following:

- What will my employment rights be while on the break?
- Will my job be guaranteed on return?
- How much responsibility will I have in putting replacement mechanisms in place?
- Can I do some work experience while on the break?
- Can I take part in training courses or undertake assignments?
- What contact can I have with my employer in order to keep in touch with changes at work?
- When do I want to return to work?
- What other benefits can I keep (e.g. membership of the social club)?

**Establishing Your Value**
Before approaching an employer, thoroughly identify the skills he or she needs most and think about the following:

- Your real value to your employer, i.e. how much has your employer invested in your recruitment, training and development?
- The skills shortages in your profession or area of work
- Your employer's future developments and planned growth
- What costs will your employer incur in replacing your skills, experience and knowledge?
- The value of employment breaks to improving employee relations, recruitment, and retention and public image.

## WHAT CAN BE ACHIEVED?

Perhaps you've always dreamed of farming alpacas, playing the harmonium, joining a circus or sailing through the Bermuda Triangle. Alternatively, you might want to stay at home to look after a new-born child or learn to paint or write a pub guide to your region. You might simply need an extended break from a demanding job or want to assess the direction of your career. Grown-ups will have their own reasons for wanting to take a gap year. The only activity which is prohibited is to sit around doing nothing.

Some will want to do their own thing while others may want a more structured break by volunteering time and knowledge to a charitable organisation at home or overseas. Many possibilities are canvassed in the chapters that follow.

To take just one example, *MondoChallenge* offers career break programmes lasting two to six months for volunteers who want to have an impact on world development at a grassroots level. In the past few years, MondoChallenge has noted that the number of career break volunteers has more than doubled, mainly high flyers in their 20s and 30s looking for a new challenge in a new environment. For example **Andrew Allright,** aged 32, then a manager at Abbey National's Market Risk division in London worked, alongside his fiancée Lili, in a small rural school set in the Himalayas near Darjeeling:

> *It was such a joy to teach these children and to see them developing. We lived with the local teacher and his family and really felt part of the community. People there have so little, yet they help each other in a way we don't see here in the UK. Stepping outside your comfort zone forces you to grow and achieve things you did not think possible. It was an amazing experience where we learnt so much about ourselves. I think I felt I made a difference volunteering, and coming back to work did not feel like that all. I am back in an office job but still think something is missing.*

**Shirley Graham**, a 38 year old communications manager for Unilever, was impressed by the same spirit of community when she spent two months through the same agency working at the Niketan School for orphans and street children. The positive adjectives tumble out when she describes her time in Nepal as 'illuminating, fascinating, fun, challenging, emotional, fulfilling and deeply satisfying' and concluded that the loving and inclusive community way of life was much more real than the stressful existence most people endure in London.

It is important to strike a good balance between slavishly following a predetermined programme and starting off with no idea of what you're hoping to achieve. Sometimes, a gap year can lead you in unexpected directions. Unpredictability is part of the adventure. During travel or time spent living in a foreign city, difficulties and frustrations are bound to crop up when dealing with different languages, customs, laws and hazards like theft or illness. Research and planning in advance are absolutely essential. **Fiona Carroll,** a software engineer and IT manager who took time off from her job in Switzerland to concentrate on her love of painting while winding down from stress, warns that 'planning is important or the time just goes.'

Be prepared for unfamiliar challenges. However well planned your break, chance events can blow it off course. A real break will assist your appreciation of your personal gifts and understanding of your weaknesses. You should be aware in advance that project funding can run out, a security situation may suddenly deteriorate or a crisis at home may require your presence. All of these will require far more flexibility than your normal life does.

Taking a career break affords a unique opportunity to experience an aspect of life that would otherwise be inaccessible to you in the course of your professional life. For some, taking a career break has had a profound effect on their values in life and on their futures.

# Nuts and Bolts

## Preparing to Take Off

Having made a commitment to negotiate a sabbatical or even resolved to leave your job altogether, the next step is to clarify your position financially and personally. Everything can fall into place with the right preparations. How are you going to finance your leave? What are the implications for long term financial security? How can you look after the house if you are going to be away for many months or even a year or more? Will your mortgage lender permit you to rent out your house to tenants? What can be done with the dog, cat or goldfish if you plan to be away from home? These are some of the many considerations any individual or family needs to consider before stepping away from their work and regular income.

All the improving talk of renewal and rejuvenation during a gap year must be balanced with an unflinching look at the down side. Organising the mechanics of a long stay abroad will take scores of hours. A family spending a year's sabbatical in Paris estimated that even eight months into their stay, one of them was having to spend at least an hour a day on what they termed 'administration'. Their situation was not made any easier by a rapacious landlady whose flat they were intending to rent but then they changed their mind. Not content to keep their €1,000 deposit, she sued them in the petty courts for breach of contract and lost at the first hurdle but not before causing the couple from Cambridge some months of anxiety.

## How to Afford a Gap Year

Financial resources may prove to be a stumbling block. But have you truly explored all the options to take that dreamed of break? Have you set out a rigorous budget for yourself to increase your level of savings? If you intend to do something charitable during your break, have you thought about fundraising activities such as those described below?

Everyone's circumstances and responsibilities will vary. Being younger with fewer financial obligations is naturally going to be an advantage, but you are probably likely to have fewer savings and no income-generating property to finance the break. As this book illustrates, people take gap years at different points in their lives depending on what their priorities are.

It is crucial to recognise that taking a gap year is probably easier in practical terms than you imagine. It may sound glib to claim that there are ways round most potential obstacles, but others who have gone before have found solutions and you can learn from their experiences. As you start to prepare to take your leave, make an audit of all your responsibilities outside work that will need to be sorted out or put into mothballs. Your life is poised to change from your usual routine and this will have an impact on all aspects of your life.

Inevitably, funding a period of time in your life without a salary is going to be expensive, especially if this time includes extensive travel or voluntary work abroad. It would be misleading to gloss over the considerable costs involved, although you have to bear in mind that the cost of living in a developing country might end up being less than it would be if you just stayed at home. Before deciding on his gap year projects, long-time teacher **Nigel Hollington** calculated that his average monthly spending at home left not much change from £1,000. So he was quite content to pay the required fees to join a series of interesting projects, starting with a 10-week conservation project in Zambia with Greenforce. He did not begrudge the cost since he knew that some of his fee would be used to support a worthwhile conservation cause.

Tempted as you might be by the idea of a gap year, you might be deterred by the assumption that a period of time without a salary would be out of the question in your circumstances. But before you put the idea out of your head or procrastinate yet again, you should be aware that there are many ways of keeping the cost down. This might involve working for a charity abroad that pays a stipend sufficient to support you in, say, the local economy of India. It might mean you could concentrate your energies on finding paid work abroad even if it was only pocket money. This might involve taking a job in a bar or using your fluency in English to teach the language (see chapter *Working and Living Abroad* for more details).

Perhaps it will be possible to obtain a grant or loan to help you obtain another qualification that might increase your earning powers when you return to work. Alternatively, you may want to use some savings you have accumulated or you might be able to take advantage of capital growth in your property by increasing your mortgage. If you are in rented accommodation, think how much you would save if you gave it up and maybe moved in with your boyfriend (as Jane O'Beirne did in anticipation of their six-month round-the-world trip) or even into your mother's attic (as Paul Edmunds did after renting out his house to a young couple in order to pay for his trip to Africa).

If you have a young child in full-time childcare, think of saving that huge expense every month. If you gave up smoking, drinking, the gym, whatever other vice, think how much richer you would be after six or twelve months. If you are a property owner, imagine renting it out for a sum that would cover the monthly mortgage payments with some to spare for your spending money.

**Some people are lucky enough to benefit from a windfall. The Whitlock family, who took a year out to go round the world (see 'Personal Case Histories'), made theirs stretch as far as possible:**
*My Grandmother died about a year and a half before we left. She left me £25,000 in her will, and this prompted us to plan the trip. At first we couldn't believe it. It seemed such a lot of money, but really, given the fact that a decent, large, family car can cost that much in itself, we couldn't work out how best to spend it. We wanted it to change our lives for the better in some way. The plans for the trip began as dream-talk, but grew and grew, until it would have been a let-down (not least to Gran's memory) not to have gone ahead with it... Some colleagues thought it was rather a reckless thing to do, but most of their concerns seemed to centre on our policy of selling/chucking away all of our possessions. Frankly, to me, that was the least traumatic thing of all.*

*We were strict throughout the trip from the point of view of budget, everything from long distance bus journeys and accommodation to loose change given to beggars being tapped into a calculator memory and added to the 'books' at the end of each day. This was boring and a constant drag, but it was necessary and it worked. The whole trip in fact fitted into our £25,000 overall budget, with the flights for the four of us costing about £8000, and a daily spend of £42, after buying insurance, rucksacks, immunisations and other essentials. At the end of the trip, it was a source of pride to us how well we felt we'd handled the finances. There were relatively few occasions when we had to compromise on excursions/activities (a notable one being the Galapagos Islands, which Nick would love to have visited). On the whole, by 'roughing it' in cheap accommodation, etc., we balanced those books without missing out.*

## DOs AND DON'Ts WHEN TAKING A CAREER BREAK

According to Anthony Lunch, Managing Director of non-profit volunteer sending agency MondoChallenge, the following practical considerations will help to ensure a smooth and rewarding gap year.

**Plan early**

- Research your destination thoroughly before you go and buy a good guidebook and maps. Also look at the advice given by the Foreign Office (www.fco.gov.uk).
- Be aware of the laws, customs and dress code for the country. Your guidebook should provide all this information.
- If you wish to return to your job on your return, contact your employer as early as possible about the opportunities for taking a sabbatical.

Your company may offer paid or unpaid sabbaticals. Emphasise the positive benefits your career break will bring to your company e.g. you will return to work more motivated and energised having learned new skills and gained more confidence.

- Online banking is a great way to manage your finances while you are away. But many internet cafés are slow and access may not always be easy so don't leave important transactions until the last minute. Set up standing orders for key items (e.g. household utilities, credit card minimum payments).
- Calculate how much money you will need for your trip and make sure you have some extra. Find out if you can use a credit or debit card to withdraw money at your destination. It's best to have a combination of credit/debit card, travellers cheques, sterling and maybe some US dollars.
- Visit your doctor for advice on vaccinations and medication needed.
- Contact the relevant embassy or consulate for advice on obtaining a visa. Many have online forms and often visas can be obtained on arrival although having one in your passport ahead of time can be comforting. If you plan to visit lots of countries, make sure your passport has plenty of blank pages, or get a new one well before you leave.
- Shop around for travel insurance and make sure you are covered for everything you intend to do e.g. white water rafting.
- Make photocopies of your passport (including visa pages), insurance details and air tickets. Leave copies with family/friends and take copies with you.
- Make sure your family or friends at home are aware of your travel itinerary.
- If you intend to use your mobile phone, contact your operator to check whether you will have coverage. If not you will need to take it into a shop to have the phone 'unlocked'. Warn friends not to call your UK mobile while you are away - you will be paying for all incoming calls from abroad (but see below for alternatives).
- Take a good international plug adaptor (or two).
- If you are volunteering through an organisation, ask for the contact details of the most recent volunteers on your project. They will be able to give you the best advice about what to expect on the project.

**On Arrival**

- Register your details with your embassy on arrival. This can simply mean sending them an email to inform them that you are in the country.
- If you are volunteering with an organisation ensure that local managers are aware of your plans e.g. if you decide to go away for the weekend.
- Keep your photocopies of important documents (passport, insurance info, plane tickets) in separate bags from the original copies.
- Take advice from your local manager about your personal safety and where best to keep your valuables.

- Keep your valuables out of sight. Combination locks are useful for your bags.
- Ensure you respect local customs in regard to dress code, personal relationships, smoking and drinking alcohol. It is important for you, the organisation you are with and the other volunteers that you do not cause offence.
- If you are staying in one country for several weeks, consider getting either a cheap local mobile phone or a local SIM card for your UK mobile. Don't forget to alert friends back home to the new number. Local texts and calls tend to be very cheap and incoming calls from abroad are free, which avoids the massive charges when using your UK mobile. Even better, ensure your UK contacts have the special access codes available for low cost dialling to your country (try Telediscount or Just Abroad).

# THE FINANCIAL IMPLICATIONS

Taking a career break will have substantial implications for your personal finances. Whatever the purpose of your career break, it means that your financial affairs will be undergoing a period of flux that requires some planning. If you own your home, you are likely to have a mortgage to maintain. Other financial concerns may include a pension, insurance policies, standing orders and direct debits from your bank account to cover regular household costs like the utilities or personal activities like club memberships, charitable donations and journal subscriptions. All of these financial commitments will need re-adjusting if you are going away. Even if you are staying at home, you might need to make financial provisions for the loss of income.

Usually, a career break effectively means living without a salary for the duration unless you're taking maternity leave, in a job with paid sabbaticals or you've been awarded an academic grant or scholarship for a course or research. When evaluating how much money you will need to pursue your ambition, you might consider cashing in those premium bonds your grandparents bought for you as a child or some shares that have risen in value. Perhaps a relative has left you a bequest.

Other ways to raise revenue include selling assets like cars or a valuable painting you once inherited but never really liked. A sensible option for homeowners who wish to travel is to make use of the empty property to generate income (see detailed section later in this chapter). This may be possible even if you are not going away for your career break; you could think about taking in a lodger to defray expenses. If you live in a town which has English language schools, contact them to see if they are looking for rooms for their foreign language students. You can increase your income by as much as £100 a week if you're prepared to have halting conversations in English over breakfast.

## Managing Your Affairs

If you are planning to be away for some time, it is useful to set up direct debit arrangements on the television licence, the water rates and all the other bills that might arrive in your absence. Find out how much flexibility is built in to your mortgage and pension since the regulations allow some leeway (see below).

Naturally, you'll need to leave enough money in the relevant accounts to cover expenses plus an extra stash for unforeseen emergencies like a tree blowing on your roof, a flood in the basement or a defaulting tenant.

Make an audit of all your additional regular expenses and decide which ones to pay and which to cancel. Unless you have very few ties, shifting your life for a career break will take some military style planning to ensure your departure is smooth. Note that some organisations like private insurers and gyms might allow members to suspend payments until they return home without losing the initial joining fee.

It cannot be denied that clearing the financial decks can involve a certain amount of tedium and drudgery. But a personal dream to accomplish a goal outside a career should not be set aside just because some of the preparations might be considered tiresome. When the list of obligations is drawn up, the task may seem somewhat overwhelming. But if you leave plenty of time and tackle one at a time you will soon have dealt with them all and be able to chime in with the breezy departure of Sir Cedric (from Roy Gerrard's charming children's stories):

> *There was rushing and fussing and bustling and packing,*
> *and cancelling the milk the last day.*
> *Then the cat was put out and they all gave a shout*
> *For at last they were off on their way.*

## Money Matters

One of many advantages of the Internet is the ability to use online banking. All the major banks and building societies offer their websites with encryption to account holders whereby you can access your personal account and check your balance, make financial transactions and payments and set up direct debits. Furthermore online banks like Smile (www.smile.co.uk) and Egg (http://new.egg.com) give favourable rates of interest. Nowadays you can also correspond with most institutions by e-mail to sort out the inevitable glitches. Technological and human errors are likely at some point to delay payment of bills and cause aggravation, usually while you're crossing Mali or Mexico.

**Paul Edmunds** knew that he did not have enough savings to cover his six-month break, the first three months of which he spent travelling and volunteering in Africa. He had no intention of returning to the workplace he had left after more than 20 years (Gatwick Airport) and was prepared to take a cut in income, even after he returned to work in a freelance consultant capacity. He therefore went in to talk to his bank manager who arranged an overdraft for him so that he avoided paying expensive interest charges.

Consider consulting a financial adviser if you don't already use one, to help you prepare a financial strategy for your career break so that the time away from paid work can have minimal impact on your long-term financial security. Arguably, the most important aspect of taking a gap year from any corporate employment is to research how a break will affect your benefits. Companies often offer a pension, private health insurance, life assurance and income protection for their employees. Will these be affected by a break? If you're taking a sabbatical as an employee with a job being held open for you it's important to understand whether these in-house benefits will be affected. In all probability your company benefits will not be diminished during your absence, particularly if the company has a formal sabbatical scheme, though you'll certainly have to hand back the company car. Typically a career break of more than 12 months may require you to resign from your current position with the promise of a job at the same level being available to you on your return, and this can affect your entitlement to important benefits such as redundancy payments.

## How Will my Plans Affect my Mortgage?

For homeowners, a mortgage is likely to be the greatest financial obligation during their working lives. Maintaining monthly payments is a crucial feature of financial planning. The good news is that mortgage policies are becoming increasingly flexible, precisely because the banks and building societies recognise that the working population needs greater choices to reflect greater competition and changes in the nature of employment.

Many of the leading mortgage companies now offer flexible mortgages, allowing suspension of payments for a few months, colloquially known as a 'payment holiday'. Specific options vary according to each policy and you will need to check with your mortgage lender.

Mortgage specialist David Hollingworth, of London and Country Mortgages Ltd (www.lcplc.co.uk), recommends thinking about this question a long way in advance to give you a chance to change your mortgage before taking a gap year:

> *It's important to look at the small print of your agreement and to be very upfront with your lender about your plans. Try to contact the lender as soon as you have made a decision to take a break or least before you actually leave work.*

Your mortgage conditions must count as the major financial factor in evaluating whether you can afford to suspend your regular salary. A logical and simple solution is to find a paying tenant for the duration of your absence from the country (see 'Renting Out Your Property' below). Remember though that if you decide to rent out the property the payments may increase depending on your mortgage rate (explained below).

If in the past few years you have taken out a flexible mortgage, it might give you the opportunity to take back capital you have put in above the mandatory interest payments. For example, if every year you pay in an extra thousand pounds to decrease the total loan, you might be able to take some of that money back in cash. Every policy will offer different benefits and detailed enquiries will have to be made before reaching any decisions about altering the terms of your mortgage. Setting up an offset mortgage which will allow you to take money out of your mortgage account without penalty can be the best course of action.

Another option for raising capital is by taking advantage of your home's increased value to extend your mortgage. If for instance you have a £50,000 loan, you may after five years of ownership be able to increase that loan to £70,000 which would cover any mortgage payments during a break and provide cash for travel or educational expenses in the time off work. Most lenders will allow you to increase the mortgage up to 75% of the current market value. But don't just renegotiate the mortgage with your current lender. Now might be the right time to shop around and switch your mortgage to take advantage of a lower rate or a more flexible policy to assist your gap year finances. Visit a broker and take advantage of the various deals available in the mortgage marketplace. Each borrower will have unique requirements and the challenge is to find a policy that suits you during your career break but which will also accommodate any foreseeable career plans after your return.

**Paul Edmunds** had problems with his mortgage lender, Abbey National, who were reluctant to allow him to continue paying a low rate of interest under his flexible mortgage arrangement if he was sub-letting to tenants while he went to Africa and then re-thought his future. Although he persuaded the building society to let him keep paying at the low interest rate for a limited time, they told him that after a certain period they would double the rate. With hindsight, he wishes that he had given three months notice and moved his mortgage to a different kind of account or to a different building society, before his gap year started when he gave up his income.

Unfortunately, flexibility may not apply to older mortgage policies. Certainly endowment mortgage payments must be maintained regardless of circumstances. Effectively, you are locked into regular payments until the policy matures. The only alternative is to close the policy but this will incur heavy penalties. Endowments are best left until they mature because, at least in theory, the fund proportionately gains most value during the final years. Similarly, traditional repayment mortgages will require that you maintain regular contributions. Remember that life assurance payments must be kept up especially if they are attached to a mortgage.

## Pensions

Pension funding is another important feature of any plan to take a gap year from employment. Until 2001, taking a career break had a deleterious effect on your pension because only earned income put into a pension would qualify for the government's tax relief. With the introduction of stakeholder pensions, it is possible for anyone whether in employment or not to contribute up to a ceiling of £3,600 gross (i.e. £2,808 from you, the rest from the government in tax relief) per year. This contribution is not a great amount but is better than relying on the state pension. According to Anna Bowes of Chase De Vere's Financial Planning department:

> *The stakeholder pension is helpful for non-working mothers or fathers and likewise for people on a career break because they don't need to forgo the government's contribution while they have no earned income. It's common for the newer pensions to allow for a break in contributions, allowing the holder to take premium holidays for up to a year. Unfortunately, some older policies may not grant this period of suspension.*

Chase de Vere are affiliated with the informative website www.moneyextra.com (click on Pensions).

Charles Bailey of Jelf Independent Financial Management (www.jelfifm.com) has helped several clients prepare for a gap year or career break. He advises anyone contemplating a substantial break to investigate how the employer's final salary pension scheme might be affected. Ask the HR department during any negotiations if a long absence from contributions will reduce the total number of years' service with the company, which is used to calculate the pension when you retire or leave the company. The worst situation is if your employer treats you as having left the scheme. So many final salary schemes are being abolished that it might disappear in your absence. But ideally there will be no break in benefits, especially regarding pensions.

Other individuals may work freelance or for companies that are too small to offer pension schemes. In this case you'll probably be contributing to a private money purchase scheme. Once again, you'll need to check whether there are any penalties if you wish to suspend contributions until you return to regular employment. From the mid-1990s pension companies began to introduce flexible pensions with provisions for 'premium holidays', a period each year when you might want to halt contributions without paying a penalty. If your pension predates this change, you will probably have to maintain payments or face some extra charges.

If taking a break of a year or more, some employers expect you officially to resign while promising to re-employ you on your return. Make sure that benefits that have been accrued are merely frozen temporarily rather than suspended.

## National Insurance

Another factor to consider is the possible effect of a break on your state pension. Projections for the state pension are dispiriting and all but a few have stopped relying on it to provide for retirement. Nevertheless it's still a benefit you're contributing to through compulsory National Insurance contributions. If you fail to make National Insurance contributions while you are out of the UK, you will forfeit entitlement to benefits on your return. You can decide to pay voluntary contributions at regular intervals or in a lump sum in order to retain your rights to certain benefits.

The normal projected figure is calculated to represent contributions from 90% of your working life. A career break will have implications although it is likely to be marginal. But you will need to check first to see how the state pension will be altered by any suspension of National Insurance contributions. If you are out of the country for an extended period, you are not obliged to continue paying National Insurance Contributions, however you might choose to make voluntary contributions all the same if you want to maintain your rights to a state pension and other benefits (though this won't entitle you to sickness or unemployment benefit). Voluntary (Class 3) contributions currently stand at £7.55 per week (from 2007). Check HM Revenue & Customs' website for further information (www.hmrc.gov.uk) or if you are self-employed and want to pay Class 2 NICs, ring 084591 54655.

As in many important choices in life these decisions all depend on individual preferences and priorities. Achieving a balance between the imperatives of living a full life right now and making sacrifices for retirement should be the aim. One source of valuable information on pension allowances, stakeholder pensions, and the state pension is the government's public service portal www.direct.gov.uk. The site enables you to access bodies that regulate taxation and personal finance.

## Red Tape in the EU

If you are a national of the European Economic Area and will be living or working in another member state, you will be covered by European Social Security regulations. The information leaflet SA29 'Your Social Security Insurance, Benefits & Health Care Rights in the European Economic Area' was last updated October 2004 and can be read online at www.dwp.gov.uk/international/sa29 or obtained from the Centre for Non Residents, Room BP1301, Benton Park View, Newcastle-upon-Tyne NE98 1ZZ (0845 915 4811; www.hmrc.gov.uk/cnr). The booklet *The Community Provisions on Social Security* can be read on the European Union website (http://europa.eu.int/comm/employment_social/soc-prot/schemes/guide_en.pdf).

## Taxation

Taxation is probably the most complex area of personal finance to be affected by any prolonged absence from the UK. As anyone faintly familiar with taxation knows, there's a professional industry dedicated to helping the individual navigate the murky waters of tax. It must be expected that your taxation will be different if you take a gap from full-time employment, since your earnings are likely to drop substantially. Because tax calculations are based on previous earnings, it may be that after your break you will be eligible for a rebate.

Calculating your liability to tax when working or living outside your home country is notoriously complicated so, if possible, check your position with an accountant or financial planner. Everything depends on whether you fall into the category of 'resident', 'ordinarily resident' or 'domiciled' in the UK'. Career breakers are normally considered domiciled in the UK even if they are away for more than a year. Formerly it was possible to claim a 'foreign earnings deduction' (i.e. pay no tax) if you were out of the country for a full 365 days. However the legislation has changed so that you are eligible for this only if you have been out of the country for a complete tax year (6 April to 5 April) though you are allowed to spend up to 62 days (i.e. one-sixth) of the tax-year back in England without it affecting your tax position. Anyone who is present in the UK for more than 182 days during a particular tax year will be treated as resident with no exceptions.

HM Revenue & Customs leaflets which might be of assistance are IR20 'Residents and Non-Residents: Liability to Tax in the UK' and IR139 'Income from Abroad? A guide to UK tax on overseas income'. HMRC also has a good website if you have the patience to look for the information you need (www.hmrc.gov.uk); it lists the relevant contact offices that deal with specific issues.

Any profit from rented property is subject to income tax. Note that there is no penalty for stopping contributions to your existing ISAs (Individual Savings Account) and Unit Trusts. You can put in as little as you like. Halting contributions will only affect your fund's rate of growth.

If you decide to stay for a prolonged period of time in another country you will need to check out the requirements for establishing residency. For example in Spain, any person who spends more than 183 days a year in Spain is considered a resident and is liable to pay Spanish tax, though Spain has a double taxation treaty with the UK. Almost all countries have double taxation agreements with Britain so it is most unlikely that you will be taxed twice; but it is a wise precaution to keep all receipts and financial documents in case problems arise.

If you plan to live and possibly work in another country, contact the Consulate and ask for the relevant dossier of information. The financial planning company the Fry Group (Crescent Road, Worthing, W Sussex BN11 1RN; 01903 231545; www.thefrygroup.co.uk) specialises in advising UK expatriates and can offer expert tax advice on questions of residency. The big five accountancy firms in the UK all have international offices across the world giving you the advantage of drawing on both UK and foreign expertise: Accenture (www.accenture.com), Deloitte (www.deloitte.com), Ernst & Young (www.ey.com), KPMG (www.kpmg.co.uk) and PricewaterhouseCoopers (www.pwcglobal.com).

## Banking

Advice on how to carry your money while travelling and how to transfer funds in an emergency is included later in this chapter. One way of getting money which will not inconvenience the folks back home works best for those who know in advance where they will be when their funds will run low. Before setting off, you open an account at a large bank in your destination city, which may have a branch in London. Most won't allow you to open a chequing account so instant overdrafts are not a possibility. But knowing you have a fund safely stashed away in Sydney, San Francisco or Singapore is a great morale booster. It can also assist with other red tape problems like obtaining a reference to be a tenant.

If you are planning to spend your sabbatical away from home, you should prepare the ground with your bank. If you are asking family or friends to conduct business on your behalf while you're away, it might make it easier to arrange power of attorney so that your signature is not required. Even something as simple as cancelling a lost or stolen credit card can be tricky for a third party to do.

And while you're at it, update or draw up a will. If you die intestate the government takes an automatic 40% of your estate in inheritance tax and lawyers will get much of the rest as they apportion your wealth according to fixed rules. DIY will-writing kits are readily available though you may feel happier paying for the services of a professional will writer (not legally trained) or a solicitor.

## Fundraising Ideas

Once you have resolved to meet a particular target, say £2,500, it is surprising how single-mindedly you can pursue it. The ingenuity which adult gappers have demonstrated in organising money-making events, etc. is impressive, for example the guy who got everybody he knew to sponsor him to stay up a tree for a week. You may choose to shave your head, jump out of an aeroplane, organise a fancy dress pub crawl or a thousand other ways to raise money. Publicise your plans and your need of funds wherever you can. Local papers and radio stations will usually carry details of your planned expedition, which may prompt a few local readers/listeners to support you. Ask family and friends to give cash instead of birthday and Christmas presents. Consider possibilities for organising a fundraising event like a concert or a ceilidh, a quiz night, wine tasting or auction of promises. (If you have ever been active in your children's school, you may have previous experience of some of these.)

Target organisations and companies with which you have some links, such as your old school or college, to ask for sponsorship. Local businesses are usually inundated with requests for donations and raffle prizes and are unlikely to give cash but some might donate some useful items of equipment. Keep track of all the individuals and businesses who have helped you and be sure to send them a thank you note later on describing the success of your fundraising trip.

**Sarah Elengorn's** most lucrative event, held a few weeks before her departure for Mexico to work with street kids, was a netball tournament organised through her club at home in Middlesex (which gave her use of the premises free of charge). Twelve teams paid £40 to enter. The event was on a Mexican theme with a bar, raffle, etc. Sarah had been hoping to raise £500 but instead made £800.

**Wendy Burridge** who went to Uganda with Madventurer also organised two raffles, one in her home town and another for brokers on the London art market with whom she had dealings through her job in art insurance. The raffles generated support from many companies who donated excellent prizes like a £100 hamper, a gym membership and an evening of drinks. As the support grew so did her fundraising ambitions. She wrote to every Premiership football team asking for signed photographs and had fantastic support from Liverpool, the FA,

Everton, Tottenham and Arsenal. The raffle raised just under £1,000.

If you want to go down the route of applying to trusts and charitable bodies, consult a library copy of the *Directory of Grant Making Trusts* (new edition published each April) or contact the Association of Charitable Foundations (020-7255 4499; www.acf.org.uk) which can offer advice on how to approach grant-giving trusts. Another possible source of useful information is the website www.funderfinder.org.uk/advice_pack.php. Also check the National Charities Database on www.charitiesdirect.com or search www.caritasdata.co.uk. In fact not many are willing to support individuals and so you may meet mostly with rejections. (One enterprising fund-raiser got his friends and family to sponsor him for every rejection.) If you are going through a registered charity, always include the charity number in your letter of request since this may be needed by their accountant.

The *Winston Churchill Memorial Trust* (15 Queen's Gate Terrace, London SW7 5PR; www.wcmt.org.uk) awards about 100 four to eight week travelling fellowships to UK citizens of any age or background who wish to undertake a specific project or study related to their personal interests, job or community. The deadline for applications falls in October. Past winners are listed on the website with their ages and diverse topics of study; for example in 2006 a twenty-eight year old candidate was given funding to explore the River Niger in the footsteps of the explorer Mungo Park and a 49 year old woman was planning to travel to China, Turkey and Italy to study the craft of pebble mosaics.

## ACCOMMODATION MATTERS

Younger individuals may decide to break their careers before taking on the large financial commitment of a mortgage. Going away for them may simply involve giving up rented accommodation. The only major logistical hurdle is finding a place to store your possessions. Disposing of furniture is difficult but even if your worldly goods consist only of clothes, books, CDs, photographs and letters, you'll have to find a place for them. It will be a time of shedding superfluous possessions (think of car boot sales, eBay and so on) and will feel like a symbolic counterpart to putting work to one side as you prepare to head off into the unknown. With luck you'll find a willing parent or friends with spare space in a garage or attic for your clobber.

But for many people in their 30s, 40s and 50s, travelling or living abroad will entail serious plans for the care of their homes. Just as making the arrangements to put a job on hold or to leave an employer is a major hurdle, so is solving the problem of what to do with your abode while you're taking a sabbatical abroad. The process of making the necessary arrangements to rent out the property or in a more radical move to sell it will take many months so it is essential to plan a long way in advance.

Five solutions can be considered: leaving the property unoccupied, finding a friend to stay in it rent-free but keeping an eye on it, finding a tenant either independently or through a letting agency, registering with a house swapping agency or using the services of a housesitting agency. The latter is so expensive as to be of interest mainly to the seriously wealthy (see below). Not everyone is comfortable with the idea of strangers living in their house, whether paying tenants or house-swappers. In the end it will be a personal decision, but be assured that tens of thousands of people have been delighted with the ease with which it can be accomplished.

## Renting out Your Property

Assuming you are a property owner, your house or flat is probably your greatest financial asset. It is also your home, a place of emotional and physical security which you will not want to hand over to strangers lightly. However, if you want to spend all or part of your gap year travelling or living overseas, renting out your home can go a long way to covering your costs and is usually worth the bother. Renting to tenants also neatly solves the problem of security and makes use of the home to provide a revenue stream at a time when you may not be drawing an income. If you are lucky you will find a tenant through the 'mates network' (which can be accessed very simply through your e-mail address book) as Mike Bleazard did when he wanted to leave home for six months. Mike was very happy to rent his flat to the colleague of a friend at somewhat below the market rate for Cambridge, i.e. at £800 a month including all the bills apart from council tax and telephone. This worked out easier all round because it meant that Mike didn't have to worry about meter readings or disconnections when he left and returned.

During the 1960s and 1970s the problem of sitting tenants who refused to leave at the end of the rental period became notorious. The Housing Act of 1988 and a subsequent amendment have virtually solved this abuse, ensuring that a contract between landlord and tenant explicitly sets out terms for the rental, for example the prohibition of pets, and makes the time limit legally binding.

Try to avoid switching to a buy-to-let mortgage (as some lenders may try to impose on you) which is almost always more expensive and will force you to pay all the costs of remortgaging (legal fees, valuations, etc.) Make sure your lender knows that you will be returning to occupy the property within a specified period. They should give you a 'permission to let' for which there may be a fee (usually under £100) but will allow you to carry on with the same mortgage terms.

Above all, it is essential to notify both your mortgage lender and your insurance company that you intend to rent out your home before agreeing to any tenancy. Any changes to the normal habitation must be cleared first. Most insurance companies are amenable to making provision for your time abroad but they may want to re-assess risk if there is a change of occupancy. Mike Bleazard was glad that he had topped up his contents insurance before renting out his flat, making sure the policy would cover tenants, because the flat was burgled while he was on his gap year.

If you put many valuable items like furniture or pictures into storage for the duration of a tenancy this might actually lower the cost of contents insurance. Your insurer will prefer and occasionally even insist that you use a registered agency or at least delegate responsibility for keeping a regular check on the property to a trustworthy person close by.

When notifying the mortgage lender, you need to know whether you have a 'residential mortgage rate' and if so whether you can retain these preferable terms while you're renting the property instead of becoming liable for the more expensive 'standard variable rate'. Normally you will be permitted to maintain your mortgage status if you sign a form stating that you are renting to a private individual on an 'Assured Shorthold Tenancy'. With hindsight **Paul Edmunds** realises that he made an error in accepting his tenants' suggestion of paying six months' rent in a lump sum at the beginning of their tenancy. This meant that he had to declare the rental income for tax purposes in that tax year, whereas if their payments had been staggered or paid later, in the next tax year when his income was much lower, he would have had to pay considerably less tax.

## Using a Rental Agency

Putting your home into the hands of professionals often imparts peace of mind even if it cuts into your financial gain. Most agencies charge a fee of at least 10% of the rent plus VAT. The Association of Residential Letting Agents (ARLA) advises – and of course it is in their members' interests to do so – that you use a professional agency to manage the tenancy while you are away. Homeowners often find comfort in knowing that any problems that arise over money or maintenance can be delegated to an impartial intermediary. Also agency fees are an allowable expense that can be offset against tax.

A letting agency will screen potential tenants according to particular criteria to ensure that you let your home to responsible people. They may for example have regular company customers who rent property on behalf of company employees, diminishing the likelihood of any disputes over unpaid rent. A company let is safer because the company in question becomes legally responsible for any transgressions by the tenant.

Letting agencies are increasingly experienced at working with private homes being placed on the rental market for a set period of time. Short lets are possible to arrange if you are intending to be away for less than six months. Even if renting out your home is a novelty and feels rather risky, there is plenty of professional help available to make it a viable proposition, allowing you to benefit from the property's intrinsic value while maintaining all your legal rights to possession.

If you are using an agency, find out if it is a member of ARLA and therefore obliged to follow a professional code of conduct. These registered agents are bonded which ensures that any misuse of your rental income or of the tenant's deposits is guaranteed by the Association's special fund. If there are any financial irregularities you can go straight to ARLA for compensation. You can ring ARLA for information about where to find a local agent or with specific questions about letting your home. It also publishes a helpful pamphlet called 'Trouble Free Letting: What Every Landlord and Tenant Should Ask' (see Letting Resources listing below) which is available from ARLA or from one of the Association's 1,723 member agencies throughout the UK.

## Renting Independently

Of course it is possible to take the independent course and organise the rental yourself and thereby save a substantial sum of money. Managing your own rental will be more difficult if you plan on being abroad. However with the rise of the Internet it is easier to locate suitable tenants and with advances in communications, it is possible to keep tabs on a tenant via email.

The tried and tested method of finding a tenant is to advertise in the local newspaper or to target a magazine read by the kind of people you want as tenants (ramblers, stamp collectors, vegetarians, alumnae of your old university, etc.) Even people who do not happen to live in prime tourist locations can often rent out their houses to people who have come to work at the local hospital, or been transferred by their employer and are renting for a time while they look around to buy. A 57-year old kitchen fitter from the small Midlands town of Measham who was planning a long break in New Zealand recognised that there was not much of a rental market in his town, though he discovered that the local Council was looking for properties to rent out for a minimum of a year. The rent of about £250 was low but they guaranteed to find tenants.

Always ask prospective tenants to supply references from their current employer, bank and previous landlord and follow them up because dodgy tenants have been known to fabricate references. Holding one month's rent as a deposit is standard practice. This can be used to pay outstanding bills at the end of the tenancy and to cover any potential damage, and then the difference is returned. Depending on the nature and duration of the tenancy, you can consider putting the utilities in the tenant's name (which is a major hassle) and asking them to pay the council tax. Together, you and your tenant should also draw up an inventory of all the items in the property, which you should both sign in front of a witness. You will want to ask a neighbour (preferably a nosy one) to contact you in the event of problems especially in an emergency like theft or fire.

**The following practical steps should be considered when renting out your house independently and going away for an extended period:**

- Notify your mortgage lender that you intend to let the property. They will want you to sign a form stating that you are renting to a private individual on an Assured Shorthold Tenancy.
- Remember you will be liable for tax on the rental income minus the mortgage payments, letting fees and other expenses.
- Agree a method of rent payment with the tenant, possibly asking for evidence that a standing order into your account has been set up or asking for a set of post-dated cheques which you (or a trusted proxy) can pay in to your account.
- Read the utility meters at the last minute before departure. If they are not accessible, request that the electricity and gas supplier take interim readings.
- Telephone the phone company for an interim reading. You can leave a cheque made payable to the phone company to cover your share of monthly or quarterly calls and leave the tenant in charge of paying the phone bill.
- Put away valuables such as computers and paintings plus any items you would be heart-broken if damaged. It may be that you can store such items in the smallest room which can be declared off-limits (assuming this has been agreed with the tenant beforehand).
- Prepare a file with all relevant instruction manuals, guarantees or insurance cover for appliances.
- If tenants are new to the area, a few tips on local shops, services, pubs and restaurants, doctor's surgeries, etc. would be appreciated.
- Ask a friend or neighbour to keep an eye on the property and ask them to contact you by phone or e-mail if anything seems amiss.
- Obtain a mail forwarding application form from any post office; the current fees within the UK are £6.90 for one month, £15.10 for three, £23.25 for six and £34.90 for 12; fees for forwarding mail abroad are double. These fees apply per surname.
- Cancel subscriptions to newspapers, book clubs, the cleaner, window washing services, etc. after ascertaining that the tenant does not want to retain them.

**Philip Hardie** was due a sabbatical term and decided to take it away from Cambridge. His twin sons were in their last year of primary school and this seemed like a good opportunity for a change. Although Australia is not the first destination to spring to mind when classicists plan a sabbatical, he had several friends in the department at the University of Sydney who assured him that the welcome would be warm and the library resources adequate for the book he wanted to research.

The family's first thought was to arrange a house swap for their four-month trip since there is plenty of sabbatical traffic in the other direction, Sydney to Cambridge. However, matching dates was going to present problems and it seemed simpler to rent out the family house in central Cambridge and find a place to rent in Sydney. Universities often have an accommodation office that caters to visiting academics and Cambridge is no exception. The rather grandly titled Society for Visiting Scholars tries to match accommodation requests from abroad with furnished houses and flats for rent. They are simply an introduction service rather than an agent and charge no commission, though they welcome donations if their services are appreciated. Usefully, the office gives its clients a template of a letting contract.

The family house was registered early in the year for a September departure with an expectation that expressions of interest would roll in. By July, the family had had just one enquiry that had come to nothing, and the university office could guarantee nothing. Realising that departure was less than eight weeks away, Philip began to panic and discovered a local website for Cambridge accommodation on which he posted (free of charge) brief house details. Within 48 hours he had had three replies, one coincidentally from Sydney, two others from people already in Cambridge and therefore available to come to see the property. One took it for precisely the dates it would be empty. The family appreciated the chance to meet the tenant in the flesh, especially when they discovered that she was the daughter of a family friend of a neighbour. References (one work, one personal, one bank) were requested and produced, an Assured Shorthold Tenancy Agreement was signed in the presence of witnesses and all went ahead smoothly.

On the family's return, they found their house not only in one piece but mostly unchanged from when they had left it. Inevitably a few dishes had been broken, a saucepan ruined, a lampshade torn, a wall gouged (the tenant had a two-year old daughter), but they felt that this was fair wear and tear from tenants paying £700 a month and thereby covering all their rental expenses in Sydney.

As for organising the paying of bills, the Hardies had continued to pay the electricity and gas bills by standing order. On their return they read both meters themselves then calculated the number of units used over the whole rental period and added the pro-rated standing charge.

The telephone bills had been slightly more problematic. Rather than change the billing name, the bills were forwarded to the owners (since they had organised all mail to be forwarded by the post office). After marvelling at how high their tenants' phone bills were, they sent them on to the tenant and trusted her to pay them. If for some reason she had not paid them, she is the one who would have suffered the inconvenience of having the service cut off. As soon as they returned home, they contacted the telephone company for an interim reading and were told the amount owing at that time was a whopping £300. This amount together with the total amount owed for utilities came in at about £50 less than the deposit of a month's rent, so there was no need to extract extra money from the tenants after they had gone.

## Letting Resources

*Association of Residential Letting Agents (ARLA),* Maple House, 53-55 Woodside Road, Amersham, Bucks. HP6 6AA (0845 345 5752; www.arla.co.uk). ARLA publishes 'Trouble Free Letting – What Every Landlord and Tenant Should Ask,' a booklet which will answer all your initial questions about fee structures, inventories, repossession, legislation and insurance cover. Enclose a stamped addressed envelope when requesting it.

*The Complete Guide To Letting Property* by Liz Hodgkinson (Kogan Page, 2004, £10.99). The author writes from personal experience as a professional journalist who runs rental flats on the side as an investment. Contains forthright advice about how to manage a rental yourself, from finding the right tenant to whether you should rent out the property furnished or unfurnished.

*The Which? Guide To Renting and Letting* by Peter Wilde and Paul Butt (2003, £11.99). This comprehensive guide tackles all the common problems that arise between landlord and tenant, and explains how the law operates to help avoid most of them.

## House Swapping

Another option to explore is swapping your home and sometimes also your car with an individual, couple or family in a city or country you want to visit. Exchanging houses with a homeowner abroad will not only save accommodation costs, it immediately takes you off the tourist trail and sets you down in a real neighbourhood. The two main requirements are that you be willing to spend at least a few weeks in one place and that you have a decent house in a potentially desirable location. You also have to be someone who can plan ahead since most swaps are arranged six months in advance. And of course you must be prepared to bring your housekeeping up to an acceptable standard.

Many home exchange agencies are in the business of trying to match up compatible swappers. Swaps are usually arranged for short holiday breaks up to about a month in the summer (especially popular with school teachers) but much longer ones are possible too. The great advantage of a home swap is that this is not a commercial transaction, so the costs are minimal. You are effectively leveraging the value of your home to secure cost-free lodging abroad.

The more desirable your home location is, the easier it will be to attract interested swappers. People who live in central London, Sydney or New York or in a Cotswold village or near a Californian beach will certainly have an advantage. But families and individuals might be looking not just for historic or culturally interesting destinations but for a specific university town or a home with easy access to the countryside. Even if you don't live in a popular destination, it is worth registering since you might just happen to find someone who is looking for a property just like yours in your particular area of the country.

It is easy to register with an agency (listed below) online. You simply complete a questionnaire describing your home and its location and pay the registration fee. Most agencies have stopped distributing printed directories because of the enormous cost and operate totally in cyberspace, which has brought annual membership down in most cases to £20-£30. Once you have subscribed, you can search the company's listings and make direct contact with the owners of properties that interest you. The vast bulk of this communication now happens by e-mail. The final stage is an exchange of formal letters of agreement.

*Green Theme International* is one of the pioneering companies in this field and has an environmental motivation. By encouraging house swaps it is hoping to limit the demand for package destinations and the appeal of second homes. The founder, Kathy Botterill, says success in finding a suitable match is often due to good luck, particularly if you have your heart set on a particular destination.

As home swapping is a form of bartering, it's entirely possible to swap your home for an extended stay, provided you can find someone willing to live in your home for that length of time. The cost will be exactly the same as if you swapped for a fortnight. In the past, Green Theme has helped residents of Australia and New Zealand swap homes for periods of one and even two years.

*Homelink International* is one of the largest agencies with more than 13,500 properties worldwide on its website. They send out three directories per year as well as maintaining web listings. The longest established company is Intervac whose list includes 8.000 properties in 50 countries though, as with most of the companies, the majority are in North America. *HomeExchange.com* has a purported 10,000 listings in 85 countries, while the *Special Families Trust* can provide a list of properties for people with a physical disability. The main organisations can arrange travel insurance specifically tailored for home swaps, covering such problems as cancellation owing to illness, marital collapse, etc.

If you are taking children with you, it's best to check whether the house you're going to live in is safe or suitable for them. Likewise, if a family with children is coming to stay in your home try to check if it meets safety standards. If possible swap with another family or couple who mirror your lives to some extent, for example, if they have children of a similar age.

It's a wise precaution to notify your insurance company too. Check to see if your home contents and building insurance covers any potential damage. Legally, people on a house swap are classified as guests not tenants. It is also sensible to put into storage your most valuable possessions to avoid accidental damage or breakage. If a car is included in the swap the guests will need to be added to the policy and details given of their driving licences.

## Home Exchange Contacts

*Green Theme International,* 94 Fore Street, Bodmin, Cornwall PL31 2HR. Contact in France: 9, rue des Insurgés, La Maillerie Ouest, Linards 87130; (tel/fax +33-5-55 08 47 04; www.gti-home-exchange.com). Modest fee of £21/$39 fee for one-year online listing.

*Holi-Swaps Vacation Home Exchanges and Rentals Worldwide* – based in Phoenix, Arizona (480-767-2753; www.holi-swaps.com). Web-based membership is $35. You can check listings before registering.

*Home Base Holidays,* 7 Park Avenue, London N13 5PG (020-8886 8752; www.homebase-hols.com). Annual fee of £29 for online listing.

*Homelink International,* 7 St. Nicholas Rise, Headbourne Worthy, Winchester, Hants. SO23 7SY; 01962 886882; www.homelink.org.uk. 13,500 members worldwide. Annual membership fee of £115 includes copy of 900-page directory as well as online listing.

*Intervac International,* 24 The Causeway, Chippenham, Wiltshire SN15 3DB (01249 461101; www.intervac.co.uk). UK membership £65 online only, £85 for entry in printed directory as well. International website is www.intervac.com.

*HomeExchange.com,* PO Box 787, Hermosa Beach, CA 90254, USA (310-798-3864; www.homeexchange.com). $60 per year. Very detailed information about properties and families.

*Special Families Home Swap Register,* Erme House, Station Road, Plympton, Plymouth, Devon PL7 3AU (01752 347577; www.mywebpage.net/special-families/home.html). Small-scale Home Swap Register for people with disabilities.

## Leaving Your Property Empty

You will need to make careful preparations to ensure that your home is well cared for and protected in your absence. Assuming you have decided against renting or lending it out to a lodger or student, can you arrange for a neighbour, relative or friend to make regular visits? How important is it for the garden to be cared for in your absence if only to have the grass mown so it looks occupied? Preventing burglary and guarding against burst pipes in winter are real considerations.

Naturally, friends or relatives may not be able or willing to commit the same amount of time or apply the same degree of professional expertise as an agency. Appointing a friend as agent can strain good relations if anything goes wrong. A bottle of wine and box of chocolates are probably not enough compensation for the anxiety the job may have caused them.

## Cars

If you own a vehicle that you do not intend to sell, you can either take it off the road for the duration of your absence or lend it to a friend/tenant. Motor insurance in the UK is less flexible than in many countries (like the US and Australia) since it covers named drivers rather than the vehicle. It can be expensive adding one or more names to the car insurance for an extended period, an expense which should be passed on to the borrower. If you have a no-claims bonus, try to find out if it can be protected in the event of another driver having an accident.

If you are taking your car off the road, you will obviously want to store it in a safe place, perhaps a friend's unused garage or driveway. Some homeowners prefer to leave their vehicle in their own drive to disguise the fact the property is empty.

If a vehicle is off the road for more than a calendar month, it is possible to reclaim the unused months of road tax by declaring SORN (Statutory Off Road Notification). Simply ask at a post office for form V14 and send it to the Driver and Vehicle Licensing Agency in Swansea (Refunds Section, DVLA, Swansea SA99 1AL).

## Pets

Taking a gap year abroad will pose a special challenge for pet owners. Most pets are well-loved friends especially for children. Your dog or cat is virtually a member of the family and it will be very hard to imagine leaving them behind. The good news is that the Passport For Pets scheme is now well established and allows you to take a dog or cat (or rodent, rabbit, reptile or ornamental tropical fish) abroad to a number of approved countries, without subjecting the animal to six months quarantine when you return. Check to see whether your destination is included in the scheme. After several years of delay, the United States and Canada are now included in the scheme.

If you plan to take a dog or cat abroad, give yourself plenty of time to make the necessary preparations to comply with the regulations of the pet passport scheme. A dog or a cat will need to be vaccinated against rabies and have a microchip implanted by the local vet which gives the animal a unique number, procedures which will run to several hundred pounds. Essentially, you have to prove that an animal is clear of rabies for the six months following the blood test after the vaccination. It's a slightly convoluted process but nevertheless is a dramatic improvement on the previous rules which made quarantine compulsory for six months. You can obtain an information pack by calling the Department for Environment, Food and Rural Affairs or by consulting the DEFRA website, which lists all the approved countries in the passport scheme (see below).

On some journeys, like a walking pilgrimage over the Pyrenees to Santiago de Compostella in Spain, it might be wholly appropriate to take your dog for company. You'll never be far from shops or veterinary care in Europe. On other trips like driving across Africa, it wouldt be completely impractical. If you are renting or swapping your house, you can hold out for a tenant who is willing to take on the care of your animal. Another option is to put the pet into a boarding kennel. To find one, ask your vet for a recommendation and then check if it is licensed by the local council. An alternative would be to find a foster family, perhaps a good friend or a relative willing to take on the care.

## Housesitting

Ideally you might hear of someone via the grapevine who is looking for temporary accommodation and who would be willing to look after your house, pet and garden in exchange for a rent-free stay. Graduate colleges and teaching hospitals are just two places with a mobile population and potential housesitters. If you do not know the person beforehand, ask for references just as you would of a rent-paying tenant.

You might want to investigate other possibilities. A journal called *The Caretaker Gazette* published in the US has been listing properties that need live-in caretakers since 1983 (address below). An annual subscription to the magazine costs $29.95.

A final solution is to hire a housesitter, who will take care of the pets and provide a range of light domestic support like simple cleaning and gardening, all for a large fee. Effectively you'll be hiring an individual or a couple to act as housekeepers. But if you can afford it and perhaps own a home that requires special care owing to age or an outstanding garden or a menagerie of animals, this might be the best solution (see Animal Aunts below).

This is certainly not a cheap option and can cost £500 a fortnight plus expenses. In return the companies will guarantee that the employee will care for your animals according to any instructions you leave.

## Useful Contacts

*DEFRA* – 0870 241 1710; www.defra.gov.uk/animalh/quarantine/pets/index.htm. DEFRA is responsible for the Pet Travel Scheme.

*Animal Aunts,* Smugglers Cottage, Green Lane, Rogate, Petersfield, Hampshire GU31 5DA (01730 821529; www.animalaunts.co.uk).

*Home & Pet Care Ltd,* Nether Row Hall, Hesket Newmarket, Wigton, Cumbria CA7 8LA (016974 78515; ww.homeandpetcare.co.uk). Provide an alternative service to people who might otherwise put their pets in a kennel or cattery.

*Minders Keepers Ltd,* 17 High Street, Shepreth, Royston, Herts. SG8 6PP (01763 262102; www.minders-keepers.co.uk). Fee of £30 per day.

*The Caretaker Gazette,* PO Box 4005-M, Bergheim, TX 78004, USA (830-336-3939; www.caretaker.org). Subscribers pay $29.95 and receive a magazine containing housesitting and caretaking opportunities, about 150 per issue.

*www.HouseCarers.com* – Housesitting database. Annual membership $32.

## Staying in Private Homes

If you are not in a position to swap your own accommodation for someone else's, you might like to consider a homestay or some variation on that theme. A number of worthy organisations dedicated to promoting world peace and understanding match up people interested in hosting foreign travellers with those on the move. Socially it can be a gamble but financially it is brilliant since expenses are minimal.

Servas International is an organisation begun by an American Quaker, which runs a worldwide programme of free hospitality exchanges for travellers, to further world peace and understanding. Normally you don't stay with one host for more than a couple of days. To become a Servas traveller or host in the UK, contact Servas Britain, 68 Cadley Road, Collingbourne Ducis, Marlborough, Wilts. SN8 3EB; 020 8444 7778 (www.servasbritain.u-net.com) who can forward your enquiry to your Area Co-ordinator. Before a traveller can be given a list of hosts (which are drawn up every autumn), he or she must pay a fee of £25 (£35 for couples) and be interviewed by a co-ordinator. Servas US is at 11 John St, Suite 505, New York, NY 10038 (212-267-0252; www.usservas.org). There is a joining fee of US$85 and a refundable deposit of $25 for host lists in up to five countries.

Hospitality exchange organisations can make travel both interesting and cheap. **Bradwell Jackson** had been mulling over the possibility of travelling the world for about a decade before he finally gave up his drug abuse counselling job in the US to take off for an indeterminate period of time but at least a year. On his earlier travels he had discovered the benefits of joining Servas and two other hospitality exchange programmes Global Freeloaders (www.globalfreeloaders.com) and the Hospitality Club (www.hospitalityclub.org). His first destination was Mexico where to his amazement he found English teaching work at the first place he happened to enquire in Mexico City:

> *I really must say right away that Servas is not simply for freeloading in people's homes. However, once you take the plunge and commit to wandering the earth, things just start to fall into place. If you belong to clubs such as Global Freeloaders, Hospitality Club, or any of the other homestay organisations, don't be surprised if the family you stay with invites you for an extended stay. The first such family I stayed with in Mexico invited me to stay for six months. All they asked is that I help with the costs of the food they prepared for me and hot water I used.*

When you register with the Hospitality Club, Global Freeloaders or the Couchsurfing Project (www.couchsurfing.com), all of which are completely free, you agree to host the occasional visitor in your home in order to earn the right to stay with other members worldwide. Another possibility is the Hospitality Exchange, 822 W. Watson St, Lewistown, Montana 59457 (406-538-8770; www.hospex.net) which charges $20 for a year's membership.

Members of the Globetrotters Club are often willing to extend hospitality to other globetrotters. Annual membership of this travel club costs £15/$29; contact the Globetrotters via their postal address BCM/Roving, London WC1N 3XX or on the web www.globetrotters.co.uk. Members receive a bi-monthly travel newsletter and a list of members, indicating whether or not they encourage other members to stay with them.

Other hospitality clubs and exchanges are worth investigating. Women Welcome Women World Wide (88 Easton St, High Wycombe, Bucks. HP11 1LT;

tel/fax 01494 465441/ www.womenwelcomewomen.org.uk) enables women of different countries to visit one another. There is no set subscription, but the minimum donation requested is £25/$45, which covers the cost of the membership list and three newsletters in which members may publish announcements. There are currently 2,500 members (aged 16-80+) in 70 countries.

A number of agencies arrange homestays in conjunction with a language course (see section on 'Learning a Language' in the chapter *New Skills and New Projects*). Major language course agencies can usually arrange for clients to live with local families as paying guests which is a great way to improve a language in the context of family life. This is commonplace throughout Latin America but can also be arranged in France, Germany, Spain and so on.

## Finding Accommodation at the Other End

As if it weren't enough trying to work out what to do with your property while you're away, you will have to worry about where you can afford to stay while you're abroad. If you intend to spend your gap year travelling, see the chapter *Travel & Adventure* for some information about where to stay on the road.

If you have organised a house swap, your accommodation has already been taken care of. Renting a flat or house abroad will be miles cheaper than staying in hotels or other travellers' accommodation but it is sure to be more complicated (unless you are lucky enough to find something through a personal contact). Property agencies normally charge steep fees and are legalistic about checking the inventory, etc. Numerous online rental agencies offer properties in Europe and worldwide for short or longer-term lets, and their fees tend to be lower and in a few cases non-existent. Try tapping 'self-catering' and your destination into google.

Agency fees can be avoided by answering ads in local newspapers, though this can be discouraging in an unfamiliar city. You can end up wasting a lot of time going to see flats in areas you might deem too seedy or unsafe to live in. Furthermore, competition for accommodation advertised in daily papers will be fierce. To stand any chance you might have to buy a morning paper as soon as it goes on sale the night before and act quickly first thing in the morning.

If you are willing to consider student-style accommodation, it is worth contacting the student housing office or checking notice boards in student unions, preferably one aimed at graduate students and therefore with notices of accommodation a little more grown-up than undergraduate digs.

One of the main drawbacks of renting is that you will be expected to sign a lease, typically for a minimum of six months which locks you into staying in one place for longer than you might have chosen. You will probably be required to pay a sizeable bond, usually at least one month's rent, which will be held back if you leave before the lease expires or if you leave the property in less than immaculate condition. Some flat-letting agents will give shorter leases for higher rents. You may be asked to provide a bank reference or evidence of a reliable income.

# Practical Advice for Travellers

The best advice comes from other people who've done it first. They've learnt the hard way, so talk to your friends, colleagues and acquaintances who have hit the road or volunteered abroad, and make use of the Internet to locate travellers who have gone before. Spending time in travel chatrooms like Lonely Planet's thorntree or www.gapyear.com (Career Gap section) might turn up gems of little-known travel wisdom or put you on your way to connecting up with a like-minded companion. Of course you don't always have to act on their advice, some of which will be too cautious/daring for your tastes, may conflict with other reports and even be downright wrong. Be prepared to cherry pick what makes sense to you.

While travelling, be open to meeting the locals and other travellers because they are a valuable source of information. But the same limitations apply to their advice. You may meet an educated professional in Islamabad who warns you against going up the Karakoram Highway on the grounds that it is populated by bandits. The same day you might meet a hardened traveller who encourages you to wander at will in the hills of the Hunza Valley on that same highway. You will have to choose your own course between these extremes and try to filter out advice based on prejudice on the one hand or bravado on the other. All the information and contacts in the world are useless unless you make a personal approach to every particular situation. If you have elected for a placement with a local NGO, you will be able to benefit immediately from local advice.

It is amazing how far the English language can take you in even remote corners of the world. But it is a gesture of respect to learn at least a few local phrases and words. In some cases, it may be essential, for example in finding the local WC or if you're vegetarian and want to avoid eating meat. At least carry a relevant phrase book or mini-dictionary.

Many single women would love to take a gap year travelling but are intimidated by perceived danger. Statistically the chances of serious mishap are negligible but it still takes courage to organise a solo trip especially without prior experience. Of course women should only undertake to travel in a way with which they're comfortable. Travelling in Islamic countries where women are barely seen in public presents special problems.

If contemplating an ambitious trip, it might be worth trying a few trips closer to home or of shorter duration to see if you can enjoy your own company and the delights of choosing an itinerary with reference to no one but yourself. As mentioned earlier, many suitable companions will be met along the route. Both women and men who remain unconvinced that they could enjoy travelling alone might prefer to travel with an organised expedition (see section on *Adventure Travel* in the chapter on Travel & Adventure chapter).

Visas and vaccinations may be a pain in the backside but neither can be ignored without giving rise to inconvenience (and worse) later in your gap year. They will also be a pain in your pocketbook. Be prepared to spend a lot of time and money: it took Paul Edmunds a full week of commuting up to London to get four African visas.

# RED TAPE

## Passports

A ten-year UK passport costs £51 for 32 pages and £62.50 for 48 pages, and should be processed by the Identity and Passport Service within three weeks. The one-week fast track application procedure costs £77.50 and an existing passport can be renewed in person at a passport office but only if you have made a prior appointment by ringing the Passport Agency on 0870 521 0410 and are willing to pay £96.50 (£104.50 for 48 pages). Passport office addresses are listed on passport application forms available from main post offices. All relevant information can be found on the website www.passport.gov.uk.

## Documentation

With more than 150 nations crammed onto this minor planet, you can't continue in one direction for very long (unless you are a national of the European Union travelling in Europe) before you are impeded by border guards demanding to see your papers. Post September 11th, immigration and security checks are tighter than ever and many countries have imposed visa restrictions, particularly on North Americans in retaliation for all the new restrictions the US has implemented. Embassy websites are the best source of information or you can check online information posted by visa agencies. For example Thames Consular Services in London (www.thamesconsular.com) allows you to search visa requirements and costs for UK nationals visiting any country. An equivalent source of visa information in the US is Travisa (www.travisa.com) with offices in Washington, New York, Chicago, LA, Houston, Miami and London. Travel Document Express in the US (www.traveldocument.com) carries visa application forms that can be downloaded and can process visa and passport applications or try Travel Document Systems in Washington, New York and San Francisco (www.traveldocs.com).

Getting visas is a headache anywhere, and most travellers feel happier obtaining them in their home country. Set aside a chunk of your travel budget to cover the costs; to give just a few examples of charges for tourist visas for UK citizens applying in London: £30 for India, £30 for China, £11 for Jordan, £23 or £38 for Vietnam (depending on whether you have a letter of authorisation), £35 for Armenia, £45 for Pakistan, £50 for Rwanda, £43.50 for Nigeria, £30 for Haiti (visa recommended). Requirements for American travellers are completely different, for example no visa is required for Haiti (nor for the majority of Latin American countries), $115 for Brazil, $65 for India, $55 for China (or $85 for rush issuance), $21.50 for Jordan, $70 for Vietnam, $105 for Nigeria, etc. Last-minute applications often incur a much higher fee, for example a Russian visa costs £30 if applied for three weeks in advance, but £80 for three-day processing. If you do not want to pin yourself down to entry dates, you may decide to apply for visas as you travel for example from a neighbouring country, which in many cases is cheaper, though may cause delays.

If you are short of time or live a long way from the Embassies in London, private visa agencies like Thames Consular mentioned above can undertake the footwork for you, at a price. Other visa agencies include the VisaService, 2 Northdown St, London N1 9BG (020-7833 2709/fax 020-7833 1857; www.visaservice.co.uk) and Global Visas (020-7009 3800; www.globalvisas.com). In addition to the fee charged by the country's embassy, there will be a service charge normally of £35-£45 per visa. Travel Document Systems in the US charges $45 per visa plus FedEx delivery charge.

If you intend to cross a great many borders, especially on an overland trip through Africa, ensure that you have all the relevant documentation and that your passport contains as many blank pages as frontiers which you intend to cross. Travellers have been turned back purely because the border guard refused to use a page with another stamp on it.

Information about documents needed for working abroad can be found in the chapter *Working and Living Abroad*.

## Accessing Money Abroad

Once you are resolved to save for your gap year, set a realistic target and then go for it wholeheartedly. If you are participating in a scheme through a recognised charity, you will be able to fund-raise (see section in chapter *Doing Something*

*Worthwhile*). Estimate how long it will take you to raise the desired amount, set some interim deadlines and stick to them. If you are lucky enough to be in a position to rent out property while you're away, you will have to make arrangements for transferring the income abroad (covered earlier in this chapter).

The cost of a trip varies tremendously, depending on modes of transport chosen, your willingness to sleep and eat modestly and to deny yourself souvenirs. It is of course always a good idea to have an emergency fund in reserve or at least access to money from home in addition to a return ticket should you run into difficulties. To estimate daily expenses, it might be helpful to know that the average budget of a travelling student is roughly £25 a day, though older more affluent gap-year travellers can easily spend twice that and much more.

Whatever the size of your travelling fund, you should plan to access your money from three sources: cash, credit cards and travellers' cheques. Travellers' cheques are safer than cash, though they cost an extra 1% or 2%. They are a useful standby if you happen to find yourself stranded in a place without an ATM. American Express have monopolised the market and their cheques are sold by most banks plus Thomas Cook (who used to have their own brand). Try to avoid frequent transactions since suitable banks outside big cities are not always easy to find and encashing them can incur a service charge.

The most straightforward way to access money abroad is by using your bank debit card in hole-in-the-wall ATMs. There is usually a minimum fee for a withdrawal so you should get larger amounts out at one time than you would at home. Read the fine print on those boring leaflets that come with your debit card because it may be that your bank will gouge you with various loading fees, withdrawal fees and transaction fees. For example the transaction fee for withdrawing foreign currency abroad or paying at point-of-sale with a standard Maestro card is 2.65% in addition to the ordinary exchange rate disadvantage plus cash machine withdrawals cost 2.25% of the sterling transaction up to a maximum of £4 (no minimum). The Point of Sale charge is a more reasonable 75 pence. If you are going to be abroad for a considerable period drawing on funds in your home account, it would be worth shopping around for the best deal which is at present offered by the Nationwide whose FlexAccount debit card is the only one currently on the market that can be used abroad for free (www.nationwide.co.uk). The website www.moneyfacts.co.uk carries a comparative list of commission charged by the main providers (search for 'Travel Money').

American Express sells a Travellers Cheque Card which is a prepaid, reloadable card that can be used at ATMs and most shops but is not linked to your bank account. You must purchase the card (£20) and then load it up with a minimum of £200 in credit (or equivalent in Euros or dollars). It is a little like using a plastic card instead of travellers' cheques. Be aware that the exchange rate used for these card transactions is not at all favourable (currently 4% worse than the exchange rate used by American Express in other contexts). Similarly Visa's TravelMoney scheme available through Travelex (www.travelex.co.uk), which also operates like a phonecard that you top up with cash, charges steep exchange rates so it is probably preferable to rely on your ATM card. Note that an American Express card cannot be used to obtain cash in an emergency unless there is a local AmEx office.

It is advisable also to keep a small amount of cash handy. Sterling is fine for most countries but US dollars are preferred in much of the world such as Latin America, Eastern Europe and Israel. The easiest way to look up the exchange rate of any world currency when planning your travels is to check on the Internet (e.g. www.xe.net/ucc) or to look at the Monday edition of the *Financial Times*. Most banks require a few days' notice to obtain a foreign currency for you. Marks & Spencer's *Travel Money* offers favourable exchange rates with no commission or handling charges on currency or travellers' cheques. Furthermore these can be ordered online and posted to your home.

A credit card is useful for many purposes, provided you will not be tempted to abuse it. For example it could be invaluable in an emergency. Few people think of crediting their Visa, Access, etc. account before leaving and then withdrawing cash on the credit card without incurring interest charges (since the money is not being borrowed). Even in remote countries like Niger in West Africa, it is possible to draw money on them The international banking network is limited in Africa and parts of Asia, so some banks and businesses will only accept American Express and/or Visa cards. Check the respective websites or your card issuer to see where your card is accepted abroad.

For information on what to do if you need to have money sent to you in an emergency, see the section below on Theft.

# WHAT TO TAKE

## Backpacking Equipment

Outdoor equipment shops carry an enticing range of shiny new products though if you are operating on a tight budget, you should first check out ebay or the small ads in the online or paper version of the free-ads paper*LOOT* (www.loot.com) or scour army surplus and charity shops, where for example you should be able to pick up a serviceable dome tent for less than £50.

For your main luggage, Paul Goodyear of the excellent Nomad Travel Store (www.nomadtravel.co.uk) recommends the new travel sack over the traditional rucksack, which he compares to a tunnel you have to push everything into. By contrast the 50-litre or 65-litre travel sack can be slung over the shoulder and immediately offers the advantage of making you look less like other backpackers. The travel sack can also be opened at the back for easy access and is designed to be more comfortable for your back during long walks. Another advantage is that it includes a daypack which can be zipped off to carry essential items like passports and money for a day trip.

Packing for travelling as a backpacker will always entail compromises because you will be limited in the amount of clothes and equipment you can take with you. When you're buying a backpack/rucksack in a shop try to place a significant weight in it so you can feel how comfortable it might be to carry on your back, otherwise you'll be misled by lifting something usually filled with foam.

Another important consideration is what you take for sleeping. Paul Goodyear recommends a tropical quilt for equatorial areas instead of a sleeping bag. Either you can spread out the quilt as a bed to sleep on or it can be folded to create a lightweight sleeping bag. The other advantage is that it is much lighter to carry and takes up less room in your luggage. Alternatively, it can be wrapped around your shoulders for warmth in an air-conditioned space or on a chilly evening in the mountains, though it will not provide enough warmth if you're planning to travel at high altitudes. A down vest might be a solution for travelling at altitude and can also double up as a comfortable pillow.

Other handy equipment includes a travel towel which can be used to dry or wash yourself. Unlike a conventional towel which occupies space and turns smelly in the heat and damp of the tropics, this one will dry very quickly after it has been wrung out.

In the heat of the tropics you should carry at least two litres of water in order to prevent dehydration. The best water bottles are soft-sided bladder-style ones (look for the Platypus brand); some have small separate compartments for a purifying agent like chlorine or iodine (mentioned below). Belts with zips worn under a shirt are very handy for carrying money unobtrusively. A bandana is also advisable in the tropics to keep the sun off your head, to mop up sweat or to put round your face in windy desert conditions. Some even have backgammon and chess sets printed on them to provide portable entertainment.

When packing it's best to roll rather than fold clothes to save space and put the heaviest objects at the bottom of the pack. Always carry liquids (like shampoo or water) inside a plastic bag in case they leak.

Do not panic that you will be cut off from the products you love. Prior to leaving for her voluntary placement in a law office in Belize, **Sara Ellis-Owen** emptied the shelves of Boots and also stocked up on favourite foodstuffs like marmite and Earl Grey tea. She later realised that Belize City already had everything that she needed; the local supermarket even stocked Waitrose supplies, so try to do some research about the shopping facilities at your destination before weighing down your luggage.

Other specialist travel merchandisers include the award-winning Itchy Feet in Bath (4 Bartlett St, Bath; 01225 337987) and London (162 Wardour St; 020-7292 9750); www.itchyfeet.com), and the mail order Catch 22 in Lancashire (01942 511820; www.catch22products.co.uk).

**Handy Travel Tips for Backpackers**

- Keep a record of vital travel documents like passport numbers, driving licences, travellers' cheque serial numbers, insurance policy, tickets, emergency number for cancelling credit cards, etc. Make two copies: stow one away in your luggage and give the other to a friend or relation at home. An even shrewder method is to take a scan of your passport and store it digitally in your e-mail account so that you can access it instantly in an emergency.
- Make sure your passport will remain valid for at least three months beyond the expected duration of your trip; some countries require six months worth of validity.
- Carry valuable items (like passport, essential medicines, digital cameras and of course money) on your person rather than relegating them to a piece of luggage which might be lost or stolen.
- Only take items you are prepared to lose.
- When deciding on clothes to take, start at your feet and work your way up the body; then try to shed up to half. If you find that you really need some missing item of clothing, you can always buy it en route.
- Take waterproof and dustproof luggage.
- Remember to ask permission before taking photographs of individuals or groups. In some cultures it can be insulting.
- Take advantage of the loos in hotels and fast food chains.
- Use the libraries of the British Council which can be found in most capital cities. The luxuries on offer include British newspapers and air-conditioning.
- Take a list of consular addresses in the countries you intend to visit in case of emergency.

## Maps and Guides

Good maps and guides always enhance one's enjoyment of a trip. If you are going to be based in a major city, buy a map ahead of time. If you are in London, visit the famous map shop Edward Stanford Ltd. (12-14 Long Acre, Covent Garden, WC2E 9LP; 020-7836 1321) whose searchable catalogue is now online at www.stanfords.co.uk; and Daunt Books for Travellers (83 Marylebone High Street, W1M 4DE; 020-7224 2295). The Map Shop in Worcestershire (0800 085 4080/01684 593146; www.themapshop.co.uk) and Maps Worldwide in Wiltshire (01225 707004; www.mapsworldwide.co.uk) both do an extensive mail order business in specialised maps and guide books.

Dozens of travel specialists throughout North America exist, including the Traveller's Bookstore (75 Rockefeller Plaza, 22 W 52nd; 212-664-0995) which sells guides, maps, travel-related books and products (free catalogue available). Also in Manhattan The Complete Traveller Antiquarian Bookstore (199 Madison Ave, New York, NY 10016; 212-685-9007; www.completetravellerbooks.com) has a very knowledgeable staff and an impressive collection of antiquarian travel books. In Boston try the Globe Corner Bookstore in Harvard Square (www.globecorner.com) and in Canada, Wanderlust (1929 West 4th Avenue, Kitsilano, Vancouver, BC, V6J 1M7; 1-866 739 2182; www.wanderlustore.com).

Phrase books, dictionaries and teach-yourself language courses can be more useful once you arrive in a country than at home.

## Electronic Items

Few serious travellers will want to leave home without a decent camera. These days most people prefer digital cameras (and possibly a high-tech box which can store thousands of images in no space at all) though traditionalists still prefer 35mm Single Lens Reflex technology.

Try to minimise the gadgets you are carrying. If you can't live without your hair dryer or travel iron, find out what the voltage and frequency are in the countries you intend to visit and invest in an earthed adaptor. Plug adaptors suitable for North American, British and European plugs can be bought from major electrical stores. For converting voltage (e.g. between European and North American equipment) you need a transformer.

The miniaturisation of gadgetry these days means that travellers will not be weighed down too much if they load up their iPod with music before leaving home. You may want to consider travelling with a laptop or palmtop computer. If you are going to be based in one place and are fairly comfortable with the idea of doing some troubleshooting, it is probably a good idea. It may be necessary to find someone to plumb it in, i.e. take apart a wall socket or telephone. Once you're connected, you simply sign up with a local or international Internet Service Provider (ISP). For technical details about getting hooked up from far-flung places, see the online manual at www.roadnews.com.

## Medications

Prescribed drugs (except contraceptives) that you take with you should be accompanied by a doctor's letter explaining why you need them. Do not carry non-prescribed drugs stronger than aspirin or anti-malarials, and then only in the original packs. Customs officers are highly sensitive about drugs of all kinds, and can be suspicious of some available over the counter in Britain but that are available only on prescription in other countries.

If you are planning a long trip, take a prescription from your doctor. It can be endorsed by a doctor abroad and used to obtain drugs.

## Gifts

When you encounter the kindness of strangers it is sometimes appropriate to bestow a small gift to acknowledge your appreciation. In developing countries, a supply of post cards from your hometown or stamps to give to children as a memento of your visit are often appreciated. Symbols of American culture like T-shirts and baseball caps are highly prized by many.

After spending some months working as a volunteer in Cambodia, Polly Botsford knew what she would do differently another time:

> *When I go back I will take a lot more presents from England. Ask your host country contacts if there is anything which is particularly expensive/unobtainable where you are going and bring bucket loads of whatever it is.*

Choosing what to take for friends or relations, or to ingratiate yourself with friends-of-friends on whom you wish to impose, is an art. If your beneficiaries are British expats, then virtually anything British might be appreciated, from a copy of *Private Eye* to Marmite to Scotch whisky.

Scott Burke, founder of *Cosmic Volunteers*, suggests taking something that few would think of, especially if you are going to be working with children in a school or orphanage. When suffering acute culture shock in Nepal and in danger of abandoning his plan to become a volunteer English teacher, he found the solution:

> *What ended up saving me was...Mr. Bubbles. That's right, a four-ounce bottle of bubbles I had brought with me to Nepal on the advice of a friend. A great icebreaker with kids, she had said. I took the bottle, walked outside and started blowing bubbles alone in my front yard. Sure enough, in a few minutes several children appeared, seemingly from nowhere. Without exchanging even one word for the next two hours, the children and I blew bubbles and laughed and ran around. Back in my room, I sat back down on that bed, took a deep breath and thought to myself: Maybe I can do this.*

All sorts of obscure items can come in handy though few are likely to follow Hannah Stevens's example and remember to pack a nit comb.

# STAYING IN TOUCH

The revolution in communication technology means that you are never far from home. Internet cafés can be found in almost every corner of the world where, for a greater or lesser fee, you can access your e-mail or check relevant information on the web. Internet cafés can easily be located on arrival in virtually any place in the world simply by asking around. *The Rough Guide to the Internet* (£7.99) contains a wealth of practical advice and, for updated listings, check www.world66.com/netcafeguide, home to the Net Café Guide with a searchable database of Internet cafés worldwide or the revealingly named www.cybercaptive.com whose database at the time of writing included 5,763 verified cybercafés, public Internet access points and kiosks in 161 countries.

The technically minded might wish to take a digital camera in order to be able to send photos home electronically or set up their own website or blog (i.e. web log) to share their travel tales with family and friends. Lots of companies will help you create your own blog, for example www.blogger.com/start (which is free) while http://community.webshots.com is designed for people to upload their photos (also free for storing up to 240 photos). Rough Guides has launched some travel planner software called intouch (www.roughguidesintouch.com) which might be worth investigating (cost £20).

## E-mail

Fixing yourself up with a web-based e-mail account before leaving home is now virtually compulsory. This allows you to keep in touch with and receive messages from home and also with friends met on the road. It is also very handy for managing your finances and stay in touch with professional resources.The most heavily subscribed service for travellers is still hotmail (www.hotmail.com or www.hotmail.co.uk) though its popularity occasionally places strains on the system. A popular alternative, also free, is provided by Yahoo (http://mail.yahoo.com) with which British users can register for a yahoo.co.uk address.

The danger for people who rely too heavily on the new technology is that they spend so much time tracking down and inhabiting cybercafés that they end up not having the encounters and adventures they might have otherwise. Just as the texting generation is finding it harder to cut ties with home knowing that a parent or a school friend is only a few digits away wherever they are, so too travellers who spend an inordinate amount of time online risk failing to look round the destination country in depth. They are so busy communicating with their fellow travellers that they miss out on meeting locals in the old-fashioned, strike-up-a-conversation, getting-in-and-out-of-scrapes way. They will also be deprived of another old-fashioned treat: arriving at a poste restante address and experiencing the pleasure (sweeter because deferred) of reading their mail.

## Telephone

A plethora of companies sell pre-paid phone cards intended to simplify international phone calls as well as make them cheaper. After registering, you credit your card account with an amount of your choice (normally starting at £10 or £20), or buy a card for $10 or $20. Then you are given an access code which can be used toll-free from any country. Credit can be topped up online or by phone with a credit card. To find companies just search online for 'Prepaid Phone Cards'.

Lonely Planet, the travel publisher, has an easy-to-use communications card called ekit which combines low cost calls, voice mail, e-mail and Internet and travel information. For information ring 0800 028 2402 or log on www.lonelyplanet.ekit.com.

Friends and family at home may wish to investigate the companies that offer low cost dialling to overseas numbers. For example with an access code from Telediscount (www.telediscount.co.uk) you can call landlines in Africa for as little as 10p pence per minute or 15 pence to a mobile.

Roaming charges for mobiles used abroad can cost an arm and a leg e.g. £2 just to receive a call. If you are going to be a frequent visitor to a country or stay for more than a few weeks, you can either buy a local mobile or invest in a country-specific SIM card. A company called 0044 (www.0044.co.uk) sells foreign SIM cards which allow you to take your mobile with you and call at local rates while you're away. For example the price of a SIM card for Spain (with up to €30 credit and free Nokia unlocking) costs £30 including delivery. All your contacts will have to be informed of your new number.

**These are the steps Debra Fuccio followed, in vaguely chronological order, in preparation for a trip to Guatemala in May 2006, as recorded on her blog (http://blogs.bootsnall.com/travelgoddess).**

- Followed gut feeling and decided it was time to head down to Guatemala
- Researched volunteer opportunities and Spanish schools
- Bought plane ticket
- Sub-let my rented San Francisco apartment through Craigslist.com. Created a 3-page sublet agreement that would make my lawyer boss from a decade ago proud. I will be a long way away, and don't want to think about my SF life when I am down there.
- Looked for travel partners, for parts of the trip via Lonely Planet Thorn Tree, Bootsnall, and ad on Craigslist SF community page
- Started to contact locals and expats who live in Guatemala
- Gave notice at present job
- Spent time going over my budget with a fine tooth comb. My usual method of travel is to save money then travel or, if planning a long period of travel, work along the way to finance, come home and work more. This time I am not travelling on savings so much as travelling on rent money.
- For peace of mind I am paying May and June bills before I go, since I may not be working right away when I return. I hope I do, but you never know with temping.
- Set up this blog
- Researched necessary immunisations and travel advisory warnings.
- Downloaded all music into iTunes, in case I do break down and take an iPod. I prefer to listen to local music/radio when I am in a place, but I have also noticed that familiar sounds are settling during times of strong culture shock or stress.
- Sorted through tons of papers lying around my apartment, sorting out what projects I can realistically complete before leaving in 2 weeks, and what needs to be postponed till my return. Breaking down projects no matter how big or small and assigning a day to work on them has helped a lot in the past few months. I also noticed that if there is a project that I keep putting off, then it tends to go into the 'better off as an idea than reality' pile.
- Made a packing checklist that included travel towel, earplugs (essential), sunblock and other things I might forget.
- Researched travel insurance. So many choices, and prices vary a lot. Used Google and followed links from respectable travel websites like Lonely Planet, Rough Guides, Bootsnall and Budget Travel Magazine. Will probably reject the one you can't extend once you are on the trip. My main concerns this time are health (since I will be doing some hiking) and theft protection (since I am taking my digital camera and iPod).

# TRAVEL ARRANGEMENTS

Those who are joining an organised voluntary or expeditionary scheme will no doubt receive plenty of advice on how to book their flights and travel. Independent travellers should be looking at discounted tickets, last minute bargains and no-frills airlines (see chapter *Travel & Adventure* for detailed advice).

## Accommodation

Places where travellers tend to congregate always have a good selection of reasonably priced accommodation. In many parts of the world, the status of backpacking is rising, and the growing range of facilities pitched at this important sector of the more mature backpacking market is impressive.

Joining the Youth Hostels Association is highly recommended even if you do not imagine yourself the type. Those who haven't stayed at a hostel since their student days will be surprised at the revolution that has taken place. Hostels generally offer higher standards of comfort than a generation ago and have become far more attractive to older travellers (not least because they have abolished the dreaded compulsory chore). Nowadays many hostels offer single, double and family rooms in addition to the standard dormitories. In major cities, youth hostels often represent the cheapest accommodation and in remote areas, they often represent the most beautiful. Many are located in prime sites and some are in beautifully restored old buildings.

YHA membership for people over 18 costs £15.95, £22.95 for two people sharing an address. In some countries, especially Australia and New Zealand, travel enterprises from bus companies to cafés, give good discounts to YHA members, which makes the price of membership well worthwhile for those who are long past possessing a student card. The YHA for England and Wales is based at Trevelyan House, Dimple Road, Matlock, Derbyshire DE4 3YH (0870 770 8868; www.yha.org.uk) or you can join at any YHA hostel throughout the UK. Seasonal demand can be high, so it is always preferable to book in advance if you know your itinerary. You can pre-book beds over the Internet on www.iyhf.org or through individual hostels and national offices.

A growing number of privately-owned hostels provides lively competition for the International Youth Hostels Federation; check the website www.hostels.com, www.hostelworld.com or www.hostels.net for a selection worldwide. VIP Backpacker hostel group (www.vipbackpackers.com) includes hostels in Australia, New Zealand, South Africa and Europe; a membership card costs £16.

For many travellers, hostels are the key to an excellent holiday. Not only do they provide an affordable place to sleep (typically £10-£15+ in the first world, much less in developing countries), they provide access to a valuable range of information about what to see, how to get there and who to go with. Additional services are often provided such as bicycle hire or canoeing and trekking trips.

The cheapest accommodation of all is a tent, an attractive option if you're travelling into remote areas like national parks where accommodation is in short supply or if you are using a means of transport like walking, cycling or hitch-hiking which might leave you stranded at nightfall. The drawback of course is the extra weight of a tent and sleeping bag. Discretion is always recommended when camping by the side of the road. If you are camping outside campsites, always seek permission from the local farmer or ask in the local pub. Finding a supply of water may present problems. Never be tempted to camp in a dried-up river bed, since a flash flood can wash you away.

## TRAVEL INSURANCE

European nationals are eligible for reciprocal emergency health care. However outside Europe a good insurance policy is absolutely essential. Increased competition among travel insurers has brought costs down over the past few years, though it will still be necessary to set aside a chunk of your travel fund. Travel policies do not automatically cover certain activities deemed to be dangerous such as winter sports and manual work (e.g. on a volunteer project). Anyone wanting to engage in adventure or extreme sports like bungy jumping, scuba diving or sky diving should do some comparison shopping since by studying the fine print, they may find a company that will cover their preferred activity without the need of investing in special cover. You are expected to inform your insurer ahead of time if you plan to indulge in any potentially risky activities.

The UK has reciprocal health agreements with more than 40 countries worldwide that entitle you to emergency care, though it is still recommended to have your own comprehensive private cover which will cover extras like loss of baggage and, more importantly, emergency repatriation. Many countries in Africa, Asia, Latin America and the USA do not provide any reciprocal cover. Travelling without travel insurance can literally break the bank. Medical care in an emergency might cost an individual tens of thousands of pounds.

All travellers must face the possibility of an accident befalling them abroad. In countries like India, Turkey and Venezuela, the rate of road traffic accidents can be as much as twenty times greater than in the UK. Certain activities obviously entail more risk. For example, broken bones are common on ski treks and evacuation can be difficult in mountainous areas where trekking is popular. If you are thinking of travelling with a tour group, ask the company how they deal with medical emergencies and whether repatriation is included in their group policy.

If you're travelling independently, you will find that almost every enterprise in the travel business will be delighted to sell you insurance because of the commission earned. Ring several insurance companies with your specifications and compare prices. Europ-Assistance Ltd (0870 737 5720; www.europ-assistance.co.uk) is the world's largest assistance organisation with a network of doctors, air ambulances, agents and vehicle rescue services managed by 208 offices worldwide offering (at a price) emergency assistance abroad 24 hours a day. The Voyager Travel policy covers periods from 6 to 18 months and the policy is invalidated if you return home during the period insured.

Many companies charge lower premiums, though you will have to decide whether you are satisfied with their level of cover. Most offer a no-frills rate which covers medical emergencies and a premium rate which covers extras that might be considered non-essential like loss of personal baggage. If you are not planning to visit North America, the premiums will be much less expensive. Note that if the Foreign & Commonwealth Office advises against travelling to a certain country, your travel insurance will be invalidated if you ignore this advice.

Some companies to consider are listed here with a rough idea of their premiums for 12 months of worldwide cover (including the USA). Expect to pay in the region of £25 per month for basic cover and £35-£40 for more extensive cover.

## Useful Contacts

*Alexander Forbes World Service,* 6 Bevis Marks, London EC3A 7AF (020-7933 0000; www.afiaws.com). Providers of International Loss/Damage Vehicle Insurance for people of any nationality living or working outside their country of origin, including travellers on expedition, diplomats, expatriates, teachers, aid workers and journalists, in their key markets of Africa, South America, Asia, the Middle East and Eastern Europe.

*Austravel* – 0870 166 2020; www.austravel.com. Specialist in travel to Australia and New Zealand sells a range of competitively priced insurance policies for both the family and the budget traveller. Cover for adventure sports is available too.

*Club Direct,* Dominican House, St John's St, Chichester, W Sussex (0800 083 2466; www.clubdirect.com). £310 for year-long cover including baggage cover; £220 for backpacker cover.

*Columbus Direct,* 17 Devonshire Square, London EC2M 4SQ (020-7375 0011/ 08450 761030). One of the giants in the field of travel insurance chosen by *Rough Guides* as their partner. From £280 for twelve months worldwide cover.

*Direct Line Insurance* – 0845 246 8910; www.directline.com. No upper age limit on single trip cover but maximum duration of 42 days for clients over 60.

*Downunder Worldwide Travel Insurance,* 3 Spring St, Paddington, London W2 3RA (0800 393908; www.duinsure.com). Special gap year 12-month policies for people under 45, start at £250; £350 for Adventurer policy (which includes activities like hang gliding, parasailing, sand yachting, diving and rock climbing).

*Endsleigh Insurance,* Endsleigh House, Cheltenham, Glos GL50 3NR (www.endsleigh.co.uk). Offices in most university towns. 12 months of essential worldwide cover costs £287, comprehensive cover from £431.

*Europ-Assistance Ltd,* Sussex House, Perrymount Road, Haywards Heath, W. Sussex RH16 1DN (0870 737 5720; www.europ-assistance.co.uk). Voyager cover for 1 year would cost £580.

*gosure.com* – 0845 222 0020. Explorer one-year policies for 18-34 year olds cost £216 with no baggage cover, £240 with.

*MRL Insurance,* Lumbry Park, Selborne Road, Alton, Hants. GU34 3HF (0870 876 7677; www.mrlinsurance.co.uk.) £119 for 4 months, £219 for 12 months for under 35s. Also offer policies to travellers up to age 90.

*Travel Insurance Agency,* Suite 2, Percy Mews, 755B High Road, North Finchley, London N12 8JY (020-8446 5414; www.travelinsurers.com). £275.

Recommended US insurers for extended stays abroad are International SOS Assistance Inc with offices in Philadelphia, Houston, Singapore, London and many others (1-800-523-8930; www.internationalsos.com) which is used by the Peace Corps and is designed for people working in remote areas. A firm which specialises in providing health insurance for Americans living overseas is Wallach & Company (107 West Federal St, PO Box 480, Middleburg, VA 20118-0480; 1-800-237-6615; www.wallach.com).

Emergency medical claims are normally processed efficiently but if you have to make a claim for lost or stolen baggage, you may be unpleasantly surprised by the amount of the settlement eventually paid, especially if you have opted for a discount insurer. Loss adjusters have ways of making calculations which prove that you are entitled to less than you think. The golden rule is to amass as much documentation as possible to support your application, most importantly medical receipts and a police report in the case of an accident or theft.

# HEALTH AND SAFETY

Travel inevitably involves balancing risks and navigating through hazards real or imagined. But with common sense and advice from experts, you can minimise potential problems. In addition to issues involving red tape, another major area of concern is health and if you are planning to travel outside the developed world, you will have to research what precautions are possible. You will also have to consider how to minimise loss or theft of money and belongings, something to be considered when you are deciding what to pack.

The Foreign & Commonwealth Office runs a regular and updated service; you can ring the Travel Advice Unit on 0870 606 0290 or check their website www.fco.gov.uk/travel. This site gives frequently updated and detailed risk assessments of any trouble spots, including civil unrest, terrorism and crime. If you have access to BBC Ceefax look at pages 470 and following. Several years ago the FCO launched a 'Know Before You Go' campaign to raise awareness among backpackers and independent travellers of potential risks and dangers and how to guard against them, principally by taking out a water-tight insurance policy. The same emphasis can be detected on the FCO site launched in 2005: www.gogapyear.co.uk. Adult gap year travellers will be reassured (unless they are parents of gappers) by the MORI poll statistic that the younger the traveller the more likely (up to 50% more likely) they are to get ill, hurt or become caught up in a civil disturbance.

General advice on minimising the risks of independent travel is contained in the book *World Wise – Your Passport to Safer Travel* published by Thomas Cook in association with the Suzy Lamplugh Trust and the Foreign Office (www.suzylamplugh.org/worldwise; £6.99 plus £2 postage). Arguably its advice is over-cautious, advising travellers never to ride a motorbike or accept an invitation to a private house. Adult travellers will have to decide for themselves when to follow this advice and when to ignore it. In the US, the State Department publishes its warnings and advisories on its website www.travel.state.gov. This same information is available in recorded messages on 202-647-5225.

A couple of specialist organisations in the UK put on courses to prepare clients for potential dangers and problems on a gap year. Needless to say, these are normally aimed at naïve 18 year olds whose parents are paying for the course. Managing director John Cummings of provider Safetrek (East Culme, Cullompton, Devon EX15 1NX; 01884 839704; www.safetrek.co.uk) notes that more grown-ups have been requesting their personal safety and awareness training. The over-40s are interested not just in what to do when abroad but how to leave homes secure. He acknowledges that a lot of it is common sense but not necessarily common practice. People in the older age group are undoubtedly more confident than their gap year counterparts straight out of school but more worried about things going wrong at home in their absence. John Cummings also suspects that older men are more inclined to react too quickly to an incident thereby making matters worse, so thinks that they could benefit from the training which urges them to remain calm and walk away.

Another training provider in this area is Planet Wise (10 Swan Street, Eynsham, Oxfordshire OX29 4HU; (0870 2000 220; www.PlanetWise.net) which runs one-day travel safety and awareness courses (£160) which can be tailored to an older age group (55+). Travellers of whatever age might feel reassured by rehearsing what to do in a crisis, such as the best course of action when getting out of a burning building; what to do if drugs are planted on you, etc.

News of tragedies affecting gap year students crop up in the news from time to time (murders, abductions, fatal illnesses, accidents) but seldom in the case of more mature travellers. However at the beginning of 2006, 50 year old nurse Jennifer Pope from Greater Manchester stopped making contact with her family after four happy months of working and travelling in South America and went missing, probably in Ecuador.

## Travellers' Health

No matter what country you are heading for, you should obtain the Department of Health leaflet T7.1 *Health Advice for Travellers* (updated May 2006). This leaflet should be available from any post office or doctor's surgery. Alternatively you can request a free copy on the Health Literature Line 0870 155 5455 or read it online at www.dh.gov.uk, which also has country-by-country details.

The old E111 certificate of entitlement to medical treatment within Europe has been superseded by the European Health Insurance Card (EHIC). In the first phase of introduction, the new card will cover health care for short stays. By 2008, the electronic card will take the place of the current E128 and E119 which cover longer stays. At present this reciprocal cover is extended only to emergency treatment, so private insurance is also highly recommended, not least to cope with theft.

If you have a pre-existing medical condition it's important to anticipate what you might require in a crisis. Ask your GP or specialist support group for advice before you leave. If you're travelling with a tour operator let the company know about your condition in advance. Under extreme climatic conditions chronic or pre-existing conditions can be aggravated. Try to ascertain how easy it will be to access medicines on your trip, whether you'll be able to carry emergency supplies with you and how far you will be from specialist help. Always carry medications in their original containers and as a precaution you might carry a note from your doctor with an explanation of the drugs you're carrying and the relevant facts of your medical history. This could also include details of any allergies for example an intolerance of penicillin. This might be of use if you are involved in an accident or medical emergency.

In an age of mass communication it is usually possible to manage a medical condition while travelling or erect a safety net. If you plan to travel to an area with poor medical standards and unreliable blood screening, you might want to consider equipping yourself or your group with sterile syringes and needles. The Department of Travel Medicine at the Hospital for Tropical Diseases recommends that you should carry a specially prepared sterile needle kit in case local emergency treatment requires injections; MASTA (see below) sells these for £17-£31.

Any visits beyond the developed world, particularly to tropical climates, require careful preparation. You will face the risk of contracting malaria or waterborne diseases like typhoid and cholera. You will need to provide your medical practitioner with precise details about where you intend to travel. Visit a medical centre at least a month before departure because some immunisations like those for yellow fever must be given well in advance.

Some of the advice given below may seem intimidating. While preparing for travelling in the developing world, you might begin to feel as if you're joining an SAS induction course. Expert medical advice is widely available on how to avoid tropical illness, so you should take advantage of modern medicine to protect yourself. And be prepared to pay for the necessary inoculations which are not normally covered by the NHS. It is always worth asking at your surgery since if they are able to give good advice (and the Internet has made that possible for any doctor or practice nurse worth his or her salt), the injections may be considerably cheaper than at a private specialist clinic where you are likely to pay between £30 and £50 per vaccine.

## Inoculations and Prophylaxis

Depending on where you live, it is entirely possible that your GP will not be keeping abreast with all the complexities of tropical medicine particularly malaria prevention for different areas of the world, etc. Some are downright ignorant. The only disease for which a vaccination certificate may be legally required is yellow fever. Many countries insist on seeing one only if you are arriving from an infected country, though it is a good idea to get protection if you are planning to travel to a yellow fever zone (much of Africa and parts of Latin America).

One of the best sources of health advice for travellers is MASTA (Medical Advisory Service for Travellers Abroad) which was set up in association with the London School of Hygiene and Tropical Medicine to meet the needs of the eight million international visits made every year from the UK. MASTA (0906 822 4100; www.masta.org) prepares health briefs for prospective travellers who provide their dates and destinations (up to ten countries). These can be obtained via their website for a fee of £3.49, by ringing their premium rate line as above or by visiting one of their affiliated health clinics throughout the UK. MASTA sells a range of practical products like insect repellents, mosquito nets and water purifiers; and runs 24 specialist travel clinics throughout the UK. You can ring MASTA's interactive Travellers' Health Line (see Contacts below) with up to ten destination countries and they will send you a basic health brief by return, for the price of the telephone call (60p per minute).

Private specialist clinics abound in London but are thin on the ground elsewhere. Most charge both for information and for the jabs (for details see Contacts listed below). A worldwide searchable listing of specialist travel clinics is maintained by the International Society of Travel Medicine (www.istm.org) though many countries are not included.

For routine travellers' complaints, it is worth looking at a general guide to travel medicine such as *Bugs, Bites and Bowels* by Dr. Jane Wilson Howarth (Cadogan, 2006, £9.99), Americans seeking general travel health advice should ring the Center for Disease Control & Prevention Hotline in Atlanta on 1-877-394-8747; www.cdc.gov. CDC issues travel announcements for international travellers rated from mild to extreme, i.e. minimal risk to a recommendation that non-essential travel not take place.

For advice on protecting your sexual health, Marie Stopes International (020-7574 7400; www.mariestopes.org.uk) is helpful; they have published a free guide to traveller's sexual health called the *Back Pocket Guide*. The government's free booklet *Drugs Abroad* and the National Drugs Helpline (0800 776600) can give information on drugs laws abroad.

## Malaria

Malaria is undoubtedly the greatest danger posed by visits to many tropical areas. The disease has been making a comeback in many parts of the world, due to the resistance of certain strains of mosquito to the pesticides and preventative medications which have been so extensively relied upon in the past. Because of increasing resistance, it is important to consult a specialist service like MASTA (Medical Advisory Services for Travellers Abroad) or the Hospital for Tropical Diseases. The Malaria Prevention Advice Line 09065 508908 can be dialled 24 hours a day (£1 per minute). You can also become better informed by looking at specialist websites such as www.preventingmalaria.info/prevention/index.htm. You need to obtain the best information available to help you devise the most appropriate strategy for protection in the areas you intend to visit. Research indicates for example that the statistical chance of being bitten by a malarial mosquito in Thailand is once a year, but in Sierra Leone it rises to once a night. Start your research early since some courses of malaria prophylaxis need to be started up to three weeks before departure. It is always a good idea to find out in advance if you are going to suffer any side effects as well.

Falciparum malaria is potentially fatal. On average between 2,000 and 2,500 travellers return to the UK with malaria every year, and between ten and twenty will die. The two main drugs can be obtained over the counter: Chloroquine and Proguanil (brand name Paludrine). In regions resistant to these drugs, you will have to take both or a third line of defence such as Maloprim or Mefloquine (or Larium) available only on prescription. Because of possible side effects it is important that your doctor be able to vary the level of toxicity to match the risks prevalent in your destination. A relatively new (and expensive) drug called Malarone is used as an alternative to mefloquine or doxycycline, and is recommended for short trips to highly chloroquine-resistant areas. New drugs are being developed all the time and sometimes there is a time lag before they are licensed in the UK or USA. For example in her gap year in Madagascar, Karen Hedges twice contracted malaria but was quickly treated with an effective drug called Coartem, expensive by local standards, and not yet licensed in the UK.

Unfortunately these prophylactic medications are not foolproof, and even those who have scrupulously swallowed their pills before and after their trip as well as during it have been known to contract the disease. It is therefore essential to take mechanical precautions against mosquitoes. If possible, screen the windows and sleep under a permethrin-impregnated mosquito net since the offending mosquitoes feed between dusk and dawn. (Practise putting your mosquito net up before leaving home since some are tricky to assemble.) Some travellers have improvised with some netting intended for prams which takes up virtually no luggage space. If you don't have a net, cover your limbs at nightfall with light-coloured garments, apply insect repellent with the active ingredient DEET and sleep with a fan on to keep the air moving. Try to keep your room free of the insects too by using mosquito coils, vaporisers, etc.

Deet is strong enough to last many hours. Wrist and ankle bands impregnated with the chemical are available and easy to use. Cover your limbs as night falls (6pm on the equator). Wearing fine silk clothes discourages bites and keep the repellent topped up. Scientists have established that mosquitoes tend to be drawn to carbon dioxide vapours, heat and body odours. Avoid wherever possible using deodorants, soap and perfumes which can attract the insects. Ben's Insect Repellent offer four different products that contain Deet including creams,

lotions and wipes as well as Ben's Natural, a chemical-free repellent suitable for children of 12 months or more. These are available from www.afterbite.co.uk or telephone 0800 1957 400.

**Paula Donohue** is a doctor in Canada as well as an inveterate traveller, with a cautionary tale. She and her 13 year old son decided to take an extended trip to Madagascar, partly because Gabriel was attracted to the exotic name and partly because they had met some charming Madagascan musicians at the annual jazz festival in New Orleans earlier that year. Naturally she was more familiar with the health risks than most and researched them thoroughly. Given the worrying side-effects of anti-malarials, especially in children, and the care with which she intended to prevent mosquito bites, she decided not to take antimalarial drugs. They came back from a wonderful month in Madagascar unscathed. Gabriel felt a bit feverish a couple of days after returning to Ontario but it was assumed that he had caught the same flu that his stay-at-home sister and her friends all had. Four days later he was hooked up to every high tech machine in the hospital and was fighting for his life. Six months later he had regained the 25 pounds he lost and returned to full strength and vigour but it was a horrible experience and, as his mother admits, forced her to give back the Mother-of-the-Year award she had received for organising their Madagascar trip. Paula now thinks she knows the occasion on which their defences were penetrated: on a day when they went for a walk to spot lemurs in the bush, Gabriel had forgotten his long trousers, refused to borrow a pair because of the heat and as a consequence got bitten. Paula says that the next time she takes her children to a malarial zone she will steel herself to the possible side effects and prescribe the recommended anti-malarials.

TravelPharm (www.travelpharm.com) markets an impressive range of medications and equipment for the prospective traveller to tropical countries. TravelPharm is an independent private pharmacy based in Devon and the website conveys country-by-country advice on anti-malarials, etc.

In the case of malaria, prevention is vastly preferable to cure. It is a difficult disease to treat, particularly in its advanced stages. If you suffer a fever up to twelve months after returning home from a malarial zone, visit your doctor and mention your travels, even if you suspect it might just be flu.

## Food and Water

Tap water throughout the developing world is unsafe for travellers to drink because there is always a chance that it contains disease organisms to which the Westerner has had no chance to develop immunities. Do not assume that you can get by with substitute beverages such as coke or tea or even bottled soda water. In hot climates, it is imperative to drink large quantities of water to avoid dehydration, possibly as much as six pints a day. The most effective method of water purification is boiling for at least five minutes. However this is seldom convenient and in hot weather the water never gets cooler than lukewarm.

A more manageable method of water sterilisation is to use chemical purifiers. Simply pick up the appropriate chlorine tablets or tincture of iodine from a chemist before departure, checking how long they take to become effective (ten minutes is preferable to 30 in a hot climate when you're gasping for a cold drink). You can buy a product that neutralises the unpleasant taste of iodine. Remember that ice cubes however tempting should be avoided. Drinking water can also be purified by filtering. MASTA and Nomad market various water purifiers; among the best are the 'Aquapure Traveller' (£40+) and the 'Trekker Travel Well' for £70.

Deciding what food is safe to eat is not always easy. You should aim to eat only freshly cooked food and avoid raw vegetables unless they have been peeled or washed thoroughly in purified water. Many people are nervous to eat street food in the third world. In fact food served in such places is usually safe provided it has been thoroughly cooked and does not look as though it has been hanging around in a fly-invested environment. A vegetarian diet is less likely to give trouble than meat or fish. Try to eat lots of yoghurt since the bacteria help to combat the bugs in the stomach.

## Diarrhoea

Up to 50% of travellers will suffer the trots or 'Delhi belly' and a mild case of diarrhoea is virtually inevitable for travellers outside the developed world. Doctors warn that however many precautions with food and water you take, it is simply impossible to guard against it completely. If left to its own devices, most bouts clear up within two or three days, although in an extreme case the fluid loss may leave you weak and tired. You should keep drinking to avoid dehydration. This is particularly important for the young or the elderly. Rehydration tablets, which replace lost salt and sugar in the right proportions, are a possible item for your first-aid kit.

Diarrhoea will clear up more quickly if you can get a lot of rest and stop eating altogether. When you begin eating again, stick to as simple a diet as possible, e.g. boiled rice and tea (without milk). If the problem persists, try a recommended medication such as kaolin and morphine or codeine phosphate. The antibiotic Ciprofloxacin can speed up recovery, but you'll need to obtain a prescription from a doctor before you leave.

## Culture Shock

Not all travellers' ailments are as straightforward to treat as mild diarrhoea. Enjoying yourself won't be easy if you are suffering the adverse psychological effects of culture shock. Adult gappers who elect to spend time in a developing country are invariably shocked to some degree by the levels of poverty and deprivation. Shock implies something which happens suddenly, but cultural disorientation more often creeps up on you. Adrenalin usually sees you through the first few weeks as you find the novelty exhilarating and challenging. You will be amazed and charmed by the odd gestures the people use or the antiquated way that things work. As time goes on, practical irritations intrude and the constant misunderstanding caused by those charming gestures – such as a nod in Greece meaning 'no' or in Japan meaning 'yes, I understand, but don't agree' – and the discomfort of those impossibly crowded buses may begin to get on your nerves.

However, most mature gappers who have taken the trouble beforehand to research their destination or volunteer situation, find the cultural differences they encounter entertaining, moving, exhilarating. While volunteering in Cambodia, **Dale Hurd** met a man called Ratana on one of her many memorable bus journeys and was invited back to his village to meet his family:

> *As guest of honour, I was more or less force fed until I could hardly move and so was quite relieved when told that I was tired and had to rest. However, to my embarrassment, I found that I was to rest in solitary state on a kind of low platform with only a rock-hard bright orange cushion for company, lulled to sleep by the sound of five incontinent cows two*

*inches from my head. The rest of the increasing hordes sat round and admired my resting techniques. It felt rather like being dead and lying in state. After about 15 minutes or so, it seemed interminable, a dog fight broke out so I could assume wakefulness and leapt up with false cries of renewed vigour. However, to my horror, I told that I now had to bath as it was so hot, which cast doubts upon my personal hygiene. Ratana led me over to the house and gave me a sarong sewn up like a tube and said I knew what to do with it. Well no, actually, I hadn't got a clue.*

On a subsequent trip back from visiting temples in the north of the country, Dale experienced the pungent terror of the open road:

*As it was a right hand drive, the driver couldn't see a thing. I, however, sitting on the left, could see everything as clear as crystal. Sensibly he chose to drive at one speed, i.e. flat out, undeterred by any of the riff raff cluttering up the highway such as motor bikes, children or cows. The lady on my right was very good about my clutching her arm at regular intervals and ignored the little comments I sometimes felt compelled to make. After a bit I decided to take a keen interest in the passing scenery rather than the oncoming vehicles, and if there's anything you want to know about the number, distribution or condition of banana trees between Sisophon and Battanbang, I'm your girl.*

An appreciation of cultural differences usually goes much deeper as it did for **Nikki D'Arcy** from Watford who volunteered in a home for the elderly in Peru with *Cross-Cultural Solutions*. Only gradually did she overcome her fears that she would be able to cope and, like so many other westerners who have immersed themselves in a developing community, was left full of admiration:

*Despite considering myself an independent, confident person, the thought of completely immersing myself in another culture was still slightly daunting. I won't lie. During my time there, I saw some things that saddened and shocked me, I didn't realise that people could live in such poverty. But I also got to know those people and saw such amazing strength in them. They were so happy to invite me into their lives, to share their stories and were so full of life, it put me to shame for moaning about the tiny problems we have. Even after a few days, I felt my attitudes and perceptions changing. I began to really understand what is important in life. Not the material things that so many of us seem to become obsessed with, but family and friends and enjoying life. Don't get me wrong, I already knew that, but I don't think you can fully understand it until you see people who have nothing, and I mean literally nothing, sometimes not even a roof, but yet they meet up with their friends and dance and sing and laugh like they don't have a care in the world. They are truly inspirational.*

## Useful Contacts

The *Foreign & Commonwealth Office* maintains a Travel Advice Unit helpline on 0870 606 0290 and posts information and risk assessments at www.fco.gov.uk/travel. At the time of writing it was advising against all travel to Chad, Somalia,

Ivory Coast and East Timor and recommending foreigners not to travel to parts of 13 other countries including Albania and Colombia.

*MASTA* – enquiries@masta.org; www.masta.org. – has already been recommended. Calls to the Travellers' Health Line (0906 822 4100) are charged at 60p per minute (average cost of call £2). With its database of the latest information on the prevention of tropical and other diseases, MASTA is one of the most authoritative sources of travellers' health information in Britain. The practical information accessible on its website and helpline is impressive. It can provide personalised advice depending on your destinations, which can be either e-mailed or posted to you. Here you can find explanations about protection against malaria, guidelines on what to eat and drink, and how to avoid motion sickness, jet lag and sunburn. MASTA's network of travel clinics administers inoculations and, like their online shop, sells medical kits and other specialist equipment like water purifiers and survival tools. MASTA also co-operates with the Blood Care Foundation, a charity that aims to deliver properly screened blood and sterile transfusion equipment to members in an emergency.

*Hospital for Tropical Diseases* – Mortimer Market Building, Capper Street, Tottenham Court Road, London, WC1E 6AU (020-7388 9600 for appointments at Travel Clinic or the Travellers Healthline Advisory Service on 020-7950 7799; www.thehtd.org).

*Travelpharm,* Unit 10 D, Mill Park Industrial Estate, White Cross Road, Woodbury Saiterton, Devon EX5 1EL (01395 233771; www.travelpharm.com). Extensive range of mosquito nets, anti-malaria drugs, water purification equipment and travel accessories available via online store.

Other travel clinics include:

*British Airways Travel Clinic,* 213 Piccadilly, London W1J 9HQ (0845 600 2236). Walk-in service operates Monday to Saturday; consultation charge £15. Their prices are posted on the website www.britishairways.com/travel/healthclinprods/public/en_gb. Prices range from £25 for a combined diphtheria and tetanus shot to £65 for tick-borne encephalitis

*Fleet Street Travel Clinic,* 29 Fleet Street, London EC4Y 1AA (020-7353 5678; www.fleetstreetclinic.com). Travel advice to the stars, or at least to film crews and high-risk journalists. £45 for a 15-minute consultation.

*Nomad Travel Clinics,* 52 Grosvenor Gardens, Victoria, London SW1W 0AG (020-7823 5823); 3-4 Wellington Terrace, Turnpike Lane, London N8 OPX (020-8889 7014); 43 Bernard St, London WC1N 1JL (020-7833 4114; www.nomadtravel.co.uk) and also in Bristol and Southampton. Walk-in and appointments. 10-minute consultation costs £5 which can be deducted from cost of vaccinations.

*The Royal Free Travel Health Centre,* The Royal Free Hospital, Pond St, London NW3 2QG (020-7830 2885; www.travelclinicroyalfree.com). Well-regarded private clinic.

*Trailfinders Travel Clinic,* 194 Kensington High St (020-7983 3999; www.trailfinders.com/clinic.htm).

Increasingly, people are seeking advice via the Internet; check for example www.fitfortravel.scot.nhs.uk; www.tmb.ie and www.travelhealth.co.uk. The website of the World Health Organisation www.who.int/ith has some information including a listing of the very few countries in which certain vaccinations are a requirement of entry.

## Theft

From London to La Paz crooks lurk, ready to pounce upon the unsuspecting traveller. Theft takes many forms, from the highly trained gangs of children who artfully pick pockets all over Europe to violent attacks on the streets of American cities. It is also not unknown to be robbed by fellow-travellers from hostels, beaches, etc. nor by corrupt airport officials in cahoots with baggage handlers.

How to carry your money and valuables should be given careful consideration. The first rule is not to keep all your wealth in one place. A money belt worn inside your clothing is good for the peace of mind it bestows. If buying a money belt avoid anything too bulky and therefore indiscreet. In fact, a simple money belt can easily be manufactured at home by any handy seamstress from a left-over length of cotton or silk (preferable to man-made fibres). Just cut a strip of cloth several inches longer than your waist with a six-inch bulge in the middle large enough to accommodate bank notes and traveller's cheques folded lengthwise. If heavy rain is a possibility, put the money in a plastic bag first. Use Velcro to close the flap over your money and also to fasten the belt round your waist under your clothes. It is a good idea to wear your belt for a few days before departure to make sure that it is comfortable and to prove to yourself that it won't fall off. Keep large denomination travellers' cheques and any hard currency cash there plus a large note of the local currency. Then if your wallet or purse is stolen, you will not be stranded.

To reduce the possibility of theft, steer clear of seedy or crowded areas and moderate your intake of alcohol. If you are mugged, and have an insurance policy which covers cash, you must obtain a police report (sometimes for a fee) to stand any chance of recouping part of your loss.

If you end up in dire financial straits without a cash or credit card, you will have to contact someone at home to send you money urgently. You can contact your bank at home (by telephone, fax or online) and ask them to wire money to you. This will be easier if you have set up a telephone or Internet bank account before leaving home since they will then have the correct security checks in place to authorise a transfer without having to receive something from you in writing with your signature. You can request that the necessary sum be transferred from your bank to a named bank in the town you are in – something you have to arrange with your own bank, so you know where to pick the money up.

If a private individual has kindly agreed to bale you out, they can transfer money in several ways. *Western Union* offers an international money transfer service whereby cash deposited at one branch by your benefactor can be withdrawn by you from any other branch or agency, which the sender need not specify. Western Union agents – there are 245,000 of them in 200 countries – come in all shapes and sizes (e.g. travel agencies, stationers, chemists). Unfortunately it is not well represented outside the developed world. The person sending money to you simply turns up at a Western Union counter, pays in the desired sum plus the fee, which is £14 for up to £100 transferred, £21 for £100-£200, £37 for £500 and so on. For an extra £7 your benefactor can do this over the phone with a credit card. In the UK, ring 0800-833833 for further details, a list of outlets and a complete rate schedule. The website www.westernunion.com allows you to search for the nearest outlet.

Thomas Cook, American Express and the UK Post Office offer a similar service called *MoneyGram* (www.moneygram.com). Cash deposited at one of their foreign exchange counters is available within ten minutes at the named destination or can be collected up to 45 days later at one of 60,000 co-operating agents in 160 countries. The fee is £12 for sending £100, £18 for up to £200, £24 for up to £300, £46 for between £750 and £1,000 and so on. Ring 0845 722 3344 for details or check the Post Office website (www.postoffice.co.uk).In an emergency, your consulate can help you get in touch with friends and relations, normally by arranging a reverse charge call. British Consulates have the authority to cash a personal cheque to the value of £100 supported by a valid banker's card.

## CONSULAR HELP IN EMERGENCIES

Widespread confusion persists concerning the help available from the UK government to its citizens in a crisis. In the first place it is the Consulate or Consular Services department which is responsible for looking after UK nationals, whereas the Embassy does business with the host country.

*A British Consul can:*

- Issue an emergency passport.
- Contact relatives and friends to ask them for help with money or tickets.
- Tell you how to transfer money.
- Cash a sterling cheque worth up to £100 if supported by a valid banker's card.
- As a last resort give you a loan to return to the UK.
- Put you in touch with local lawyers, interpreters or doctors.
- Arrange for next of kin to be told of an accident or death.
- Visit you in case of arrest or imprisonment and arrange for a message to be sent to relatives or friends.
- Give guidance on organisations who can help trace missing persons.
- Speak to the local authorities for you.

*But a British Consul cannot:*

- Intervene in court cases.
- Get you out of prison.
- Give legal advice or start court proceedings for you.
- Obtain better treatment in hospital or prison than is given to local nationals.
- Investigate a crime.
- Pay your hotel, legal, medical, or any other bills.
- Pay your travel costs, except in rare circumstances.
- Perform work normally done by travel agents, airlines, banks or motoring organisations.
- Find you somewhere to live or a job or work permit.
- Formally help you if you are a dual national in the country of your second nationality.

# Doing Something Worthwhile

## Becoming a Volunteer

The impulse to 'give something back' can ring in the ears as an empty cliché. But in the aftermath of recent devastating natural disasters like the Tsunami and earthquakes in Pakistan and Java, and increasing global awareness of the discrepancy between rich and poor created by the Make Poverty History campaign, among others, there has been a subtle shift among travellers with a social conscience. Many prefer to combine travel with making a contribution to overseas relief rather than pursuing hedonism and relaxation. They are signing on with companies that offer a chance to participate in some worthwhile way (if only briefly) rather than just gawp and lounge.

According to a National Survey of Volunteering, 11 million people would volunteer if only they were asked. In an age when the old jobs-for-life contract between employer and employee is breaking down, individuals are increasingly looking for rewarding experiences outside work that will add value to their lives. They want to find activities that can bestow pride and a sense of achievement. Work may provide an outlet for some of these yearnings, but many individuals prefer to search elsewhere and the voluntary sector at home and abroad is a major beneficiary.

The first tentative step that working people might take in this direction is to volunteer locally. In the UK, many companies like Marks & Spencer and HSBC have long run programmes to encourage their employees to take an active part in their communities. Major companies promoting social responsibility in this way such as Barclays, PricewaterhouseCoopers and Nike are co-operating with *CSV* (Community Service Volunteers) to encourage staff to become involved, for example in literacy and numeracy projects in schools. Nike allows its employees to take six extra days off per year for volunteering.

On this topic, the *Guardian* quoted an employee of a legal firm, 'There are so many benefits to volunteering; most of the time you get so caught up with work and working life that you forget what really matters.' The British government strongly supports corporate initiatives to promote volunteering; see www.employeevolunteering.org.uk for case studies. Self-employed people working from home can benefit enormously from stepping outside their daily working grind intermittently or for an extended period to join a voluntary project.

Hardly anyone can be entirely unmoved by news reports of disasters or by appeals from local and international charities on behalf of the struggling and the suffering – abandoned children, needlessly blind farmers, performing bears and so on. Usually a feeling of responsibility flickers past our consciences and is quickly suppressed. A career break allows you to believe that you can get usefully involved. But stepping in to right such wrongs is never straightforward and potential volunteers soon learn that a willingness to help is not sufficient. Aid work is a difficult field to break into, and agencies are increasingly cautious in the selection process for candidates to go overseas. You might think that being able-bodied and financially privileged might be sufficient but relevant experience and professional qualifications are almost always required.

The Tsunami Disaster of Boxing Day 2004 focused minds on helping in an emergency in an unprecedented way. The outpourings of financial help from around the world were reinforced by an upsurge in the number of people wanting to donate their time to help. As with all emergency relief work, skilled and experienced professionals are in demand while well-meaning amateurs potentially just get in the way. In the immediate aftermath, the United Nations Volunteers (www.unv.org) drew up an emergency roster of potential volunteers keen to help in the relief effort and reconstruction in Southeast Asia. To be included on that, you had to have had experience in disaster response, be available at short notice, have worked in South Asia, be at least 25 years of age with a completed technical/university degree and fluent in English with some knowledge of local languages. Quite a tall order.

If all of this sounds discouraging, ordinary mortals should be aware that many organisations offer fee-paying volunteers the chance to experience life in the developing world by working alongside local people for a short period. The next chapter has details of programmes of dozens of charities and companies that can make it easy for the man or woman who is tired of the commute on the Northern Line or the M42 to go abroad as a volunteer, provided that the ex-commuter is willing to pay, normally about £2,500-£3,000 for 10-16 week projects.

It is also possible to bypass the middleman, i.e. the agency or charity in your country, and go direct to small grassroots projects, some of which are experienced at incorporating paying volunteers from the developed world. It is for each individual to weigh up the pros and cons of paying a fee to a mediating agency which is what **Polly Botsford,** a lawyer from London, did when arranging a project in Cambodia through *Outreach International* as part of her six-month gap year:

> *I went to a couple of extraordinarily off-putting open days full of anxious sixth formers and their less anxious parents. It may be that you do not need to go through an organisation. Many people I met had just turned up in a country and got a feel for what was going on. Organisations can be expensive and could be spoon-feeding. I do feel quite sorry for students who really do want to go and discover the world for themselves because sometimes it can be over-packaged, particularly perhaps for the 'maturer' traveller. On the other hand, the agency did provide useful contacts and structure and was particularly good in finding friendly language tutors, which was invaluable. There was no way I would have picked up Khmer as much as I did without that tuition.*

If you decide that you do not need the safety net of a sending organisation in your own country, the Internet makes it possible to connect with local charities in a way that has never been possible before. **Geoffroy Groleau** is an economist and consultant from Montréal who decided to spend some months in India and wanted to dedicate part of his time to volunteering in the development field. He stumbled across the website of an Indian NGO and arranged to work for a month with Dakshinayan which works with tribal peoples in the hills of Rajamhal and nearby plains.

**Although Geoffroy Groleau ended up thinking that his enjoyment took precedence over his usefulness, he still enjoyed his 'gap' from professional life enormously:**

*The application process is simple and can be conducted fully over the Internet. The registration fee which must be provided before setting out for the project is the primary source of revenues for Dakshinayan. So there I was, stepping onto a train from New Delhi heading to Jharkhand.*

*The project provides an opportunity to acquire a better understanding of the myths and realities surrounding poverty in the developing world, and specifically about the realities of rural India. The tribal people of these villages do not need or want fancy houses or televisions, but simply an education for their children and basic healthcare in order to improve the life they have been leading in relative isolation for centuries. It was interesting for me to see that they lead a quiet and simple life based on the rhythm of harvests and seasons, in marked contrast to most westerners. The primary role for volunteers is to teach English for a few hours every day to the kids attending the three Dakshinayan-run schools. I should also mention the numerous unforgettable football games with enthusiastic kids at the end of sunny afternoons. One should be aware that Dakshinayan is an Indian NGO fully run by local people, which in my view is another positive aspect. But it also means that volunteers will have to adapt to Indian ways.*

*Volunteers should expect to learn more from the people than they will ever be able to teach. Remember that the villagers know much more about their needs than we do, and they have learned long ago to use effectively the resources around them. On the other hand, the contacts with the outside world that the volunteers provide is a valuable way for the villagers to begin to understand the world that surrounds them. In my experience, the hardest things were to adapt to the rather slow rhythm of life and to the fact that as a volunteer you will not manage to change significantly the life of the villagers other than by putting your brick in a collective work that has been going on for many years.*

*Dakshinayan* can be contacted c/o Siddharth Sanyal, F-1169 Ground Floor, Chittarangan Park, New Delhi 110019 (+91 9431397178; www.dakshinayan.org). Volunteers join grassroots development projects every month and contribute $300 for a month.

## Rewards of Volunteering Overseas

A career break provides an opportunity to live and work abroad with a purpose that offers the potential for enormous satisfaction, one that allows the individual to integrate into a foreign society rather than just pass through on a holiday. By volunteering somewhere in the world on a humanitarian or environmental project, you can give your career break a structure and a goal. Importantly, you will also acquire skills that are not available during the course of your normal professional life. A career break offers the chance to stretch yourself and make an enduring contribution if not to the world at least to your own development. If you want to use a career break to discover a country or culture, then volunteering is an attractive option.

Volunteers who return from stints abroad frequently rhapsodise about their experience and regard their time as a volunteer as an extraordinary episode in their lives. During a holiday in South East Asia last summer, **Dale Hurd** was enormously impressed by the friendliness and dignity of the people and the beauty of a culturally fascinating country, but at the same time appalled by the poverty and deprivation.

**Having long before decided to do some voluntary work overseas as soon as she retired from teaching, Dale Hurd knew immediately that she had no alternative but to return to Cambodia to do something more constructive than sightseeing. Through *Outreach International,* she devoted six months to a project training Khmer teachers and working with children who work on a rubbish dump in Phnom Penh, which in normal circumstances you would not expect to prompt someone to write about their experiences under the title 'The Time of my Life':**

*Sitting here, back in the freezing English spring, I look at my hundreds of photographs and dream I'm back in Cambodia in Phnom Penh, dripping in sweat, dodging motodops, blinded by the radiant smiles of the enchanting Khmer people. I had elected to train teachers at a French school called Pour un Sourire d'Enfant which rescues children living near a vast rubbish dump, spending their days and most of their nights scavenging what bits of junk they can sell to finance their survival. They were in considerable danger from hypodermics, from pressurised tins that can blow up in their faces and from the huge machines that sometimes carelessly run them down. I visited the dump early one morning when the stench was suffocating, the sight of small filthy children dragging round the mounds of squalor unforgettable. I was warned to be careful when I filmed as the adults felt insulted and degraded; theirs was not a life they had made through choice but through desperation. Despite this situation where humanity seemed to have hit rock bottom, the children smiled and laughed, eager to communicate and make friends.*

*The Vocational school, where I spent most of my time, comprised 7 sectors: mechanics, gardening, secretarial, hairdressing and spa, maternity nursing, hotel work/housekeeping and restaurant. The beauty of this was that not only did they get a general education but also were able to graduate fully trained to go straight into a job. I'll never forget the graduation ceremony when I not only got a huge lump in my throat, but thought: one less prostitute, one less drug pusher, as I watched each immaculate, smiling student receive a certificate.*

*I could go on indefinitely about the experiences I had. I learnt an enormous amount about Cambodia and about myself. I found depths of tolerance within me that I never knew I had: when in England would I ever happily sit and wait for a bus for three hours, munching bananas and watching the world go by as I did at Snoul? When before had I got as much job satisfaction, or feel daily like a princess when the students said ' Oh, Dul, you are so beautiful today,' when all I'd done was put on a clean shirt. I miss – terribly- the camaraderie and laughter of the teachers. I miss the heady fragrance of the Jacaranda and the tantalising smells of cooking food in the streets; I miss Raidth running up from downstairs calling 'Mummee' with something delicious to eat; I miss Naieng the landlady playing badminton every night in the yard and nursing me so kindly when I was ill; I miss my students who greeted me so joyfully every day; I miss the landscape, slowly turning from blinding greens to dull golds and browns. Above all I miss the Cambodian smile. I miss everything. I had the time of my life and I can't wait to go back.*

Later in 2006, Dale intends to return to Cambodia as a trusted volunteer, having used the Outreach International placement as a stepping stone into the world of international development and longer term humanitarian work. Little did she know that her whole life would change in the most radical way.

In addition to the energising break in routine, you may be able to improve or acquire a language skill and to learn something of the customs of the society in which you are volunteering. You may also gain practical experience in the fields of construction, conservation, archaeology or social welfare. A number of organisations are offering integrated programmes that might combine work, adventure and language learning. For example *Trekforce* (see Directory entry) has a five-month programme in Central America for candidates of all ages, consisting of a conservation work attachment in Belize followed by an intensive Spanish language course in neighbouring Guatemala and a period of teaching English in a Belize primary school. Meanwhile *Frontier* actively assists volunteers to pursue a career in conservation by offering a BTEC qualification in Tropical Habitat Conservation. Although these and similar organisations are popular among young people taking a gap year between school and university, they encourage older volunteers to participate as well.

## Career Break or Career Development?

Does the term 'career break' do justice to the range of experiences obtained and new skills acquired by those who venture forth on a volunteering sabbatical? 'Almost certainly not,' says Anthony Lunch, founder of *MondoChallenge,* 65% of whose volunteers fit this category. The need to get away is frequently a desire to challenge oneself in new directions, to move outside one's comfort zone, to experience different ways of life and to work in a new geographical location. There is usually also an element of wanting to put something back, of doing something useful for people less fortunate.

Undertaking a challenge of this kind often turns out to be more of a career *development* experience than just a break in one's normal routine. New skills are learned very quickly. Teaching in a small school in India, for example, when one has never taught before, provides daily practice in planning and rapidly hones communication skills. For women, the ability to work effectively in what is often a male-orientated society, provides a sharp focus on negotiating skills and on the art of diplomacy.

Volunteers taking part in a small business programme face other challenges. 'They can forget the excel spreadsheets and three-year plans', say Anthony Lunch. 'It is today's actions and tomorrow's plan that really matter when trying to create livelihoods.' A Proctor & Gamble marketing manager once likened his experience on an HIV business project in Tanzania to a 'six week MBA programme,' which illustrates how a career break can be qualitatively different from a long holiday.

## Agency Fees

As soon as you start to search for volunteering opportunities in books (like this) or on the Internet, you will quickly conclude that volunteering is expensive. Mediating agencies charge fees that are sometimes very high. Participants must either pay the fees themselves or fund-raise. Most organisations provide much detailed advice on how to obtain sponsorship and raise money.

The internet search engines are dominated by the high profile international volunteer operations offering a packaged volunteer experience which may not suit everyone. Paying to volunteer is an issue with which adult gappers have to grapple. Attitudes to the fees charged by sending agencies differ enormously from a feeling that they are good value (a typical monthly cost approaches £1,000) to a conviction that they are a complete rip-off. Some companies are far more commercial than others and it is usually easy to tell from their style and literature. Essentially some are tantamount to specialist tour operators and charge accordingly for the infrastructure they provide. Occasionally suspicions are aired in the media and elsewhere that the service offered by the big agencies does not justify the fee. For example the BBC Radio 4 consumer interest programme *You and Yours* unearthed some disgruntled grown-up gappers a couple of years ago who maintained that they had been dropped into schools or orphanages in the developing world where there was no structured programme for volunteers. One woman who was sent to an orphanage in Bolivia was given a box with a few pencils and a skein of wool and was told to get on with teaching and supervising the children. Not surprisingly she resented the £1,700 fee she had paid to the agency for matching her with this 'project'. Often problems arise because of a mismatch of expectations between aspiring volunteer and third world venture, and it is of course the responsibility of the sending agency that collects the volunteer fee to provide as clear and honest a briefing as possible about what the volunteer should expect.

Most volunteers who have gone abroad through one of the sending agencies agree that they could (or would) not have had the experience without the backing of an organisation. Indeed certain grassroots development charities and NGOs in the developing world will not accept foreign volunteers unless they are connected to a sending organisation. Once the initial attachment has been organised through an agency, it is often possible to return independently once your commitment has been proven.

Of course it is not impossible to make direct contact with small local organisations in the developing world which actively look for self-funding volunteers abroad. Certain websites will be of use in this search, for example www.volunteersouthamerica.net, founded in 2005 by Steve McElhinney who was looking for 'grass-roots, zero-cost volunteer work' in Argentina. Finding volunteering opportunities that did not involve paying a large amount of cash to a middle-man or third party was more difficult than he anticipated and he spent dozens of hours trying to track them down. He then posted his findings on a site which eventually became volunteersouthamerica.net. A similar not-for-profit site was launched in 2006 with a somewhat wider brief; try www.truetravellers.org.

Older travellers with experience of the developing world may conclude that they do not need the safety net of a sending agency. **Till Bruckner** is a veteran world traveller who has developed a strong preference for fixing up teaching and voluntary placements independently after arrival rather than with the help of an agency. In fact he did go to Africa initially through a London-based organisation and later regretted that he hadn't put the £500 fee he had paid the agency into a donation box, since he feels that the money would have been much better spent by an international charity than on his placement as a teacher in a relatively privileged setting.

> *If you sign up as a volunteer with an organisation in your home country, it's hard to tell if you're needed at all. It might be run by a local businessman who wants to polish his ego and reputation by seeming charitable, or it might simply fail to address local needs. Some companies are offering nothing more than cultural adventure holidays with a politically correct twist and CV value. Nothing wrong with that, as long as people don't delude themselves that they're contributing to a better world by flying halfway around the planet (spraying the ozone layer with kerosene as they go).*
>
> *My advice to anyone who wants to volunteer in Africa (or anywhere else) is to go first and volunteer second. That way you can travel until you've found a place you genuinely like and where you think you might be able to make a difference. You can also check out the work and accommodation for yourself before you settle down. If you're willing to work for free, you don't need a nanny to tell you where to go. Just go.*

However for those who find this prospect daunting (and unless you are a mature and seasoned traveller you probably will), you will want to pre-arrange a more structured placement.

## Caution

Potential volunteers should not get carried away imagining that they will be able to change the world. It is undoubtedly the case that some of the promotional literature, distributed by profit-making companies out to enlist paying volunteers, shamelessly tries to exploit people's altruistic urges. The reality is that the experience of volunteering overseas is invariably of more benefit to the volunteer than to the community being helped. Some people argue that volunteer-tourism is the new colonialism, that poor suffering communities are being exploited as do-gooders' playgrounds. This negative interpretation should be resisted because all it does is quash the impulse to help others. It may be true that some volunteer schemes have been set up with the needs of the foreign volunteers taking priority over those of the local community. The local people may well enjoy the presence of the foreigners but in terms of contributing to ongoing change or building infrastructure, many of the programmes have little lasting impact. But this is not colonial exploitation. Nothing is removed from the foreign village except the experience for the western participant, which can be transforming.

The insights gained by volunteers are often the most important long-term effect, resonating long after a gap year is over. Even those who have given the matter little thought when they are signing up for a £3000 volunteering adventure in Africa or Southeast Asia often end up with their eyes being opened to the difficulties of delivering aid across cultural divides. A typical gap year volunteer might find him or herself working in a school in Ghana or Nepal or Costa Rica. Every day for three months he/she will stand in front of a class of 60 or 80 children trying to help them improve their spoken English by devising games for them to rearrange sentences in order, teaching them Beatles songs or nursery rhymes and having them compose haikus or put on a play. You could take a jaundiced view and say that in the scheme of things this contribution is negligible and mainly provides a chance for the classroom teacher to put her feet up in the staff room. But our volunteer is sure to go home with a heightened sensitivity to cultural differences. Even if the development outcomes that follow on from a typical short volunteer placement are limited, foreign participants usually bring variety and laughter to the lives of children and adults they meet, forming bonds along the way. These issues are worth thinking through before committing yourself, so that you are more likely to choose with care your sending agency. A good agency will promote worthwhile programmes which grow out of local input while avoiding local rascals and rip-off merchants.

Some of the glossy marketing material distributed by specialist 'voluntourism' operators shows only pristine beaches, jolly campfires and smiling black babies, with an upbeat text to match. It might be instructive to quote a more realistic version taken from the literature of an Icelandic exchange organisation (EXIT):

> *As much as we would like Peru to live up to European standards, we have to warn you that institutions do not prepare for your arrival by organising a weekly work schedule or other special instructions. It's a big challenge to live and work in a poor Latin American country. It demands courage, some experience and the ability to adapt. It can be overwhelming, especially at first, to have to adjust to completely new conditions, communicate in a foreign language, etc. Things are not as you are used to, the climate, the food, the atmosphere – everything is different. During your work you will be faced, daily with a harsh social reality and experience things very differently from the way a tourist would.*

Voluntary projects abroad often demand a large measure of flexibility. More mature volunteers with experience of the working world are often better placed than young students to cope in situations where the tasks are not pre-determined and where you may be left not knowing what you are supposed to do or be asked to carry out tasks for which you are ill-prepared.

Privately-run projects are particularly susceptible to causing disappointment if the individuals in charge fail to maintain high standards. For example volunteers have travelled to remote corners of the world to work on eco-projects only to find that the managers run them for profit. One eager volunteer turned up for an eight-week music project in Rio de Janeiro only to find that it was the summer holidays and then Carnaval and the college was deserted most of the time. Another was promised a garden design placement in Sri Lanka where the only task was weeding the headmistress's private garden because local males were not permitted to do this chore. Occasionally eager volunteers are forced to conclude that the voluntary organisation under whose auspices they are working charge volunteers well in excess of essential running costs. Nowadays the large number of voluntary organisations competing with one another for paying volunteers means that it is wise to investigate as thoroughly as you can the proportion of your fee that goes to the needy project and how much goes towards administration and in some cases profit. An increasing number of mediating agencies do not have charitable status and are simply profit-making travel companies specialising in volunteer placement. Ask for a breakdown of where your payment goes and if you are in any doubt about an organisation, ask for the names of past volunteers whom you can contact for an informal reference. Any worthy organisation should be happy to oblige.

People who work in the developing world often experience just as much culture shock on their return home as they did when they first had to adapt to difficult conditions abroad (see chapter *Back to Normal or A Change for Life?*). Anyone who has spent time living amongst people for whom every day is a struggle to survive may find it very difficult to return to their privileged and comfortable life in the west. Many returned volunteers claim to feel sickened by the excesses of consumer culture and misplaced value systems. After returning from an HIV education programme in Zambia, **Carolinen Kippen** commented, 'I really value what is important in life now, although that makes things difficult managing my expectations now I am back home – people just don't see things the same way I do now!'

Volunteering is nothing like a conventional holiday and even volunteers for organisations with glossy seductive brochures often find the tasks they are assigned to be more physically and emotionally demanding than they anticipated. Teaching English to a group of smiling eight-year olds in a West African village sounds fun and exotic when contemplated at home, but can land you in a very testing situation which might involve few creature comforts and demand a measure of stoicism. During a longer-term placement some volunteers are bound to face homesickness, loneliness or illness.

Raleigh International stresses that for its volunteer expedition leaders, attitude of mind, not age, is the crucial factor in coping with the tough conditions of the Chilean Andes or the Mongolian steppes. If you have any concerns about physical endurance, it's best to consult your GP for a full medical. Explain the conditions you are likely to face and ask for advice.

Regional crises also flare up making volunteering potentially risky. For example Maoist insurgency is a continuing problem in Nepal and most volunteer agencies have withdrawn from troubled Zimbabwe. Try to research in advance any local issues that may be causing concern. As mentioned, the Foreign &

Commonwealth Office runs a regular and updated service; you can ring the Travel Advice Unit on 0870 606 0290 or check their website www.fco.gov.uk/travel to get advice about travelling to regions and countries experiencing conflict, instability or high crime.

# VOLUNTEERING ABROAD THROUGH A UK AGENCY

A growing number of British companies and organisations makes it possible for people of all backgrounds to take a career break of three, six or twelve months volunteering abroad. While some specialise in fixing up placements for gap year students between school and university, others cater to an older age group and many accept volunteers on a year out whatever their age.

Because the student gap year market has almost reached saturation and has been experiencing some shrinkage with the introduction of top-up fees in 2006, many mediating agencies for 18 year olds have broadened the scope of their programmes to appeal more specifically to an older clientele. For example one of the leading companies, *i-to-i,* which has grown tremendously over the past ten years with offices in the USA, Australia and Ireland as well as Leeds, reports that its real growth market has been among the over-30s with the over-50s close behind. Since 2004 it has sent more than 2,000 adult gappers (defined as anyone over 25) overseas, with this group accounting for around 35% of all i-to-i travellers. The most popular destinations among their grown-up clients are ranked as follows: Kenya, Costa Rica, Bolivia, Sri Lanka, India and South Africa. Teaching and conservation placements are the most popular among adults followed by care work.

Similarly, *Madventurer,* which started life as an organisation catering to university students, has noticed such a marked increase in the number of people joining as part of a career break that they now run projects just for adults (25+) taking a gap from their careers (see www.careerbreaker.com). *MondoChallenge* has always encouraged older volunteers to join its range of community-based projects on three continents. Its volunteer profile indicates that as many as 65% of volunteers are on a career break, 21% are post-university and 3% are retired, while the rest are students. Each agency has its own application procedures and it is best to telephone or look to their websites for detailed instructions. Many of these volunteer recruitment companies hold open days when you can meet the permanent staff and hear from former volunteers. If you have anxieties, try to establish precisely what safety net is in place in case of difficulties or emergencies.

Before you apply to join an agency that sends volunteers abroad, it's best to research the options available to you and try to match them with your objectives. What skills do you have to offer and what do you expect to achieve? Are you prepared to accept a different quality of comfort? Are you adaptable to foreign cultures? Can you work alone or in a team? The appeal of applying to a large, well-established sending agency is that you can be reasonably sure that your interests will be handled professionally and with attention to the safety and welfare of participants. Accommodation will be arranged, insurance provided and the logistics in place. You will have the benefit of being put in touch with other volunteers who have been sent out by the same agency.

Organisations that impose few restrictions on skills but charge a joining fee include the following, all of which have Directory entries in the next chapter: *Changing Worlds, i-to-i, Madventurer, MondoChallenge, Outreach International, Raleigh International, Real Gap, Teaching & Projects Abroad, Travellers Worldwide,* and *Venture Abroad*. Any upper limits may be flexible and should be challenged by a keen and energetic candidate.

# OPPORTUNITIES FOR PROFESSIONALS

Commitment, no matter how fervent, is not enough to work in an aid project in the developing world. You must normally be able to offer some kind of useful training or skill unless you are prepared to fund yourself and don't mind that your effort to help will be more a token than of lasting benefit. Mainstream voluntary bodies like VSO (Voluntary Service Overseas), International Service, Skillshare Africa and Hands Around the World act as matching agencies for overseas partners looking for specialist skills and expertise from the developed world.

## Voluntary Service Overseas (VSO)

VSO is an international development charity which works on long-term partnerships with overseas organisations which is perhaps the most famous and longest established of volunteer sending agencies in the UK. Doing a stint as a volunteer with VSO is a classic career break which thousands of Britons apply to do every year. Every year VSO recruits over 750 people from around the world. Volunteers are recruited from the UK, Ireland, Europe, North America, India, the Philippines and Kenya. Enquiries should be sent to VSO, 317 Putney Bridge Road, London SW15 2PN (020-8780 7500; enquiry@vso.org.uk; www.vso.org.uk).

During nearly 50 years VSO has earned a reputation for the success of its programmes and its professional approach to recruiting volunteers. Recruitment is rigorous and intended to make sure that volunteer skills are matched most effectively with projects in the developing world. The advantage of volunteering with VSO is that its track record means that it is relatively well funded. Volunteers have their expenses covered and are also given a salary in line with local salaries plus various grants such as an equipment grant, national insurance, extensive training, reasonable accommodation with a private room and return travel. Most reassuringly, the health insurance package is described as the 'rolls-royce' of policies, providing comprehensive coverage. Additionally, a payment is made on the return home to act as a cushion.

This level of support requires a corresponding level of commitment and responsibility because applicants will be asked to dedicate one or two years of their lives. Recently VSO merged with the volunteering charity BESO (British Executive Service Overseas) and is now able to offer shorter assignments for people with experience of working overseas in development, and who are available at short notice. VSO's Business Partnership Scheme encourages company bosses to allow volunteers to work overseas for shorter periods of between three and 12 months, partly in response to a shortfall of volunteers. Companies like Accenture, PricewaterhouseCoopers, Randstad and Shell have participated (see an account in the *Personal Case Histories* at the end of the book of **Alefiya Rajkotwala**, an Accenture manager who spent nine months in Rwanda).The average age of VSO volunteers has been steadily rising and is now 38. A fifth of volunteers recruited in 2005 were over 50; the maximum age is about 75, although some roles have a ceiling of 55 years according to local retirement ages. Many older volunteers have taken early retirement. VSO recruits volunteers in the fields of education, TEFL, health, natural resources, technical trades and engineering, business and social work and many others. About half of all VSO projects worldwide are related to education. Likewise there is a growing need for expertise in IT and small business advisers.

The selection procedure takes place in several stages. Applications are assessed initially on paper to match volunteer skills to the requests made to VSO by its partners. If a certain skill does not meet a requirement then an application might be put on hold until opportunities arise. Then an assessment is made about each applicant's personal situation to see whether it affects their suitability. For example, does the applicant have children, a partner, financial stability, emotional stability? Often a couple will apply and only one of the couple will be able to find a suitable placement. References from current employers are checked at this stage and also a routine check takes place with the police to ensure that the applicant doesn't have a criminal record. Successful applicants then undergo intensive training in the UK and after arrival to prepare them for their assignments, including workshops on health and language immersion.

**An IT trainer in her late 40s, Jan Lee decided that before she turned 50 she was going to finally follow through on her New Year's resolution to do something different:**

*After spending some time searching the Internet I discovered that VSO seemed to offer me all that I wanted – the opportunity to travel; the chance to live in and experience at first hand another culture; an appropriate job where I could fully utilise my skills and share my knowledge with local people in a developing country; and, perhaps most importantly for a 50 year old single female embarking on her first real adventure, the protection and support of a large and well-respected organisation.*

*I soon began the process of filling in application forms; attending the selection day which weeds out those who are not fully committed, those with marked prejudices, those who are burning with a desire to change the world and other inappropriate candidates; and attending the various training offered by VSO to prepare you as much as possible for what you might meet overseas. My medical showed up a previously unknown condition which involved an operation and a six-month delay to my departure, but by November of that year I was ready to depart for Laos (which I learned is in Southeast Asia and not Africa) as an IT adviser to a government department dealing with Agriculture and Fisheries.*

**Polly Page** worked for seven years with a charity providing services to people with HIV and had risen to the position of senior manager of volunteer services. At the point where her job was effectively being downgraded to meet funding cuts, she decided to take voluntary redundancy. VSO seemed an attractive next step since it gave her a positive purpose while she made significant changes in her life. Initially, she misunderstood VSO's needs and believed that because she was not a trained medic a placement would not be found for her. However, like many people with professional experience, she was told by VSO that they could use her expertise and Polly was placed as a manager with an eye clinic in Nepal.

As many other newly arrived volunteers have found in developing countries, she felt that the impact she was having was not as significant as she had hoped:

*There were some frustrations, particularly during the first year. It's difficult to integrate into a different culture and you will always be seen as an outsider. Invariably you have more money than the people you work with and in a medical emergency they know you will be flown out. The organisation I was assigned to also found it difficult to make good use of my skills and they were resistant to my suggestions. The biggest challenge for a volunteer in this situation is to find an appropriate niche within the organisation they are ostensibly assigned to help.*

Despite making many suggestions for change to improve the delivery of medical care, Polly finally realised that the organisation would only change if the staff first understood what the problems were and then were persuaded to push for change themselves. To help her achieve this she borrowed a technique that had been developed in Bangladesh which was to stage a play in which the problems were dramatised and the staff were invited to intervene in the show to illustrate how a problem could be resolved. By this method, Polly became a facilitator for change. Only by encouraging the staff to think differently could she have the impact she desired.

Polly's advice to other volunteers is to find out as much as possible about the organisation they are being sent to assist and, if the placement is not working out, not to sit around feeling frustrated and unhappy. Try to negotiate improvements and if that fails think about leaving or changing jobs in-country. VSO programme offices can help with problems.

Any potential volunteer needs to know that the relationship with the host group will be delicate. Cross-cultural differences will be a challenge to accommodate and it is you who will have to do more adapting than the host project. Sometimes the advertised role will be different from the one you expected. Inevitably some local attitudes to volunteers are ambivalent. On the one hand a placement from a charity like VSO is prestigious and lends credibility to the indigenous programmes but on the other you might be perceived as something of a nuisance, a disruptive challenge to the established hierarchy. The trick is to earn the trust of your co-workers and to act as a catalyst for change rather than simply imagine you can act in an executive fashion.

Looking back Polly is very clear about the frustrations but she also acknowledges that her VSO placement was tremendously beneficial too. She met her partner there and also learnt to speak almost fluent Nepalese. Living in Kathmandu the capital, she had some comforts like privacy and use of a laptop. At the outset she felt the placement failed to use her skills, but in time the struggle taught her the importance of effective teamwork. During the last six months of the placement, Polly finally felt the rewards of her patient efforts to find a role and she began to see the clinic make progress in the way it functioned.

## Other Agencies Recruiting Professionals

A range of charitable organisations supports 'operational' agencies such as Oxfam, UNICEF, UNHCR, etc. by recruiting for certain positions within their programmes. The types of assignment for which the client agencies need personnel almost always require previous field experience, typically at least six months with a known non-governmental organisation (NGO) in a developing country. The mediating agencies find people for specific jobs not jobs for specific people. They receive many requests from those without previous field experience who wish to do short-term assignments but it is increasingly rare for such people to be placed, especially if they are first-timers who cost the agencies a lot of money in training and travel expenses. Competition for such placements is high, and aid work has rapidly turned into a very serious profession. Agencies are increasingly cautious in the selection process for candidates to go overseas because they have to ensure that the donor's money is being spent in the best possible way. Even with a relevant degree and further specialist qualifications, it can still be difficult to secure a position in the aid field.

RedR-IHE is an international NGO that provides recruitment, training and support services for humanitarian professionals across the world. RedR originally stood for Engineers for Disaster Relief merged several years ago with International Health Exchange (IHE). For example, following the Indonesian earthquake in May 2006, RedR-IHE mobilised relief personnel from its online database in preparation for deployment to the region.

Within most professions, an organisation refers specialists to appropriate volunteer vacancies overseas, including vets, dentists, pharmacists, pilots, even accountants. **Debbie Risborough** (see her Case History at end of book) got her job with Concern in Sudan through MANGO, Management Accountants for NGOs – not to be confused with the fashion label – see www.mango.org.uk. A list of these professional agencies has been drawn up by Médecins sans Frontières and may be found on www.uk2.msf.org/aboutus/Links/OtherAgencies.htm. Meanwhile reliefweb.int carries a current list of humanitarian vacancies for professionals.

*Skillshare International* (www.skillshare.org) can help first-time volunteers, mostly related to the medical profession. It sends qualified and skilled staff to work professionally in partnership with local people on development work throughout southern Africa and also India. Positions are varied and have included teachers for agricultural studies, business advisers, curators, fund-raisers, catering tutors, ceramics/3D design lecturers, physiotherapists, engineers, bricklaying instructors and so on. Placements are for two years, and flights, national insurance payments, a modest living allowance/salary, rent-free accommodation, health insurance, small home savings allowance and equipment grants are provided. Applicants should be between the ages of 21 and 62 and should have relevant qualifications and at least two years post-qualification work experience. Many other agencies receive requests for volunteer input from projects worldwide which they try to match with suitable volunteers on their register of willing professionals. Disaster relief organisations work in a similar way; for example, *Merlin,* the international medical relief agency, maintains a register of health professionals and logisticians willing to be considered for emergency relief work and also offers specialist courses.

If you are spending time in one place in the developing world you are bound to make the acquaintance of the aid community who will be plugged into the needs of local NGOs and international agencies. While **Till Bruckner** was staying in the Sudan he noticed that overseas branches of Oxfam, Save the Children, etc. had huge volumes of reports to write, something that the local staff sometimes struggled to do in polished English. He discovered that his assistance was welcomed by some and so advises others to do likewise (see chapter *Back to Normal or a Change for Life?* for further ideas from Till Bruckner on how to break into the world of professional development).

## Listing of International Voluntary Organisations

*British Red Cross,* 44 Moorfields, London EC2Y 9AL (0870 170 7000; www.redcross.org.uk). Maintains a register of skilled, experienced delegates who are available to work overseas on a fixed-term, salaried basis.

*Concern Worldwide,* 52-55 Lower Camden St, Dublin 2, Ireland (+353 1-417 7700; www.concern.net). See website for UK offices. Recruits mostly qualified professionals over 21 for development projects in Africa and Asia.

*IESC Geekcorps,* Suite 1010, 901 15th St. NW, Washington, DC 20005 (202-326-0280; geekcorps@iesc.org; www.geekcorps.org). Geekcorps was set up by a group of IT professionals to help small businesses and institutions in the developing world. Although it is based in the US, IT specialists do not need to be American citizens to apply. Most volunteers work for periods of three months.

*Hands Around the World,* PO Box 62, Lydney, Gloucestershire GL15 6WZ (tel/fax 01594 560223; info@hatw.org.uk; www.hatw.org.uk). Run three to six month assignments primarily in Africa in a range of fields including for physiotherapists, radiographers/ultrasonographers, pharmacists, lab technicians, IT specialists and dairy farmers.

*International Service,* Hunter House, 57 Goodramgate, York YO1 7FX (01904 647799/ fax 01904 652353; is@internationalservice.org.uk/ www.internationalservice.org.uk. Founded as the United Nations Association, IS recruits professionals for two-year placements in Bolivia, Brazil, Burkina Faso, Mali and the West Bank and Gaza.

Médecins du Monde UK, 34th Floor, One Canada Square, London E14 5AA (020-7516 9103; www.medecinsdumonde.org.uk). Must have a minimum of two years healthcare experience post-qualification and a working knowledge of French would be useful. Minimum placements are three months, maximum one year.

*Médecins Sans Frontières (UK),* 67-74 Saffron Hill, London EC1N 8QX (020-7404 6600/fax 020-7404 4466; office-ldn@london.msf.org/ www.msf.org). MSF sends 2,000 volunteers to 70 countries providing medical support to victims of war and disaster, normally for 9-12 months. Most opportunities are for qualified medical professionals though there are also places for administrators, engineers, and accountants. A knowledge of French is an asset.

*Merlin,* 12th Floor, 207 Old St, London EC1V 9NR (020-7014 1600; www.merlin.org.uk).

*Oxfam,* Volunteering Team, Oxfam House, John Smith Drive, Cowley, Oxford OX4 2JY (0870 333 2444; www.oxfam.org.uk/what_you_can_do/volunteer/internship.htm). Oxfam recruits only full-time professionals for overseas but relies on volunteers in the UK. Internships are available in several divisions and are mostly based in Oxford.

*RedR/IHE,* 1 Great George St, London SW1P 3AA (020-7233 3116; www.redr.org/london).

*Skillshare Africa,* 126 New Walk, Leicester, LE1 7JA (0116 254 1862; www.skillshare.org).

*United Nations Volunteers,* Postfach 260 111, D-53153 Bonn, Germany (+49 228-815 2000; www.unvolunteers.org).

*VSO,* 317 Putney Bridge Road, London SW15 2PN (020-8780 7500; enquiry@vso.org.uk; www.vso.org.uk). Ireland office: VSO Ireland, Carmichael Centre, Brunswick St, North, Dublin 7 (01872 7173; info@vso.ie; www.vso.ie). Office for North America: VSO Canada, 806-151 Slater Street, Ottawa ON K1P

5H3 (1-888-876-2911 or 613 234-1364; inquiry@vsocan.org; www.vsocan.org). Office in Netherlands for Europe: VSO Nederland, Oorsprongpark 7,3581 ET Utrecht (+31-30 23 20 600; recruitment@vso.nl; www.vso.nl).

# SHORT-TERM VOLUNTEERING

## Workcamps

Voluntary work in developed countries often takes the form of workcamps which accept unskilled people of all ages for short periods.The term 'workcamp' is falling out of favour and is often replaced by 'project'. As part of an established international network of voluntary organisations they are not subject to the irregularities of some privately run projects. As well as providing volunteers with the means to live cheaply for two to four weeks in a foreign country, workcamps enable volunteers to become involved in what is usually useful work for the community, to meet people from many different backgrounds and to increase their awareness of other lifestyles, social problems and their responsibility to society.

Within Europe, and to a lesser extent further afield, there is a massive effort to co-ordinate workcamp programmes. This means that the prospective volunteer should apply in the first instance to an organisation in his or her own country. The vast majority of camps take place in the summer months, and camp details are normally published in March/April with most placements being made in April/May. Understandably, these organisations charge £4-£6 for a printed copy of their international programmes though a great deal of information is available online. It is necessary to pay a registration fee (usually £80-£130 for overseas camps) which includes board and lodging but not travel.

Many projects are environmental and involve the conversion/reconstruction of historic buildings and building community facilities. Interesting projects include building adventure playgrounds for children, renovating an open-air museum in Latvia, organising youth concerts in Armenia, constructing boats for sea-cleaning in Japan, looking after a farm-school in Slovakia during the holidays, helping peasant farmers in central France to stay on their land, excavating a Roman villa in Germany, forest fire spotting in Italy, plus a whole range of schemes with the disabled and elderly, conservation work and the study of social and political issues. It is sometimes possible to move from project to project throughout the summer, particularly in countries such as France or Morocco where the workcamp movement is highly developed.

Service Civil International is the largest workcamp organisation with links to 40+ countries. The UK branch is International Voluntary Service (IVS) (addresses below).

*International Voluntary Service (IVS Field Office),* Old Hall, East Bergholt, Colchester, Essex CO7 6TQ (01206 298215; www.ivs-gb.org.uk). IVS North: Oxford Place Centre, Oxford Place, Leeds LS1 3AX (0113-246 9900; ivsnorth@ivs-gb.org.uk) and IVS Scotland: 7 Upper Bow, Edinburgh EH1 2JN (0131-226 6722; scotland@ivs-gb.org.uk). Programme of camps published online in April. The cost of registration on workcamps outside the UK is £145 which includes £30 membership in IVS.

*Concordia Youth Service Volunteers Ltd,* Heversham House, 20-22 Boundary Road, Hove, East Sussex BN3 4ET (tel/fax 01273 422218; www.concordia-iye.org.uk). Registration costs £90-£115.

*UNA Exchange,* United Nations Association, Temple of Peace, Cathays Park, Cardiff CF10 3AP (029-2022 3088; www.unaexchange.org). Majority of camps cost £110-£160 to join.

*Youth Action for Peace/YAP,* 8 Golden Ridge, Freshwater, Isle of Wight PO40 9LE; 01983 752557; www.yap-uk.org). Formerly the Christian Movement for Peace. Medium and longer term projects for older volunteers (minimum 21/23) as well as short workcamps.

## Archaeology

Taking part in archaeological excavations is another popular form of voluntary work, but volunteers are usually expected to make a contribution towards their board and lodging. Also, you may be asked to bring your own trowel, work clothes, tent, etc. Archaeology Abroad (31-34 Gordon Square, London WC1H 0PY; 020-8537 0849; www.britarch.ac.uk/archabroad) is an excellent source of information, as they publish details of excavations needing volunteers on CD-ROM in spring and autumn; in the past year between 700 and 1,000 definite places on sites were offered to subscribers. They do stress however that applications from people with a definite interest in the subject are preferred. An annual subscription costs £20.

Another valuable list of over 200 digs worldwide needing volunteers is the *Archaeological Fieldwork Opportunities Bulletin* published by the Archaeological Institute of America in Boston and now searchable on their website www.archaeological.org). For those who are not students of archaeology, the chances of finding a place on an overseas dig will be greatly enhanced by having some digging experience nearer to home. Details of British excavations looking for volunteers are published in *British Archaeology* magazine from the Council for British Archaeology (St. Mary's House, 66 Bootham, York YO30 7BZ; 01904 671417; www.britarch.ac.uk). The magazine is produced six times a year and lists archaeological digs to which volunteers can apply; an annual subscription costs £23. Digs are also listed on their website.

A huge number of digs take place throughout France in the summer months. Every May the Ministry of Culture (Direction de l'Architecture et du Patrimoine, Sous-Direction de l'Archéologie, 4 rue d'Aboukir, 75002 Paris, France; 01-40 15 77 81) publishes a national list of excavations requiring up to 5,000 volunteers which can be consulted on its website (www.culture.fr/fouilles). Most *départements* have *Services Archéologiques* which organise digs. Without relevant experience you will probably be given only menial jobs but many like to share in the satisfaction of seeing progress made.

Israel is another country particularly rich in archaeological opportunities, many of them organised through the universities. Digs provide an excellent means of seeing remote parts of the country though Israeli digs tend to be more expensive than most, typically US$35-$40 a day plus registration.

# CONSERVATION

Saving the planet is an issue that is slowly climbing up the international agenda. Scaling down one's consumption is often part of a gap year spent travelling or learning. But to make a more lasting contribution, it is worth slotting into a conservation project at home or abroad. Most fix up a placement in advance though this is not essential. One enterprising visitor to South Africa looked up the 'green directory' in a local library, contacted a few of the projects listed in the local area and was invited to work at a cheetah reserve near Johannesburg in exchange for accommodation and food.

For a directory of opportunities in this specialised area, consult the book *Green Volunteers: The World Guide to Voluntary Work in Nature Conservation* published in Italy and distributed by Vacation Work (www.vacationwork.co.uk) in Europe. Related titles from Vacation Work are *Working with the Environment* and *Working with Animals* (both £11.95). Many of the projects listed in *Green Volunteers* are ideally suited to people on a gap year. To take just one example, the Wakuluzu Trust in Kenya needs volunteers over the age of 22 who can stay for at least three months to work to save the Angolan Colobus monkey and preserve its coastal habitat. The cost of participating is modest: €400 per month plus about €15 a week for food. (Details are available from the Colobus Trust, PO Box 5380, 80401, Diani Beach, Kenya; tel/fax: +254 40 320 3519; www.colobustrust.org.

Animal lovers will find a wealth of opportunities. To take just one of the main conservation organisations, *Global Vision International* (see entry; www.gvi.co.uk) can arrange for people to work with vervet monkeys in South Africa, big game in Kenya, turtles in Costa Rica, orangutans in Sumatra and collect species data in the Galapagos Islands. Elsewhere, the six-week expeditions in Borneo with the *Orangutan Foundation* are popular with career breakers, as are wildlife assignments in Africa with the main agencies listed in the Directory of Specialist Programmes in the chapter that follows. Phil Bond's lack of fitness in hot humid Borneo was instantly forgotten when an orangutan came over to him, put her hand in his lap and her baby played with the zip on his pocket.

**Neil Munro** was in his 60s (see 'Case Histories' at end of book) when he joined a lion-breeding project at a game park in Zimbabwe called Antelope Park (www.antelopepark.co.zw). He gravitated to two cubs who had had a traumatic start in life, perhaps because he had just emerged from a four-year family trauma in his own life. Neil knew nothing about lions before he went and had had limited contact with animals, but discovered to his pleasure that he was a natural. He was not overly frightened of the lions. Even on the occasion that two cubs did jump on him, he didn't lose his nerve, only hit them on the side of the face as the guides had instructed to show them who was in command. He was good at 'thinking like a lion' and worked patiently and devotedly to win the trust and affection of the two damaged cubs in which he was put in charge, for instance by crawling under prickly bushes with them (until one of them would sleep over his legs), adjusting their feeding routines and greeting them by rubbing heads, as lions do. He had lots of adventures in the bush – rode horses to inspect the perimeter fences and to check for poachers' snares, rode elephants to look at game, saw a deadly two-meter long Egyptian cobra (which made a fellow volunteer scream and jump into his arms), a python (not so dodgy because not poisonous), watched impala, wildebeest, hartebeest, zebra, giraffes, etc. For the most part he got on very well with the other volunteers who were of many nationalities and mostly young. Over time, his interaction with the lion cubs Casper and Cleo had a healing effect on them and unobtrusively on him too. The cubs gradually learned to play and not to be so dependent on each other. He thinks that because he (unlike most of the other volunteers) has children of his own, he was more understanding of their situation. He has been back since his original stay to visit 'his' cubs who clearly remembered him. He is now looking into the possibility of selling some land to fund further long term stays in this beautiful corner of Africa.

Short-term conservation holidays are available through the *BTCV (British Trust for Conservation Volunteers)* which runs a programme of mainly 2-week International Conservation Holidays in 25 countries including Iceland, France, Bulgaria, USA, Cameroon, Japan and China. Further details are available from BTCV, Conservation Centre, Balby Road, Doncaster DN4 0RH (01302 572244; information@btcv.org.uk; http://shop.btcv.org.uk). Accommodation, meals and insurance are provided from £385 to £880 a fortnight on international projects or about £150 a week in the UK including training in conservation skills.

The *Involvement Volunteers Association Inc.* arranges short-term individual, group and team voluntary placements in many countries including Australia, New Zealand, California, Hawaii, Fiji, Thailand, India, Lebanon and Germany. Many projects are concerned with conservation, while others assist disadvantaged people. Projects can be arranged back-to-back in different countries for a fee.

Conservation work in New Zealand is offered by the New Zealand Volunteer Programme run by NZ Job Search (www.nzjs.co.nz); see the directory listing for *Beyond Backpackers*.

Well-known organisations like Raleigh, Frontier, Trekforce and Coral Cay recruit expeditionary groups, which operate as a project team for a period of two to three months. These agencies help and staff scientific expeditions by supplying fee-paying volunteers. These are in effect specialist tour operators, and it seems that there is a booming market for this sort of working holiday among the affluent who are looking for a holiday with a difference or a platform from which to launch a career break. Scientific expedition organisations and wildlife programmes that use self-financing volunteers include the following (most with entries in the 'Directory of Specialist Programmes').

*African Conservation Experience* (www.conservationafrica.net) sends people to game and nature reserves in South Africa, Zimbabwe and Botswana for between one and three months where they have the chance to assist rangers and wardens and get some first-hand experience of animal and plant conservation. The participation fees are approximately £2,700 for one month, £4,000 for three months including airfares.

*Biosphere Expeditions* (www.biosphere-expeditions.org) organise wildlife conservation research expeditions to many parts of the world. Volunteers with no research experience assist scientific experts. Fees start at £990.

*Blue Ventures* (www.blueventures.org) conducts marine research and grassroots conservation projects in Madagascar.

*Coral Cay Conservation* (www.coralcay.org) recruits paying volunteers to assist with tropical forest and coral reef conservation expeditions in Malaysia, Honduras, the Philippines and Fiji. A sample six-week project for a dive trainee is £1,900.

*Earthwatch Europe* (www.earthwatch.org/europe). International non-profit organisation that recruits over 4,000 volunteers a year for 130 expeditions to assist scientific field research around the world. Prices range from £150 for a short local project to £2,450 for helping to monitor greenhouse gases in Canada.

*Ecovolunteer,* First Floor, 577/579 Fishponds Rd, Bristol BS16 3AF (0117-965 8333; www.ecovolunteer.org.uk). Travel agent that specialises in matching paying volunteers with short-term wildlife conservation projects worldwide.

*Frontier Conservation* (www.frontier.ac.uk) operates a conservation programme to preserve coral reefs, savannas, forests and mangrove areas in Tanzania, Madagascar, Cambodia, Fiji & the Pacific Islands and Nicaragua.

*Global Vision International* (www.gvi.co.uk) offers research and conservation expeditions of varying lengths worldwide.

*Greenforce* (www.greenforce.org) specialises in environmental expeditions: terrestrial projects in Amazonian Ecuador and Nepal; marine projects in Borneo, Fiji and the Bahamas.

*Operation Wallacea* (www.opwall.com) runs marine, rainforest or desert research projects in Sulawesi (Indonesia), Honduras, Egypt, Amazonian Peru, South Africa and Cuba.

*Personal Overseas Development* (www.thepodsite.co.uk) runs Amazon jungle conservation programme in Peru as well as other opportunities IN Tanzania, Thailand and Nepal (see entry).

*Trekforce Expeditions* (www.trekforce.org.uk) offers projects in Belize, Guyana, Peru and Borneo to research endangered rainforests and wildlife.

**As the head of science of a secondary school in Cornwall, Tom Inger was interested in ecology and wanted to explore a reef system. The *Operation Wallacea* expedition to Indonesia allowed him to qualify for an Open Water PADI qualification and then to work alongside a research team studying the health of the reef.**

*Our task was to monitor numbers of species of bugs and lobsters, starfish and invertebrates. Bomb-fishing has irreparably damaged the coral and the damage needs to be quantified. OpWall shares the research results with the local communities in an attempt to change harmful practices.*

*There were 80 volunteers, mainly British and many of 'teacher age' including a family with two children aged five and six; the father is a diver and the mother a sociologist who was more interested in studying the local Bajo people. I had an absolutely brilliant time living in such a remote corner of the world, and also feel that the experience was professionally worthwhile too. Some of the Key Stage 3 and 4 lessons that I have given this year have been greatly improved by my first-hand experience.*

## Organic Farms

With an upsurge of interest in organic foods, the organic farming movement is attracting a rapidly increasing following around the world, from Tunbridge Wells to Turkey with an ever-rising number of farms converting, at least partially, to organic methods of production. Organic farms are labour-intensive operations and everywhere they take on volunteers. Various co-ordinating bodies go under the name of WWOOF – World Wide Opportunities on Organic Farms. WWOOF has a global website www.wwoof.org with links to the national offices in the countries that have a WWOOF co-ordinator. WWOOF organisations exist in the UK, Denmark, Sweden, Germany, Switzerland, Austria, Czech Republic, Italy, Slovenia, Turkey, Australia, New Zealand, Canada, Mexico, Ghana, Uganda, Nepal, China, Japan and Korea. Individual farm listings in other countries, i.e. those with no national organisation, are known as WWOOF Independents. It is necessary to join WWOOF before you can obtain addresses of these properties (£15 for Internet access to addresses, £20 for printed booklet).

National WWOOF co-ordinators compile and sell a worklist of their member farmers willing to provide free room and board to volunteers who help out and who are genuinely interested in furthering the aims of the organic movement. Each national group has its own aims, system, fees and rules but most expect applicants to have gained some experience on an organic farm in their own country first. WWOOF is an exchange: in return for your help on organic farms, gardens and homesteads, you receive meals, a place to sleep and a practical insight into organic growing. (If the topic arises at immigration, avoid the word 'working'; it is preferable to present yourself as a student of organic farming organising an educational farm visit or a cultural exchange.)

Before arranging an extended stay on an organic farm, consider whether or not you will find such an environment congenial. Many organic farmers are non-smoking vegetarians and living conditions may be primitive by some people's standards, so if you are used to slipping out from work for a cappuccino or a burger for lunch, you might want to think carefully before organising a career break on an organic farm.

If you are starting in Britain, send an s.a.e. to the UK branch of WWOOF (PO Box 2675, Lewes, Sussex BN7 1RB; 01273 476286) who will send you a membership application form. The active Australian branch of WWOOF publishes its own *List of Independent Hosts* of farms and volunteer work opportunities in those countries with no national WWOOF group, which will be sent to addresses overseas for A$32(WWOOF Australia, 2166 Gelantipy Rd, W Tree, Via Buchan, Vic 3885; 03-5155 0218; www.wwoof.com.au),

A free internet-based exchange of work-for-keep volunteers can be found at www.helpx.net where the majority of farms are located in Australia and New Zealand.

## Communal Living

A short or long stay on a commune, at a peace centre or similar may be of interest to people whose spirits have been flagging in a frenetic workplace. Many communities (formerly known as communes) welcome foreign visitors and willingly exchange hospitality for work. The details and possible fees must be established on a case-by-case basis. See chapter *Spiritual Development* for more contacts.

Perhaps the most famous kind of community is the kibbutz. The wind has largely gone out of the sails of the kibbutz movement of Israel, which has been moving away from the old socialist model. In fact in 2006, the long established Kibbutz Representatives office in London ceased sending volunteers to kibbutzim. Yet some are still attracted to these settlements where they can exchange their labour for accommodation, food, perks and a chance to experience the Middle East. Placement of volunteers takes place in Tel Aviv where you can register at the official volunteer placement office, the Kibbutz Program Center (18 Frishman St, Cnr. 90 Ben Yehuda St, Tel Aviv 61030; 03-527 8874/ fax 03-523 9966; kpc@volunteer.co.il/ www.kibbutz.org.il/eng/welcome.htm). Volunteer stays last between two and six months and the registration fee is $60.

# VOLUNTEERING WITHOUT MALARIA PILLS

Going abroad is not essential to becoming a volunteer. Thousands of opportunities within the UK do not require volunteers to pack a rucksack or learn survival skills. If the thought of leaving home for an extended period and living in some wild and woolly place is unappealing, daunting or just plain unmanageable, volunteering closer to home may easily be incorporated into a gap year.

Some of the people most desperately in need of a career break (and uniquely placed to arrange one) are those people who work from home, freelance cartoonists, web designers, translators, crafts people, childminders, copy editors and so on. For many, feelings of isolation can be overwhelming, and they think back with fondness on the busy camaraderie of the office life left behind. Many feel that their social (not to say love) lives have gone into hibernation and they long for some new social outlets. One way of achieving this end is to join a congenial local project as a volunteer.

You might want to use a career break to find out about a different profession through volunteering. For anyone considering a career in youth and community work, counselling or social services, it has become standard practice to spend time initially as a volunteer. Some people combine local voluntary work with a career break motivated by other reasons, e.g. raising children or looking after a family member.

Anyone contemplating taking time out of the workplace this way can start gradually by volunteering his or her spare time while working full-time. This is becoming easier with the creation of schemes like Business in the Community (www.bitc.org.uk) which has persuaded hundreds of companies to donate some of their employees' time to a local charity or community group. The best place to start familiarising yourself with volunteering opportunities at home is to consult your local Volunteer Centre which forms part of Volunteering England (www.

volunteering.org.uk) linking volunteer centres all over the country. For example each London borough has its own. Each office is staffed by professional advisers who will develop a profile of your abilities and interests and then match you up with a local organisation. They act as a high street recruitment agency for local charities, non-profit bodies and community groups and on average have databases containing between one and three thousand opportunities. The last national survey discovered that half a million people had spent time volunteering after consulting their local volunteer recruitment office. Scotland's equivalent is called Volunteer Development Scotland (www.vds.org.uk).

Other sources of information include public noticeboards in libraries, the local hospital, etc. Local councils also work with volunteers and it's worth approaching the department that interests you, e.g. social services.

**Volunteering England, which advises voluntary bodies, suggests you consider these issues first:**

- Before making contact with an organisation, think about what you want to know from them, and what they are likely to ask you.
- How much time can you give? At what time of day?
- What do you want to get from volunteering, e.g. meeting people or gaining new skills?
- What skills or experience can you offer?
- Will out-of-pocket expenses be paid? Does the organisation insure its volunteers?
- Are you receiving any form of state benefit?

Volunteering in the UK can be a stepping stone to opportunities abroad or provide a taster of work in the field of development as it did for **Jen Dyer**. Although Jen had been enjoying her work in the office of a conservation expedition company, she decided to take a break to find out more about careers in the humanitarian and development sector. After much research, she discovered that an internship was the best option, since proper jobs required previous experience and qualifications she didn't have. She applied for all of the different internships Oxfam was advertising at the time and was interviewed by two departments, the Programme Resource Centre and the Media unit:

> *My internship was for 3+ months for 3 days a week. I lived with a friend who was located conveniently close to Oxford which meant that I had lower rent and could finance my internship by continuing to work part-time for Operation Wallacea in Lincolnshire. Oxfam paid my expenses, which meant my living costs were very low and I just had to resist unnecessary items.*
>
> *The best part of my internship may be yet to come. I have gained many contacts through Oxfam and am hoping that when I travel to Honduras with Opwall this summer I will be able to visit Oxfam's agricultural scale-up programme and see development work firsthand. I had one week where I was less excited about the work I was doing at Oxfam. I was helping with the migration of intranet pages to a new system which involved a lot of repetitive computer work without having much interaction with staff but I made up for that by attending the myriad of lunchtime talks available on Oxfam's work and pestering other staff members to have coffee and chats with me to hear their experiences and how their career in this sector came about…*

*The experience has helped me decide on my next course of action. I have now applied for a Masters degree at Manchester Uni in Environment and Development. Eventually I will look for employment in a sector which has now been revealed to me in more detail. I have enjoyed my internship entirely and it has been a wonderful experience where I have learnt an inordinate amount, not just about Oxfam's work but about working in a large NGO, and in fact in a large company, as well as making some great friends.*

## Practicalities

The choices for volunteering in the UK are infinite and include both residential and non-residential work. Residential posts range from a week (say helping at a holiday centre for disabled children or rebuilding a dry stone wall) to a year (for instance at an outdoor centre for disadvantaged youths or at the Centre for Alternative Technology in Wales). By piecing together short stints as a volunteer in different places, it is possible to experience a range of activities and settings on a gap year within the UK.

Many organisations arrange accommodation, sometimes free as in the residential social care placements made by *CSV* (www.csv.org.uk/fulltimevolunteering; see entry), sometimes at a modest cost, as in the week-long conservation projects organised by the *BTCV (British Trust for Conservation Volunteers).* Most BTCV conservation holidays for paying volunteers are for short periods of a weekend or a week, but it is also possible to become a volunteer field officer for up to a year at one of BTCV's centres. Long term volunteers are not restricted by age or qualification and are eligible for income support for the duration of their placement.

*CSV* places volunteers away from home around the UK for 4-12 month placements in a large variety of projects in the social care field. This includes working with the homeless, schools and hospitals, and mentoring young offenders and teenagers in care. Volunteers are given free board and accommodation and paid pocket money of £30 per week. CSV aims to recruit individuals up to the age of 35, though they also run a Retired & Senior Volunteers Programme for volunteers over 50. The CSV Employee Volunteering programme encourages companies to release employees on a part-time basis to volunteer locally in schools, etc.

**Peter Luckham** was at the upper end of the age range when he decided to give his managerial job in IT a rest and become a CSV volunteer, a scheme he remembered hearing about at university. For the first part of his six-month sabbatical he supported 63-year old Eddy who is partially blind and has learning difficulties. His next project was to work as a learning mentor at a special school in Hackney for boys with emotional and behavioural difficulties. It was while working there that he decided to resign from his job in London with a big investment bank and now works on a self-employed basis for a small IT consultancy that serves local small businesses in and around Bournemouth.

For some years, Peter had not felt motivated in the IT world and he began to see that his life lacked balance. Following his volunteering he has returned to a career in IT, but on a different basis and with a different client base, learning new skills at a technical level, and 'no longer a small cog in a big machine as I was in the corporate world':

*Originally I felt as though I was living in an isolated world, worrying about mortgages and pensions, but disconnected from the world around me.*

*Now I'm in a continuous process of discovery. Volunteering has helped me have a wider experience of dealing with different people. It has helped me prove that I can do other things outside the IT world and that I don't need to be as dependent on the perceived security that a very commercially focussed career provides. The experience of being a volunteer provided the space and a new structure to find out a little more about me, and what I really want. I wanted to give something back – maybe I have a little middle class guilt complex.*

## VOLUNTEERING RESOURCES

If you are interested in short or long-term voluntary projects around the world, you might start by browsing through relevant publications such as the *International Directory of Voluntary Work* by Victoria Pybus (Vacation-Work, 2006; £11.95). The current edition describes the voluntary requirements of 700+ organisations. Other useful sources of voluntary opportunities include the website www.do-it.org.uk. Do-it was launched in 2001 as a national database of volunteering opportunities in the UK. Try also new web portal www.responsibletravel.com on which a search for 'Volunteer Travel' results in nearly 250 possibilities. Heavy Internet users should consider using everyclick.com as their search engine, since every click benefita your nominated charity.



The *World Service Enquiry* of the respected charity Christians Abroad, Bon Marché Centre, Suite 237, 241-251 Ferndale Road, London SW9 8BJ (0870 770 3274; www.wse.org.uk) provides information and advice to people of any faith or none who are thinking of working overseas, whether short or long term, voluntary or paid. *The Guide* contains a useful listing of 350+ organisations in the UK and overseas that use short-term volunteers; the 2006/7 edition can be ordered by sending a 68p SAE plus £5.

Since 2004 the Scottish charity Challenges Worldwide has been running a free advisory service 'Ask an Expert' through a partner site www.intervol.org.uk. Intervol is sponsored by CWW together with the government volunteering agency Timebank (www.timebank.org.uk). Free, impartial advice is provided to anyone wanting to volunteer internationally including information on reasons for using a volunteer sending agency, why it is necessary to pay to volunteer, training provision for volunteering overseas, the roles and responsibilities expected for and by volunteers, etc. The website also includes a number of case studies.

*2Way Development* offers a different kind of service to people looking for international voluntary experiences. They provide independent, professional support to volunteers in the organisation of placements overseas, in all sectors of work. The one-off fee of £850 includes personal consultation, referral to ethical volunteering opportunities with NGOs, assistance with preparation and ongoing support.

*Working Abroad Projects,* PO Box 454, Flat 1, Brighton, BN1 3ZS, E. Sussex or WorkingAbroad, 7 rue d'Autan, 11290 Montreal d'Aude, France (tel/fax +33-4-68 26 41 79; Victoria.McNeil@workingabroad.com; www.workingabroad.com). As well as being a web-based resource of voluntary opportunities worldwide, the Brighton-based Workingabroad.com will prepare a personalised report after you complete a detailed request form; the fee is £29/$52 by email, £36/$65 by post.

*Returned Volunteer Action,* 1 Amwell St, London EC1R 1TH (retvolact@lineone.net). RVA gives guidance to potential volunteers through its various publications which draw on the experience of many volunteers who have worked abroad. RVA does not offer individual assistance or placement.

*Christian Vocations* (St James House, Trinity Road, Dudley, West Midlands DY1 1JB; 0870 745 4825; www.christianvocations.org) publishes a searchable online directory of short-term opportunities with Christian agencies.

## Sources of Information

The revolution in information technology has made it easier for the individual to become acquainted with the amazing range of possibilities. One of the best website directories is www.traveltree.co.uk. It covers gap year ideas and volunteering opportunities worldwide as well as internships and educational travel. *Transitions Abroad* magazine maintains great online resources for volunteering (www.transitionsabroad.com). The best of the websites have a multitude of links to organisations big and small that can make use of volunteers. For example www.idealist.org (from Action Without Borders) is a US-based easily searchable site that will take you to the great monolithic charities like the Peace Corps as well as to small grassroots organisations. It lists 20,000 non-profit and community organisations in 150 countries.

The website of Volunteering England (www.volunteering.org.uk) has a listing of UK agencies that send volunteers abroad, as well as disseminating a great deal of other information about volunteering generally. Worldwide Volunteering for Young People (7 North Street Workshops, Stoke sub Hamdon, Somerset TA14 6QR; 01935 825588; www.wwv.org.uk) has developed an authoritative search-and-match database of volunteering opportunities for 16-35 year olds which is available individually online via their website or by subscription (online or CD) for schools, colleges, universities, careers offices, volunteer bureaux, etc.

Although TimeBank is primarily intended to match British volunteers with UK projects, it has developed an online overseas directory (www.timebank.org.uk/givetime/overseas.htm). The Japan-based Go Make a Difference (www.gomad.org) has links to unusual voluntary projects while www.eVolunteer.co.uk includes small British and international grassroots organisations. The search engine at www.do-it.org is very useful for finding suitable projects in the UK.

REACH (89 Albert Embankment, London SE1 7TP; 020-7582 6543; www.reach-online.org.uk) brings together voluntary organisations in the UK and volunteers with career skills, mainly mature professionals and executives who are not in full-time work.

## Sources of Information for North Americans

*Volunteer Vacations* (Chicago Review Press/Independent Publishers Group, 814 N Franklin St, Chicago, IL 60610; 800-888-4741/www.ipgbook.com). Updated every other year; $17.95.

*Alternatives to the Peace Corps: A Directory of Third World and US Volunteer Opportunities* (by Paul Backhurst, Food First Books, 11th edition, 2005; $11.95).

*IVPA (International Volunteer Programs Association)*, 71 West 23rd St, 17th Floor, New York, NY 10010-4102 (www.volunteerinternational.org) has links to all the mainstream US organisations operating internationally.

*VolunteerMatch* based in San Francisco runs a website that aims to link volunteers with projects throughout the USA via www.volunteermatch.org.

*InterAction* based in Washington DC posts vacancies in international relief and development agencies; a one-month e-subscription costs $20 (www.interaction.org/jobs).

*Quaker Information Center*, 1501 Cherry St, Philadelphia, PA 19102 (215-241-7024; www.quakerinfo.org) maintains lists of Quaker and other organisations that need short- and long-term volunteers.

In Canada, the mediating agency *Horizon Cosmopolite* (3011 Notre Dame Ouest, Montréal, Quebec, H4C 1N9; 514-935-8436; www.horizoncosmopolite.com) maintains a database of opportunities abroad, most of them voluntary and tries to match clients with suitable placements. The registration fee of C$345 or C$495 plus tax guarantees placement plus varying fees payable to the chosen volunteer organisation.

The first voluntary agency to spring to an American's mind is the *Peace Corps* (1111 20th St NW, Washington, DC 20526; 1-800-424 8580/202-692-1800; www.peacecorps.gov) which sends volunteers, normally with appropriate skills and experience, on two-year assignments to 70 countries. It has undoubtedly done good work over the years though some volunteers come away with reservations about its focus.

**Kristie McComb was a Peace Corps volunteer in Burkina Faso and gradually concluded that the programme places less emphasis on development than on cultural exchange, i.e. sharing American culture with the host country nationals and then sharing the culture of your host country with Americans on your return:**

*The cool thing for Americans is that you don't have to be qualified in anything to be accepted by the Peace Corps. There are many generalist programmes where you can learn what you need to know once you get there through the three-month pre-service training. I would encourage interested parties to be honest about what they can and cannot tolerate since not all volunteers are sent to live in mud huts. In a world changed by terrorism it is comforting to know how much of an active interest the US government takes in the safety and well being of its citizens abroad.*

*However some people might find this stifling and not adventurous enough. How well PC keeps tabs on volunteers in any given country depends on the local PC leadership but, regardless, you are still in a high profile group of well locatable people. Risk reduction is the buzz word in Washington these days.*

*Overall I am happy with my experience though I am often frustrated by the inertia, the corruption and bureaucracy that make me question whether anything will ever change. But you do gain a lot by (if nothing else) witnessing poverty on a regular basis. You quickly learn to recognise the difference between a problem and an inconvenience and to see how lucky we are as Americans to have some of the 'problems' we have.*

Other key North American organisations that send self-funding volunteers to various projects worldwide are listed at the end of the Directory chapter.

# Directory of Specialist Programmes

Specialist agencies and organisations can arrange the logistics and save you a great deal of time and anxiety. They make placements, provide orientation and sometimes group travel and, crucially, provide back-up, usually in the form of an in-country representative who can sort out problems. Mediating agencies come in all shapes and sizes. Some are ethical non-profit charities that have links with local grassroots projects; some are bastions of the establishment with longstanding programmes in a range of countries. Still others are profit-making companies and are always seeking new projects in developing countries to which they can send paying volunteers. It is not always easy telling the difference between the various types of sending agency.

A plethora of organisations both charitable and commercial offers a wide range of packaged possibilities, from work experience placements in US businesses to teaching in Himalayan schools. Many of these organisations focus on the gap year market, targeting school leavers taking a year off before university. The boom in year-out travel for 18 year olds heading abroad after doing their A levels has resulted in an explosion of specialist companies. An increasing number of programmes from Siberia to Sulawesi is available to almost anyone able to pay.

Competition among the companies has become acute especially since university fees at UK universities tripled. This has prompted many of the agencies into trying to broaden the appeal of their programmes to an older clientele. The directory that follows gives brief details of the programmes offered by companies, agencies and charities that place mature candidates in voluntary positions worldwide, sometimes integrated with language courses, expeditions, diving courses, etc.

With the marked growth in the number of adults undertaking such projects, the mediating agencies are beginning to design programmes for the older age range. There has been a recent tendency for projects of shorter duration, e.g. three to six weeks, to be introduced to cater for the well-heeled older person who does not want to take off more than a few weeks at once. Organisations that started out offering experiences to either adults or students realised that without changing anything except how they package and market their experiences, they can attract another population. It is possible that the majority of participants on a given scheme will be school-leavers which might potentially limit the social pleasures in store for a career-breaker. Anyone who is concerned about this possibility should simply enquire of the sending agency what the average age and full age range will be on the project that interests him or her. On her otherwise fantastic 14-month gap year, 38 year old **Debbie Risborough** did not experience the buzz she expected to from a diving expedition she had booked in Fiji:

> *All the other people on the trip were in their gap year prior to uni so I was the odd one out, which I found very difficult. I would have preferred a wider age range in the group. One of the low points was knowing that I was stuck on an island with 15 x 18yr olds for company for weeks and weeks and it really didn't matter how nice they all were.*

While 18 is usually quoted as the minimum age, an upper age limit is seldom specified. Even if an agency specifies 30 or 40, these upper limits tend to be flexible and an energetic candidate may have little trouble in being accepted. Most of these programmes are open to anyone with an adventurous spirit, good health, reasonable fitness, a willingness to rough it and enough money to pay for it. Many mature volunteers end up not minding working alongside eighteen year olds as much as they thought they would. **Nigel Hollington** knew that he wouldn't mind since he had always enjoyed the company of young people during his long teaching career. Over the ten weeks of his wildlife project in Zambia with Greenforce, differences of age and background seemed to melt away and he enjoyed the company of his 18 year old roommate Mark. Stereotypes of carefree youth versus cautious middle age were overturned when they set off together to do a bungy jump. Nigel knew that Mark was absolutely terrified but felt that he could help him by remaining calm, so they achieved it together.

Another grown-up gapper, 43 year old **Paul Edmunds**, worked on the outskirts of Accra in Ghana with mainly gap year students. He feels that the 18 year olds who choose to do something worthwhile like this are a self-selecting group and tend to be more sensible and plucky than typical 18 year olds. However because of his age, he did sometimes feel impatient with the emphasis placed by his agency (*Travellers Worldwide*) on safety and security. Occasionally he found living in a family, who assumed it was their role to act *in loco parentis,* rather claustrophobic and he sometimes regretted that he wasn't able to live independently, kind and welcoming as his host family was. For example he struggled with the Ghanaian diet and sometimes found the meals served by his host inedible, yet it was awkward going out to find a more palatable alternative.

## CHOOSING AN AGENCY

Unless you have a reasonably specific plan for your gap year, you can become overwhelmed by the number of possibilities out there. Career gapper **Polly Botsford** has come to distrust the current mantra of extending choice and feels that there are too many destinations and options. 'You have this sense that you want to be original. My approach was to let the plans evolve. I let ideas sit awhile and talked to lots of people over the course of about a year.'

Of course there is no better starting point than this book for providing a survey of the options. In 2005/6, two specialist websites were launched: www.careerbreakcafe.com and www.thecareerbreaksite.com carrying lots of useful information, links and first-hand accounts. Ben Keene who runs careerbreakcafe.com aims to develop the site into an evolving info guide for career breakers as well as a community for people to meet and discuss the issues, challenges and what they plan to do with their time out.

The longer established website www.gapyear.com has a special section for 'Career Gappers' with recommended organisations (all included below) and a few case studies. Although the website, started and still run by Tom Griffiths, was originally aimed only at school-leavers, it has been expanding its provision for older gappers since they are the fastest growing gap year market. Gapyear.com's main rival on the web is FindaGap.com though it remains loyal to its original constituency of young gappers.

The non-profit trade association, the Year Out Group (www.yearoutgroup.org) is working towards models of good practice and seeking to maintain high standards of quality among its member agencies. So far it has confined its role to promoting structured gap years for pre-university students, though many of its founding member companies also accept older participants. Their website contains useful guidelines and questions to ask when comparing providers, most of which are common sense, e.g. find out whether it is a charity or a profit-making company, look at safety procedures and in-placement support, ask for a breakdown of costs, and so on. Gapadvice.org provides independent and unbiased information, research and advice on gap years for people of all ages.

A growing number of UK organisations make it possible for people of all backgrounds to take a career break of 3, 6 or 12 months volunteering abroad. Each organisation has its own application procedures and it is best to telephone or look to their websites for detailed instructions. Many of these volunteer bodies hold open days when you can meet the permanent staff and hear from former volunteers. People planning a career break might try to visit one of the annual specialised travel shows such as One Life Live held in March in London (www.onelifelive.co.uk) or the Times Gap Year Show in London and Manchester held in November (www.gapyearshow.com) which in 2006 promoted the idea of sabbaticals as well as student gap years. These exhibitions are designed to hone your enthusiasm and give you the chance to talk to companies offering career break travel and listen to specialist talks on the subject.

**Hannah Stevens** wanted to leave her life in London and planned a one-year break which included a volunteering stint in Cambodia through *Outreach International:*

*I spent a long time looking for an organisation that fitted my requirements, and when I found it, it just felt right. I passed the interview to see if we could handle living in a third world country with flying colours, and then sought sponsorship from friends and family. Moving into a village for six months forces a whole new way of thinking, and I have loved adapting myself to those surroundings, and reassessing what is important in life. Whether our being there has done anything, I will never know, but I have giggled and laughed with people who'd never seen white skin, and it's those moments that I'll take with me.*

Practical considerations will revolve around the size of the fee and whether what is included justifies the expense. Usually accommodation will be arranged for you, insurance provided and logistics put in place, all of which is likely to cost several thousand pounds. The publicised fees charged by commercial agencies of £2,500-£3,500 do not generally include airfares from the UK to your destination.

People with a church affiliation and Christian faith have a broader choice of opportunities since a number of mission societies and charities are looking for Christians. For example World Exchange (St Colm's International House, 23 Inverleith Terrace, Edinburgh EH3 5NS; 0131-315 4444; www.worldexchange.org.uk) arranges for people to work as volunteers worldwide for 10-12 months.

Whereas some religious organisations focus on practical work, such as working with street children, orphans, in schools, building libraries, etc., others are predominantly proselytising, which will only appeal to the very committed. Andreas Kornevall of Working Abroad Projects in Brighton (see Resources at end of previous chapter) warns potential volunteers to avoid working with any group that advocates a cultural or religious superiority or acts insensitively to local customs. Some religious groups are prone to take this attitude, although he adds that there are distinctions to be made, noting that some religious charities and organisations are doing superb work in the developing world.

When trying to differentiate among gap year providers, the guidelines provided on www.gapyearresearch.org/ethicalvolunteering.htm might prove helpful. The academic Kate Simpson has compiled a searching list of questions under the heading 'How to be an ethical volunteer: Picking the worthwhile from the worthless'. A good organisation should be able to tell an applicant exactly what work they will be doing and precise contact details for the overseas project. Assuming you care about such things (and even if you don't beforehand, you probably will after spending some time in a developing country), ask the company what financial contribution they make to the voluntary project. Some gap year companies wait until a paying customer has signed up before finding a placement abroad and these are often less satisfactory. The new sending agency *People and Places* is aware of the pitfalls and has tried to address them, primarily by being transparent about how the fees are spent. They aim to match volunteers' skills to community needs on sustainable projects on which volunteers work alongside not instead of local people.

## Careers Teacher Turned Volunteer

Because of the glut of year-out provision, it is possible to join interesting projects at short notice. Long-time teacher **Nigel Hollington** decided that the time had come for him to take a year out of teaching. After negotiating with his head, who promised to keep a teaching job open for him in his Hertfordshire comprehensive where he was a valued member of staff, Nigel's first step was to rent out his house which would force him into action. Normally the expression 'burning your boats' means cutting yourself off, destroying your means of escape. But in the context of taking a major step like deciding to rent out your house to finance some serious travels or volunteer projects, it can mean exactly the opposite. Paradoxically you might have to burn your boats (give up your job, move out of your house) to catch a boat to freedom and adventure.

Nigel had no fixed ideas of what he wanted to do or where he wanted to go, though he knew he wanted to fill the year with constructive things and not just bum around. By November, only a few weeks before he had to give up his house, he still had nothing fixed up and began to take a closer interest in the literature that passed through his hands in the careers room at school. *Greenforce's* details caught his eye and he was impressed with their projects. He had an open mind about destinations and was soon signed up for the first expedition they had available, a 10-week conservation project in Zambia. Organisations whose literature contains dire warnings of the consequences of procrastination often have last minute vacancies, so it is worth ringing around whenever you decide you want to go for it.

# Directory of Specialist Programmes

*The Directory sets out the programmes of charities and companies that are equipped to arrange all or part of a gap year. Organisations that specialise in placing North American volunteers are listed at the end of this chapter, though some US organisations (like Travel Alive in Nicaragua) welcome all nationalities onto their programmes.*

## 2WAY DEVELOPMENT

**Unit 4, 25a Vyner Street, Bethnal Green, London E2 9DG. ☎/fax: 020-7193 7228. E-mail: volunteer@2way.org.uk. Website: www.2way.org.uk.**

**Programme description:** 2Way Development arranges skilled, long-term volunteer placements within local not-for-profit organisations in the developing world that work in pursuit of sustainable development and social justice. Skills and desires of volunteers are matched with the areas of need. Some are looking to gain experience in international development.

**Destinations:** Worldwide, especially sub-Saharan Africa.

**Number of placements per year:** 50.

**Prerequisites:** Nationalities include British, American, Canadian, Australian and New Zealand. Average age 28. Educational and/or professional background in a skill (not specified) is needed.

**Duration and time of placements:** 3-24 months (8 months average).

**Selection procedures and orientation:** Interviews not essential, but informal interviews and event days are held every month in central London, where volunteers can meet staff to evaluate their decision.

**Other Services:** Volunteers are supported while preparing for their placement before leaving home, e.g. are provided with a training manual. Assistance given with visa preparation. Other training courses can be recommended on request.

**Cost:** £850.

**Contact:** Katherine Tubb, Director.

## ABLe VOLUNTEERS INTERNATIONAL FUND (AVIF)

**AVIF (UK) Fair Mount, Hartwith Avenue, Summerbridge, North Yorkshire HG3 4HT. ☎0777 171 2012. E-mail: volunteer@avif.org.uk. Website: www.avif.org.uk.**

Corresponding charity in Nairobi is KPDP (Kenya Programmes of Disabled Persons): www.kpdp.kabissa.org.

**Programme description:** Summer Programme targets disabled children, especially females, as well as vulnerable and poor children and their families, to provide life skill teaching, general classes, inspiration, and basic IT training at primary and secondary summer schools in rural Kenya. Volunteers are encouraged to integrate HIV/AIDS and sexuality education into their teaching.

**Destinations:** Kenya.

**Number of placements per year:** Up to 35 for 300+ children in 5 venues per summer.

**Prerequisites:** Enthusiasm, tolerance and dedication. Background in education would be helpful but even fully qualified teachers sometimes lack the necessary tolerance for work in Kenya.

**Duration and time of placements:** 4 week placement in July/August following orientation.

**Selection procedures and orientation:** Deadline for applications is June. Online interviews via email & Skype. Successful candidates are given 3-day orientation in Nairobi and 24-hour support service.

**Other Services:** Teachers are given housing but must currently be self-sufficient with regard to meals. Accommodation varies among host schools from shacks with bore hole water-source, school dormitories to country hotels. End-of-programme tented safari.

**Cost:** International airfares plus subsistence. AVIF hoping to raise sufficient funding to pay for volunteers' meals but this is not the case at present.

**Contact:** Ms. Alison Lowndes, Founder Trustee.

## ADVENTURE ALTERNATIVE

**31 Myrtledene Road, Belfast BT8 6GQ. ☎/fax: 02890 701476. E-mail: office@adventurealternative.com. Website: www.adventurealternative.com.**

Three-month programmes primarily for gap year students, career breakers, medical students or medical professionals in Kenya and Nepal.

**Programme description:** Combine 8-12 weeks of teaching/community or medical work, group activities (e.g. climbing, trekking, rafting, safaris) and independent travel. In Kenya participants teach and work in clinics and primary education in rural and slum schools or in an orphanage. In Nepal, participants help to build a village school or work in a Kathmandu primary school. Medical electives also available for doctors.

**Destinations:** Rural Kenya and Himalayan Nepal.

**Number of placements per year:** 30 for Kenya, 30 for Nepal.

**Prerequisites:** Hard-working committed enthusiastic volunteers who are not fazed by the hardships of living in a developing country. All nationalities/ages welcome.

**Duration and time of placements:** 8 weeks (Nepal), 12 weeks (Kenya) but can be flexible.

**Cost:** £1,800 (includes food and accommodation) plus £300 in-country expenses (email, telephone, souvenirs) plus £600 for flights, insurance and other necessities.

City trader James Garner takes time out to work with beekeepers in Gambia

Volunteers in Tanzania get involved with adult literacy classes, improving their chances of getting jobs

MondoChallenge volunteers find themselves becoming part of local communities, often in remote and beautiful locations

MondoChallenge volunteers help with English teaching in schools in the beautiful valleys of northern Chile

Arts and crafts are a great way to get Nepalese children involved in creative learning

Volunteering in rural areas of the Himalayan foothills does have its advantages

Teddy bears were donated through the MondoChallenge Foundation to Sri Lankan children who had lost everything in the 2004 tsunami

MondoChallenge volunteers teach all ages and get involved with extra-curricular activities

A grants scheme in Tanzania is helping families affected by HIV/AIDS to sustain livelihoods

MondoChallenge volunteers live and work in rural areas and stunning locations

**Contact:** Gavin Bate, Director; Chris Little or Andy MacDonald, Expedition Co-ordinators.

Africa & Asia Venture
AV
"Total adventure... with a purpose"
• Teaching
• Sports Coaching
• Community Work
• Conservation
Share the experience... on challenging projects and adventures in Africa, India, Nepal and Mexico from 5 weeks to 5 months.
call us or check out
www.aventure.co.uk
av@aventure.co.uk Tel: 01380 729009
YEAR OUT


**AFRICA & ASIA VENTURE (AV)**

**10 Market Place, Devizes, Wiltshire SN10 1HT. ☎01380 729009. Fax: 01380 720060. E-mail: av@aventure.co.uk. Website: www.aventure.co.uk.**

Volunteers support rural communities in Africa, the Himalayas, Thailand and Mexico, assisting with community work, teaching or conservation. Individuals combine cultural immersion with adventure as part of a small group. AV is a founder member of the Year Out Group.

**Programme description:** Volunteers are placed, usually in pairs, in rural communities (school or village) as teachers, sports coaches or in community or conservation projects for 3 months (occasionally less). 2-3 weeks are set aside after the placement for backpacking round the country followed by a week-long group safari. 5-week adventures are also available in Kenya/Uganda, combining 3 weeks of community work (building, renovating, etc.) with a week's game park safari and a further week either on the coast or climbing Mount Kenya or on camel safari.

**Destinations:** Kenya, Tanzania, Botswana, Uganda, Malawi, Himalayan India, Nepal, Thailand and Mexico.

**Prerequisites:** Minimum age 18; those over 25 should discuss options with AV.

**Duration and time of placements:** 4 months (5 in Tanzania and Mexico). 5-week shorter adventures (timings on website). Groups depart throughout the year.
**Selection procedures and orientation:** Places are allocated on application on a first-come, first served basis. Volunteers are invited to an interview aimed at matching individual to placement. 1-week orientation training on arrival in country.
**Cost:** £2,740 basic cost for 4/5 months covers insurance, accommodation, living allowance, safari, orientation course and in-country support. Fee does not include airfares, entry visas and extra spending money. Shorter adventures from £1,830.

## AFRICAN CONSERVATION EXPERIENCE

**PO Box 206, Faversham, Kent ME13 8WZ. ☎0870 241 5816. E-mail: info@ConservationAfrica.net. Website: www.ConservationAfrica.net.**
**Programme description:** Conservation work placements on game reserves in Southern Africa. Tasks may include darting rhino for relocation or elephant for fitting tracking collars. Game capture, tagging, assisting with veterinary work, game counts and monitoring may be part of the work programme. Alien plant control and the re-introduction of indigenous plants is often involved.
**Destinations:** Southern Africa including South Africa, Botswana, Namibia and Zimbabwe.
**Prerequisites:** Reserves open to people of all ages who have reasonable physical fitness and ability to cope mentally. Enthusiasm for conservation is essential. Specific projects are run for 'grown-ups' which allow for better social interaction within the group.
**Duration and time of placements:** 2-12 weeks throughout the year.
**Selection procedures & orientation:** Candidates are matched to a suitable project on the information provided on their application form but do have final say on their choice of project. Optional Open Days are held at various locations in the UK.
**Cost:** Varies depending on reserve and time of year. Students can expect an average total cost of about £2,800 for 4 weeks up to £4,500 for 12 weeks, which includes international flights (from London), transfers, accommodation and all meals. Support and advice given on fundraising.
**Contact:** Sarah Bishop, Marketing Manager.

## AFS INTERCULTURAL PROGRAMMES UK

**Leeming House, Vicar Lane, Leeds LS2 7JF. ☎0113-242 6136. Fax: 0113-243 0631. E-mail: info-unitedkingdom@afs.org. Website: www.afs.org.**
According to its mission statement, AFS is an international, voluntary, non-governmental, non-profit organisation that provides intercultural learning opportunities to help people develop the knowledge, skills and understanding needed to create a more just and peaceful world. AFS currently has 54 member countries.
**Programme description:** On the International Volunteer Programme, participants spend 6 months in another country, volunteering on a local community project and living with a local family or the project.
**Destinations:** Worldwide including Brazil, Chile, Costa Rica, Ecuador, Ghana, Guatemala, Honduras, Mexico, Peru, South Africa, Thailand and Venezuela.

**Number of placements per year:** AFS tries to place anyone eligible who applies.
**Prerequisites:** Applicants for the International Volunteer Programme are aged 18 and older. No particular qualifications or skills are needed.
**Duration and time of placements:** 6 months, departing January/February and July/August.
**Selection procedures and orientation:** Initial application form must be accompanied by a £10 fee. Selection is conducted at a group event, after which a full application will have to be completed. It is preferred that applications are sent at least six months before the intended departure to give time to raise contribution costs and for the organisation to find a suitable placement.
**Cost:** International Volunteers are requested to raise £3,300. Advice and support for fundraising are given. The money raised covers travel, medical insurance, orientation materials and events, language tuition and emergency support. The host family provides food and accommodation.
**Contact:** Bianca Chantry.

## AIDCAMPS INTERNATIONAL

**5 Simone Court, Dartmouth Road, London SE26 4RP. ☎020-8291 6181. E-mail: info@aidcamps.org. Website: www.aidcamps.org.**
**Programme description:** Teams of volunteers of all ages work with partner NGOs on range of projects such as renovating a school for disabled children, conservation work, village water projects, teaching, etc. Individual AidCamps programme introduced autumn 2006.
**Destinations:** India, Nepal, Sri Lanka and Cameroon.
**Prerequisites:** Average age of volunteers is 40. If someone has particular skills/ interests to offer, AidCamps will liaise with partner NGOs to arrange an appropriate placement.
**Duration and time of placements:** Mainly short-term projects lasting 3 weeks. Longer term scheme called 'Individual AidCamps' suitable for older gappers. Average duration is 5 weeks but can be between 1 week and several months.
**Cost:** Team participants pay £595 for 3 weeks, nearly three-quarters of which goes directly to the aid project. Homestay accommodation for Individual Aid-Camps costs roughly £35-£50 per week.
**Contact:** Marios Cleovoulou, Founder & Managing Trustee.

## AZAFADY

**Studio 7, 1A Beethoven St, London W10 4LG. ☎020-8960 6629. Fax: 020-8962 0126. E-mail: mark@azafady.org. Website: www.madagascar.co.uk.**
**Programme description:** Pioneer Madagascar programme allows volunteers to work on humanitarian, sustainable development and environmental projects. Particularly suited to adults interested in development and ecology (who may be looking for experience as an entry point into an ethical career) or who simply want to make a difference and have a meaningful holiday experience.
**Destinations:** Southeast Madagascar.
**Number of placements per year:** 10-20 per group, 4 groups per year.
**Prerequisites:** Enthusiasm and cultural sensitivity. All ages welcome; past age range 18-55. Training given. Volunteers learn basic Malagasy so that they may

work together with members of rural communities and gain a unique insight into the culture.
**Duration and time of placements:** 10 weeks starting in January, April, July and October. Shorter placements are available by arrangement.
**Cost:** Successful applicants pay for pre-project costs such as flight, insurance and visa and are required to raise a minimum donation of £2,000 (different for non-UK applicants). Applicants are provided with extensive fundraising resources and advice.
**Contact:** Mark Jacobs, Managing Director.

## BASE CAMP GROUP

**30 Baseline Business Studios, Whitchurch Road, London W11 4AT. ☎/fax: 020-7243 6222. Fax: E-mail: contact@basecampgroup.com. Website: www.basecampgroup.com.**
**Programme description:** Ski & Snowboard Instructor Courses (full- and part-time) in the European Alps and Canadian Rockies. Clients learn to become instructors while improving their all-round skiing or snowboarding. First aid courses, avalanche courses, ski technician clinics, French classes as well as a variety of trips and social events are included. Also offer performance camps including Powder Camp, Freestyle Camps and Improvement Camps.
**Destinations:** Meribel and Val d'Isère (France) and Whistler, Kicking Horse and Banff (Canada).
**Duration and time of placements:** 11-week and 4-week intensive programmes. 10-week part-time BASI ski instructor course in Val d'Isère which appeals to slightly older clientele.
**Qualifications offered:** BASI in Europe and CSIA and CASI in North America.
**Number of placements per year:** 200.
**Prerequisites:** Some skiing/snowboarding experience recommended.
**Cost:** £5,750-£6,500 excluding insurance for 11 weeks; £2,800-£3,200 for 4 weeks. Includes accommodation, ski pass, coaching, exams and courses as above.
**Contact:** Max Shepherd, Course Advisor.

## BEYOND BACKPACKERS

**PO Box 5188, Wellesley St, Auckland, New Zealand. ☎ +64 9-358 4877. Fax: +64 9-358 4872. E-mail: info@gobeyond.co.nz. Website: www.gobeyond.co.nz.**
**Programme description:** Network of superior backpacker hostels in New Zealand, offering one-stop-shop services to travellers of all ages, including onsite travel centres, New Zealand Job Search services, Internet cafés and bars. New Zealand Job Search (www.nzjs.co.nz) is located in Auckland Central Backpackers (Level 3, 229 Queen St; 09-357 3996; info@nzjs.co.nz) and operates as a job agency for backpackers. NZ Volunteer Programme available for those interested in conservation.
**Destinations:** Throughout New Zealand; hostels in Auckland, Bay of Islands, and Rotorua, Queenstown.
**Prerequisites:** Working holiday visa necessary to use NZ Job Search; unlimited number of visas valid for up to 23 months available to UK nationals aged 18-30.
**Cost:** Starter pack includes 12 months registration with Job Search, airport pick-up, two nights accommodation on arrival, etc. for NZ$290.

**BIOSEARCH EXPEDITIONS**

**Wayfarer Lodge, Welbourn, Lincs. LN5 0QH. ☎01400 273323. Fax: 01400 273003. E-mail: expeditions@biosearch.org.uk. Website: www.biosearch.org.uk.**

**Programme description:** Expeditions to track and record game in the Nyika National Park of Malawi to build up a biodiversity index for the park in cooperation with Malawi Department of National Parks & Wildlife and other institutions.

**Destinations:** Malawi. Weekend courses held at Hilltop Farm, Lincolnshire.

**Number of placements per year:** 25. Plus more attend weekend training camps in the UK.

**Prerequisites:** all nationalities accepted and range of ages from university students up to 70. Biosearch are actively encouraging more mature team members with established amateur and professional skills. Training weekends require no qualifications, just the desire to learn about adventure travel and bush living. Candidates for expeditions should have an inclination to natural history and conservation.

**Duration and time of placements:** Standard 1-month expeditions in March and July. 2-day training weekends in UK are open to all (whether or not they join a team in Malawi).

**Selection procedures and orientation:** Applications for March expeditions should be submitted by December and for July expeditions by April. Enrolment on weekend camps must be at least a fortnight beforehand. Interviews are required and are normally held at Biosearch office or at the college of students. Telephone interviews possible if applicants are not in the UK.

**Other Services:** Details of training weekends available on website. Training continues on arrival in the bush. Accommodation is in small tents on expedition, otherwise in comfortable accommodation.

**Cost:** £2,400 for African expedition, excluding travel. £199 for expedition training weekend in UK.

**Contact:** Charles Peter Overton, Project Director.

**BIOSPHERE EXPEDITIONS**

**Sprat's Water, Nr Carlton Colville, The Broads National Park, Suffolk NR33 8BP. ☎0870 4460 801. Fax: 01502 587414. E-mail: info@biosphere-expeditions.org. Website: www.biosphere-expeditions.org.**

**Programme description:** Biosphere Expeditions is a non-profit-making organisation offering hands-on wildlife conservation expeditions to all who seek adventure with a purpose. Volunteers with no research experience assist scientific experts.
**Number of placements:** 200-300.
**Destinations:** Worldwide, e.g. biodiversity survey in the Peruvian Amazon, snow leopards among others in the Altai Republic of Central Asia, cheetahs in Namibia, elephants in Sri Lanka, dolphins and whales in the Azores, Arabian leopards in Oman, jaguars and pumas in Brazil, coral reef survey in Honduras, chamois, wolves and bears in Slovakia.
**Duration and time of placements:** 11 days to 2 months, starting year round.
**Prerequisites:** No special skills or fitness required to join and no age limits whatsoever.
**Cost:** £990-£1,250 (excluding flights). Expedition contributions vary depending on the expedition. At least two-thirds of contributions benefit local project directly.
**Contact:** Paul Light, Operations Assistant.

## BLUE VENTURES

**52 Avenue Road, London N6 5DR. ☎020-8341 9819. E-mail: enquiries@blueventures.org. Website: www.blueventures.org.**
**Programme description:** Volunteers needed for marine conservation project. Blue Ventures conducts marine research, coral reef conservation and grass-roots conservation in south-west Madagascar. Volunteers participate in all research programmes and day-to-day management of field camps. Non-diving conservation work might involve cetacean surveys, accompanying local fishermen or beach clean-up operations.
**Destinations:** Village of Andavadoaka is the current Blue Ventures expedition site, in South Western Madagascar. Blue Ventures has co-ordinated marine projects in Tanzania, New Zealand, South Africa and the Comoros Islands.
**Prerequisites:** International team of volunteers are all ages and come from all walks of life. No diving or scientific background or training needed.
**Duration and time of placements:** 6 weeks, although shorter and longer stays can be accommodated.
**Cost:** £1,880 for 6 weeks for non-divers; £1,680 for PADI Advanced divers or equivalent. Volunteers will be expected to provide personal diving kit (i.e. mask, snorkel, wet-suit, fins), torch, sleeping bag, malaria prophylactics, inoculations and flights. After the initial six weeks, the first three additional weeks are charged at a cost of £245 per week and £195 per week thereafter.
**Contact:** Richard Nimmo, General Manager.

## THE BRITISH INSTITUTE OF FLORENCE

**Piazza Strozzi 2, 50123, Florence, Italy. ☎ +39 055-26 77 82 00. E-mail: info@britishinstitute.it. Website: www.britishinstitute.it.**
**Programme description:** Situated in the historic centre of Florence, the British Institute offers courses in Italian language and art history as well as life drawing, water colour painting, Tuscan cooking and Italian opera. Institute also hosts regular programme of mainly free events including lectures, concerts and films, held in the Harold Acton Library overlooking the River Arno.
**Duration and time of courses:** 1 week to 3 months throughout the year.

**Cost:** Tuition fees vary according to the course chosen, e.g. a 4-week Italian course costs €630, a 4-week History of Art course €585 and a 4-week combined Italian and History of Art course €1,120. Accommodation can be arranged as homestays, in shared flats or in *pensiones*. Prices for homestay accommodation start at about €32 per night (plus €25 fee for arranging accommodation).
**Contact:** Giovanna Ianniello, Assistant to the Director.



**BUNAC**
**16 Bowling Green Lane, London EC1R 0QH. ☎020-7251 3472. Fax: 020-7251 0215. E-mail: enquiries@bunac.org.uk. Website: www.bunac.org.**
Founding member of the Year Out Group. Primarily a non-profit national student club offering work and travel programmes worldwide, BUNAC has recently introduced programmes for older participants.
**Programme description:** Work New Zealand and Work Canada are open to 18-35 year old UK passport holders. BUNAC acts as an aide before and after arrival in the country of travel and acts as a 'security blanket' if anything goes wrong. BUNAC arranges exclusive visa that enables participants to do any job for up to 12 months. Work does not have to be pre-arranged.
**Destinations:** Canada and New Zealand (plus other countries for younger travellers).
**Prerequisites:** Ages 18-35 for both. New Work Exchange visa for New Zealand is even open to people who have previously held a NZ Working Holiday Visa.

**Duration and time of placements:** 1-12 months.
**Cost:** £5 BUNAC membership fee, plus programme fee of £450 for New Zealand (plus £50 or £70 for visa) and £160 registration fee for Canada.

### CACTUS WORLDWIDE LTD.

**4 Clarence House, 30-31 North St, Brighton BN1 1EB. ☎0845 130 4775. Fax: 01273 775868. E-mail: info@cactuslanguage.com. Website: www.cactuslanguage.com.**

Provider of language courses worldwide. In Latin America courses run in conjunction with voluntary placements. Cactus also acts as a business language and teacher training consultancy.
**Volunteer destinations:** Guatemala, Costa Rica, Peru, Ecuador, Bolivia, Brazil, Argentina, Chile and Mexico.
**Language course destinations:** Language courses in Germany, France, Spain, Italy, Greece, Russia, China and many others.
**Prerequisites:** All ages and nationalities welcome.
**Duration and time of placements:** Combination language and volunteer programme in Latin America: standard 4 week language course followed by 4 weeks volunteering but duration is flexible. Language courses from 1 week. TEFL courses usually 4 weeks.
**Cost:** From £799 for 8 weeks in Guatemala to £1,159 in Costa Rica. Language course and TEFL training course costs clearly searchable on Cactus website.
**Other services:** Admissions service and impartial advice given on recognised TEFL training courses such as the Cambridge CELTA and Trinity CertTESOL, as well as courses for experienced teachers, teachers of other languages and non-native teachers of English.

### CALEDONIA LANGUAGES ABROAD

**The Clockhouse, 72 Newhaven Road, Edinburgh EH6 5QG. ☎0131-621 7721/2. Fax: 0131-621 7723. E-mail: courses@caledonialanguages.co.uk. Website: www.caledonialanguages.co.uk.**

Established in 1994, Caledonia's main work is booking clients on short or long term language courses with accommodation (homestay or apartment) in 17 countries throughout Europe and Latin America. They also arrange voluntary placements in Latin America, and language + activity courses (e.g. Spanish + Trekking in Cuba or French + skiing in Chamonix) and language + learning (e.g. Italian + History of Art in Sicily or French + cooking in Aix-en-Provence).
**Programme description:** For language clients wanting to use their skills and experience in a constructive way, Caledonia can arrange volunteer community projects in Latin America, such as working with street children in Maceio, Brazil; in conservation projects in the cloud forests of Costa Rica; in a psychiatric hospital in Bolivia; in a kindergarten in Peru; teaching English in Ecuador. Living accommodation is with local families.
**Destinations:** Caledonia's partner language schools are in France, Spain, Portugal, Italy, Germany, Russia, Peru, Chile, Dominican Republic, Guadeloupe, Bolivia, Ecuador, Cuba, Costa Rica, Brazil, Mexico and Argentina.
**Prerequisites:** Complete beginner to advanced learners are catered for. Intermediate level of Spanish or Portuguese is needed to work on projects alongside local people.

**Duration of courses:** Minimum 1 week (or 4 weeks if combined with volunteer placement) up to 6 months. Classes start year round.
**Selection procedures and orientation:** For volunteers, a short language course is taken in the country before work can begin, for cultural and linguistic familiarisation. Briefing meetings on the proposed volunteer work and occasionally pre-placement site visits are arranged. Full back-up support is given by language school in-country.
**Cost:** Volunteers must pay for the pre-placement language course in the overseas country plus accommodation and travel. In Peru, 3 weeks intensive Spanish course plus 9 weeks voluntary work with full board homestay throughout would cost from £1,360 (flights not included).

## CAMP AMERICA

**37a Queen's Gate, London SW7 5HR. ☎020-7581 7373. E-mail: enquiries@campamerica.co.uk. Website: www.campamerica.co.uk.**
**Programme description:** Camp America has been placing people from Europe, Asia, Africa, Australia and New Zealand on American summer camps for 42 years. Camp counsellors look after the children and/or teach sports activities, music, arts, drama and dance, etc.
**Destinations:** Throughout the USA.
**Number of placements per year:** 8,000+ in 2006.
**Prerequisites:** Camp America is looking to recruit skilled adults for a variety of job choices. Experience in sport coaching, religious counselling, teaching, childcare, health care and lifeguarding is preferable.
**Duration and time of placements:** Must be willing to depart between 1 May and 27 June for a minimum of 9 weeks. Up to 10 weeks of travel time available between camp and visa expiry at the end of October.
**Selection procedures & orientation:** Face-to-face interview with locally appointed Camp America interviewer. Also Camp America host recruitment fairs allowing participants to meet and interview with Camp Directors from a variety of summer camps in London, Manchester, Edinburgh and Belfast in the late winter. Selectors aim to evaluate applicants' background, training and main skill areas to make suitable placements. Personal interview at US Embassy also required. Early application is advised.
**Cost:** Medical insurance and application fees apply. All programmes offer free return flights from London and other selected international airports to New York, along with transfer to the camp, free accommodation and meals, up to 10 weeks of travel time after camp duties, Cultural Exchange US visa sponsorship, 24-hour support, medical insurance, and pocket money which ranges from $500 to $1,000 (dependant on age, experience and kind of counsellor).

## CAMPS INTERNATIONAL LIMITED

**Unit 1, Kingfisher Park, Headlands Business Park, Salisbury Road, Blashford, Ringwood, Hants. BH24 3NX. ☎0870 240 1843. Fax: 01425 485398. E-mail: info@campsinternational.com. Website: www.campsinternational.com.**
The 'Life' programme incorporates a range of responsible travel experiences consisting of community and conservation volunteer opportunities including a healthy mixture of volunteer work, adventure and relaxation. Kiswahili lessons included.

**Destinations:** Kenya and Tanzania incorporating safari drives through National Parks, possibility of climbing Mount Kenya or Kilimanjaro and water sports on coast.
**Duration and time of placements:** 1 week to 1 month, year round.
**Cost:** 2 weeks from £850; 4 weeks from £1,550.
**Contact:** Hannah Davies, Expedition Coordinator.



## CESA LANGUAGES ABROAD

**CESA House, Pennance Road, Lanner, Cornwall TR16 5TQ. ☎01209 211800. Fax: 01209 211830. e-mail: info@cesalanguages.com. Website: www.cesalanguages.com.**

**Courses offered:** Group language courses (15-30 group lessons per week). Private tuition courses (10+ lessons per week). Open to all abilities. Courses for mature students (50+) in Spain and France; Italian/Spanish/French + Cookery; German or Spanish + Skiing; Spanish + Diving/Surfing; French + Surfing/Sailing. Languages offered: French (France & Guadeloupe), Spanish (Spain & Latin America), German, Italian, Portuguese, Japanese, Russian, Greek and Arabic.
**Duration of courses:** 1-48 weeks. At least one start date per month for general courses. Set dates apply to Language plus Activities or Mature Student programmes.
**Qualifications offered (but not compulsory):** Spain: DELE exam preparation. France: DELF, DALF, Alliance Francaise and CCIP exam preparation. Germany:

Goethe exams. Russia: TRKI exam preparation.
**Cost:** 16 weeks in Granada from £2,640 and 12 weeks in Bordeaux from £2,493, both including shared apartment accommodation.
**Accommodation:** Options include sole-occupancy apartments, hotels, shared apartments or host families. Students can also make their own arrangements.
**Contact:** Katherine Brand, Director.

## CHALLENGES WORLDWIDE

**54 Manor Place, Edinburgh EH3 7EH. ☎0845 200 0342. Fax: 0131-225 9549. E-mail: enquire@challengesworldwide.com. Website: www.challengesworldwide.com.**

Scottish charity matching skilled professional volunteers with short-term (3-6 month) placements overseas. Volunteers are placed with local governments, NGOs or community groups in order to provide technical assistance to address issues such as management, strategy, finance, research, monitoring and evaluation, social development, education and human rights issues. CWW also arranges personal and professional development assignments (6-12 weeks) for corporate clients to allow career break opportunities for their employees.
**Programme description:** Personal service matching individual skills and interests of the volunteer with local host partners overseas. Comprehensive pre-departure training provided.
**Destinations:** Bangladesh, Belize, India, Sri Lanka, Ghana, with plans to extend further into Asia and Africa (see website for current situation).
**Number of placements per year:** 100.
**Prerequisites:** Average age is late 20s although volunteers can be aged 18-65. Volunteers need to have some level of relevant education or life/work experience (some placements require less experience than others).
**Duration and time of placements:** 3 or 6 months. Recruitment takes place year round.
**Selection procedures and orientation:** Applicants are invited to attend a face-to-face interview in the UK and comprehensive pre-departure preparation and training session. Full mentor support provided by CWW UK Recruitment Officer as well as local Placement Leader in-country throughout placement.
**Cost:** Volunteers must fundraise a minimum contribution of £2,150 for 3 months, which covers pre-departure admin, training, ongoing support, accommodation, food and insurance.
**Contact:** Recruitment hotline 0845 2000 342 or email enquiry@challengesworldwide.com with contact details. CWW will respond within 24 hours.

## CHANGING WORLDS

**Hodore Farm, Hartfield, East Sussex TN7 4AR. ☎01892 770000. Fax: 0870 990 9665. E-mail: ask@changingworlds.co.uk. Website: www.changingworlds.co.uk.**

Member of the Year Out Group. Aims to provide full cultural immersion through challenging and worthwhile work placements with a safety net if required.
**Programme description:** Voluntary work placements in schools, orphanages, zoos, etc. and paid work placements in hotels and hospitality.
**Destinations:** Australia, Brazil, Canada, Chile (Patagonia), Ghana, India, Latvia, epal, New Zealand, Romania, Tanzania and Thailand.

**Number of placements per year:** 200.
**Prerequisites:** All ages. Must have initiative, determination, adaptability and social skills plus skills relevant to the job if possible.
**Duration and time of placements:** from 3 to 6 months. Placements begin throughout the year.
**Selection procedures and orientation:** Interview days held in Surrey every 6-8 weeks. All participants attend a pre-departure briefing; for those going to a developing country, this is a 2-day residential course. Participants are met on arrival in-country and attend orientation with the local representative before proceeding to placement. Local representatives act as support during placement. Volunteers teaching in Patagonia are expected to learn Spanish.
**Cost:** From £1,895. Prices include return flights but exclude insurance (approximately £200 for 6 months).
**Contact:** David Gill, Director.

## CORAL CAY CONSERVATION

**40-42 Osnaburgh St, London NW1 3ND. ☎0870 750 0668. Fax: 0870 750 0667. E-mail: info@coralcay.org. Website: www.coralcay.org.**

Founding member of the Year Out Group. Hundreds of volunteers join CCC projects each year to assist in conserving fragile tropical marine and terrestrial environments.
**Programme description:** The aim of CCC expeditions is to help gather scientific data for the protection and sustainable use of tropical resources and to provide alternative livelihood opportunities for local communities.
**Destinations:** Philippines, Trinidad & Tobago and Fiji. Participants in Fiji (for example) spend the first 7 weeks at one dive site and then choose between staying on a remote island with only 200 villagers and the research team or going to Coral Cay's other site on Castaway Island, one of the first resorts built in Fiji.
**Number of placements per year:** hundreds.
**Prerequisites:** No previous experience is required. Volunteers come from a diverse range of ages, nationalities and backgrounds Volunteers are provided with scientific and scuba diving tuition.
**Duration and time of placements:** Expeditions depart monthly throughout the year. Minimum stay 4 weeks (no maximum stay).
**Selection procedures and orientation:** A free information pack is available on request; enrolment pack can be downloaded from website. Full training is provided on location.
**Cost:** From £600. Prices vary according to time of year, project and whether participants are already dive-qualified or are dive trainees. Prices exclude flights and insurance.

## COSMIC VOLUNTEERS

**PO Box 11738, Philadelphia, Pennsylvania 19101, USA. ☎610-279-2052. E-mail: info@cosmicvolunteers.org. Website: www.cosmicvolunteers.org.**

**Programme description:** Volunteering, internships and specialist travel programmes in five developing countries. Volunteer programme includes teaching, medicine, orphanages, journalism, social work, HIV/AIDS, environment, sports, organic farming and turtle conservation.

**Destinations:** Ecuador, Ghana, India, Kenya, Nepal, Peru, Philippines and Vietnam.
**Number of placements per year:** 1,000+.
**Prerequisites:** for all ages (16-60) with average about 24. Must have open mind and be fluent in English. Medical placements available only to health professionals and trainees.
**Duration and time of placements:** 1 week to 2 years.
**Selection procedures and orientation:** Applicants accepted year round. Must sign up at least 30 days before programme start date.
**Costs:** Varies with programme, from $967 for one month's volunteering in Nepal to $1,987 for 3 months in Ecuador. Spanish language classes available in Ecuador and Peru.
**Contact:** Scott Burke, Founder (whose vivid account of his own gap year in Nepal which inspired him to start Cosmic Volunteers may be read online at www.cosmicvolunteers.org/stomping.html).

## CROSS-CULTURAL SOLUTIONS

**UK Office: Tower Point 44, North Road, Brighton BN1 1YR. ☎0845 458 2781/2782. E-mail: infouk@crossculturalsolutions.org. Website: www.crossculturalsolutions.org. US address: 2 Clinton Place, New Rochelle, NY 10801 (1-800-380-4777).**

A non-profit international volunteer organisation founded in 1995 and registered charity in the UK (Number 1106741).
**Programme description:** Opportunity for participants to work side-by-side with local people, on locally designed and driven projects. Volunteer programmes are designed to facilitate hands-on service and cultural exchange with the aim of fostering cultural understanding.
**Destinations:** Brazil, China, Costa Rica, Ghana, Guatemala, India, Peru, Russia, Tanzania and Thailand.
**Number of placements per year:** 2,200+.
**Prerequisites:** All nationalities and ages welcome. Participants must be proficient in English.
**Duration and time of placements:** 1-12 weeks. Frequent start dates run throughout the year.
**Cost:** Programme fees start at £1,389 ($2,389) for a 2-week programme and cover costs such as staffing, volunteer placement, lodging, meals, ground transport and medical and emergency evacuation insurance. International airfares are not included.

## CSV

**National Full-Time Volunteering Team, 5th Floor, Scala House, 36 Holloway Circus, Queensway, Birmingham B1 1EQ. ☎0800 374991. E-mail: volunteer@csv.org.uk. Website: www.csv.org.uk/fulltimevolunteering.**

CSV is the largest voluntary placement organisation in the UK. It guarantees a structured voluntary placement to anyone aged over 16 who commits him or herself to a minimum of 4 months full-time volunteering in a huge range of social care projects.
**Number of placements per year:** 1,000-1,500.
**Programme description:** CSV volunteers help people throughout Britain in a

huge range of social care projects, e.g. working with adults and children with physical disabilities or learning difficulties, enabling people to access leisure and community facilities, supporting students with disabilities at university; homeless people, older people, assisting in schools, enabling adults with disabilities to live independently in their own home, mentoring and befriending young people at risk of offending or exclusion from education. CSV volunteers are full-time and live away from home anywhere within Britain.
**Prerequisites:** No previous qualifications or skills are needed. Volunteers must have commitment and be flexible as volunteers are placed where their help and skills are needed most. A full UK driving licence is useful but not required.
**Duration and time of placements:** 4-12 months, beginning at any time of the year.
**Selection procedures and orientation:** Interview days are held across the UK and start dates are available throughout the year. Volunteers receive regular supervision and back-up support from their local CSV office. CSV certificate given on completion of placement.
**Cost:** No joining fee. CSV volunteers receive £30 per week living allowance plus free accommodation, meals, travel expenses and relevant training.

## DEVELOPMENT IN ACTION

**78 York St, London W1H 1DP. ☎07813-395957. E-mail: info@developmentinaction.org. Website: www.developmentinaction.org.**
Non-profit-making development education organisation (formerly Student Action India).
**Programme description:** Voluntary attachments to various Indian non-governmental organisations. Grassroots development projects ranging from teaching children in urban slums, administration and fundraising, to fieldwork and research. Volunteers are asked to produce a development education project to be used as a resource in the UK.
**Destinations:** India with projects in Pune, Udaipur, Indore, Bhopal, Pondicherry and rural placements.
**Prerequisites:** Motivation, an interest in global issues, and commitment to the aims of DiA. No upper age limit.
**Duration and time of placements:** 2-month summer placements or year-out 5-month placements beginning in September.
**Selection procedures and orientation:** University recruitment talks/careers fairs take place in January and February (see website). Application deadlines around the end ofJanuary and March; interviews held in February and April. Pre-departure training over one weekend plus one week training on arrival.
**Cost:** £550 for summer, £1,000 for 5 months (covers placement, training and accommodation). Flights, insurance, visa and subsistence costs are extra.
**Contact:** Ellen Roberts, UK Co-ordinator.

## DRAGONFLY

**1719 Mookamontri Soi Songpon 13, A. Muang Nakhon Ratchasima, 30000 Thailand. ☎/fax: +66 4128 1073. E-mail: martin@thai-dragonfly.com. Website: www.thai-dragonfly.com.**
**Programme description:** Volunteer English teaching programme.
**Destinations:** Thailand.
**Number of placements per year:** 150.

**Prerequisites:** All natives or fluent speakers of English. No qualifications or experience required as training is provided.
**Duration and time of placements:** 4-52 weeks. Usual hours of work are 8am-4pm with 15-20 hours of teaching lessons per week.
**Selection procedures and orientation:** Online applications accepted.
**Other Services:** 2 training options precede volunteer placement: 4-day intensive teacher training course or a 120-hour TEFL course with Thai training provider Text & Talk.
**Cost:** Short training course plus placement fee is £320 for 4-8 weeks plus £15 per month. Long training course plus placement fee is £1,250. Teaching is voluntary with free homestay accommodation and meals provided.
**Contact:** Martin Walsh, Project Manager.

## EARTHWATCH INSTITUTE

**267 Banbury Road, Oxford OX2 7HT. ☎01865 318838. Fax: 01865 311383. E-mail: info@earthwatch.org.uk. Website: www.earthwatch.org/europe.**

Earthwatch is an international environmental charity which offers conservation volunteering opportunities on scientific research expeditions around the world. Earthwatch Institute is a registered charity, and all volunteer contributions go directly towards supporting the scientific research.
**Programme description:** Earthwatch currently supports 130 expeditions in about 50 countries, from looking at the impacts of climate change in the Arctic, to the protection of cheetah in Namibia.
**Destinations:** Volunteer field assistants needed throughout the UK and worldwide (Europe, Africa, Asia, Australasia, the Americas). UK projects include whale and dolphin surveys in the Hebrides and mammal monitoring in Oxfordshire. International projects range from turtle conservation in Malaysia to climate change studies in the Arctic.
**Number of placements per year:** 4,000 approximately.
**Prerequisites:** Ages 16-95 and all nationalities. No qualifications needed.
**Duration and time of placements:** Projects last between 3 days and 3 weeks, throughout the year (see website for calendar of dates).
**Selection procedures:** No previous experience necessary. Volunteers fill out a questionnaire and health form before participating on the project; no interview is required.
**Other Services:** All volunteers receive a briefing pack prior to going on the expedition giving detailed information about the project, logistics and general information about the area. All volunteers receive training when they are at the expedition site before they start assisting the scientists. Accommodation provided, from huts in the Arctic to hammocks in the rainforest to safari lodges in Kenya.
**Cost:** UK projects start at £150, international projects range up to £2,450.

## ECOLOGIA TRUST

**The Park, Forres, Moray, Scotland IV36 3TZ. ☎/fax: 01309 690995. E-mail: volunteer@ecologia.org.uk. Website: www.ecologia.org.uk and www.kitezh.org.**

The Trust promotes creative change in Russia through youth, ecology and education working closely with the Kitezh Community of foster families.

**Programme description:** Volunteers including gap year students and 2 or 3 adults are placed at the Kitezh Children's Community for orphans in western Russia. Russian language is not essential although students of Russian will quickly become fluent.
**Destinations:** Kaluga, Russia and Moscow, Russia.
**Prerequisites:** Reasonable knowledge of Russian language, TEFL or experience teaching English as a foreign language, experience working with children (sports, arts and crafts, music, drama), building, cooking and gardening. An interest in children and a willingness to participate fully in the life of the community are essential. For the Moscow placement (contingent on funding), fundraising experience and a knowledge of the NGO sector particularly to do with children's issues would be useful.
**Duration and time of placements:** 1-3 months; additional months are at the discretion of the Kitezh Council. Moscow placement: 1 year.
**Selection procedures and orientation:** Introductory questionnaire followed by telephone interview required to apply. Police check in country of residence required. Extensive preparatory materials are sent including feedback from previous volunteers. Informal orientation given on arrival, weekly meeting with volunteer supervisor, and ongoing support from Ecologia Trust via e-mail.
**Cost:** 1 month costs £540, 2 months £700. Costs include invitation, visa, visa registration, transfer Moscow to Kitezh return, support from Kitezh Centre in Moscow and accommodation and food in Kitezh. Insurance and airfare not included; flights cost from £260 (depending on time of year). Cost of additional months approximately £60 per month, negotiated with Kitezh directly. Moscow placement: cover own travel costs. Accommodation and monthly stipend negotiable.
**Contact:** Liza Hollingshead, Director.

## EDUCATORS ABROAD LTD.

**5 Talfourd Way, Royal Earlswood Park, Redhill, Surrey RH1 6GD. ☎01737 785468/768254. Fax: 01737 768254. E-mail: craig@educatorsabroad.org. Website: www.educatorsabroad.org.**

Company that has been created to manage and operate the ELTAP (English Language Teaching Assistant Program) for the University of Minnesota, Morris, Minnesota 56267, USA (+1-320-589-6406; swww.eltap.org).
**Programme description:** Volunteer/college-sponsored programme open to adults as a non-credit certificate option as well as to students. Participants assist teachers and students in ESL and EFL classes by bringing their native fluency in English to schools around the world.
**Destinations:** Over 25 countries on all continents.
**Duration and time of placements:** 4-10 weeks throughout the year.
**Cost:** $300 placement fee, course fee and travel (usually totals $3,000-$4,000). Accommodation and board provided by host schools.
**Contact:** Dr. Craig Kissock, Director.

## EXPERIENCE MEXECO LTD

**38 Award Road, Fleet, Hampshire, GU52 6HG. ☎/fax: 01252 629411. E-mail: info@experiencemexeco.com. Website: www.experiencemexeco.com.**

**Programme description:** Sea turtle conservation, English teaching projects, community fundraising for special needs schools and other community-based projects.

**Destinations:** Pacific coast of Mexico.
**Number of placements per year:** 30-35.
**Prerequisites:** All nationalities and ages (average 19-26). All backgrounds welcomed as any necessary training is provided. Spanish is not a necessity as local staff speak English and Spanish.
**Duration and time of placements:** 1-3 months.
**Selection procedures and orientation:** Applications should be in no less than 1 month before desired start date though earlier preferred. Interview not required.
**Cost:** £799-£899 for 1 month, £1,899-£1,999 for 3 months covers accommodation (homestay, private or small tents on turtle project) and food throughout placement plus insurance and 24-hour in-country support, but exclude flights.
**Contact:** Daniel Patman, Director.

## FLYING FISH

**25 Union Road, Cowes, Isle of Wight PO31 7TW. ☎0871 250 2500. Fax: 01983 281821. E-mail: mail@flyingfishonline.com. Website: www.flyingfishonline.com.**

Member of the Year Out Group. Flying Fish trains water and snow sports staff and arranges employment for sailors, divers, surfers, windsurfers, skiers and snowboarders. Founded in 1993, Flying Fish provides travel, training, adventure and professional qualifications for those looking to enjoy some time out, take a gap year or start a career in watersports.
**Programme description:** A year out with Flying Fish starts with a course leading to a qualification as a surf or windsurf instructor, a yacht skipper, galley chef, divemaster and dive instructor, a ski or snowboard instructor. For those not looking to work in the sports industry, training at professional level makes a challenging recreational course offering personal adventure and the ability to perform at a high level.
**Destinations:** Training courses are run at Cowes in the UK, at Sydney and the Whitsunday Islands in Australia, Bay of Islands in New Zealand, at Dahab in Egypt, Vassiliki in Greece, and Whistler in Canada. Jobs are worldwide with main employers located in Australia, the South Pacific, the Caribbean and the Mediterranean.
**Number of placements per year:** 600, almost equal no.s of men and women.
**Prerequisites:** Ages 18-60+, from all around the world;
**Duration and time of placements:** 2-19 weeks with start dates year round.
**Selection procedures & orientation:** Applicants submit an application and, if looking for a career in the industry, may be asked to attend job interviews.
**Cost:** Fees range from 1,100 to £11,000. Accommodation and airfares are provided, with normal wages during employment.

## FRONTIER

**50-52 Rivington St, London EC2A 3QP. (020-7613 2422. E-mail: info@frontier.ac.uk. Website: www.frontier.ac.uk.**

Frontier has been involved with conservation expeditions since 1989. It aims to work with local people in order to find out as much as possible about the areas so that relevant and necessary conservation work can be pursued.
**Programme description:** Frontier offers the opportunity to work in coral reefs, savannas, forests and mangrove areas as part of conservation programmes in far-

off destinations. Programmes are established in response to problems; surveys of damaged areas are carried out so that possible solutions can be identified. For example, dynamite fishing in Tanzania was damaging the web of delicate marine life. Frontier volunteers carried out more than 6,000 dives, resulting in the establishment of a Marine Park where the marine life is protected.
**Destinations:** Tanzania, Madagascar, Cambodia, Egypt, Thailand, Vietnam, Fiji, Nicaragua, Costa Rica, Belize, Mexico and Peru.
**Prerequisites:** Minimum age 17. No specific qualifications required as training is provided. Marine expeditions include free scuba diving training. Possibility of studying in the field for a BTEC Advanced Diploma in Tropical Habitat Conservation or a BTEC Advanced Certificate in Expedition Management.
**Duration and time of placements:** 4, 5, 8, 10 or 20 weeks.
**Selection procedures and orientation:** Open days are held twice a month (check website for dates) where interested parties can find out more from past volunteers. After an application has been submitted and a telephone briefing, applicants will hear within a week whether they have been accepted. Prior to the expedition, a briefing weekend is held in the UK.
**Cost:** Depending on location and duration, international volunteers raise £695-£1,600 for 4 weeks, £1,700-£2,300 for 8 weeks, £2,000-£2,800 for 10 weeks and £3,000-£3,800 for 20 weeks, which covers all individual costs, including a UK weekend briefing, scientific and dive training, travel, visas, insurance, food and accommodation but excludes flights.

## FRONTIERS FOUNDATION-OPERATION BEAVER

**9781-127th Street, Surrey, BC, Canada V3V 5J1. ☎(604) 585-6646. Fax: (604) 585-6643. E-mail: frontwest@shaw.ca. Website: www.frontiersfoundation.ca. Toronto office: 419 Coxwell Ave, Toronto M4L 3B9 (416-690-3930).**

Non-profit charitable organisation which since 1968 has been recruiting international groups of volunteers to come to Canada to work in Native communities in the far north.
**Programme description:** Volunteers work as tutors and teaching assistants, recreation workers, along with assisting in First Nations offices. Tutoring in maths, science, English, music, drama, etc.
**Destinations:** Low-income communities in Canada, including Native communities in isolated northern areas. Some Operation Beaver projects take place on wilderness camps for Native children or schools in the three northern territories (Yukon, Northwest Territories and Nunavut).
**Prerequisites:** Minimum age 19, no maximum. Energetic and motivated volunteers needed, with a strong interest in meeting new people and learning about a new culture. A university degree and/or experience of working with young people or working in an education setting would be assets. Previous volunteer experience also helpful.
**Duration and time of placements:** Placements coincide with academic year – 10 months from early September.
**Cost:** All expenses paid within Canada, volunteers must pay for international airfares. Medical insurance is paid and a living allowance of $50 a week provided for spending money.
**Contact:** Don Irving.

## FUNDACIÒN PRONIÑO ('FOR THE CHILDREN')

**Barrio El Centro, Edificio Ecocentenario, El Progreso, Yoro, Honduras. ☎/fax: (504) 647 3424. E-mail: proninohonduras@yahoo.com (for volunteer enquiries); streetkidshonduras@yahoo.com. Website: www.streetkidshonduras.org; www.pronino.org.**

**Programme description:** Proniño has two centres for street children based in El Progreso, Honduras. Las Flores provides for the initial needs of a child; Montaña is more of a home environment, where the children go to school and receive vocational training for their futures in society.
**Destinations:** El Progreso, Honduras.
**Prerequisites:** Ages 19-60. The most important quality needed is an ability to love, care and support the children. Any transferable skills that are appropriate to children are useful, e.g. for the education programmes at both centres (especially computer and English classes). People with a professional skill (like psychologists or people with a building trade) are welcome to suggest a specific project they would like to set up.
**Duration and time of placements:** Minimum 4 months, usually 6-12 months.
**Selection procedures and orientation:** Applications accepted year-round. Telephone interviews arranged after email application submitted. Participants receive a welcome pack with information about Proniño and the culture of Honduras. Exposure to the different centres and the office during the first 2-3 weeks so volunteer can decide where they can best help.
**Cost:** Volunteer house is comfortable and classic Honduran, and costs approximately $120 per month; personal spending and living expenses about $50 per month.
**Contact:** Claire Rollings, Volunteer Coordinator.

## GAP SPORTS

**Willowbank House, 84 Station Road, Marlow, Bucks. SL7 1NX. ☎0870 837 9797. E-mail: info@gapsports.com. Website: www.gapsports.com.**

**Programme description:** Specialist organisation that offers a number of sports and non-sports opportunities overseas, including sports coaching and outreach projects in Africa and Latin America, ski/snowboard instructor courses and adventure training in Canada, and professional sports development programmes at international golf, rugby, cricket, football and scuba academies.
**Destinations:** Ghana, South Africa, Costa Rica and Canada.
**Number of placements per year:** 500-800.
**Prerequisites:** No previous experience needed. Open to people from all walks of life including career breakers. GAP SPORTS Career Breaks are aimed at qualified professionals and full-time workers who want the chance to take some time out from work to play the sports they love or gain the skills needed to enter a new career path.
**Duration and time of placements:** 3-4 months on average though it is possible to stay up to 12 months. 5-week projects are also available.
**Selection procedures and orientation:** Applications should be submitted at least 6 weeks before departure. Interviews not required. A free training weekend is organised one month before departure. GAP SPORTS is planning to launch in Australia in 2006/7.

**Cost:** Approximately £1,295-£1,795 for community projects; £2,500-£5,000 for sports instructor coaching.
**Contact:** James Burton, Director.

## GAPYEAR.COM

E-mail: info@gapyear.com. Website: www.gapyear.com/25plus. Largest gap year community in the UK dedicated to helping people plan and prepare for a gap year. Special section of website devoted to 'career-gappers'. Users of the website can create profiles, find travel mates, access a database with thousands of opportunities, compare insurance policies and pose questions on the message boards. Gapyear.com also runs gapyearshop.com (specialist gap year travel kit site).

## GAP YEAR FOR GROWN UPS

**1st Floor, Zurich House, Meadow Road, Tunbridge Wells TN1 2YG. ☎01892 701881. Fax: 01892 523172. E-mail: info@gapyearforgrownups.co.uk. Websites: www.gapyearforgrownups.co.uk / www.realgap.co.uk.**

Part of the Real Group including Real Gap for the 18-30 market.
**Programme description:** Can choose a core of work, volunteer and travel options around the world, including a bespoke 'design-your-own-gap-year' service. Range of travel and volunteer programmes includes working with children and adults in deprived communities, paid work in China, conservation volunteering, working with wildlife in Africa or Latin America; or learning a new skill such as a language, PADI dive course or working on an outback property. Other travel and volunteering options available worldwide including packages for people under 30 who are eligible for working holiday visas to Australia, New Zealand, Japan or USA.
**Destinations:** Australia, New Zealand, USA, Canada, Africa, South America, Asia and Round-the-World.
**Prerequisites:** Programmes vary but most are open to all ages and backgrounds.
**Cost:** Varies with programme. Sample fees £549 for 4 weeks conservation work in Australia, £899 for an adventure in Thailand, £959 working on the Galapagos Islands saving Giant Tortoises and £799 for 4 weeks working with orphans and street children in Africa.

## GLOBAL ADVENTURES PROJECT

**38 Queen's Gate, London SW7 5HR. ☎0800 0854197 (freephone). E-mail: info@globaladventures.co.uk. Website: www.globaladventures.co.uk.**

A division of the American Institute for Foreign Study (AIFS), an educational and cultural exchange organisation founded in 1964 which also oversees Camp America and Au Pair in America.
**Programme description:** 3 to 12-month programmes provide choice of round-the-world ticket and the opportunity to join up to four work, study and/or volunteer programmes in the USA, Brazil, Europe, South Africa, India, Peru, Borneo, Belize, Canada, China and Australia/New Zealand with time for independent travel in between. Some trips particularly designed for career breakers.

**Destinations:** Core destinations are USA (as camp counsellors), Canada (as camp counsellors or working at a summer or winter resort), Brazil (conservation volunteer), Europe (language learning in France, Austria or Spain), South Africa (study at Stellenbosch University and volunteering in townships), India (volunteering or paid internships), China (language course and voluntary teaching), Peru (Spanish language and rural volunteering), Borneo (voluntary teaching and PADI dive course), Belize/Guatemala (Spanish course and voluntary teaching) and Australia/New Zealand (paid work).
**Prerequisites:** Minimum age 18 at time of departure so available to gap year students and people taking a career break.
**Duration and time of placements:** Each placement lasts 3 months (with the exception of Australia/New Zealand which can last up to 9 months) and departures from UK take place in January, April, June and September.
**Selection procedures and orientation:** Applications should be sent at least 3 months before departure with £100 fee. Individual consultations arranged to discuss preferences and later two-day orientation session.
**Cost:** From £3,195 (for two core options) to £5,295 (for up to four core options).
**Contact:** Heather Thompson, Director.

## GLOBAL VISION INTERNATIONAL (GVI)

**Amwell Farmhouse, Nomansland, Wheathampstead, St. Albans, Herts. AL4 8EJ. ☎0870 608 8898. Fax: 0870 609 2319. E-mail: info@gvi.co.uk. Website: www.gvi.co.uk.**
**Programme description:** 40+ conservation expeditions, volunteer projects, courses and internships throughout Africa, Latin America, Europe, Asia and the US. Courses for prospective volunteers include intensive weekend TEFL courses in the UK, Spanish lessons in Latin America and outdoor survival courses, including training to become a safari field guide in South Africa.
**Destinations:** Mexico, Costa Rica, Guatemala, Honduras, Nicaragua, Panama, Belize, Ecuador, Argentina, Brazil, Bolivia, Chile, Peru, Nepal, India, Sri Lanka, Thailand, South Africa, Kenya, Namibia, Ghana, Rwanda, Uganda, Seychelles, Tanzania, Madagascar, Indonesia, Borneo, Vanuatu, USA and UK.
**Number of placements per year:** 2,000.
**Prerequisites:** None. Minimum age 18. All nationalities welcome.
**Duration and time of placements:** 1 week to 2 years.
**Selection procedures and orientation:** Some projects require a telephone interview; others require only a completed application form online.
**Cost:** from £250 to £3,500. For example in South Africa: £795 for 4 weeks at a wildlife sanctuary, £2,450 for a 10-week wildlife research expedition and £2,995 for a year-long internship. Price for marine conservation expedition in Seychelles starts at £1,650 for 5 weeks, including scuba diving equipment, training and accommodation.

## GLOBAL VOLUNTEER NETWORK

**PO Box 2231, Wellington, New Zealand. ☎+64 4-569 9080. Fax: +644-569 9081. E-mail: info@volunteer.org.nz. Website: www.volunteer.org.nz.**
**Programme description:** Volunteers recruited for a variety of educational,

environmental and community aid programmes in 19 countries. Projects include working with children in orphanages, English teaching, environmental work, animal welfare, health and sanitation, maintenance/construction, and cultural homestays. Fund-raising hikes also offered to Everest Base Camp, Kilimanjaro, Machu Picchu and the New Zealand Alps.
**Destinations:** China, Ecuador, El Salvador, Costa Rica, Honduras, Nepal, India, Vietnam, Philippines, New Zealand, Romania, Russia, Thailand, Uganda, Tanzania, South Africa, Ghana, Kenya and USA (Alaska).
**Duration and time of placements:** 2 weeks to 12 months depending on the placement. Applications accepted year round.
**Number of placements per year:** 2,000 (aiming for 2,500 in 2006/7).
**Prerequisites:** No special skills or qualifications needed in most cases. All nationalities placed, although projects in China and Russia accept only Australians, Canadians, Europeans, Irish, British, American and New Zealand.
**Cost:** US$350 application fee to GVN covers administration, marketing and programme information. Programme fees vary from US$445 per month in Ecuador to $1,500 a month in Alaska to cover training, accommodation and meals during training and placement, transport for volunteers (but not international airfares) and supervision.
**Contact:** Colin Salisbury, Executive Director.



## GREENFORCE

**11-15 Betterton Street, Covent Garden, London WC2H 9BP. ☎020-7470 8888. Fax: 020-7379 0801. E-mail: info@greenforce.org. Website: www.greenforce.org.**

Member of the Year Out Group. Greenforce invites people from all backgrounds to work on one of their five wildlife research projects around the world. Projects work to protect endangered species and habitats on behalf of a host country authority. Establishing new protection zones and managing wildlife resources are the main objectives of these long-term conservation projects.
**Programme description:** Participants work as Fieldwork Assistants, carrying out tasks such as tracking animal movements and studying coral reef species over a 10-week project phase. All training is provided including diver training for the marine expeditions and language training for the terrestrial expeditions. Greenforce offers a traineeship to one member of each marine volunteer team;

the selected trainee stays on camp for a further expedition as a staff assistant at no further cost. The position is aimed at those seeking to develop a career in conservation.

**Destinations:** Malaysian Borneo, Fiji, the Bahamas, Zambia, Ecuador, Tanzania and Nepal/Tibet.

**Number of placements per year:** 300 per year. 4 volunteers per member of staff.

**Prerequisites:** Greenforce expeditions suit older participants because they focus on practical skills and learning experiences, rather than outward bound adventure activities and personal development. No previous experience is necessary; no qualifications required. Applicants must be over the age of 17.

**Duration and time of placements:** 4-10 weeks, commencing January, April, July and October. Limited number of 4-week placements in summer months. Flexible departure dates and durations for the Ecuador and Nepal expeditions.

**Selection procedures and orientation:** Applicants may attend one of the regular, informal open evenings. A comprehensive briefing pack is provided on application, giving information about fundraising and relevant medical advice, etc. Participants can attend a training weekend 6 weeks prior to joining the project (cost included in contribution). The first week of the expedition is spent undertaking further training and familiarisation with the project and host country.

**Cost:** From £1,500 for 4 weeks and £2,400 for 10 weeks in Ecuador and Nepal; £2,500 for 10 weeks in Zambia; £2,700 for marine expeditions. These fees cover training and instruction, food, accommodation, visas and medical insurance but not international flights. Diving equipment and training are provided for £300 if necessary.

## HEALTH ACTION PROMOTION ASSOCIATION (HAPA)

**PO Box 24, Bakewell, Derbyshire DE45 1YP. E-mail: support@volunteerafrica.org. Website: www.volunteerafrica.org.**

**Programme description:** UK charity recruits volunteers to work with village projects in Tanzania, e.g. in rural development or orphanage teaching.

**Destinations:** Singida Region of Tanzania.

**Prerequisites:** All ages above 18.

**Duration and time of placements:** 4, 7 or 10, 11 or 12 weeks.

**Other Services:** Other vacancies in Africa with various charities and aid agencies are posted on this same site.

**Cost:** Fees are £950 (4 weeks), £1,330 (7 weeks), £1,710 (10 weeks), £1,950 (11-12 weeks), a proportion of which is a donation to the host programme.

**Contact:** Moya Cutts, Volunteer Coordinator.

## HELP (HIMALAYAN EDUCATION LIFELINE PROGRAMME)

**30 Kingsdown Park, Whitstable, Kent CT5 2DF. ☎01227 263055. E-mail: help@help-education.org. Website: www.help-education.org.**

HELP enables young people from poor communities in the Himalayas (Nepal and India) to improve their employment opportunities through education by providing financial and volunteer resources to their schools.

**Programme description:** Volunteer teachers, nurses and child-carers work in needy schools targeted by HELP.

**Destinations:** Himalayan India (Sikkim, West Bengal, Uttaranchal, Ladakh and Himachal Pradesh) and Nepal (Kathmandu Valley, Pokhara abnd Chitwan).

**Number of placements per year:** 14.
**Prerequisites:** Ages 19/20-60+. Teaching experience and/or TEFL qualifications are desirable but not essential. Nurses need to be qualified. Volunteers should be mature, and resourceful people who can hit the ground running. Qualities needed include resilience and adaptability, an open mind and an interest in other cultures, good mental and physical health, plus tact and diplomacy. A love of and experience with children is vital.
**Duration and time of placements:** 2 months normally. Volunteers can stay for a maximum of 6 months (for visa reasons).
**Selection procedures and orientation:** Applications accepted year round. Telephone interview is conducted after receipt of the online application form. Volunteers receive a briefing pack. Advice is given by email and/or over the phone.
**Cost:** From £390 depending on volunteer's status and length of stay, including accommodation with host families or in school hostel.
**Contact:** Jim Coleman, Executive Director.

## HOPE AND HOME

**Nepal Volunteer Program, Panipokhari, Kathmandu, Nepal. ☎ +977 1 4415393. Fax: +977 1 4415176. E-mail: info@hopenhome.org, hopenhome@gmail.com. Website: www.hopenhome.org.**

Community-oriented volunteer opportunities for international volunteers in a quest to find sustainable solutions for education, health, conservation, and development issues through volunteering.
**Programme description:** Volunteer opportunities are in the fields of teaching English, working in an orphanage, community health and environmental programme, school and community maintenance and homestay/cultural exchange.
**Destinations:** Nepal (Kathmandu Valley, Pokhara, Chitwan and Nawalparasi).
**Number of placements per year:** 25-30.
**Prerequisites:** Ages 18-35. All that is needed is a genuine desire to help people.
**Duration and time of placements:** 2 weeks to 5 months.
**Selection procedures and orientation:** Online applications accepted year round.
**Other Services:** Language class, cultural information and project information provided.
**Cost:** Volunteer fees entirely fund programme and include homestay accommodation and food. From $250 for 2 weeks to $450 for 6 weeks to $800 for 5 months.
**Contact:** Rabyn Aryal, Director.

## IALC (INTERNATIONAL ASSOCIATION OF LANGUAGE CENTRES)

**Lombard House, 12/17 Upper Bridge St, Canterbury, Kent CT1 2NF. ☎ 01227 769007. Fax: 01227 769014. E-mail: info@ialc.org. Website: www.ialc.org.**

Language school association that accredits private language schools, with 90 members in 22 countries.
**Courses offered:** Hundreds of programmes in nine languages worldwide,

ranging from short general language courses to specialised courses combining language with culture, cookery, dance, art, sport, etc. Some IALC schools offer work experience or volunteering.

**Application procedures:** Canterbury office is not a booking office. Contact details for member schools appear on the IALC website.

**Contact:** Jan Capper.

## ICYE: INTER-CULTURAL YOUTH EXCHANGE

**Latin American House, Kingsgate Place, London NW6 4TA. ☎/fax: 020-7681 0983. E-mail: info@icye.co.uk. Website: www.icye.co.uk.**

ICYE is a registered charity (charity No. 1081907) and part of an international exchange organisation.

**Programme description:** ICYE UK run Long and Short-term exchange programmes worldwide with an emphasis on inter-cultural understanding and integration into local communities. The majority of projects are social and community based, such as working with street children, working in orphanages, HIV awareness, working in disability support, mental health, conservation work, human rights work, construction and teaching. Volunteers live on projects or with host families.

**Destinations:** Long-Term Programme destinations include Bolivia, Brazil, Colombia, Costa Rica, Ecuador, Honduras, Mexico, Mozambique, Nigeria, Ghana, Kenya, South Korea, Taiwan, India, Nepal and Uganda. Short-Term Programme destinations are India, Nepal, China, Morocco, Ecuador and Costa Rica, Nigeria, Ghana, Kenya, Mozambique and Uganda.

**Number of placements per year:** The ICYE network arranges approximately 600 exchanges in over 30 countries.

**Prerequisites:** Applicants must have a commitment to intercultural learning and the principles of ICYE. No formal qualification necessary, just enthusiasm and open-mindedness. ICYE's Long Term Programmes are open to 18-30 year old, although applicants can be considered on a case by case basis. Short Term Programmes are open to volunteers aged 18+.

**Duration and time of placements:** Long-Term Programme begins in August and January and lasts 6 or 12 months. The Short-Term Programme runs all year with monthly departures.

**Cost:** 12 months costs £3,900, amnd 6 months costs £3,300. Long Term Programme fees include the following: flights and travel costs, insurance, visas,

accommodation, food, pocket money, training, language course and administration. Prices for the Short-Term Programme vary depending on length of stay and project choice. Volunteers are supported in their fundraising efforts and a discount of up to £300 is available for online fundraising.
**Contact:** Sophie Bray-Watkins (Long-term Co-coordinator) and Cat Udal (Short-term Programme Co-ordinator).

## IKO PORAN ASSOCIATION

**Rua Dr. Julio Otoni, 571, Santa Teresa, Rio de Janeiro (RJ), CEP: 20.241-400, Brazil. ☎ +55 21-2205 1365. Fax: +55 21-2205 2765. E-mail: rj@ikoporan.org. Website: www.ikoporan.org.**
**Programme description:** Volunteers are assigned to various autonomous development projects. Iko Poran is always forging new links with Brazilian NGOs who can use the services of volunteers.
**Destinations:** Brazil (Rio, Salvador, Amazonia).
**Number of placements per year:** 250-300.
**Prerequisites:** Average age range 20-30 but accept volunteers up to 70. All nationalities welcome.
**Duration and time of placements:** 3-24 weeks, according to volunteer's availability. Maximum of 24 weeks is for visa reasons.
**Selection procedures and orientation:** Applications accepted up to one week before arrival. Volunteers fill out an extensive application form detailing their interests, abilities and reasons for joining an international volunteer programme. Police Certificate needed by volunteers who want to work with children.
**Other Services:** Upon arrival volunteers are picked up from airport and given an orientation that includes a welcome pack, info on neighbourhood facilities and public transport, maps and guides, safety tips and so on. Portuguese language lessons can be arranged.
**Cost:** Programme fee is R$1,500 (US$665/£360) which covers lodging in one of Iko Poran's comfortable volunteer houses for the first 4 weeks and a donation of R$400 to the project. Additional weeks cost R$180.
**Contact:** Luis Felipe Murray, General Coordinator.

## THE INTERNATIONAL ACADEMY

**King's Place, 12-42 Wood Street, Kingston-upon-Thames, Surrey KT1 1JY. ☎0870 060 1381. Fax: 020-8939 0411. E-mail: info@theinternationalacademy.com. Website: www.theinternationalacademy.com.**
Recently acquired by the Crystal Holiday Group.
**Programme description:** Instructor training courses worldwide in skiing, snowboarding, scuba diving and flying that lead to internationally recognised qualifications. Courses are run in partnership with the resident ski, snowboard, diving or flying schools in resort. Lead to recognised qualifications: CSIA, CASI or NZSIA ski/snowboard qualifications; PADI Divemaster or Open Water Scuba Instructor; progress towards Joint Aviation Authorities (JAA) Private Pilot License.
**Destinations:** Ski/snowboard courses in: Whistler-Blackcomb and Banff/Lake Louise in Canada or Cardrona, New Zealand. Diving: courses in Red Sea, Cyprus or Malta. Flying courses in Florida.
**Duration of courses:** 4-12 weeks depending on the activity, with various start dates throughout the year.

**Cost:** Courses include flights, resort transfers, accommodation, breakfast and evening meals, instructor training/tuition, exam fee and certification. Sample price of a 5-week ski or snowboard course in the Canadian Rockies is £4,390, whereas the 12-week course costs £6,650.

## INVOLVEMENT VOLUNTEERS ASSOCIATION INC. (IVI)

**PO Box 218, Port Melbourne, Victoria 3207, Australia. ☎ +61-3-9646 9392. Fax: +61-3-9646 5504. E-mail: ivworldwide@volunteering.org.au. Website: www.volunteering.org.au. IVUK: ivengland@volunteering.org.au. German office: IVDE, Volksdorfer Strasse 32, 22081 Hamburg (+49 4126 9450; ivgermany@volunteering.org.au).**

Established in 1988 for young or older volunteers from any country that are welcomed by the government of the country they want to visit.

**Programme description:** IVI arranges individual placements worldwide. Projects are concerned with conservation, the natural environment, animal welfare, social and community service, education and childcare.

**Destinations:** Argentina, Australia, Austria, Bangladesh, Bolivia, Botswana, Brazil, Cambodia, Cameroon, China, Colombia, East Timor, Ecuador, Egypt, Estonia, Fiji, Finland, France, Germany, Ghana, Greece, Guatemala, Guinea-Bissau, Iceland, India, Israel, Italy, Japan, Jordan, Kenya, Korea, Kosovo, Latvia, Lebanon, Lithuania, Malaysia (Sabah), Mexico, Mongolia, Namibia, Nepal, New Zealand, Peru, Poland, Romania, Samoa, South Africa, Spain, Sri Lanka, Tanzania, Thailand, Togo, Turkey, Uganda, Ukraine, USA, Vietnam, Venezuela, and Zambia.

**Prerequisites:** Anyone can volunteer, preferably with knowledge, training and experience but also possible without. Volunteers must be over 18 (unless they have parental agreement) and have 'young, enthusiastic, elastic minds'.

**Duration and time of placements:** Individual placements last 2-6 weeks at any time of the year and Group placements are usually 2-4 weeks at specific dates. Any number of placements of any type can be arranged over the period of one year from the starting date of the first placement.

**Cost:** From £295 (€425).

## IST PLUS LTD

**Rosedale House, Rosedale Road, Richmond, Surrey TW9 2SZ. ☎020-8939 9057. E-mail: info@istplus.com. Website: www.istplus.com; www.widenyourworld.org.**

Work, teaching and study abroad programmes for UK students, graduates and professionals.

**Programme description:** Programmes that are open to grown-up gappers include Professional Career Training (PCT) in the USA (for ages 20-40), Work & Travel Australia (maximum age 30), Work & Travel New Zealand (maximum age 30), Teach in China (maximum age 65) and Teach in Thailand (maximum age 65). IST Plus also arrange Language Study Abroad programmes (French, German, Spanish, Italian) in 23 destinations across Europe and Latin America for all ages.

**Number of placements per year:** unlimited.

**Cost:** Australia and New Zealand programmes cost £195. Asian teaching programmes start at £725 whereas PCT in USA starts at £500, excluding travel.

**i-to-i**

**Woodside House, 261 Low Lane, Horsforth, Leeds LS18 5NY. ☎0870 333 2332. Fax: 0113 205 4619. E-mail: info@i-to-i.com. Website: www.i-to-i.com.**

A founding member of the Year Out Group with Investors in People status, i-to-i is a TEFL training and volunteer travel organisation.

**Programme description:** Around 500 projects in 22 countries involving teaching, conservation, community work, building, sports, media placements and humanitarian tours. i-to-i also organises 20-hour weekend TEFL training courses across the UK, Ireland, Australia and the USA, and an online version accessible anywhere in the world for those who prefer to learn at their own pace. Most recent course additions are Weekend Travel Photography and Weekend Travel Writing.

**Destinations:** Argentina, Australia, Bolivia, Brazil, China, Costa Rica, Dominican Republic, Ecuador, Ghana, Guatemala, Honduras, India, Kenya, Malaysia, Mexico, Nepal, Peru, South Africa, Sri Lanka, Tanzania, Thailand and Vietnam. Teaching and conservation projects take place in most countries, whilst more career-focussed programmes including marketing, media, tourism, museums and health placements are available in selected countries. i-to-i also offers paid teaching placements in China, Poland, South Korea, Thailand and Turkey.

**Number of placements per year:** 15,000 (including course participants).

**Prerequisites:** Most projects require no experience or qualifications, although some skills development placements (e.g. media) require a CV.

**Duration and time of placements:** From one week to a full year out, starting year round.

**Selection procedures and orientation:** Venture placements include full pre-departure travel and work briefing, full project inventories and information packs, comprehensive insurance, in-country co-ordinator to help deal with emergencies, airport pick-up and orientation in-country. All teaching placements include a free i-to-i Online TEFL course, CD-ROM and teaching worksheets, TEFL Toolkit of teaching activities for any classroom, and back-up from trained TEFL teachers in the UK.

**Cost:** from £495/€695 (excluding airfares). £195/€295 for TEFL course only. Free taster TEFL course online at www.onlinetefl.com.

**I-VOLUNTEER**

**D-134, East of Kailash, New Delhi 110065, India. ☎/fax: +011-26217460. ☎+011-55672160. E-mail: seema@ivolunteer.org.in. Website: www.ivolunteer.org.in.**

**Programme description:** iVolunteer provides an Infrastructure for cost-effective and hassle-free volunteering in the Indian subcontinent in a range of fields such as poverty, livelihoods, education, health and women related issues, working with disadvantaged children and so on. Flexible tailor-made programmes.

**Destinations:** India. iVolunteer has centres in New Delhi, Mumbai, Bangalore and Chennai with links to urban and rural NGOs.

**Number of placements per year:** 15-20.

**Prerequisites:** Age range 18-30. No particular skills needed.

**Duration and time of placements:** 2 months.

**Selection procedures and orientation:** Applications are accepted round

the year. Volunteers receive one-day intensive in-country training covering volunteering and how to survive living in India.
**Cost:** £250.
**Contact:** Ms. Seema Verma, Assistant Manager.

## JAPAN EXCHANGE & TEACHING (JET) PROGRAMME UK

**JET Desk, Embassy of Japan, 101-104 Piccadilly, London W1J 7JT. ☎020-7465 6668. E-mail: info@jet-uk.org. Website: www.jet-uk.org.**
The JET Programme is a well-established initiative in the field of cultural exchange and provides opportunities for those contemplating a career break or change of career.
**Programme description:** Government-run JET Programme allows graduates to spend one or more years teaching or working with local government in Japan.
**Destinations:** Throughout Japan.
**Number of placements per year:** 400+
**Prerequisites:** Must have a Bachelor's degree, UK passport and be under 39 years of age by the time of departure.
**Duration and time of placements:** One-year contracts begin in late July.
**Selection procedures and orientation:** The application deadline is the last Friday in November. Orientations given in London/Edinburgh and Tokyo.
**Cost:** None. Return airfares provided to those who complete contract. Salary of 3,600,000 yen paid (currently about £19,000). Participants pay for rent (30,000-70,000 yen) plus 40,000 yen per month compulsory contributions.

## LANGUAGE COURSES ABROAD LTD

**67 Ashby Road, Loughborough, Leicestershire LE11 3AA. ☎01509 211612. Fax: 01509 260037. E-mail: info@languagesabroad.co.uk. Website: www.languagesabroad.co.uk.**
Parent company is Spanish Study Holidays Ltd. which recently launched a new website applelanguages.com in order to extend online services and to roll out several new languages (Arabic and shortly Chinese).
**Programme description:** In-country language courses in Spanish, French, German, Italian, Portuguese and Russian.
**Prerequisites:** All ages, including clients in their 30s, 40s and older. Club 50+ language courses are offered in a number of destinations for people in their 50s and older (details on www.languagesabroad.co.uk/third_age.html).
**Duration and time of placements:** 1-36 weeks.
**Accommodation:** Shared self-catering student apartments, private studio apartments, host families, student residences or hotels.
**Contact:** Mike Cummins (Director) or Peter Carvell (Language Travel Advisor).

## LATIN IMMERSION

**Roman Diaz 297, Providencia, Santiago, Chile. ☎/fax: +56 2-264-9604. ☎1-866-577-8693. Fax: 1-866-726-5705/ +56 2-264 9604 E-mail: info@latinimmersion.com. Website: www.latinimmersion.com. Argentina offices: Junin 1418, Recoleta, Buenos Aires; and Pasaje Gutiér-rez 843, Ciudad de Bariloche.**
**Programme description:** Spanish language courses combined with volunteer programme.

**Destinations:** Chile or Argentina.
**Number of placements per year:** 20. Most volunteers are from the US, UK and Netherlands.
**Prerequisites:** Average age 26.
**Duration and time of placements:** All enrolled language students are eligible to continue on as volunteers for 8 weeks, after 4 weeks of immersion Spanish classes or 8 weeks if complete beginners.
**Selection procedures and orientation:** Applications due 8 weeks before arrival. Student selects 3 volunteer options from list to match area of interest. Volunteer placement not guaranteed until after arrival when student visits the organisation.
**Cost:** Registration fee $75, classes $180 per week, and half-board accommodation $140 per week. No volunteer placement fee.

## LAUNCHPAD AUSTRALIA

**PO Box 2525, Fitzroy, Victoria 3065, Australia. ☎ +61 1300 851 826. Fax: +61 3-9445 9375. E-mail: workingholiday@launchpadaustralia.com. Website: www.launchpadaustralia.com.**
**Programme description:** Offers a variety of international work, study, cultural and volunteer opportunities.
**Destinations:** Worldwide possibilities for volunteers. UK, Europe and Canada for Australians.
**Number of placements per year:** 200+.
**Prerequisites:** Mainly aimed at Australians, though volunteer and language immersion programmes open to all nationalities. Average age 25+ though also caters to lots of young gappers. Many programmes offer an 'organise, pay and off you go' arrangement. Teaching English Abroad placements often require a Bachelor's degree.
**Duration and time of placements:** Language courses from one week, cultural tours in Italy at least 2 weeks, volunteering is usually a minimum of 2 weeks and work programmes can go up to a year.
**Cost:** Varies hugely depending on programme.
**Contact:** Danielle Ades-Salman, Managing Director.

## THE LEAP OVERSEAS LTD

**The Leap Overseas, 121 High Street, Marlborough, Wiltshire, SN8 1LZ ☎ 0870 240 4187/01672 519922. Fax: 01672 519944. E-mail: info@theleap.co.uk. Website: www.theleap.co.uk.**
**Programme description:** Team voluntary placements in Africa, South America, Asia and Australia, rotating through safari camp/eco-tourism lodge placements, conservation projects and community projects. For example in Kenya volunteers can escort guests on safari, track elephant in the bush and teach football or English to local kids.
**Destinations:** Placements are based in game parks, jungle and coastal locations in Africa (Kenya, South Africa, Mozambique, Tanzania, Malawi, Zambia and Botswana), South America (Guyana, Costa Rica, Argentina and Ecuador), Asia (Cambodia and India) and Australia.
**Number of placements per year:** 130 with expectation to expand to 400. The majority of participants are school-leavers aged 18-20, though career breakers

are specially catered for and sent together with others of a similar age.
**Prerequisites:** Ages 18-60. Must be committed, enthusiastic and motivated, able to work well in a team and prepared to get stuck in.
**Duration and time of placements:** Flexible departure dates. 12, 10 or 6-week team schemes including Summer Team Gap trips departing in July. 3-month solo placements in Africa only.
**Selection procedures and orientation:** Application form and attend interview or Familiarisation and Selection Course in the UK for assessment on suitability and for briefing.
**Other services:** Flights can be arranged through ATOL partner agency Safari Drive Ltd. or booked privately. Plenty of time for adventure travel.
**Cost:** £1,600 for 6-week summer trip; approx £2,600 for longer trips including accommodation, food, travel insurance, transport and back-up, excluding travel and visas.
**Contact:** Guy Whitehead, Director.



### MADVENTURER

**The Old Casino, 1-4 Forth Lane, Newcastle upon Tyne NE1 5HX. ☎0845 121 1996 or 0191-269 9495. Fax: 0191-280 2860. E-mail: team@madventurer.com. Website: www.madventurer.com; www.careerbreaker.com.**
Madventurer combines development projects and adventurous overland travel. The Madventurer ethos is 'developing together' to assist rural community development while at the same time enabling adventurous travellers to gain experience of a different culture and be encapsulated by village life. For challenging sports-coaching programmes in other developing countries, see entry below for Sportventurer.
**Programme description:** Expeditions that give career breakers, gap year individuals and students the opportunity to undertake a range of voluntary work for a grassroots community or environmental project (building, teaching, sports instruction, healthcare and conservation) with the option then to travel on an overland adventure (trekking, rafting, touring). Placements can sometimes be arranged to complement area of academic study. The specially designed career break projects are for individuals aged 24 or over who are looking for a unique experience during their time out from work.
**Destinations:** Peru, Ghana, Tanzania, Togo, Kenya, Uganda, Fiji, Tonga, Sri

Lanka and Thailand.
**Prerequisites:** Career Break projects for all ages.
**Duration and time of placements:** From 2-5 weeks (for those who want to join as part of their annual leave) to 3-month placements with various departure dates throughout the year. The most popular option is the 5-week project that costs from £1,380. Some venturers extend their stay for up to 6 months.
**Selection procedures and orientation:** Full-time crew support venturers both before departure and overseas on project sites. Thorough pre-departure information, advice, support and fundraising pack provided.
**Cost:** from £750 (not including flights).
**Contact:** any of the Madventurer team (team@madventurer.com).

## MONDOCHALLENGE

**Malsor House, Gayton Rd, Milton Malsor, Northampton NN7 3AB. ☎01604 858225. Fax: 01604 859323. E-mail: info@mondochallenge.org. Website: www.mondochallenge.org.**
**Programme description:** MondoChallenge is a not for profit organisation which sends volunteers (post-university, career break, early retired, etc.) to help with teaching and business development programmes in Africa, Asia and South America. Programmes are community-based, providing volunteers with an insight into local cultures and a chance to experience a different way of life first-hand.
**Destinations:** Nepal, India, Sri Lanka, Tanzania, Kenya, The Gambia, Senegal, Chile and Ecuador.
**Number of placements per year:** 200 approximately.
**Prerequisites:** All ages; average age is 29. All nationalities accepted; about half are non-UK based with a large number of volunteers from North America, Europe and Australia. For teaching projects, minimum qualification is A-level or equivalent in subjects to be taught. For business development, a minimum of 3 years business experience is required. Must be able to cope with remote posting and to relate to people of other cultures. Enthusiasm, flexibility and good communication skills are essential.
**Duration and time of placements:** Normal stay is 2-4 months and start dates are flexible.
**Cost:** £1,100 for 3 months. Board and lodging in local family homes costs an extra £15 (approximately) per week.
**Contact:** Anthony Lunch, Director.

## NONSTOP ADVENTURE

**Nonstop Ski & Snowboard/ Nonstop Sail, Shakespeare House, 168 Lavender Hill, London SW11 5TF. ☎0870 241 8070. E-mail: info@nonstopadventure.com. Website: www.nonstopadventure.com (nonstopski.com, nonstopsnowboard.com and nonstopsail.com).**
**Programme description:** Ski and Snowboard improvement courses in the Canadian Rockies. Professional yacht sailing courses including Yachtmaster fast track and 6-week Adventure Sailing experiences across the Atlantic, sailing around Britain, island hopping in the Caribbean or cruising the Mediterranean.
**Number of participants:** 25-50 on wintersports courses (30% are aged 30+). 5 per yacht on sailing adventures.

**Destination:** Canadian Rockies (Fernie, Banff, Red Mountain).
**Prerequisites:** Snow course participants should have at least 2 weeks snow experience. No sailing background needed for sailing courses.
**Duration:** Ski & Snowboard courses are 2-11 weeks. Sailing lasts 1-14 weeks.
**Qualifications offered:** Internationally recognised CSIA (Canadian Ski Instructor Alliance) and CASI (Canadian Association of Snowboard Instructors). Also CAA (Canadian Avalanche Association) Recreational Avalanche 1 certificate and St. John's Ambulance Basic first aid certificate. Freestyle and race coach qualifications can also be obtained. For Sail programme, all RYA qualifications including Yachtmaster.
**Other services:** Work experience may be arranged with local ski school and contacts with other ski schools for instructing jobs provided.
**Cost:** Ski and Snowboard £2,050-£6,450 which includes flights, accommodation, meals, coaching, weekend trips, first aid course, avalanche course, lift pass and more. Sail trips cost from £525 to £7,250. Ski accommodation in twin or single rooms in houses/lodge equipped with kitchens, comfortable living rooms, stereo and cable TV. Sailors sleep on board yachts.
**Contact:** Melissa Taylor, Sales & Marketing Director.

## OPERATION WALLACEA

**Hope House, Old Bolingbroke, Nr Spilsby, Lincolnshire PE23 4EX. ☎01790 763194. Fax: 01790 763825. E-mail: info@opwall.com. Website: www.opwall.com.**
**Programme description:** Marine and Rainforest scientific research projects in Sulawesi (Indonesia) and Honduras; desert and marine projects in Egypt; sailing expeditions down the Amazon in Peru; bush and marine projects in South Africa; and turtle monitoring and marine projects in Cuba. Projects aim to carry out good scientific conservation work to enable local people to protect their own environment from destructive practices. Volunteers from all walks of life and ages assist with surveys of marine, desert, bush and rainforest habitats.
**Destinations:** Southeast Sulawesi (Indonesia), Northern Honduras, Egypt, South Africa, Cuba and Peru.
**Prerequisites:** Minimum age 16. Enthusiasm needed.
**Duration and time of placements:** 2, 4, 6 or 8 weeks between June and September.
**Selection procedures and orientation:** Telephone interview. No deadlines. Dive training to PADI OW and jungle training are given (included in the cost of the expedition).
**Cost:** £950 for 2 weeks, £1,750 for 4 weeks, £2,400 for 6 weeks and £2,800 for 8 weeks, excluding flights.
**Contact:** Pippa Fawcett.

## ORANGUTAN FOUNDATION

**7 Kent Terrace, London, NW1 4RP. ☎020-7724 2912. Fax: 020-7706 2613. E-mail: info@orangutan.org.uk. Website: www.orangutan.org.uk.**
**Programme description:** Volunteers are based in the Tanjung Puting National Park in Kalimantan, Indonesian Borneo. Volunteers spend time at Camp Leakey, the historical research site of Dr Biruté Galdikas and may also work in other areas of the Park or in the Lamandau Reserve, a new release site for rehabilitated orangutans. Previous projects have included: general infrastructure repairs,

MONDO CHALLENGE
The Career Break Specialists
Volunteer programmes:
- teaching, business development, HIV/AIDS support
- from the Himalayas to Tanzania
- placements from 2 to 6 months
01604 858225
info@mondochallenge.org
www.mondochallenge.org

trail cutting, constructing guardposts, and orangutan release sites. Volunteers should note that there is no direct work with orangutans.
**Number of placements per year:** 48.
**Duration and time of placements:** 6 weeks, 4 teams of no more than 12, departing April, June, August and September. Dates for 2007/8 to be confirmed.
**Prerequisites:** Participants must be members of the Orangutan Foundation (£20 per year). They must work well in a team, be fit and healthy and adaptable to difficult and demanding conditions. There is no upper age limit.
**Selection procedures and orientation:** All potential UK volunteers are expected to attend an interview at the Foundation office in London. Phone interviews can be conducted for non-UK applicants. Successful UK applicants are expected to attend a pre-departure briefing day.
**Cost:** £550, includes all accommodation, food, equipment, materials and transport for the duration of the programme but does not include international and internal travel to the project site.
**Contact:** Claire Webber, Volunteer Co-ordinator (claire@orangutan.org.uk).

## OUTREACH INTERNATIONAL

**Bartletts Farm, Hayes Road, Compton Dundon, Somerton, Somerset TA11 6PF. ☎/fax: 01458 274957. E-mail: info@outreachinternational.co.uk. Website: www.outreachinternational.co.uk.**

Member of the Year Out Group. Outreach International is a specialist organisation that places committed volunteers in carefully selected meaningful projects.
**Programme description:** Volunteers can make a valuable contribution to their project whilst experiencing the pleasures of living and working with local people and immersing themselves in a foreign culture. The projects are all small, worthwhile, varied and handpicked. They include humanitarian and aid work, community development, helping in orphanages, teaching English, sports or computer skills to street children, teaching in schools on the Pacific coast of Mexico, helping at medical centres, working at a centre for disabled children, dance, art & craft projects, conservation work with giant sea turtles and environmental work in the Amazon rainforest. Projects are visited regularly by the Outreach director and team member. In order to minimise the cultural impact of projects, volunteers are normally placed in pairs and never in a large group.
**Destinations:** Mexico, Costa Rica, Sri Lanka, Cambodia, Ecuador and the Galapagos Islands.
**Prerequisites:** Ideal for confident people with a desire to travel, learn a language and offer their help to a humble community. Some of the projects need volunteers with skills in physiotherapy, law, report writing, computers (IT) and office management. The majority however do not need specific skills. Energy, enthusiasm and commitment are more important than official qualifications.
**Duration and time of placements:** Short and long-term placements lasting a month or more. Flexible departure dates, though the most popular departure times are January, April, June and September.
**Selection procedures and orientation:** Outreach International aims to meet all applicants within 3 weeks of applying and let them know what the chosen placement will involve. Each placement has its own project manager and volunteers have 24-hour in-country support from a full-time co-ordinator.
**Cost:** £3,650 for 3 months includes full insurance (public liability, health and

baggage), language course, in-country support, food, accommodation, local travel, all project costs, fundraising, teacher training and pre-departure briefing days in the UK. Extended stays cost approximately £450 per month.
**Contact:** James Chapman, UK Director.

## OVERSEAS WORKING HOLIDAYS (OWH)

**Level 1, 51 Fife Road, Kingston, Surrey KT1 1SF. ☎0845 344 0366 or 020-8547 3664. Fax: 0870 460 4578. E-mail: info@owh.co.uk. Website: www.owh.co.uk.**

Part of the Australian-owned Flight Centre Group.
**Programme description:** Paid work in hospitality industries of Australia and Canada, paid English teaching in Korea, China, Thailand and Poland, volunteer placements worldwide, among others (in conjunction with i-to-i, see entry).
**Number of placements per year:** 400.
**Destinations:** Australia and Canada. Other countries for Australians.
**Prerequisites:** Ages 18-30 for Australia, 18-35 for Canada, all ages for paid teaching. No specific qualifications needed. Non-UK citizens must check visa restrictions.
**Duration and time of placements:** Duration of working holiday visa, i.e. 1 year in Australia, winter or summer seasons in Canada (November-May or March-October).
**Cost:** Choice of programme fee for Australia depending on level of service: £189, £229 or £259. Canada programme fee is £349. Volunteer programme fees vary from project to project.

## PANTANAL INSTITUTE

**Rua B, No. 4, Setor Centro Sul, Morada do Ouro, Cuiabá/MT, Brazil CEP: 78053-164. ☎+55 (0) 65 3644 2331. E-mail: contact@pantanalinstitute.com. Website: www.pantanalinstitute.com.**

Institute welcomes Brazilian biologists who would like to improve their English.
**Programme description:** Institute combines School Teaching English as a Foreign Language and captive breeding facility for birds of prey, i.e. hawks. Voluntary/work experience vacancies available on conservation projects.
**Destinations:** Pantanal, a vast wetland habitat in central western Brazil.

**Number of placements per year:** 50-100.
**Prerequisites:** Ages vary, average about 40. All nationalities welcome as long as English is the mother tongue. Flexibility, enthusiasm to work with wildlife, confidence and approachability needed.
**Duration and time of placements:** 1 month.
**Selection procedures and orientation:** Deadline for applications May 30th. Interviews are recommended and held at a hotel in Manchester (UK) in July. On arrival, meet and greet service and candidates work closely with the director who is a British biologist.
**Cost:** £500 per month includes full board and lodging.
**Contact:** John Beaumont, Director.

## PEAK LEADERS

**Mansfield, Strathmiglo, Fife KY14 7QE, Scotland. ☎01337 860755. Fax: 01337 868176. E-mail: info@peakleaders.com. Website: www.peakleaders.com.**

Time out and gap year ski and snowboard instructor courses in New Zealand, Argentina, Switzerland and Canada, with possible job offers to high quality candidates on completion.
**Programme description:** Ski and Snowboard instructor courses including choice of modules on powder, moguls, free skiing, free riding, park and pipe, ski tuning, along with the services of an experienced leader throughout. Peak Leaders' Ski and Snowboard Instructor courses can also include avalanche awareness, mountain first aid, team leading, back country, freestyle, ski school shadowing and off-piste skiing.
**Destinations:** Courses are in Switzerland (Zermatt and Verbier), Canada (Whistler and Banff), Argentina (Bariloche in Patagonia) and New Zealand (Queenstown).
**Duration of courses:** 10-12 weeks. Instructor training in Argentina and New Zealand finishes in September/October and high-quality, well organised candidates can get jobs in Europe or Canada by Christmas.
**Cost:** About £6,500 inclusive of instruction, flight (not available to New Zealand or Switzerland), hotel with half board, lift tickets and certification.
**Other services:** Optional extras are offered like skidoo driving, backcountry training, Spanish and French language and stopover in Buenos Aires. Job advice available.
**Contacts:** David and Annie Hughes, Directors.

## PEOPLE AND PLACES

**1 Naboths Nursery, Canterbury Road, Faversham, Kent ME13 8AX. ☎01795 535718. Fax: 01795 539728. E-mail: info@travel-peopleandplaces.co.uk. Website: www.travel-peopleandplaces.co.uk.**

New volunteer recruitment organisation for volunteers of all ages. Also work in partnership with Saga Holidays on their newly launched volunteer programme (www.saga.co.uk/travel/general3/volunteer_intro.asp) for people aged 50+.
**Programme description:** Various volunteer placements as requested by local communities liaising with host country project management teams. Examples include: working with the Red Cross on a community AIDS care project, training programmes for the unemployed, high school student mentoring, marine

research and child care support. No volunteers replace local labour.
**Destinations:** South Africa, Gambia and Pakistan.
**Number of placements per year:** 500-1,000.
**Prerequisites:** Most volunteers are aged 35-45 with a maximum of about 70 for the projects available through the partnership with Saga, though there is no maximum age if volunteers are healthy and can do the work. All nationalities accepted. Volunteers' skills and abilities are more important than age and are matched with needs of individual projects, e.g. child counselling, education or health care training or experience, IT skills, practical and trade skills.
**Duration and time of placements:** Most are 4-8 weeks though some are shorter and others last up to 12 weeks.
**Selection procedures and orientation:** Flexible start dates; normally one month is needed for screening and placement. Telephone or face-to-face interview required.
**Other Services:** Each volunteer receives comprehensive pre-departure information, including a briefing on responsible volunteering and the communities in which they will be working.
**Cost:** £1,045 for 4 weeks including orientation, half-board accommodation (normally homestay), airport transfers and support throughout. All volunteer fees are paid direct to the host country, and the vast majority of it stays there. Volunteers are clearly told in advance how the donation element will be spent for the specific project on which they are working.
**Contact:** Kate Stefanko (Placement Director), Sallie Grayson (Director).

## PERSONAL OVERSEAS DEVELOPMENT (POD)

**Linden Cottage, The Burgage, Prestbury, Cheltenham, Glos. GL52 3DJ. ☎01242 250901. E-mail: info@thepodsite.co.uk. Website: www.thepodsite.co.uk.**

PoD provides the opportunity for people to volunteer and arranges placements and courses for people to develop their skills.
**Programme description:** Flexible programmes are designed to provide the essentials for a fulfilling break, which can also be incorporated into existing travel plans. Packages include training, support and accommodation if required. Opportunities include teaching English to primary school children, working in orphanages and care homes, working in animal rescue centres, healthcare, Amazon jungle conservation and scuba diving.
**Destinations:** Peru, Thailand, Tanzania and Nepal.
**Prerequisites:** No specific requirements for most placements, just a positive attitude.
**Duration and time of placements:** From 2 weeks to 6 months, throughout the year.
**Selection procedures & orientation:** All applicants submit a written application, receive a telephone interview and references are taken. A Criminal Records Bureau Check may also be conducted. A detailed information pack is sent to volunteers pre-departure and local training and introductions are undertaken on arrival in-country. PoD is a small organisation that believes in personal service, quality and benefit for local communities.
**Cost:** Short programmes start at £300. Sample prices include 2 months of dog and cat care in Thailand for £395, 3 months village teaching in Tanzania, £995.
**Contact:** Mike Beecham and Alex Tarrant.

## QUEST OVERSEAS

**The North West Stables, Borde Hill Estate, Balcombe Road, Haywards Heath, West Sussex, RH16 1XP. ☎01444 474744. Fax: 01444 474799. E-mail: emailus@questoverseas.com. Website: www.questoverseas.com.**

**Programme description:** Expedition specialists with projects and adventure travel to suit all ages in South America and Africa. A range of projects are on offer from working with children or animals to diving surveys to work in rainforests. Activities can include rafting, trekking, diving, snorkelling, ice climbing, sandboarding, quadbiking, bungee jumping and safari.

**Destinations:** Southern Africa, East Africa, Andean South America and Brazil.

**Number of placements per year:** 300+.

**Prerequisites:** Average age 21 though median age varies with team (an estimated 20% of clients are on career sabbaticals). No qualifications needed, just enthusiasm.

**Duration and time of placements:** Range of departures from 3 wks to 3 mths.

**Selection procedures and orientation:** Application deadline 2 weeks before departure. Interviews can be in person or by phone.

**Other Services:** All participants receive a joining pack and access to help and advice. They are also invited to 2-day training event which covers all topics in preparation for overseas travel and project work.

**Cost:** £1,800-£4,920 (South America) and £1,390-£4,240 (Africa).

**Contact:** Beth Chapman or Olivia Knight-Adams, Operations Managers.

## RALEIGH INTERNATIONAL

**Raleigh House, 27 Parsons Green Lane, London SW6 4HZ. ☎020-7371 8585. Fax: 020-7371 5852. E-mail: staff@raleigh.org.uk. Website: www.raleighinternational.org.**

Raleigh International is a youth development charity with over 21 years experience. Through its Motive8 programme in the UK, which aims to develop the skills and prospects of socially excluded young people, and its overseas programmes, the charity works with young people aged 17-25 from all backgrounds and nationalities to enable them to make a positive contribution and achieve personal and social development.

**Programme description:** Staff volunteers (aged 25+) are required on the overseas programmes to support young people in undertaking sustainable community, environmental and adventure projects. All projects are designed in partnership with government ministries, local communities or NGOs to ensure that they are worthwhile and sustainable. Staff volunteers will either be based at the headquarters in the country or on the project sites themselves.

**Destinations:** Costa Rica & Nicaragua, Ghana, Namibia and Malaysia (Borneo).

**Number of placements per year:** 300-350 staff (9-10 programmes per year).

**Prerequisites:** Applicants must be aged over 25 and have one or more relevant skills and experience in administration, building and carpentry, communications and creativity, driving, finance, logistics, medical/nursing or paramedic qualification, photography, project management, Spanish interpreting, trekking and outdoor instruction, or working with young people. A 'can-do' attitude, lots of energy and desire to benefit communities and young people from around the world also necessary.

**Duration and time of placements:** 13 weeks to include 2 weeks of in-country training before the programme begins and a week at the end for review.
**Selection procedures and orientation:** After an application has been accepted, the applicant is invited to an assessment weekend which simulates potential team challenges through physical exercises and problem solving.
**Cost:** Raleigh International is a charity so staff volunteers are asked to contribute £1,500 which will cover the costs of training and living expenses (can be reduced to about £860 by claiming on gift aid). Bursaries are available for certain key staff (e.g. doctors, nurses and qualified outdoor professionals).
**Contact:** Ana Steele, Staff Recruitment Coordinator.

## ROBBOOKER VOLUNTARY ORGANIZATION

**Box RY 655 Railways, Kumasi, Ghana. ☎ +233-24-4591378 (Mob). Fax: +233-51-34493. E-mail: robbookervoluntary_organization@yahoo-mail.com. Website: www.robborg.org.**
**Programme description:** Service/volunteer projects in Ghana for students and volunteers worldwide.
**Destinations:** Throughout Ghana.
**Number of placements per year:** 50.
**Prerequisites:** Ages 17-50. All nationalities. No special qualifications needed.
**Duration and time of placements:** 2-12 weeks.
**Selection procedures and orientation:** Written applications accepted on an ongoing basis. Pre-departure profile on Ghana is sent to volunteers weeks before departure. In-country orientation about project and host families are given to volunteers upon arrival.
**Cost:** Programme costs $1,500 (£850) including homestay accommodation, excluding flights.
**Contact:** Richmond Amoakoh, Director.

## RURAL CENTRE FOR HUMAN INTERESTS (RUCHI)

**Bandh, Bhaguri 173233, Dist. Solan, Himachal Pradesh, India. ☎ +91-1792-282454, +91-1792-282516. E-mail: ruchin5@vsnl.com; virjids@yahoo.com. Website: www.ruchin.org.**
The TOTEM programme enables people to work in one of 200 villages for spells of three weeks (or longer) as volunteers in India.
**Programme description:** Volunteers can choose between Environmental Management Programme, Social Development Programme and Health and Sanitation Development Programme.
**Destinations:** Himachal Pradesh, India.
**Number of placements per year:** 10.
**Prerequisites:** For ages 20-60. All candidates are welcome to apply. The key acceptance criterion is whether the candidate has enough international travel experience to handle the basic conditions in a grass-roots organisation.
**Duration and time of placements:** 3-week placements for working professionals, starting on fifth day of every month (though start dates are flexible). Extensions can be negotiated for up to 6 months.
**Cost:** $1,000 for 3 weeks; cost for longer placements negotiable. Fee includes transport from Delhi railway station, use of private car with driver when at RUCHI, accommodation and all vegetarian meals.

## SAGA VOLUNTEER TRAVEL

**The Saga Building, Enbrook Park, Folkestone, Kent CT20 3SE. E-mail: volunteer@saga.co.uk. Website: www.saga.co.uk/volunteer.**

New division of Saga launched 2006 linked with the Saga Charitable Trust.

**Programme description:** Volunteer placements offered in conjunction with *people and places* (see entry).

**Destinations:** South Africa (Cape Town and Port Elizabeth).

**Cost:** £1,019 for 4 weeks, £1,449 for 8 weeks.

## SPW – STUDENTS PARTNERSHIP WORLDWIDE

**2nd Floor, Faith House, 7 Tufton Street, London SW1P 3QB. ☎020-7222 0138. Fax: 020-7233 0008. E-mail: info@spw.org. Website: www.spw.org.**

European, American and Australian volunteers aged 18-28 are recruited to work in partnership with counterpart volunteers from Africa and Asia. In pairs or groups they live and work in rural communities for 4-8 months. Their input builds awareness and begins to change attitudes and behaviour to important health, social and environmental issues amongst young people and communities. All volunteers take part in training which covers health, hygiene, sanitation, nutrition and the environment, with a particular emphasis on HIV/AIDS prevention and care. SPW is a non-profit making charity.

**Programme description:** SPW runs health education and environment programmes. These programmes tackle youth problems from different perspectives. All placements are in rural villages.

**Destinations:** India, Nepal, South Africa, Tanzania, Uganda and Zambia.

**Number of placements per year:** 200 places for European, American and Australian volunteers.

**Prerequisites:** A-level or equivalent qualifications. Volunteers need to be physically and mentally healthy, hard working, open-minded, enthusiastic and have good communication skills.

**Duration and time of placements:** 4-8 months with starting dates throughout the year.

**Selection procedures and orientation:** Every applicant is required to attend an Information and Selection day in London. This also gives them the opportunity to meet staff and ex-volunteers. Following selection, volunteers are accepted on a first come first served basis, so early application is recommended.

**Cost:** Minimum donation of £3,600 to the charity. All costs are then covered by SPW including open return flight, accommodation, basic living allowance, insurance, in-country visa, UK briefings and general administrative support, and extensive overseas training and support.

## SPORTVENTURER

**The Old Casino, 1-4 Forth Lane, Newcastle upon Tyne NE1 5HX. ☎0845 121 1996. Fax: 0191-280 2860. E-mail: team@sportventurer.com. Website: www.sportventurer.com.**

**Programme description:** Sportventurer is a programme run by Madventurer (see entry above) that creates opportunities for people with a passion for sport and adventure to coach and play sport overseas. Volunteers contribute to sports development programmes in less-privileged parts of the world.

**Destinations:** Ghana, Uganda, Fiji, Tonga and Peru.

**Prerequisites:** Must have passion for sport. No experience or qualifications necessary.
**Duration and time of placements:** 2 weeks, 5 weeks or 3 months.
**Selection procedures and orientation:** Full-time Madventurer Crew support venturers both before departure and overseas on project sites. Thorough pre-departure information, advice, support and fundraising pack provided.
**Cost:** From £750 (excluding flights).
**Contact:** any of the Madventurer team (team@madventurer.com)

### STAESA (STUDENTS TRAVEL AND EXPOSURE SOUTH AFRICA)

**PO Box 15016, Dalpark 11, Brakpan 1552, South Africa. ☎ +27 73-651 8203/11-910 2654. Fax: +27 11-845 1026. E-mail: info@staesa.org/ksa_simon@yahoo.co.uk. Website: www.staesa.org.**

South African registered NGO.
**Programme description:** Provides volunteers with work placements in range of community projects, small scale industries and NGOs in South Africa and throughout sub-Saharan Africa.
**Destinations:** Mainly South Africa, also possibilities in Ghana, Benin, Togo, Senegal, Mali, Botswana, Tanzania, The Gambia, Uganda, Malawi and Kenya.
**Number of placements per year:** 400 volunteers and interns.
**Prerequisites:** All nationalites and ages over 18. Should be loving, caring, understanding, ready to share, ready to travel, open-minded, flexible, and have sense of humour.
**Duration and time of placements:** 2 weeks to 1 year.
**Selection procedures and orientation:** Acceptance year round. Orientation given on arrival.
**Cost:** From US$395 for two weeks in Ghana including host family accommodation to US$5,000+ for one year in most of the countries.
**Contact:** Rev. Simon Kudzo, International Programme Director.

### STARFISH VENTURES

**PO Box 9061, Epping, CM16 7WU. ☎/fax: 0800 197 4817. E-mail: enquiries@starfishventures.co.uk. Website: www.starfishventures.co.uk.**

Starfish Ventures is a British company founded in 2003 which specialises in supporting development projects in Thailand. Starfish is a small organisation in which volunteers work closely with Thai partner organisations (such as the Education Administration of Surin Province and Thailand's Marine and Coastal Protection Organisation). In addition to placing volunteers, Starfish delivers financial aid and provides expertise and project management.
**Programme description:** Volunteer programmes in teaching, development, animal welfare, conservation, construction and medical.
**Destinations:** Throughout Thailand including Surin, Kho Samui and Rayong.
**Prerequisites:** Ages 18-70 (older volunteers may be accepted but will need to discuss insurance cover and any medical conditions). All nationalities accepted. Criminal Records Bureau (CRB) certificate essential for UK applicants; non-UK residents must provide evidence of no criminal record.
**Duration and time of placements:** 2-12 weeks, longer placements can be arranged.
**Selection procedures and orientation:** Applicants must apply at least 6 weeks prior to the volunteer's chosen departure date. Suitable projects are suggested

on basis of applicant's CV. Volunteers joining a Teaching Venture attend a TEFL training weekend. Comprehensive briefing kit given. Thai co-ordinators help candidates orientate themselves in their new surroundings, make regular checks throughout placement and provide 24-hour support service.
**Cost:** £595 (2 weeks) to £1,695 (12 weeks). Includes preparatory TEFL training weekend, insurance, in-country co-ordinator and 24-hour support, travel within Thailand, plus accommodation in private room in privately rented house.
**Contact:** Dan Moore, Director.

## SUDAN VOLUNTEER PROGRAMME

**34 Estelle Road, London NW3 2JY. ☎020-7485 8619. E-mail: davidsvp@blueyonder.co.uk. Website: www.svp-uk.com.**
**Programme description:** SVP works with undergraduates and graduates who are native English speakers and who wish to teach English in Sudan. Teaching tends to be informal in style, with 4-5 hours of contact a day. Volunteers can plan their own teaching schemes, such as arranging games, dramas, competitions and tests for assessing skills learned by the students. Accommodation is in flats shared with other volunteers.
**Destinations:** Sudan, mostly in and around Khartoum especially Omdurman.
**Prerequisites:** TEFL certificate, experience of travelling in developing countries and some knowledge of Arabic are helpful but not obligatory. Volunteers must be in good health and be native English speakers.
**Duration and time of placements:** Preferred minimum 6 months.
**Selection procedures and orientation:** Applications accepted year round. Two referees are also required. Prior to departure, medical check-up required plus selection interviews, orientation and briefings take place. Volunteers are required to write a report of their experiences and to advise new volunteers.
**Cost:** Volunteers must raise the cost of the airfare to Sudan (currently £585) plus £60 (cost of the first 3 months insurance). SVP pays subsistence, accommodation and insurance beyond the initial 3 months.
**Contact:** David Wolton (at email above).

## TASK BRASIL TRUST

**PO Box 4901, London, SE16 3PP. ☎020-7735 5545. Fax: 020-7735 5675. E-mail: info@taskbrasil.org.uk. Website: www.taskbrasil.org.uk.**
**Programme description:** Volunteer projects in Rio de Janeiro working with children and teenagers from troubled backgrounds. Volunteers are involved in the day-to-day care of the children and in offering activities such as art, English lessons, sports, music and swimming or in outreach work on the streets of Rio. Other volunteer work takes part at the projects themselves and volunteers are assisting Task Brasil staff in their work for example on the streets or in Casa Jimmy caring for teenage mums and their babies.
**Destinations:** Rio de Janeiro, Brazil.
**Number of placements per year:** 100.
**Prerequisites:** Average age 26. Experience working with children/adolescents. Ability to teach English (TEFL) and/or organise activities such as arts, sports, music or swimming is also useful.
**Duration and time of placements:** 1-12 months. Volunteers accepted year round. Should apply at least 2 months before start date.

**Selection procedures and orientation:** Interviews in UK are essential and candidates must attend induction meetings.
**Other Services:** Volunteers attend preparatory sessions including at least one meeting with ex-volunteers to discuss what volunteering consists of and to pose any questions they have.
**Cost:** Self-catering shared accommodation and food are provided. Volunteers need to pay for flights and bring their own spending money.
**Contact:** Charlotte Smith, Office Manager.



## TEACHING & PROJECTS ABROAD

**Aldsworth Parade, Goring, Sussex BN12 4TX. ☎01903 708300. Fax: 01903 501026. E-mail: info@teaching-abroad.co.uk. Website: www.teaching-abroad.co.uk.**

Founding member of the Year Out Group. Company arranges voluntary teaching posts as well as placements in care, conservation, animal care, medicine, journalism and other fields around the world. New Adventure in New Zealand programme.
**Destinations:** Argentina, Bolivia, Cambodia, Chile, China, Costa Rica, Ghana, India, Mexico, Moldova, Mongolia, Nepal, New Zealand, Peru, Romania, Senegal, South Africa, Sri Lanka and Thailand. Destinations and placements can be combined; their 'Grand Gap' combines three or four destinations.
**Number of placements per year:** 3,000.
**Prerequisites:** Volunteers range from 17 to 70. Optional UK briefing and TEFL weekend courses before departure.
**Duration and time of placements:** Very flexible, with departures year round. Placements last 1-12 months.
**Selection procedures and orientation:** Paid staff (120 in total) in all destinations who arrange and vet placements, accommodation and work supervisors. They meet volunteers on arrival and provide a final briefing before the placements.
**Cost:** Placements are self-funded and the fee charged includes insurance, food, accommodation and overseas support. Three-month placements cost between £895 and £3,000+, depending on placement and destination, excluding travel costs.

**TRAVELLERS**

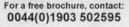

**7 Mulberry Close, Ferring, West Sussex BN12 5HY. ☎01903 502595. Fax: 01903 500364. E-mail: info@travellersworldwide.com. Website: www.travellersworldwide.com.**

Founder member of the Year Out Group. Volunteer programme for people taking a career break, gap year or want to do something constructive in retirement.

**Programme description:** Voluntary work overseas on different types of project, open to all. Projects include teaching conversational English (and other subjects like sports, music, drama, maths, geography), conservation programmes including rehabilitation of endangered species, African wildlife courses, structured work experience in sectors such as law, journalism and medicine; language courses (e.g. Spanish, Russian, Mandarin, Brazilian Portuguese) and cultural courses (meditation, photography, tango, music, martial arts).

**Destinations:** Argentina, Australia, Bolivia, Brazil, Brunei, China, Cuba, Ghana, Guatemala, India, Kenya, Malaysia, Peru, Russia, South Africa, Sri Lanka, Zambia and Zimbabwe.

**Number of placements per year:** 1,000+.

**Prerequisites:** No formal qualifications required. Open to all ages 17-90.

**Duration and time of placements:** 2 weeks to 1year with flexible start dates all year round.

**Cost:** Sample charges for 3 months in Sri Lanka are £1,345 and China £1,095. Prices include food and accommodation plus transport, airport greeting, local support and back-up by Travellers staff overseas, but do not include international travel, visas or insurance. (Travellers can arrange the latter but many volunteers prefer the flexibility of organising their own.)

**TREKFORCE EXPEDITIONS**

**Naldred Farm Offices, Borde Hill Lane, Haywards Heath, West Sussex RH16 1XR. ☎/fax: 01444 474123. E-mail: info@trekforce.org.uk. Website: www.trekforce.org.uk.**

Founding member of the Year Out Group. Registered charity, established since 1989.

**Programme description:** Challenging project-driven expeditions and placements to the rainforests of Southeast Asia, and Central and South America.

**Destinations:** Central America (Belize and Guatemala), South America (Guyana

and Peru) and East Malaysia (Sabah and Sarawak).
**Prerequisites:** Age 18+. No qualifications or experience required but all applicants must be medically fit and healthy.
**Duration and time of placements:** 1, 2, 3, 4 or 5 months, all year round. Conservation expeditions last for 1-2 months, with extended programmes of up to 5 months for those who opt for Spanish language learning in a second country, and teaching in rural communities such as the Maya, Kelabit or Amerindian communities.
**Selection procedures & orientation:** Interested participants can attend an informal introductory day or visit the Trekforce office for an introductory meeting. A briefing event is held prior to departure, and in-country training is provided for all expedition members.
**Cost:** Fundraising targets begin at £1,600 and go up to £3,900 for 5-month programmes. Funding covers project costs, food, transport, accommodation, training, comprehensive medical cover, expedition staff and in-country support (excluding international flights).
**Contact:** Robert Driver.

### TWIN WORK AND VOLUNTEER ABROAD

**67-71 Lewisham High Street, London, SE13 5JX. ☎0800 804 8380. Fax: 020-8297 0984. E-mail: workabroad@twinuk.com. Website: www.workandvolunteer.com.**
**Programme description:** Range of volunteer programmes in developing countries. Project types include community development, conservation, medical and teaching. Also Work Experience programmes, both paid and unpaid, mostly in Europe (including government-funded vocational training programmes).
**Destinations:** Volunteer programmes in Asia, Africa and South America. Work Experience in Europe.
**Number of placements per year:** 100-120.
**Prerequisites:** Average age of participants 25, with plans to develop the older market. All nationalities accepted, subject to visa requirements. Generally there are no specific skills required, just enthusiasm, an open mind and a willingness to get involved.
**Duration and time of placements:** From 2 weeks to 1 year.
**Selection procedures and orientation:** Some programmes require 3 months

notice, others need much less processing time. Interviews are not required, but some programmes include a UK-based induction programme. All programmes have some form of orientation/induction/training in the host country.
**Other Services:** Accommodation varies. Some programmes offer comfortable fully furnished rooms with en-suite facilities; in other cases, participants will be camping in the wilderness for short periods with limited facilities.
**Cost:** Varying programme costs.
**Contact:** Dai Williams or Caroline Norman.



**VENTURECO WORLDWIDE**
**The Ironyard, 64-66 The Market Place, Warwick CV34 4SD. ☎01926 411122. Fax: 01926 411133. E-mail: mail@ventureco-worldwide.com. Website: www.ventureco-worldwide.com.**
Specialists in Career Gap and Gap Year Ventures in Latin America, Africa and Asia. Unique three-phase Ventures combine a language and cultural orientation, a community development project and a wilderness expedition. ATOL license 5306. Member of the Year Out Group. Development projects are funded by the VentureCo Trust, a UK registered charity.
**Programme description:** Combination of language course, projects and expeditions allows Career Gap travellers to explore off the beaten track, learn about the host country and give something back to the communities where they stay.
**Destinations:** VentureCo have 13 itineraries operating in 19 countries across Latin America, Africa and Asia.
**Number of placements per year:** 175.
**Prerequisites:** Career Gap Ventures for those 21 and over. Gap Year Ventures for ages 17-20. No upper age limit. Must have motivation, enthusiasm and desire to be part of a Venture team.
**Duration and time of placements:** Ventures range from 2 to 15 weeks. Departures year round.
**Selection procedures & orientation:** Open Evenings in London on the first Tuesday of every month. Selection is by an informal induction workshop held in Warwick. Experienced VentureCo leaders accompany small teams of Venturers and provide full expedition training. Planning, leading and organisation roles throughout the Venture are shared amongst the team.

**Cost:** Venture costs range from £500 for a 2-week introductory course, to £1,995 for a 6-week Summer Venture and £4,515 for a full 15-week Career Gap Venture. Cost includes a 3-day Travel Safety Course, all food, accommodation, in-country transport, language tuition, project funding and all expedition activities. Not included: Flights, airport taxes, insurance and visas.
**Contacts:** Helen Pearson, Venture Co-ordinator.

## VOLUNTEER AFRICA – see Health Action Promotion Association

## VOLUNTEER PETEN

**Parque Ecologico Nueva Juventud, San Andres, Peten, Guatemala. ☎(502) 5711-0040. E-mail: volunteerpeten@hotmail.com. Website: www.volunteerpeten.com.**

Not-for-profit organisation which recruits volunteers to help protect and manage a 150-acre reserve in San Andres, to provide environmental education to all the schools in the area, to aid and assist small community organisations, schools, and families, and to provide quality volunteer opportunities for travellers and students.
**Programme description:** Volunteer projects are concerned with Ecological Management or Education. Ecological Management includes maintaining a 150-acre reserve, trail management, gardening, tree nursery management, medicinal plants, reforestation projects, and ecological restoration projects. Education includes environmental education, general education in local schools, library management and activities, extracurricular activities, and adult education. Volunteers also work on various construction projects throughout the year.
**Destinations:** San Andres, Peten, Northern Guatemala.
**Number of placements per year:** 180.
**Prerequisites:** Average age 25. Volunteers should be open-minded and hard working.
**Duration and time of placements:** 4-12 weeks.
**Selection procedures and orientation:** Rolling acceptance of volunteers. Orientation, tour of facilities and projects, use of equipment and tools, and daily supervision by staff.
**Cost:** $350 for 4 weeks, $650 for 8 weeks and $900 for 12 weeks, which includes room and board with local family, training, all activities, and use of resources on a project.
**Contact:** Matthew R. Peters, Director.

## THE VOLUNTEER SITE

**6 Greencroft Avenue, Corbridge, Northumberland, NE45 5DW. ☎01434 632255. E-mail: info@thevolunteersite.com. Website: www.thevolunteersite.com.**

**Programme description:** The Volunteer Site works with small community-based projects to give volunteers the chance to make a contribution to needy causes. Choice of teaching, community work and conservation placements.
**Destinations:** Mexico, including Guadalajara (protecting street children, teaching English, working on an English language newspaper), Tapalpa (education for

indigenous community, work in local state schools), Cuyutlán (preserve coastal and marshland habitats) and Careyes (sea turtle protection).
**Number of placements per year:** 25.
**Prerequisites:** No upper age limit. Patience, flexibility and a willingness to help are essential. Some projects require volunteers to speak Spanish. Experience is useful but not essential.
**Duration and time of placements:** Average 3 months, 1-6 months possible.
**Selection procedures and orientation:** Continuous applications. Pre-departure guidance and in-country induction.
**Cost:** From £1,195/$2,245 for 1 month conservation to £1,795 for 3 months teaching. Prices include homestay with Mexican family and $175 monthly donation to the project. Fundraising advice on application.
**Contact:** Thomas Maskell, Director.

## VSO (VOLUNTARY SERVICE OVERSEAS)

**317 Putney Bridge Road, London SW15 2PN. ☎020-8780 7500. Fax: 020-8780 7300. E-mail: enquiry@vso.org.uk. Website: www.vso.org.uk.**
International development charity which works on long-term partnerships with overseas organisations worldwide. Offices also in Dublin, Ottawa and Utrecht. More detailed information about VSO may be found in the chapter *Doing Something Worthwhile.*
**Programme description:** Volunteers are assigned to suitable projects abroad, primarily in the fields of education, health, natural resources, technical trades and engineering, IT, business, management and social work.
**Destinations:** Worldwide.
**Number of placements per year:** 750+.
**Prerequisites:** Must have professional skills or experience that can be matched with an overseas need. Average age of volunteers is 38; maximum age about 75. High level of commitment required.
**Duration and time of placements:** 1-2 years. Short-term specialist assignments now available for highly experienced professionals who can work at senior levels. Business partnership placements for volunteers from the corporate world who can be seconded for periods of 6-12 months.
**Selection procedures & orientation:** Rigorous selection procedures and extensive training provided.
**Cost:** None. Volunteer receives living expenses and wages in line with local workers, plus various benefits on returning home.

## WORLD CHALLENGE EXPEDITIONS

**Black Arrow House, 2 Chandos Road, London NW10 6NF. ☎020-8728 7200. E-mail: leaderinfo@world-challenge.co.uk. Website: www.world-challenge.co.uk.**
World Challenge Expeditions run skills development programmes for schools and individuals including month-long expeditions worldwide for young people aged 16-18 which require expedition leaders.
**Destinations:** Over 30 destinations in Africa (including Tanzania and Madagascar), Central Asia (including the Himalayas and Mongolia), Southeast Asia (including Borneo and Thailand), and South & Central America (including the Andes and Amazonia).

**Prerequisites:** Expedition leaders must be suitably qualified. Leader Development Programme delivered via World Challenge Leadership & Development Centre, Manchester Road, Buxton, Derbyshire SK17 6ST (01298 767900). Training combines formal training courses (e.g. Mountain Leader training) and selected placements on existing expeditions, either in UK or abroad.
**Duration and time of placements:** 4 or 6 weeks in July/August.
**Contact:** Charlie Eustace, Overseas Leader Recruitment Coordinator.

## WORLDWIDE EXPERIENCE

**Guardian House, Borough Road, Godalming, Surrey GU7 2AE. ☎01483 860560. Fax: 01483 860391. E-mail: info@worldwideexperience.com. Website: www.worldwideexperience.com.**

**Programme description:** Global conservation and community development combined programmes. Worldwide Experience specialises in conservation projects in South Africa working on some of the world's leading Game Reserves, National Parks and Ocean Research projects.
**Destinations:** South Africa, Kenya, Namibia, Sri Lanka, Scotland.
**Number of placements per year:** 100-150.
**Prerequisites:** No particular skills needed but should be passionate about conservation. All nationalities accepted.
**Duration and time of placements:** 2, 4, 8 or 12 weeks. Summer holiday or gap year.
**Selection procedures and orientation:** Applications accepted year round. Interviews are informal and can be done by telephone. Occasional open days are arranged e.g. at South African High Commission in London to meet potential volunteers. Full medical and personal checklist is supplied during preparation.
**Cost:** from £2,100 for a 4-week placement; £4,200 for a 12-week placement, inclusive of international flights, meals, accommodation (furnished and comfortable, shared between two) and placement activities.

## YHA

**Youth Hostels Association Recruitment Department, Trevelyan House, Matlock, Derbyshire DE4 3YH. ☎01629 592656. E-mail: jobs@yha.org.uk. Website: www.yha.org.uk.**

Seasonal hostel assistants are required to help run the YHA's 227 youth hostels in England and Wales.
**Employment available:** Assistants undertake various duties including catering, cleaning, reception work and assisting the manager with all aspects of the day-to-day running of a hostel.
**Number of placements per year:** 300.
**Prerequisites:** Minimum age 18. Experience in one or more of the relevant duties is essential, as are enthusiasm and excellent customer service.
**Duration of employment:** Between February and October.
**Wages:** £720 per month plus accommodation (food optional at £97 per month).
**Selection procedures and orientation:** Recruitment mainly in December and around Easter, with some recruitment and selection events across the winter.

**YOUTHREACH**

**11 Community Centre, Ground Floor, Saket, New Delhi 110017, India. ☎/fax: +91 11-26533520/25/30. ☎+91 11-41649067; +91 11-41664084/5. E-mail: yrd@youthreachindia.org. Website: www.youthreachindia.org.**

**Programme description:** Youthreach matches volunteers with NGOs working to assist disadvantaged children, women and the environment. Tasks for volunteers range from reading to children, teaching academic subjects and art and craft, to skilled professionals contributing their time by building the capacities of the staff/ grassroots workers of NGO partners.
**Destinations:** India.
**Number of placements per year:** 17 foreign volunteers were placed in 2005/6.
**Prerequisites:** Age range 20-40+. All nationalities welcome. Many skills can be put to use from graphic design to occupational therapy (see website).
**Duration and time of placements:** Very flexible – 2-52 weeks.
**Selection procedures and orientation:** Ongoing acceptance. Volunteer expresses preferences before arrival but on arrival visits some possible projects so that a structured volunteering programme can be worked out.
**Other Services:** No accommodation provided. Most foreign volunteers live in guest houses.
**Cost:** nil.
**Contact:** Shveta Bakshi, Manager, NGO partnerships.

# KEY US ORGANISATIONS

Of the thousands of organisations large and small offering programmes of possible interest to North American grown-ups planning a gap year, here is a small selection of important ones for prospective volunteers, travellers or learners:

*Adelante LLC,* 601 Taper Drive, Seal Beach, CA 90740; 562-799-9133; info@adelanteabroad.com; www.adelanteabroad.com. Internships, volunteer placements, teaching abroad, language classes and semester placements from 1-12 months in Spain (Barcelona, Madrid, Seville and Marbella), France (Pontlevoy in the Loire Valley), Costa Rica (San José), Mexico (Oaxaca), Uruguay (Montevideo) and Chile (Vina del Mar/Valparaiso). Prices from $1,650 for 1 month in Chile or Mexico to $5,595 for a semester in Seville.

*AFS International Youth Development,* National Service Center, 198 Madison Avenue, 8th Floor, New York, NY 10016 (800-AFS-INFO; www.usa.afs.org). Full intercultural programme lasting 4/6-12 months in 54 countries for volunteers aged 18-29. Most programmes include language training prior to volunteer placement, homestay accommodation and participation in local voluntary projects.

*Agriventure,* International Agricultural Exchange Association, No. 105, 7710 5th Street SE, Calgary, Alberta T2H 2L9, Canada (canada@agriventure.com). Details of the international farm exchange may be found in the chapter *Working and Living Abroad.*

*AIPT – Association for International Practical Training,* 10400 Little Patuxent Parkway, Suite 250, Columbia, Maryland 21044-3510 (410-997-3069; www.

aipt.org). Short- and long-term placements in more than 80 countries through the International Association for the Exchange of Students for Technical Experience (IAESTE) available to students in science, engineering, math, agriculture or architecture. Other work exchange schemes with selected countries. For example US citizens who have been offered a full-time position in their field of study or experience in the UK may apply for a work permit through the AIPT.

*Alliances Abroad Group,*3 Barton Skwy, Suite 250, 1221 South Mopac Expressway, Austin, TX 78746 (512-457-8062 or 1-888-6-ABROAD; www.allianceabroadgroup.com). Variety of overseas placements including work placements in the UK, France and Australia, teaching in Spain, China and Argentina, and volunteer placements in Ecuador, Costa Rica, Brazil and Peru. Participants pay fees to cover placement, accommodation and emergency insurance, e.g. $850 for summer placement teaching in China, $1,090 for up to a year in Spain living with a family and $1,600 for 3 months in Argentina.

*AmeriSpan,* PO Box 58129, Philadelphia, PA 19102 or 117 S 17th St, Suite 1401, Philadelphia, PA 19103 (800-879-6640 or 215-751-1100; fax (215) 751-1986; info@amerispan.com; www.amerispan.com). Language training organisation operating worldwide that arranges internships lasting 2 weeks to 6 months in many Spanish-speaking countries.

*BUNAC USA,* PO Box 430, Southbury, CT 06488 (800-462-8622; www.bunac.org). Administer a number of work exchange programmes (some open only to students).

*CCUSA (Camp Counselors),* 2330 Marinship Way, Suite 250, Sausalito, CA 94965 (www.ccusa.com). Work Experience programmes in Australia/New Zealand (18-30) and summer camp counsellors in Russia (no upper age limit).

*CDS International Inc,* 871 United Nations Plaza, 15th floor, New York, NY 10017-1814 (212-497-3500; info@cdsintl.org). Executive level internships for young American professionals aged 23-34 in Germany. Programmes also in Russia (ages 25-35), Argentina, Spain and Switzerland.

*CIEE* – Boston: 3 Copley Place, 2nd Floor, Boston, MA 02116 (617-247-0350; info@councilexchanges.org / http://us.councilexchanges.org). Work Abroad programme to Ireland, Canada, Australia, New Zealand, China and Thailand.

*Cross-Cultural Solutions,* 2 Clinton Place, New Rochelle, NY 10801 (1-800-380-4777; info@crossculturalsolutions.org; www.crossculturalsolutions.org). Volunteer projects in Brazil, Costa Rica, China, Ghana, Guatemala, India, Peru, Russia, Tanzania and Thailand.

*Earthwatch Institute,* 3 Clocktower Place, Suite 100, PO Box 75, Maynard, Massachusetts 01754 (1-800-776-0188; www.earthwatch.org). International environmental charity which recruits over 4,000 volunteers a year to assist professional, scientific field research expeditions around the world. Prices range from $700 to $3,600 excluding air travel to location.

*EIL (Experiment in International Living),* Kipling Road, PO Box 676, Brattleboro, Vermont 05302-0676 (802-257-7751; eil@worldlearning.org; www.usexperiment.org). Community service programmes lasting 3-5 weeks include some language training.

*ELTAP (English Language Teaching Assistant Program),* University of Minnesota, Morris, Minnesota 56267 (320-589-6406; craig@educatorsabroad.org; www.eltap.org). Participants bring their native fluency in English to schools in over 25 countries on all continents. Placements last 4-10 weeks throughout the year. $300 placement fee, plus course fee and travel (total usually $3,000-$4,000). Accommodation and board provided by host schools. Available to students and non-credit certificate option for adults.

*Experiential Learning International,* PO Box 9282, Denver, CO 80209 (303-321-8278; www.eliabroad.com). Volunteering programmes in Argentina, Ecuador, India, Ghana, Kenya, Mexico, Nepal, Philippines and Poland; plus intern placements in Ecuador, India, Ghana and Nepal. Sample price for 2 weeks of teaching English at Polish summer school is $995, or in the Philippines $495 placement fee plus $50 a week.

*Explorations in Travel Inc,* 2458 River Road, Guildford, VT 05301 (802-257 0152; www.volunteertravel.com). International volunteers for rainforest conservation, wildlife projects, etc. in Ecuador, Costa Rica, Belize, Guatemala, Puerto Rico, Mexico, Nepal, Australia and New Zealand. Other placements in animal shelters, on small farms and in schools. Placement fees start at around $1,000.

*Foundation for Sustainable Development,* 870 Market St, Suite 231, San Francisco, CA 94102 (tel/fax 415-288-4873; info@fsdinternational.org; www.fsdinternational.org). Short summer and longer term internships for anyone over 18 in the field of development in Argentina, Bolivia, Peru, Ecuador and Nicaragua. Normally volunteers will be expected to converse in Spanish.

*Global Citizens Network,* 130 N Howell St, St. Paul, MN 55104 (800-644-9292; www.globalcitizens.org). Teams of paying volunteers are sent for 1-3 weeks to rural villages in Kenya, Nepal, Mexico, Guatemala, Tanzania, Arizona and New Mexico; programme fee is $1,250-$1,950 plus airfares.

*Global Crossroad,* 11822 Justice Avenue Suite A-5, Baton Rouge, LA 70816 (225-295-4950; info@globalcrossroad.com; www.globalcrossroad.com). Volunteer teaching and internships in 20 countries. Paid teaching in Thailand (3-12 months) and China (1-12 months). Placement fees from $799 for China to $4,399 for 3 months internship in South Africa.

*Global Experiences,* 1010 Pendleton St, Alexandria, VA 22314 (1-877-GE-ABROAD or 1-877-432-2762; admin@globalexperiences.com/ www.globalexperiences.com). Offices in Florence (Italy) and Sydney (Australia). Range of internships for young professionals in Italy, Australia and Ecuador. Intensive language course in Italy followed by work placement. Internships may be in graphic design, business, marketing, IT, fashion, etc. 2-month programme in Florence costs from €3,940.

*Global Service Corps,* 300 Broadway, Suite 28, San Francisco, CA 94133 (www.globalservicecorps.org). Co-operates with grass-roots organisations in Thailand and Tanzania and sends volunteers and interns for two or three weeks or longer.

*GVI Projects International Inc,* Unit 4, 252 Newbury Street, Boston, MA 02116 (888-653 6028; info@gviusa.com; www.gviusa.com). US office of British company of same name (see entry above).

*Global Volunteers,* 375 E Little Canada Road, Little Canada, Minnesota 55117, USA (651-482-0915/toll-free 1-800-487-1074; e-mail@globalvolunteers.org; www.globalvolunteers.org). Non-profit voluntary organisation that sends 1,500 paying volunteers a year to scores of projects lasting from one to three weeks in Africa, Asia, the Caribbean, the Americas and Europe.

*Institute for Cultural Ecology,* PO Box 991, Hilo, Hawaii 96721 (808-640-2333; www.cultural-ecology.com). Academic internships in Fiji, Thailand and Hawaii working on marine biology projects, environmental advocacy or custom-designed projects in participant's field of interest. 4, 8 or 12 weeks. Sample fees: $1,895 for 4 weeks, $3,850 for 12 weeks; 6 weeks of reef mapping on the Fiji coast costs $3,175.

*InterExchange Inc,* 161 Sixth Avenue, New York, NY 10013 (212-924-0446; info@interexchange.org/ www.interexchange.org). Various work programmes including interning in France, the UK and Costa Rica, working in Australia, volunteering in Peru, South Africa, etc. Fees from $495-$3,495.

*International Cultural Adventures,* 81 Jewett St, No. 2, Newton, MA 02458 (888-339-0460; info@ICAdventures.com; www.ICAdventures.com). Cultural, educational and volunteer service experiences in Peru, India (Sikkim) and Nepal. Fees for 6-week summer programmes from $3,050 and from $4,050 for 12-week extended programmes beginning in March, July and September.

*i-to-i,* 190 E 9th Avenue, Suite 350, Denver, CO 80203 (800-985-4864; usca@i-to-i.com). US office of British company i-to-i (see entry in Directory).

*Kibbutz Program Center,* 114 West 26th Street, Suite 1004, New York, NY 10001 (212-462-2764; mail@kibbutzprogramcenter.org). Volunteer placement service for people aged 18-35 for Israeli kibbutzim; $100 registration fee, $250 programme fee.

*Living Routes,* 79 South Pleasant St, Suite 302, Amherst, MA 01002 (413-259-0025; www.LivingRoutes.org). Semester, summer and year-abroad programmes based in eco-villages around the world that help people of all ages gain the knowledge, skills and inspiration to build a sustainable lifestyle. Current programmes in India, Scotland, Australia, Senegal, USA, Mexico, Peru and Brazil.

*NRCSA – National Registration Center for Study Abroad,* Box 1393, Milwaukee, WI 53201 (414-278-0631; inquire@nrcsa.com; www.nrcsa.com). Website has links to study and volunteering or career-focussed internship programmes in Latin America plus Spain, France and Germany.

*Operation Crossroads Africa,* PO Box 5570, New York, NY 10027 (212-289-1949; www.operationcrossroadsafrica.org). 7-week summer projects in Africa and Brazil. $3,500 including airfares.

*Peace Corps,* 1111 20th St NW, Washington, DC 20526 (1-800-424 8580/ www.peacecorps.gov). Sends volunteers on two-year assignments to 138 countries; the average age of volunteers is 28.

*Projects Abroad,* 347 W 36th St, Suite 901, New York NY 10018 (888 839-3535; www.projects-abroad.org). US office of British company Teaching & Projects Abroad (see entry above).

*ProWorld Service Corps,* PO Box 21121, Billings, MT 59104-1121 (877-733-7378; www.proworldsc.org). Internships in Peru, Belize and Mexico lasting 2-26 weeks provide professional experience in variety of fields from business to journalism. $2,485 for first 4 weeks; extendable.

*Schools Without Borders,* 115 Cottingham St, Toronto, Ontario M4V 1B9, Canada (514-284-1929; www.schoolswithoutborders.com). Registered Canadian charity dedicated to fostering youth leadership through 6-month cross-cultural educational and volunteer programmes in Brazil, Nepal, India, Kenya and Thailand.

*Travel Alive Inc,* 1177 S. Lombard Avenue, Oak Park, IL 60304 (toll-free 866-551-1929; info@travelalive.com; www.travelalive.com). Provides Spanish language study, family stay and volunteer opportunities in the community of Ocotal, Nicaragua. Sample prices $1,595 for 4 weeks, $3,125 for 10 weeks.

*Where There Be Dragons,* PO Box 4651, Boulder, CO 80306 (800-982-9203; www.wheretherebedragons.com). 6-week summer programmes including homestays, trekking, service projects, language training, etc. in China, Thailand, Vietnam, Laos, Cambodia, Tibet, India, Mongolia, Mexico, Guatemala,

Peru, Bolivia And Senegal. Adult-only trips are 2-3 weeks and cost from $3,600 (excluding flights).

*Wildlands Studies,* 3 Mosswood Circle, Cazadero, CA 95421 (707-621-5665; www.wildlandsstudies.com). Conservation projects lasting 6 weeks in the US (including Alaska and Hawaii), Belize, Thailand, Nepal, etc.

*World Endeavors,* 2518 29th Avenue South, Minneapolis, MN 55406 (612-729-3400; www.worldendeavors.com). Volunteer, internship and study programmes lasting 2 weeks to 2 months in Brazil, Costa Rica, Ecuador, Philippines, China, Nepal, India, Thailand, Ghana and Jamaica.

*WorldTeach Inc.,* Center for International Development, Harvard University, 79 John F Kennedy Street, Cambridge, MA 02138 (617-495-5527/ 1-800-483-2240; www.worldteach.org). Non-profit organisation that places paying volunteers as teachers of EFL or ESL in countries which request assistance. Currently, WorldTeach provides college graduates for 6 or 12 months to Poland, Costa Rica, Ecuador, China, Namibia, Chile, Guyana, the Micronesian state of Pohnpei and the Marshall Islands for the summer or for the academic year. Prices vary from free (the governments of the Marshall Islands and Pohnpei fully fund volunteer teachers) to $6,000 for a year in Namibia.

# Working and Living Abroad

Who has not dreamed of living in a place far from home, perhaps a favourite holiday destination or a place that lives in your imagination? Perhaps you want to try living elsewhere as an experiment to gauge how you might cope with moving abroad indefinitely. But how can you translate this yearning into the reality of spending an extended period of time somewhere else, of transforming yourself from a tourist into a temporary resident? The choices at your disposal are simply to set up home and stay there, which is expensive without an income (unless you are living in a country with a very low cost of living), to find paid work or to undertake some formal studies. (Volunteering is covered in a separate chapter.)

The reasons why people choose to settle temporarily in a foreign place are multitudinous. Climate is the reason most often cited. Often it's something as straightforward as wanting to be near a partner who comes from that place or been posted there. Living abroad is by far the best way to master a foreign language. Sometimes the urge to spend time abroad is motivated by a simple craving for novelty and curiosity about a place and culture which has caught your attention. Two-week holidays can be unsatisfactory from many points of view and may have engendered a desire to experience a foreign culture from the inside rather than as an onlooker.

Using a gap year to dip your toe into foreign societies and cultures needs to be distinguished from becoming an expatriate, which by definition means that you have taken up residence in another country. On a personal level, it all depends on what you classify as home and how you regard your time abroad. Calling your time abroad a 'career break' implies that you are suspending your normal professional routine temporarily and intend to return to 'real life'. Inevitably these definitions can become blurred over time. It is very common for people who are lucky enough to own a holiday home abroad to increase the percentage of time they spend there.

# Working Abroad

If seeing the world is your motivation for a career break, finding an opportunity to live and work in a foreign country might give you the most rewarding experience. Travelling on its own may not answer your need to get under the skin of a different culture. By setting up a temporary home abroad you'll have the chance to make new friends, learn another language and experience, not just observe, how people in different parts of the world actually live. It will be a challenging experience as you'll need to learn fast and find ways of landing on your feet in a place where customs and laws will be different from those back home.

For those who aren't going to be able to save enough beforehand to fund a long holiday from work or can't rely on an income by renting out their house, money may have to be earned. Taking up paid work on the road may bridge any looming financial crises. This may involve the most menial jobs like picking grapes to more skilled work such as translating technical and academic papers. The latter kind is not always preferable, as **Chris Miksovsky** concluded. He found well paid computer work in both Sydney and Melbourne offices with ease. However after a few months he realised that the reason he had left home was to get away from spending his days in an office, so he headed north to work on a sheep or cattle station and was thrilled with the contrast.

For others, finding work abroad acts as an admission ticket to an unfamiliar society. Above all, if you're hoping to learn a foreign language, it's arguably the best way of creating your own crash course. It will give your gap year structure, particularly if you are spending a lengthy period of time in one place, and it will be a chance to meet the locals in their own habitat and make new friends.

Another great advantage of working abroad is that it will look good on a CV, which is important if you're concerned that a career break might be viewed as an indulgence or wasted time by a prospective employer on returning home. Of course the acquisition of a language will be a plus. So too an intimate knowledge of another country can be used to your advantage in many areas of commerce and the media.

Thirty-year old Australian **Paul Jones** had already given up a full-time position in the IT industry in order to go freelance so had 'gotten over' any anxieties about having a secure job. So when he took the decision to go overseas for a while, he was lucky enough to have the freedom to choose when:

*Having been working for a number of years and having transferable skills in IT, it made sense to find work in Europe in my field to finance my trip. Prior to leaving, I found a job by using the Internet and having interviews over the phone. I still like the fact that I got my first job by having an interview on my mobile phone that was the clearest while standing on a city street that provided a nice drowning out kind of noise. Not the best conditions for an interview but it worked. The job happened to be in the Netherlands where I hadn't particularly wanted to go but that was the job that I was accepted for first, so I took it as a stepping stone. After a number of months in a job I didn't like in a country that I never found an affinity for, I found a job in Bristol which has since been my base and will be until the end of 2006.*

For some fortunate individuals, their employer will arrange for them to live and work abroad. In this case help is automatically provided to navigate the problems of legal status, housing and adapting to a strange culture. However, the nature of your profession or the absence of international postings within a company may prevent you from effortlessly going off to work in New York, Rome or Hong Kong. Many individuals will need to find alternative ways of immersing themselves in a foreign culture without the help of an employer.

Volunteering is popular (see earlier chapter *Doing Something Worthwhile*) because much of the logistical support is set up, either by a charity for whom you'll be working or by a mediating agency that recruits fee-paying volunteers on behalf of local projects. Joining a voluntary project simplifies the process of finding a radically different niche from your usual one. Trying to find some kind of paid work will be more difficult but not impossible.

Working abroad is one of the means by which people can immerse themselves in a foreign culture, to meet foreign people on their own terms and to gain a better perspective on their own culture and habits. The kind of job you find will determine the stratum of society in which you will mix and therefore the content of the experience. The professional who is engaged in a job swap with someone in their profession or who is attached to an overseas office of their old employer will have a less radical break than the adult on a gap year who decides to do something entirely different like teach English in the Far East or scuba dive in the Red Sea.

Sweeping generalisations about the valuable cultural insights afforded by working in a foreign land should be tempered with a careful consideration of the reality of doing a job abroad. True 'working holidays' are rare, though they do exist. For example people have exchanged their labour for a free trip with an outback Australian camping tour operator or a free stay in a Spanish hill resort merely by promising to speak English (mentioned later in this chapter). This is easier if you have certain skills like mechanical or culinary ones. But jobs are jobs wherever you do them, and there is little scope for visiting art galleries and historic sights or even developing a social life if you are stranded in an obscure industrial town teaching English six days a week or manning reception in a damp caravan for a camping holiday operator.

## Visas and Permission to Work

The great hurdle to overcome in gaining work abroad, particularly in popular destinations like the United States and Australia, is obtaining the legal right to work. The situation is much more favourable in the European Union where citizens of any member country can work, live and study in any of the other member states with a minimum of bureaucracy. This is perhaps one of the greatest benefits of the single market, making a working stint in Denmark, Greece, Hungary, Malta, etc. wholly feasible.

The European Union consists of the original 15 member states (Austria, Belgium, Denmark, Finland, France, Germany, Greece, Ireland, Italy, Luxembourg, the Netherlands, Portugal, Spain, Sweden and the United Kingdom) plus the ten that joined May 2004 (Cyprus, Czech Republic, Estonia, Hungary, Latvia, Lithuania, Malta, Poland, Slovakia and Slovenia). Reciprocal transitional controls may be in place in some of the accession states; the consular representatives will be able to advise.

The standard situation among all EU countries is that EU nationals have the right to look for work in any member state for up to three months. At the end of that period they should apply to the police or the local authority for a residence permit, showing their passport and job contract. The residence permit will be valid for five years if the job is permanent or for the duration of the job if it is for less than one year.

Work permits/work visas outside the EU are not readily available. It is easy to understand why most countries in the world have immigration policies that are principally job protection schemes for their own nationals. Nevertheless it can be frustrating to encounter bureaucratic hassles if you are merely taking a break from your employment at home and want to earn a little money by picking up a job here and there on your travels.

The standard procedure for acquiring a work permit or work visa is to find an employer willing to apply to the immigration authorities on your behalf months in advance of the job's starting date, while you are in your home country. This is usually a next-to-impossible feat unless you are a high ranking nuclear physicist, a foreign correspondent or are participating in an organised exchange programme where the red tape is taken care of by your sponsoring organisation. In some countries, an exception is made for special employment categories such as teachers of English and live-in child-carers.

Official visa information should be requested from the Embassy or Consulate of the country you intend to visit; the *Diplomatic List* contains up-to-date contact details for all diplomatic representations in London and is published in print and online by the Foreign & Commonwealth Office (0870 600 5522 to order it from the Stationary Office; www.fco.gov.uk). Being caught working illegally in any country potentially jeopardises any chance to work there in the future or even to visit as a tourist, and may even result in the ignominy of deportation.

For specific information on the red tape governing work in the USA and Australia, see relevant sections below.

## Planning in Advance

At the risk of oversimplifying the range of choices, anyone who aspires to work temporarily abroad must either fix up a definite job before leaving home or take a gamble on finding something on-the-spot. Some jobs can be pre-arranged either through private contacts or by enlisting the help of a mediating organisation or agency but, as in any job hunt, it is much easier to land a job if you can present yourself face-to-face to a prospective employer, which is worth more than any number of speculative applications from home. If nothing else your presence in the flesh reassures the employer that you are serious about working and available to start as soon as a vacancy crops up.

'Easy' ways to fix up a job abroad do exist, for example to teach English in Taiwan, work on an organic farm or look after children for a European family. The price you pay for having this security is that you commit yourself to a new life, however temporary, sight unseen. Wages in these cases are negligible so that these are tantamount to volunteer jobs even if they do require eight hours of work a day.

It is a truism to state that the more unusual and interesting the job, the more competition it will attract. For example it is to be assumed that only a small percentage of applicants for advertised jobs actually get the chance to work as history co-ordinators for a European tour company, assistants at a museum bookshop in Paris or underwater photographic models in the Caribbean. Whereas other less glamorous options can absorb an almost unlimited number of people, for example working as a counsellor or sports instructor on an American children's summer camp.

Secretarial and employment agencies from Brussels to Brisbane can be especially useful to those with the right qualifications. For example Manpower has several thousand branch offices in 72 countries; most addresses are linked from their UK or US sites (www.manpower.co.uk/ www.manpower.com) or try other multinationals like Drake (www.drakeintl.com) and Adecco (www.adecco.com) with 6,600 branches in 70 countries. No matter how briefly you have worked for an agency, request a letter of reference or introduction which may allow you to bypass the typing and other tests if you work for the same company elsewhere.

Reputable international recruitment agencies in Britain, the USA and elsewhere may be looking for personnel qualified in your area of expertise for short-term contracts in fields like accountancy and IT. For example Robert Walters plc with 23 offices in 13 countries (www.robertwalters.com) specialises in recruiting contract staff for jobs worldwide in the fields of accountancy and finance, banking, legal, information technology, sales and marketing, human resources, support and administration. Interviews can be pre-arranged for candidates at their city of arrival and in the case of high calibre candidates, tele-conference links are set up.

## Improving Your Chances

A number of specific steps will improve your chances either of being accepted on an organised work scheme or of convincing an employer in person of your superiority to the competition. For example, before leaving home you might take a course in a foreign language or acquire a portable skill like teaching English as a foreign language, cooking, data processing or sailing – all skills which have been put to good use by people on a gap year working abroad.

Even if you are not lucky enough to have friends and family scattered strategically throughout the world, it is always worth broadcasting your intentions to third cousins, pen friends to whom you haven't written since you were twelve and visiting professors, in case they divulge the addresses of some useful contacts. The more widely publicised your work and travel plans are, the better your chance of being given a lead. Any locals or expatriates you meet after arrival are a potential source of help. Any skill or hobby from jazz to running (e.g. seek out the Hash House Harriers popular with expatriates worldwide) can become the basis for pursuing contacts.

## Job Hunting on Arrival

Not all jobs are found by word-of-mouth or contacts. Local English language newspapers like Mexico City's *The News*, the *Bangkok Post* or the *Athens News* may carry job advertisements appropriate to your situation, or may be a good publication in which to place an advertisement offering your services. If (for example) you want a job translating documents in a company office or teaching English in a school but there appear to be no openings, volunteer to do some unpaid translation or assist with a class one day a week for no pay and if you prove yourself competent, you will have an excellent chance of filling any vacancy which does occur.

Public libraries can be helpful as proved by the Briton who found a directory of wildlife and environmental organisations in a South African library and went on to fix up a board-and-lodging job at a game reserve.

The ease with which you can find work may depend partly on your knowledge of the language, though neither this nor a circle of ready-made friends is essential. The independent and confident traveller quickly accumulates names of contacts and advice from travellers, expats and residents in preparation for setting up a home from home abroad. With the advent of the Internet it's possible to carry out an enormous amount of research and make online contact with relevant companies and organisations before leaving home.

## Seasonal Work

For a complete break from the stresses of a professional life, perhaps casual or seasonal work is the answer. Two categories of employment appeal most to seasonal workers because they appeal least to a stable working population: agriculture and tourism. Farmers from Norway to Tasmania (with the notable exception of developing countries) are not able to bring in their harvests without assistance from outside their local communities, though piece-work apple-picking in Tasmania or strawberry-picking in Denmark is unlikely to appeal to many career breakers. The tourist industry in many areas could not survive without a short-term injection of seasonal labour. Big cities create a wealth of employment opportunities for people not driven to compete in a professional capacity.

While opening up an enormous range of possibilities, the Internet can be a bewildering place to job-hunt. One of the best specialist recruitment websites is www.seasonworkers.com, a site that has been designed to help people conduct a tailored search for a summer job, outdoor sports job, ski resort job, gap year placement or course quickly and easily. In 2004 it won in the 'Best Recruitment' category in the Travel and Tour-ism web awards. Their search system differentiates between courses, gap year placements and paid jobs in many categories, and their chatrooms are busy which helps users get a first hand view of the activity they are considering.

PGL Travel Ltd (Alton Court, Penyard Lane, Ross-on-Wye, Herefordshire HR9 5GL; 0870 401 4411; www.pgl.co.uk/recruitment) run outdoor activity holidays for children in locations around the UK, France and Spain. They employ over 2,500 seasonal staff a year for a huge range of jobs from sailing instructors to drivers, catering staff to French-speaking tour guides.

# TEACHING ENGLISH

Although the English language is still the language which literally millions of people around the world want to learn, finding work as an English teacher has become more difficult in recent years, as an increasing number of people of all ages are acquiring specialised training. The number of public and private institutes turning out certified TEFL teachers in the UK, North America and the Antipodes has greatly increased, creating a glut of teachers chasing the good jobs, especially in the major cities of Europe like Paris and Prague.

Having sounded that warning note, there are still areas of the world where the boom in English language learning seems to know no bounds, from Ecuador to China, Slovakia to Vietnam. A university degree is sufficient to find a respectable job in Thailand, Japan, China, Taiwan and a few others. In small private schools and back-street agencies, being a native speaker and dressing neatly are sometimes sufficient qualifications to get a job. But for more stable teaching jobs in recognised language schools, you will have to sign a contract (usually a year to qualify for a visa). **John Routledge** describes how English teaching can fill a gap year and beyond on the website www.onestopenglish.com:

> *I had been working in south London as a software developer and had had enough of the whole 9 to 5 job culture (it was more like 8 to 6 every day). So I went to Chiang Mai, Thailand's second city. I had only planned to stay for a few months at the most and hadn't considered teaching English. My sister was a teacher in England and from what she told me, it really didn't seem like my kind of thing – lots of lesson planning, low pay and not much respect from the students. Four years and five months later, I'm still here and fully immersed in TEFL teaching. I went for an interview at the university and to my surprise they weren't at all interested in my CELTA or my three years' experience at the private language school. They were most interested with my honours degree. I'm still teaching there now and really enjoying it and never wake up dreading going to work.*

## TEFL Training

The only way to outrival the competition and make the job hunt (not to mention the job itself) easier is to do a training course in Teaching English as a Foreign Language (known as TEFL, pronounced 'teffle'). Intensive Certificate courses are typically delivered over four weeks and cost between £800 and £1000. In the UK the two standard recognised Certificate qualifications that will improve your range of job options are the Cambridge Certificate in English Language Teaching to Adults (CELTA) administered and awarded by the University of Cambridge Local ESOL Exam Unit (address in Resources listing below) and the Certificate in TESOL (Teaching English to Speakers of Other Languages) offered by Trinity College London. Both courses involve at least 100 hours of rigorous training with a practical emphasis (full-time for four weeks or part-time over several months which might suit grown-ups who are not ready to give up their jobs but want to equip themselves for a future break). Although there are no fixed pre-requisites apart from a suitable level of language awareness, not everyone who applies is accepted.

A listing of the 237 centres offering the CELTA course is available from the University of Cambridge in exchange for a large s.a.e. or can be searched on their website www.cambridgeesol.org/teaching. Here is a small selection:

*Basil Paterson Edinburgh Language Foundation,* 66 Queen St, Edinburgh EH2 4NA (0131-556 7695; www.basilpaterson.co.uk). 10 courses per year; £900.

*Ealing, Hammersmith & West London College,* Gliddon Road, London W14 9BL (0800 980 2185; www.hwlc.ac.uk). £805.

*Embassy CES,* International Teacher Training Institute, Gensing Manor, Dane Road, St. Leonards on Sea, Sussex TN38 0QJ (01424 464820; training@studygroup.com). Full-time CELTA courses offered monthly in Hastings, Cambridge and New York.

*Embassy CES,* International Teacher Training Institute, 8 Grange Road, Cambridge, CB3 9DU (01233 311344; lmiller@studygroup.com). Full-time CELTA courses offered four times a year.

*International House,* 16 Stukeley St, Covent Garden, London WC2B 5LQ (from 2007); 020-7518 6928; www.ihlondon.com. Certificate course runs at least monthly; £1,195. Also offers courses at IH Newcastle.

*Language Link,* 181 Earls Court Road, Earls Court, London SW5 9RB (020-7370 4755; www.languagelink.co.uk). £745 full-time, £850 part-time over 12 weeks. Places Certificate holders in its network of affiliated schools in Slovakia, Russia, Vietnam and China.

*St Giles College Highgate,* 51 Shepherd's Hill, London N6 5QP (020-8340 0828; www.tefl-stgiles.com). £925. Also offered at St. Giles in Brighton.

*Stanton Teacher Training,* Stanton House, 167 Queensway, London W2 4SB (020-7221 7259; www.stanton-school.co.uk). £765 including UCLES registration fee of £90.

Centres offering the Trinity College Certificate include:

*EF English First Teacher Training,* 26 Wilbraham Road, Fallowfield, Manchester M14 6JX (0161-256 1400; www.englishfirst.com). EF aims to recruit successful trainees to work for EF schools worldwide. Train and teach programmes available in the UK, Spain, Italy, Czech Republic and South Africa which provides subsided training provided candidates sign 12-month contracts for Indonesia or China, or 9-month teaching contract in Russia.

*The Language Project,* 27 Oakfield Road, Clifton, Bristol BS8 2AT (0117-909 0911; www.languageproject.co.uk). £1,275 including moderation fee. Also offer Introduction to TEFL/TESL (£245 for two-day course).

*Golders Green Teacher Training Centre,* 11 Golders Green Road, London NW11 8DY (020-8731 0963; www.goldersgreen-college.co.uk). 5 week course, £649 plus £105 exam fee.

*Inlingua Teacher Training & Recruitment,* Rodney Lodge, Rodney Road, Cheltenham, Glos. GL50 1HX (01242 253171; training@inlingua-cheltenham.co.uk). £995. Can help place successful candidates in posts in inlingua schools in Ecuador, Italy, Germany, Russia, etc.

*Windsor TEFL,* 21 Osborne Road, Windsor, Berks. SL4 3EG (01753 858995; www.windsorschools.co.uk). Also in London (1-2 Ramillies Street, Off Oxford Street, London W1F 7LN), Barcelona and Madrid. Cost is £906.

Cambridge CELTA courses are offered at nearly 150 overseas centres from the Middle East to Queensland, including ten in the US, among them the following:

*Embassy CES,* 6th Floor, 330 Seventh Avenue, New York, NY 10001 (212-497-8324; www.studygroup.com/embassyces/english).

*International House USA,* 155 'B' Avenue, Suite 220, Lake Oswego, 11, Portland, OR 97034 (503-675-7700; teachertraining@ih-portland.com; www.ih-usa.com). Also offers courses in San Francisco and Santa Monica. $2,200.

*St Giles Language Teaching Center,* One Hallidie Plaza, Suite 350, San Francisco, CA 94102 (415-788-3552; www.stgiles-usa.com). $2,790.

Other centres for American readers to consider are *Transworld Schools,* 701 Sutter St, 6th Floor, San Francisco, CA 94109 (1-888-588-8335/415-928-2835; www.transworldschools.com), San Diego State University/American Language Institute, 50 Campanile Drive, San Diego, CA 92115-1914 (619-594-8740;

www.americanlanguage.com/home.html) and the Boston Language Institute (648 Beacon St, Boston, MA 02215; www.teflcertificate.com) which offer highly regarded *sui generis* certificates with extensive job placement assistance.



Many advantages can be gained by signing up for a TEFL course in the place where you want to work, from Barcelona to Bangkok. Most TEFL training centres have excellent contacts with language schools and can assist with the job hunt. For example the Boland School offers intensive teacher training diploma programmes in Brno (Czech Republic), Hong Kong and two locations in China; contact details on www.boland-czech.com and www.boland-china.com. Demanding 148-hour 4-week graded courses lead to an International TEFL Diploma qualification. The cost is €1,300 in the Czech Republic (plus €285 for accommodation) and €1,250 in China (plus €285-€300 for single-room accommodation).

Scores of other independent providers provide TEFL training courses of varying lengths, including:

*Bridge-Linguatec Language Services,* 915 S. Colorado Blvd, Denver, CO 80246, USA (tefl-celta@bridgelinguatec.com; www.bridgetefl.com). Language training company which offers TEFL teacher certification and job placement programmes in Asia, Europe and Latin America. Also offers online TEFL course. TEFL training (2-4 weeks) available in Argentina, Brazil, Chile, China, Costa Rica, Czech Republic, Mexico, Peru, Spain, and the USA.

*TEFL International,* 1200 Belle Passi Road, Woodburn, OR 97071, USA (866-384-8854; http://teflinternational.com). Also office in Thailand: 38/53-55 Moo 1, Klaeng, Muang Rayong 21160 (+66 38-652280; info@teflint.com). 130-hour certificate course offered in Thailand and many other countries including England, France, New Zealand, Egypt and China. $1,390-$1,490 (excludes private accommodation).

*World TEFL School,* Head Office: 122-126 High Road, London NW6 4HY (0800 073 1028 or 020-7692 4217; USA: 214-347-4406; www.worldteflschool.com). Weekend and 4-week Advanced TEFL courses can be taken in the UK, France, Spain, Italy, Greece, Czech Republic, Thailand, Australia, Argentina or Costa Rica. Cost of Advanced 120-hour course varies among locations but mostly £800-£900 apart from Buenos Aires (£570). Weekend course costs £225 or £294 with personal career consultation. Volunteer teaching programmes available in Thailand, Vietnam, Cambodia, Costa Rica and Sri Lanka.

A number of centres worldwide offer TEFL training which varies enormously in quality and price. Short introductory courses are mainly intended to act as preparatory programmes for more serious courses; yet many people who hold just a short certificate go on to teach.

*i-to-i,* Woodside House, 261 Low Lane, Horsforth, Leeds LS18 5NY (0870 333 2332; www.i-to-i.com). Intensive 20-hour weekend TEFL training courses at venues throughout the UK, Ireland, USA and Australia (£195). Online TEFL course also available from any location worldwide. Online courses include online tutor back-up and CD ROM. Price £195/US$295. Free taster TEFL course online at www.onlinetefl.com. i-to-i also arranges paid teaching placements in China, Poland, Korea, Thailand and Turkey.

*INTESOL (International TESOL Training),* 4 Higher Downs, Knutsford, Cheshire WA16 8AW (01565 631743; www.intesoltesoltraining.com). Distance Learning Introductory Certificate in TESOL: £195. Also offer combined programme with residential fortnight following 2 weeks home study available in Leeds, Barcelona, Prague, Singapore, Crete and Cusco. Partnered with Hunt-esl.com which advertises TEFL vacancies (e.g. in Korea) of interest to 'career gappers, university graduates and travellers'.

*Saxoncourt Teacher Training,* 59 South Molton St, London W1Y 1HH (020-7499 8533; www.saxoncourt.com). 5-day foundation TEFL course available free to graduates who have a job offer to teach in Japan, Taiwan or China with Shane English Schools.

## TEFL Resources

*Teaching English Abroad* by Susan Griffith (Vacation-Work, £12.95). The 2007 edition is the definitive guide to short and long-term opportunities for trained and untrained teachers.

*British Council,* Information Centre, Bridgewater House, 58 Whitworth St, Manchester M1 6BB (0161-957 7755; www.britishcouncil.org). Distributes information on getting started in TEFL (www.britishcouncil.org/english/quals.htm).

*University of Cambridge ESOL Examinations,* 1 Hills Road, Cambridge CB1 2EU (01223 553355; esol@ucles.org.uk; www.cambridgeesol.org/teaching. Administers the Cambridge Certificate in English Language Teaching to Adults (CELTA) and other specialised qualifications in English Language Teaching.

*Trinity College London*, 89 Albert Embankment, London SE1 7TP (020-7820 6100; www.trinitycollege.co.uk). Administers the Certificate in TESOL (Teaching English to Speakers of Other Languages). Course locations provided on website.

## What English Teaching Involves

It is difficult to generalise about what work you will actually be required to do once hired. At one extreme you have the world traveller who is hired by a businessman to correct English pronunciation on a one-to-one basis and at the other you get teachers contracted to teach a gruelling 30 hour week split between early morning and evening classes requiring extensive preparation.

Native speaker teachers are nearly always employed to stimulate conversation rather than to teach grammar. Yet a basic knowledge of English grammar is a great asset when pupils come to ask awkward questions. The book *English Grammar in Use* by Raymond Murphy is recommended for its clear explanations and accompanying student exercises (2004 edition, £15.56 excluding postage from CUP with CD-ROM and practice book; www.cambridge.org). Other useful books for unsupported English teaching placements include *Getting Beginners to Talk* by Jim Wingate (Prentice Hall) and *Lessons from Nothing* by Bruce Marsland (Cambridge).

Each level and age group brings its own rewards and difficulties. Beginners of all ages usually delight in their progress which will be much more rapid than it is later on. Not everyone, however, enjoys teaching young children (a booming area of TEFL from Portugal to Taiwan) which usually involves sing-songs, puzzles and games. Intermediate learners (especially if they are adolescents) can be difficult, since they will have reached a plateau and may be discouraged. Adults are usually well-motivated though may be inhibited about speaking. Teaching professionals and business people is almost always well paid. Discipline is seldom a problem, at least outside Western Europe. In fact you may find your pupils disconcertingly docile and possibly also overly exam-oriented.

Most schools practise the direct method (total immersion in English) so not knowing the language shouldn't prevent you from getting a job. Some employers may provide nothing more than a scratched blackboard and will expect you to dive in using the 'chalk and talk' method. If you are very alarmed at this prospect you could ask a sympathetic colleague if you could sit in on a few classes to give you some ideas. Brochures picked up from tourist offices or airlines can be a useful peg on which to hang a lesson. If you're stranded without any ideas, write the lyrics of a pop song on the board and discuss.

The wages paid to English teachers are usually reasonable, and in developing countries are quite often well in excess of the average local wage. In return you will be asked to teach some fairly unsociable hours since most private English classes take place after working hours, and so schedules split between early morning and evening are not at all uncommon.

It is also possible to arrange an informal exchange of English conversation for discounted accommodation or lessons in the destination language. Englishtown is a unique programme whereby a holiday village in Spain (between Madrid and Barcelona) is 'stocked' with native English speakers and Spanish clients who want to improve their English. The English native-speaking volunteers participate alongside the Spanish adults in an intensive eight days of activities, sports, games and group dynamics and, in exchange for making English conversation, receive free room and board. All they have to do is cover the travel expenses to Madrid and then agree to chat and exchange stories. Participants come from all over the world and the average age is 40. More information is available from Vaughan (Pueblo Inglés Vaughan, Rafael Calvo 18, 4ºA, 28010 Madrid, Spain; +34 91-391 3400; www.vaughanvillage.com).

Of course many people on an extended break teach English on a voluntary basis. For them adulation is better than wages. **Peter and Debra Hardy** from Devon aged 46 and 51 decided to take time out to do some voluntary teaching in Thailand through *Starfish Ventures*. Pete had to negotiate unpaid leave from his job as a veterinary practice manager, which was the major limiting factor on their time:

> *We can both honestly say that it was one of the great experiences of our lives, and if anybody is debating whether to embark on a Starfish project, then do it. I have never taught before, but the intensive weekend TEFL course set me up well for the job. I was a bit apprehensive on my first day teaching, but I needn't have been. The Thai kids are wonderful – very keen to learn, very respectful, and a total joy! After a busy but hugely enjoyable English Camp at one school, we even taught the kids to play rounders and cricket! My only regret was that we were only there for one month – I could happily have stayed for many more. The Starfish organisers in Surin were a fountain of knowledge and helped us arrange trips on our days off to Kho Samet, Cambodia and Kho Chang (don't miss that one!)... We are now trying to persuade all our friends to get off their backsides and be volunteers!*

Pete's wife Debra sounded an equally enthusiastic note and reflects on the after-effects of the experience:

> *We had always wanted to undertake voluntary work overseas, but were restricted by a perceived lack of qualifications, experience and funds. With our offspring away at university, it suddenly seemed like a good time to dip our toes in the water. We met so many interesting and inspiring people, experienced wildly different cultures first hand, and found we could survive being completely outside our comfort zone. Working as part of a community is completely different to being a tourist, just being a tourist seems very detached or superficial now! The combination of the two works very well though. Interestingly, on our return, Peter is really energised. We have never been very materialistic, but we are both even less interested in possessions now; living perfectly well with minimal belongings reinforced this. Witnessing true poverty – families with hardly any belongings let alone furniture, carpets, etc. – certainly makes you think about our insatiable western appetites for 'things'. I wonder if I need so many serving bowls, candles as decorations, drawers and drawers of stuff....*

## English for Specific Purposes

English for Specific Purposes (ESP) refers to the practice of teaching groups of employees the specific vocabulary they will need in their jobs, preferably by a native speaker of English with experience of that job. This means that anyone with a professional background such as business, banking, tourism, medicine, science and technology, secretaries, etc. can try to be matched to an appropriate group of language learners from airline staff to exporters. They want lessons in which they can pretend to be telephoning a client or chasing a missing order. People on a gap year are often far more suited to this kind of teaching than a freshly qualified TEFL teacher would be.

When applying to an organisation which serves this business market, try to demonstrate your commercial flair with a polished presentation including a business-like CV. **Andrew Sykes** felt that he owed the success of his job-hunt in Tours to his experience of accountancy rather than to his TEFL Certificate:

> *I wrote to lots of schools in France and elsewhere that didn't stipulate 'experience required' and was fairly disheartened by the few, none-too-encouraging replies along the lines of 'if you're in town, give us a call.' Sitting in a very cheap hotel bedroom halfway down Italy in early November feeling sorry for myself and knowing that I was getting closer and closer to my overdraft limit and an office job back in the UK, I rang the schools that had replied. 'Drop in,' the voice said, 'and we will give you an interview'. So I jumped on the next train, met the director on Monday and was offered a job on the Tuesday morning, initially on an hour-by-hour basis and then in December on a contract of 15 hours which was later increased to 20 hours a week.*
>
> *What got me the job was not my TEFL certificate nor my good French. It was the fact that I was an ex-accountant. I had been one of the thousands enticed by the financial benefits of joining an accountancy firm after graduation. But I hated the job and failed my first professional exams. Ironically the experience gained during those years of hell was invaluable because in France most employers are looking for business experience (whereas in Italy they want teaching experience).*

You will in the end be teaching people not objects, and any experience you can bring to the job (and especially the job interview) will help. However ashamed you may be of telling everyone in the pub back home that you were once a rat catcher, it may be invaluable if the school's main client is Rentokil.

## The Job Hunt

Printed advertisements have been largely replaced by the Internet, so it is hardly worth checking ads in Tuesday's *Guardian* (which at one time carried many TEFL ads, especially between February and June) when you can check TEFL jobs online at http://jobs.guardian.co.uk. Most advertisers are looking for teachers who have some training or experience but in some cases, a carefully crafted CV and enthusiastic personality are as important as EFL training and experience.

For schools, a website advert offers an easy and instantaneous means of publicising a vacancy to an international audience. People looking for employment can use search engines to look for all pages with references to EFL, English language schools and recruitment. CVs can be e-mailed quickly and cheaply to advertising schools, who can then use e-mail themselves to chase up references. Arguably it has become a little too easy to advertise and answer job adverts online. At the press of a button, your CV can be clogging up dozens, nay, hundreds of computers. But everywhere you look on the Internet, potentially useful links can be found, many of them leading to Dave Sperling's ESL Café (www.eslcafe.com) which so expertly dominates the field that it is hard for others to compete (though dozens try). 'Dave' provides a mind-boggling but well-organised amount of material for the future or current teacher including first hand accounts. It also provides links to specific institutes and chains in each country.

After sweating his way through a CELTA course one summer, **Fergus Cooney** (an aspiring musician from Scotland) turned to the Internet to find a job:

*After installing myself in the cheapest net café in Edinburgh I began reading and posting e-mails here, there and everywhere. I also posted a message on Dave's eslcafe.com, a message stating 'Qualified teacher seeking job'. Within two days I was inundated with many dozens of replies requesting my CV and, more surprising, with job offers everywhere from Andorra to Zonguldak, through Italy, Poland, Turkey, Russia and too many to count from Korea, Taiwan and China. Jackpot, I thought. (I have since realised that many schools/agents must have an automatic reply system that e-mails those who advertise in the way I did.) I quickly began sifting through the replies but not as quickly as they kept arriving in my inbox. Before a few days had passed, I had become utterly confused and had forgotten which school was which, which Mr. Lee-Soo was which, etc. So I deleted them all, got a new e-mail address and posted a second more specific message on Dave's: 'Teacher with degree + CELTA seeks job in Italy/Spain.' This had the desired effect. A couple of days later my inbox began to fill though not overflow with replies. I still had to delete many from China etc. but could work with the rest and chose a school in Calabria…*

A choice he later came to regret but that is another story.

Among the most productive and popular ELT recruitment sites are www.TEFL.com; www.jobs.edufind.com; www.englishjobmaze.com; www.free-esl.com; www.eslemployment.com and www.esljobs.com. Other websites that are country-specific include www.ohayosensei.com (jobs in Japan) and www.ajarn.com (teaching in Thailand).

A wealth of opportunities exists for untrained but eager volunteers willing to pay an agency to place them in a language teaching situation abroad. For example *IST Plus* runs the Teach in Thailand and Teach in China programmes for graduates up to the age of 65. *i-to-i* (address above) has a host of teaching placements in countries around the world, as do *Teaching & Projects Abroad, Travellers Worldwide, Sudan Volunteer Programme* and others with entries in the Directory.

On the basis of **Sheona Mckay's** time off, she would thoroughly recommend gap year projects for personal development and fun. However she is not sure why most gap year companies charge such a huge amount to the volunteers. She managed to set up her own project as a volunteer teacher in Peru through a personal contact for free:

*Especially for people wanting to teach English, I think it is easy enough to find out the names of some schools in an area you are interested in working in. Then you can e-mail the school directly and hopefully come to an agreement with them. On the other hand maybe for first-time travellers the security of back-up from an organisation is necessary and worth the money. I wasn't expecting the school I taught in to be so well off and perhaps another time would try to find a poorer school where I would feel as though I had made a bigger difference to the children's education and lives.*

## On the Spot

Jobs in any field are difficult to get without an interview, and English teaching is no different. In almost all cases it is more effective to go to your preferred destination, CV in hand, and call on language schools and companies. Consult the British Council in your destination and the *Yellow Pages* online in order to gather together a list of addresses where you can ask for work. Read the adverts in the English language papers. Contact business schools and major businesses particularly in a field with which you are familiar to find out if they can use a teacher of commercial English or English for Specific Purposes.

## Freelancing

An alternative to working for a language school is to set yourself up as a freelance private tutor. While undercutting the fees charged by the big schools, you can still earn more than as a contract teacher. Normally you will have to be fairly well established in a place before you can attempt to support yourself by private teaching, preferably with some decent premises in which to give lessons (either private or group) and with a telephone.

It is always difficult to start teaching without contacts and a good working knowledge of the language. When you do get started, it may be difficult to earn a stable income because of the frequency with which pupils cancel. It is unrealistic for a newly arrived freelancer to expect to earn enough to live on in the first six months or so.

Getting clients for private lessons is a marketing exercise, and all the avenues that seem appropriate to your circumstances have to be explored. Here are some ways you can market yourself:

- Put a notice up in schools and universities, supermarkets or corner shops, and run an advertisement in the local paper if you have the use of a telephone.
- Send neat notices to local public schools, announcing your willingness to ensure the children's linguistic future.
- Compile a list of addresses of professionals (lawyers, architects, etc.) who may need English for their work and have the resources to pay for it. Then contact them.
- Call on export businesses, distribution companies, perhaps even travel agencies.

These methods should put you in touch with a few hopeful language learners. If you are good at what you do, word will spread and more paying pupils will come your way, though the process can be slow.

If you are more interested in integrating with the local culture than making money, exchanging conversation for board and lodging may be an appealing possibility. This can be arranged by answering (or placing) small ads in appropriate places. The American Church in Paris notice board is famous for this.

# WORKING IN TOURISM

The travel and tourism industry employs a staggering 72 million people. A season of working as a tour guide, holiday rep or sports instructor might exactly suit someone taking a gap year though, on the whole, the work is hard and the pay low.

For people pursuing a career related to travel and tourism, it would be worth looking at another Vacation-Work Publications title *Working in Tourism* (£11.95). A selection of recruitment websites offer job-seekers access to global seasonal employment opportunities at all levels within the catering, leisure & travel industries.

Everywhere you look on the Internet, potentially useful links can be found. A surprising number of tour operators and other travel company home pages feature a Recruitment or Human Resources icon which you can click to find out about jobs with that operator. A host of websites promises to provide free online recruitment services for people looking to work overseas; search for jobs in Travel & Tourism on some of the big recruitment sites like www.voovs.com, www.doctorjob.com and www.hotrecruit.co.uk. For non-professional openings abroad, check out the non-commercial free Jobs Abroad Bulletin (www.payaway.co.uk), www.anyworkanywhere.com, www.jobsmonkey.com (especially for North America) and www.transitionsabroad.com, among many others. JobSlave.com, newly launched by findaGap.com, aims to cover everything from bar jobs in Sydney to IT internships in America.

The glossy independent travellers' monthly magazine *Wanderlust* (01753 620426; www.wanderlust.co.uk) advertises vacancies with adventure travel companies. In its Job Shop column you might expect to find ads for tour leaders in the Eastern Mediterranean or in Latin America for Spanish speaking guides aged 25-35. Opportunities for cycle holiday leaders or hill-walking guides are also notified in specialist outdoor magazines. Often a first aid certificate and driving licence are required and in some cases a specialist certificate such as the MLTB (Mountain Leader Training).

Many tourist destinations are in remote places where there is no local pool of labour. Itinerant job-seekers have ended up working in hotels in some of the most beautiful corners of the world from the South Island of New Zealand to Lapland. People with some training in catering will probably find themselves in demand. In addition to hotel and restaurant kitchens, cooks and chefs can put their talents to good use in a range of venues from luxury yachts to holiday ranches, safari camps to ski chalets.

## Resorts

It is not at all unusual for people who have been working in business or industry for a few years to want to work in the sun for a while. Mediterranean resorts in places like the Canaries, Ibiza and Corfu are bursting at the seams with tourist establishments that need to be staffed – mostly by young party animals.

But if you target the right resorts and the right companies, you can find something suitable for a grown-up gap year. More mature candidates may be appreciated by companies catering to that market, a hope expressed by a woman from Yorkshire who posted a request for relevant information on the 'Living and Working Abroad' branch of Lonely Planet's Thorntree website (http://thorntree.lonelyplanet.com):

> *I've done the career thing: 17 years in banking, finishing up as a relatively senior manager. But I'm opting out of the rat race now with a handy redundancy payment in my pocket. I passionately want to live on an unspoilt Greek island. I don't mind being paid peanuts, a pit for accommodation is fine, and a bicycle is an improvement on the transport I'll have in the UK (my feet). I haven't applied to just an ordinary holiday company but rather*

*to a specialist in unspoilt Greek islands. Their prices are a little higher and their clientele a little older. I should know since I've holidayed with them four times. Each time the rep was over 30 and once he was over 50 so I don't worry about being too old.*

## Hostels

At the age of 29, it hadn't occurred to **Debra Fuccio** to strap on a backpack until she spent time working in a travellers' hostel in San Francisco and met a series of creative travellers. They inspired her to save like mad and make a trip to the part of Italy from which her family originates. By making use of the international hostel site www.hostels.com, Debra had little difficulty pre-arranging a hostel job:

*I was working at a really cute, small hostel in Rome called Hostel Casanova and was working 7 days a week (I was a bit scared about running out of money since this was the first leg of the trip). As well as getting to stay there for free, they paid me 20 euros per day in cash which was really nice. Rome was so cheap (from a San Francisco point of view) and with great weather, it was easy to save. I came to Italy with $700 cash and a plane ticket, I left with about $600 and a plane ticket to England and Ireland. I was there about 5 weeks total.*

So smitten was Debra with the travelling life that since then she has worked in hostels in Ireland and San Francisco, set up an e-magazine about travelling, taught English in Taiwan, studied Spanish in Argentina and in 2006 is taking more Spanish lessons, trekking and travelling around Guatemala while blogging on http://blogs.bootsnall.com/travelgoddess.

## Tour Operators

A list of special interest and activity tour operators (to whom people with specialist skills can apply) is available from AITO, the Association of Independent Tour Operators (33A St Margaret's Road, Twickenham TW1 1RG; www.aito.co.uk). In the US, search the website of the *Specialty Travel Index* (www.specialtytravel.com).

**When Roger Turski came to a crisis in his career and wanted a gap year, he knew immediately that he wanted to go to Africa to work at a safari lodge, and was able to arrange this with the help of a small agency that specialises in making placements in eco-tourism in Africa and Asia:**

*I decided I needed a career sabbatical and wanted to combine this with my passion for the African Bush. At 39 years of age my desire was to spend time through voluntary work at a Game Lodge in Southern Africa. Within a few clicks of the Internet I came across The Leap, and after a call to the director, I knew I had found the kind of thing I was looking for. I was thrilled at the type of experiences on offer which were much closer to the career sabbatical I was after than some normal gap year projects.*

*My time in Botswana was nothing short of magical. The safari company has four lodges as part of their operation (three in Botswana and one in Zambia) and I spent time in all of them learning and experiencing a life that few imagine possible. Realising that I was there to work, I was quite happy to be given tasks that utilised some of my city-borne skills. Initially I helped the company resolve some logistical issues they were having with maintaining correct levels of food and general supplies within each lodge. In doing this I picked up some new skills along the way and have come away with a rudimentary but solid knowledge of how to run a safari operation. Eventually I moved on to helping with relief management of the camps whilst the permanent managers were on leave. This was quite a responsibility as the guests pay a premium price for a luxury safari holiday and demand the service that goes with it. I did of course have many, many opportunities to see the wildlife. Some events will stay with me for the rest of my life. Coming across your first pride of lions, alone in a completely open vehicle, is quite an experience.*

## Special Events

Great bursts of tourist activity take place around major events which require armies of people to work. For example the last Olympic Games in Athens relied on an army of tens of thousands of people to work as volunteers. As is commonplace at high profile international sporting events, people who work on-site are normally doing so merely for the thrill of being part of the action. Volunteers who are neither paid nor provided with accommodation are invited to work eight-hour shifts for a minimum of ten days. Sports lovers planning a career break in 2008 might like to keep their eye on the press for opportunities in Beijing or Vancouver in 2010 where the Winter Olympics are due to take place.

## Overland Tour Leaders

Leaders are needed to escort groups on tours within Europe by a range of companies. Drivers need to have a Passenger Carrying Vehicle (PCV) or a Heavy Goods Vehicle (HGV) licence, which costs several hundred pounds to obtain. Working in Africa, Asia and Latin America as an adventure tour leader is usually only for people in their late 20s and 30s willing to train for one of the specialist licences and with some knowledge of mechanics. Competent and well-travelled expedition staff (including cooks) are in demand by the many overland companies and youth travel specialists which advertise their tours and occasionally their vacancies in magazines like the London giveaway *TNT* (www.tntmagazine.com/uk/jobzone) or in the Jobshop column of *Wanderlust* magazine.

Here is an annotated list of overland operators; others are listed on the Overland Expedition Resources website www.go-overland.com.

*Dragoman Overland Expeditions,* Operations Department, Camp Green, Kenton Road, Debenham, Suffolk IP14 6LA (01728 861133; www.dragoman.co.uk). Have a good reputation and look for leader drivers over 25 willing to train for the PCV licence in their workshops (if they don't already have one). Minimum commitment of two years for expeditions to Africa, Asia, South and Central America.

*Exodus,* Grange Mills, Weir Road, London SW12 0NE (0870 240 5550; www.exodus.co.uk/vacancies.html). Suitable candidates (aged 25-32) can acquire the appropriate licence during the months of training. Ages 25-32. Knowledge of Italian, Spanish, French or Japanese highly valued.

*Explore Worldwide Ltd,* Nelson House, 55 Victoria Road, Farnborough, Hampshire GU14 7PA (0870 333 4002; www.explore.co.uk/worldwide/

tourleaders.jsp). Europe's largest adventure tour operator employing more than 100 tour leaders for Europe, Africa, Asia and the Americas. Must obtain first aid certificate and preferably have a second language. Training given.

*Intrepid Travel* – www.intrepidtravel.com/employmentgrp.php. Applications accepted online only. 'Intrepid Group Leaders come from all walks of life – corporate executives, nurses, landscape gardeners, even rock band roadies'.

*Kumuka Worldwide,* 40 Earl's Court Road, London W8 6EJ (020-7937 8855; www.kumuka.com). Looking for qualified diesel mechanics with a PCV licence to be drivers. Tour leaders (age 23+) chosen according to experience and personality.

*Tucan Travel,* 316 Uxbridge Road, Acton, London W3 9QP (020-8896 1600; www.tucantravel.com). Tour drivers and tour leaders hired for South American trips.

The job of expedition tour leader may sound glamorous but it can be daunting unless you know well the countries and places through which you will be expected to chaperone your group. The journalist Rosemary Behan who took her own gap year in 2006 gave an account in the *Daily Telegraph* of a small group tour she joined in southwest China:

> *Our group numbered seven plus our Australian guide. We were concerned to learn that she had never been to China before, but we hoped for the best. It soon became clear that our guide was seriously out of her depth, barely managing to shepherd us on to local buses and trains, let alone give us the expert insight into the country we had all hoped for. On the other hand, simply having someone to take responsibility for our daily transport and accommodation needs did allow us more time for reflection.*

Any competent sailor, canoeist, diver, climber, rider, skier, etc. might be able to market his or her skills abroad. If you would like to do a watersports course with a view to working abroad, you should investigate courses by *Flying Fish, Plas Menai and Nonstop Adventure*; for further information see relevant entries in the Directory and also the sections on Sports Courses in the chapter 'New Skills and New Projects'.

## Ski Resorts

Ski resorts generate many vacancies in the tourist industry. Staff are needed to operate the ski tows and lifts, to be in charge of chalets, to patrol the slopes, to dispense and maintain hired skis and of course to instruct would-be skiers. Either you can try to fix up a job with a British-based ski tour company before you leave (which has more security but lower wages and tends to isolate you in an English-speaking ghetto), or you can look for work on the spot where there will be a lot of competition from the young and footloose.

Specialist online ski recruitment agencies will be of interest: Free Radicals (www.freeradicals.co.uk), Natives (www.natives.co.uk), www.findaskiresortjob.com and the smaller Ski Staff (www.skistaff.co.uk) all match job-seekers with alpine vacancies. Free Radicals for example calls itself a one-stop shop for ski season jobs for Europe and America, while Natives.co.uk declares itself simply to be the 'Season Workers' website', where many ski jobs as well as summer jobs are posted before the season.

The sixth edition of *Working in Ski Resorts* (Vacation Work, 2006; £12.95) contains many addresses of ski companies and details of the job hunt in individual European and North American resorts. In response to the thousands of enquiries about alpine jobs which the Ski Club of Great Britain receives, it distributes *The Alpine Employment Fact Sheet*; send £3 and an s.a.e. to the SCGB, 57-63 Church Rd, Wimbledon SW19 5SB; 020-8410 2000; www.skiclub.co.uk).

For ski instructing courses see entries for *Basecamp Group, International Academy, Nonstop Adventure* and *Peak Leaders.*

**Rhona Stannage,** a Scottish solicitor, and her husband Stuart applied to all the companies they could find addresses for:

> *Only one company gave us an interview. No one else would touch us because we were too old (i.e. 28), married and had no experience in the catering trade. Skibound gave us both jobs as chalet girls (yes, Stuart signed a 'chalet girl' contract) working in a four-person chalet with a manageress and a qualified chef. The wages were dire (as expected) but we got free ski passes, accommodation in our own apartment and food. Stuart was a bit worried about the uniform but it was only a purple T-shirt.*

Some chalet companies hire older applicants; for instance Snowline (140-142 Wandsworth High St, London SW18 4JJ; 020-8870 4807; www.snowline.co.uk) welcomes applications from 'couples and mature applicants' to do a winter season in Val d'Isère, Méribel, La Tania or Morzine. Le Ski (www.leski.com) is another company that will consider older applicants to manage chalets in France. In fact a few seasons ago they hired **Susan and Eric Beney** (who were old enough to have a daughter the same age as Rhona in the previous quotation):

> *We took pot luck with the resort and on reflection should have done a bit more homework on resorts. La Tania was very limited; La Plagne would have been one hundred percent better. We worked long hours, six days a week, and were probably a bit too conscientious due to our age (we have just become grandparents). It's still a good way to experience a season in the Alps, but just be prepared to be overworked and underpaid. Listen to the young folk who have got the work down to a fine art and really know how to cut corners since they are there to ski and socialise.*

## Resources for Living and Working Abroad

*Vacation Work* (www.vacationwork.co.uk) publishes the 'Live and Work' series for specific regions/countries: Australia & New Zealand; Belgium, Netherlands & Luxembourg, China, France, Germany, Ireland, Italy, Japan, Portugal, Saudi & the Gulf, Scandinavia, Scotland, Spain, and finally the USA & Canada, all between £10.99 and £12.95.

*Live and Work Abroad: A Guide For Modern Nomads* by Huw Francis and Michelyne Callan (Vacation Work, £11.95). By two experienced expats, everything you need to know about finding your feet as the resident of a foreign country.

*Work Your Way Around the World* by Susan Griffith (Vacation Work, £12.95). The definitive guide (if I am permitted to say so) to picking up short-term work to pay for your adventures.

*Working Abroad: The Complete Guide to Overseas Employment* by Jonathan

Reuvid (Kogan Page, 2006, £12.99).

*Careers Europe,* Onward House, Baptist Place, Bradford BD1 2PS (01274 829600; www.careerseurope.co.uk). Produce the Eurofacts and Globalfacts series of International Careers Information, and Exodus, the Careers Europe database of international careers information, all of which can be consulted at local Connexions and Jobcentre Plus offices in the UK.

*EURES (EURopean Employment Service)* – http://europa.eu.int/eures/index.jsp. Searchable database of vacancies. Europe-wide employment service operates as a network of EuroAdvisers who have specialist expertise on living and working in other member states.

*Payaway.co.uk* – Non-commercial website dedicated to international short term work. It has a free e-mail newsletter, the monthly *Jobs Abroad Bulletin,* with specific vacancies round the world.

## INTERNATIONAL JOB EXCHANGES

Even though you will be performing the same job on a job swap as you do at home, it will involve a significant change in your life and therefore qualifies as a gap year for grown-ups. You'll have the chance to relocate abroad, meet new colleagues and put yourself in a new, challenging environment. If you're keen to live abroad without giving up your job and its income then this could be an ideal way of taking a break from the usual routines at home and work.

Employees of multinational companies are sometimes lucky enough to be offered a posting abroad so that their career break is laid on for them. Other professions can benefit from specific exchanges, for example teachers.

### Teacher Exchanges

The UK government supports the idea of teacher sabbaticals and LEAs may even make funding available. Qualified teachers can join a post-to-post exchange through the government-sponsored *League for the Exchange of Commonwealth Teachers* (7 Lion Yard, Tremadoc Road, London SW4 7NQ; www.lect.org.uk) which places Commonwealth teachers with at least five years experience in one-year or shorter posts, in any one of 20 Commonwealth countries. Teachers continue to be paid their normal salaries which makes it very difficult for teachers from India, Barbados, etc. to survive. So most of the vacancies for British teachers are in Australia, Canada and New Zealand. Currently about 50 teachers, sometimes accompanied by their families, take part every year, though LECT manages a number of other professional development programmes for teachers.

The British Council runs a post-to-post teacher exchange programme with Europe. Modern language teachers swap their jobs and homes for a period of one year. British teachers will continue to draw the same salary and their regular benefits plus pay British income tax and national insurance. Details are available from Teacher Exchange Europe, British Council, 10 Spring Gardens, London SW1A 2BN (020-7389 4447; www.britishcouncil.org/learning-teach-in-a-european-school.htm). The Council also administers the Fulbright US/UK Teacher Exchange which funds British teachers at any level to spend a term or a year in the US. Alternatively investigate the Visiting International Faculty (VIF) Program (PO Box 3566, Chapel Hill, NC 27516; 919-967-5144; www.vifprogram.com) which last year placed about 1,700 teachers in 1,000 schools throughout the US.

Teacher exchanges can also be arranged independently. **Anne Hogan** was teaching at a college of further education when it occurred to her that she would love to spend a term in the US. She wrote to about ten English departments which were strong in her field of interest (children's literature) and received several replies. The most promising was from a college in North Carolina. Further investigation revealed that it looked a good place to spend the winter months. She negotiated directly with her counterpart who was satisfied to exchange a big house for a small one, and wasn't unduly concerned that Anne didn't own a car.

## Overseas Opportunities for Qualified Teachers

Organisations involved in teacher recruitment including the British Council and VSO normally welcome applications only from trained and experienced teachers. Similarly, the long established *CfBT* (address below) recruits teachers on behalf of foreign Ministries of Education, mainly for Brunei, Malaysia and Oman.

Certified American and international teachers seeking appointments abroad in international schools should contact *International Schools Services* which offers a recruitment/placement service year round and sponsors three large international recruitment fairs each year. Similarly *Search Associates* tries to match qualified teachers with vacancies in international schools worldwide via its website and also teacher/recruiter job fairs held in Kuala Lumpur, Sydney, Dubai, London, Toronto and others between January and July.

If you are a qualified teacher and think you might want to look for a job after arriving in an English-speaking country, you should take along your diploma and any letters of reference you have. It is a good idea to correspond ahead of time with the education authority in the district which interests you, to find out what their policy is on hiring teachers with foreign qualifications. Some countries with teacher shortages (like New Zealand and Hong Kong) advertise their vacancies abroad and even sometimes offer incentives such as a NZ$4,000 re-location grant and automatic two-year visas (www.teachnz.govt.nz/overseas_index.html). Private recruitment agencies can also help teachers find temporary jobs in other English-speaking countries (though most of the traffic is from overseas to the UK especially London).

The *Times Educational Supplement* publishes occasional articles and resources for teachers who want to organise a sabbatical (see article 'Taking a Sabbatical' at www.tes.co.uk/2070481).

## Useful Addresses for Teachers

*British Council,* 10 Spring Gardens, London SW1A 2BN (teachers.programme@britishcouncil.org; www.britishcouncil.org).

*CfBT The Teaching Agency,* 60 Queens Road, Reading RG1 4BS (0118 902 1000; enquiries@cfbt.com; www.cfbt.com).

*Christians Abroad,* Bon Marché Centre, Suite 233, 241-251 Ferndale Rd, London SW9 8BJ (0870 770 7990; www.cabroad.org.uk). Paid 1 and 2 year teaching posts in China, Hong Kong, Japan, Tanzania and Nigeria; voluntary opportunities for minimum 3 months in Kenya, Zambia, Tanzania, Nigeria and Cameroon.

*International Schools Services,* 15 Roszel Road, PO Box 5910, Princeton, NJ 08543, USA (609-452-0990; www.iss.edu).

*Search Associates* – www.search-associates.com.

*VSO (Voluntary Service Overseas),* 317 Putney Bridge Road, London SW15 2PN (www.vso.org.uk).

## International Training

Some professional organisations for law, agriculture, business, social work, etc. sponsor work exchanges for career development around the world but particularly in the US, Canada, Australia, New Zealand and South Africa.

Doctors have a well-established network of contacts for finding temporary secondments to hospitals abroad. In response to the many enquiries it receives from medics looking for a stint abroad the British Medical Association (BMA; www.bma.org.uk) carries information on planning a temporary career abroad. The *British Medical Journal* carries classified adverts for long and short-term postings abroad (www.bmjcareers.com).

Similarly, nurses and physiotherapists are a highly mobile population especially with morale so low in the National Health Service. The Royal College of Nursing (20 Cavendish Square, London W1M 0AB; www.rcn.org.uk)provides information for its members who want to work abroad. Of course many medical charities recruit volunteers (see the chapter *Doing Something Worthwhile*).

In some of the capitals of the world, specialist agencies and human resources companies can set up internships for ambitious young professionals in the field of their choice. To take just one example InterWorld in Buenos Aires has links with multinational companies who sometimes accept interns who wish to gain business skills and improve their Spanish; details from the Internship Program Manager, InterWorld (Interlatina Corp), Tucuman 1367, 4 A, Capital Federal, Argentina; interworldargentina@yahoo.com.

## International Vocational Exchanges

*Agriventure* is the name of the International Agricultural Exchange Association's exchange programme which operates in Australia, New Zealand, Canada, the United States and Japan. Agriventure has many years experience arranging for young agriculturalists up to the age of 30 to live and work with approved host families. Many types of agricultural/horticultural placements are available for between six and twelve months. Participants pay between £2,000 and £4,100 which includes airline tickets, visas, insurance, orientation seminar and board and lodging throughout with a host family. Trainees are then paid a realistic wage. Details from the IAEA, Speedwell Farm Bungalow, Nettle Bank, Wisbech, Cambridgeshire PE14 0SA (01945 450999; www.agriventure.com).

The International Exchange Programme (IEPUK, The Old Rectory, Belton, Rutland LE15 9LE; 01572 717381; www.iepuk.com) places trainees under 35 and with at least a year's hands-on practical experience in horse racing and equine work, agriculture, horticulture and oenology (wine-making) in the US, Australia, New Zealand, South Africa and Europe including Ireland. IEP can assist candidates in getting a J-1 visa for up to 18 months of working in the USA and a 416 working holiday visa for Australia; the placement fee is about £2,000 including airfares.

# WORKING IN THE US

Visas are a perennial bugbear for anyone who is interested in doing paid work in the United States. The exchange visitor visa J-1 is available only through approved exchange organisations responsible for work and travel programmes, mostly for students, and only to candidates who pass an interview at the US Embassy. Joining a Summer Camp Counsellor programme like *Camp America* (see Directory entry) or BUNAC (www.bunac.org.uk) is the most straightforward way to spend time working in the USA with a J-1.

For a brief list of approved exchanges and internship programmes in the US, including some for specific groups (from qualified lawyers to unemployed Northern Irish nationals) contact the Educational Advisory Service of the Fulbright Commission or check the website www.fulbright.co.uk/eas/workexchange/programmes.html.

Apart from the J-1 visa available to people on approved Exchange Visitor Programmes, the other possible visas must be applied for by the employer on the applicant's behalf which will take at least three months. The H category covers non-immigrant work visas in special circumstances. The H2-B is for temporary or seasonal vacancies that employers have trouble filling with US citizens. For example, the chronic shortage of workers on the ski fields of Colorado means that many employers can obtain the necessary Labor Certification confirming that there are no qualified American workers available to do the jobs. A petition is then submitted by the employer to the Immigration and Naturalisation Service (INS). The maximum duration of the H2-B visa is ten months though most come in for about six months to work at amusement parks, as lifeguards, in retail and fast food. They must work only for the employer that has petitioned for their visa.

The H-1B 'Specialty Occupation' visa for professionals with a degree is available for 'prearranged professional or highly skilled jobs' for which there are no suitably qualified Americans. The allocation of H1-B visas rose sharply a few years ago, partly to alleviate the shortage of IT specialists, but has been declining again (so that the 2006 cap is 65,000). A university degree is a pre-requisite and all the paperwork must be carried out by the American employer who must pay a training fee.

The H1-C is available only to nurses. The H-3 'Trainee' visa is the other possibility. Applicants must indicate in detail the breakdown between classroom and on-the-job time, and why equivalent training is not available in their own country.

## Internships and Work Experience

Internship is the American term for traineeship, providing a chance to get some experience in your career interest as part of your academic course. These are typically available to undergraduates, recent graduates and young professionals. Note that at the time of writing (June 2006), the US government controversially was proposing to raise the bar for participation which would limit and jeopardise many of the current programmes.

Several organisations in the UK arrange for students and young professionals to undertake internships and work experience in the US. *IST Plus* (Rosedale House, Rosedale Road, Richmond, Surrey TW9 2SZ; 020-8939 9057; www.istplus.com) runs Professional Career Training programmes for candidates aged 20-40 as well as helping full-time students to arrange course-related placements in the US lasting 3 to 18 months. IST Plus supplies practical advice on applying for work and a searchable database of internships/work placements. Those who qualify get a J-1 visa. The programme fees start at £500.

*CDS International* (871 United Nations Plaza, 15th Floor, New York, NY 10017-1814; 212-497-3500; www.cdsintl.org) offers Professional Development Program in the US lasting 2-18 months in a variety of fields including business, engineering and technology. The opportunities for internships are open to young professionals, aged 22-35. Participation fee is $1,100.

*Cultural Cube* (16 Acland Rd, Ivybridge, Devon PO21 9UR; www.culturalcube.co.uk) runs an internship programme mainly for people with a background in the hospitality industry but occasionally in other branches of business. Hospitality internships are located in and around Atlanta (programme fee $4,300 for less than 12 months, $4,750 for 13-18 months; monthly stipend $400 on top of accommodation).

Internship programmes are also available through *InterExchange* (161 Sixth Avenue, New York, NY 10013) and *Alliances Abroad Group* (1221 South Mopac Expressway, Suite 250, Austin, Texas 78746; 512-457-8062/ 1-888-6-ABROAD; www.allianceabroad.com) which can authorise J-1 visas and arrange internships in Denver, San Francisco and Washington DC.

The *Association for International Practical Training* or AIPT in Maryland (info@aipt.org) administers the UK/US Career Development Programme. This programme is for people under 35 with relevant qualifications and/or at least two years of work experience in their career field. A separate section of the programme is for full-time students in Hospitality & Tourism or Equine Studies.

The book *Internships* published by Peterson's Guides lists intern positions which are paid or unpaid, can last for the summer, for a semester or for a year. The book offers general advice (including a section called 'Foreign Applicants for US Internships') and specific listings organised according to field of interest, e.g. Advertising, Museums, Radio, Social Services, Law, etc. This annually revised book is available in the UK from Vacation-Work (www.vacationwork.co.uk) for £18.99 plus £3 postage.

## Useful Contacts for Work Exchanges in the US

*Association for International Practical Training (AIPT),* 10400 Little Patuxent Parkway, Suite 250, Columbia, Maryland 21044-3510 (410-997-3068; aipt@aipt.org/ www.aipt.org). Practical training placements for graduates and young professionals as well as university students.

*British-American Business Council,* 75 Brook St, London W1K 4AD (020-7467 7400; www.babinc.org) is able to facilitate J-1 visas for business trainees.

*BUNAC,* 16 Bowling Green Lane, London EC1R 0QH; (020-7251 3472; www.bunac.org.uk). Administers various temporary work programmes in the US on summer camps and the more general Work America Programme for students only.

*Fulbright Commission,* Educational Advisory Service, 62 Doughty St, London WC1N 2JZ (020-7404 6994; www.fulbright.co.uk). Send an s.a.e for a list of exchange programmes.

*International Legal Exchange Program (ILEX),* administered by the American Bar Association. Details from the International Projects Administrator, Section of International Law and Practice, 1620 L St, NW, Suite 825 Washington, DC 20036 (202-466-2600; www.abanet.org/intlaw/ilex/home.html). The ILEX programme places foreign attorneys who wish to receive comparative training with US law firms or in other legal offices.

*American Youth Work Centre,* AYWC Social Services Practical Training Program (practicaltraining@youthtoday.org; www.youthtoday.org/aywc). Enables foreign social service providers (human services and children and youth services) to enter the US legally to receive practical, hands-on training and experience in an American social service agency and earn the prevailing wage plus benefits for 18 months. The programme currently places around 150 British trainees in the US each year.

*US Embassy,* Visa Branch, 5 Upper Grosvenor St, London W1A 2JB (www.usembassy.org.uk).

## WORKING IN AUSTRALIA & NEW ZEALAND

Australia has reciprocal working holiday arrangements with Britain, Ireland, Canada, Netherlands and a number of other countries. Applicants must be between the ages of 18 and 30 and without children. The visa is for people intending to use any money they earn in Australia to supplement their holiday funds. Working full-time for more than six months for the same employer is not permitted (increased from three months in 2006) and full-time study or training can now last up to four months.

The working holiday visa is valid for 12 months after entry, which must be within 12 months of issue. People who have done at least three months of seasonal work in regional Australia or worked in specified primary industries are eligible to apply for a second working holiday visa. Application can be made via the Australian Immigration Service website (www.immi.gov.uk) or using a specialist agent like Visas Australia (01270 626626; www.visas-australia.com) where you will pay a premium.

It is now possible to apply for an electronic working holiday visa which can be done very simply before entry but requires a visit in person to an immigration office on arrival in Australia. The official non-refundable visa fee is currently A$180 (£85).

*Real Gap* (1st Floor, Zurich House, Meadow Road, Tunbridge Wells TN1 2YG; 01892 701881; www.realgap.co.uk) offers a range of working holiday packages to anyone eligible for the working holiday visa (under 31), from the basic Australian DIY package for £199 to a more deluxe one for £559. The cost of the inclusive New Zealand package is £599 which includes visa, insurance, job offer guarantee and many other benefits.

The dense network of 'backpackers' (i.e. private hostels) is a goldmine of information. Foreign job-seekers often find employment in the hostels themselves too. Working in the cities may not provide much of a contrast with your home situation, so consider spending time in the bush or the outback. Many gap year dreams revolve around campfires by moonlight and close contact with wildlife and nature. One way of experiencing the authentic Aussie outdoors is to sign up for a one week course as a station/farm assistant (jackaroo or jillaroo).

Horsecraft, cattle mustering, ute driving and trail biking are tasks that may occupy your days. The course organisers often provide a referral service to other stations in case you want to stay on working as a farm hand (provided you have a working holiday visa in your passport). Courses in Queensland are available from Rocky Creek Station in Biggenden, (+61 7-4127 1377; www.isisol.com.au/rockycrkfarmstay). Intensive four or five-day farm training courses will cost roughly A$125 a day. A course at the Leconfield School of Jackarooing in New South Wales (www.leconfieldjackaroo.com) is longer and therefore costs more (A$950 for 11 days).

Recently the New Zealand government has increased the number of working holiday visas available to Britons aged up to 30 who can work for up to two years. *Beyond Backpackers* with its headquarters in Auckland offers a Work & Travel Starter Package which includes 12 months registration with New Zealand Job Search (including a job offer guarantee), orientation sessions, the first few nights' accommodation and many other perks (www.gobeyond.co.nz).

# Nesting Abroad

Finding a temporary home in Marrakech or Memphis, San José or Salamanca is an idyllic dream for many, giving them the chance to enjoy a rejuvenating interlude in their lives. A stint spent living abroad is bound to be exciting and memorable as you navigate your way round a different society, interact with the locals in the bar or corner shop, adapt to a different sense of humour and come to understand how different societies develop according to history, geography and climate. On a more basic level, simply mastering the bus or postal systems or signing up for an evening class will impart a feeling of achievement. Perhaps you'll have the chance to rent your own place, even if is just a bedsit or a garret. Once you have a base in a foreign country, you will begin to feel as though you are really living there, however briefly.

Sometimes your travels will lead you into an unexpected episode of living abroad. On the road you may fall in love with a person or place and find a way to extend your stay for months. Travelling without any intention of working, Rachel Pooley and Charlie Stanley-Evans were driving through Africa when they were offered the lease on a backpacking hostel in Malawi for £1,000 which they ran for six months, living contentedly by the shores of Lake Malawi. To give themselves their own project they built a house of brick and straw and made a garden. They even considered buying the hostel outright and settling down indefinitely, but they decided that the expatriate life was not for them in the long term. But they describe this period spent managing the lodge as the most worthwhile experience of the whole trip and enabled them for a time to live in a 'heavenly place.'

After a period of volunteering in the Himalayas through HELP and working for the Orangutan Foundation in Borneo, **Natasha Allden** went on to spend three months in New Zealand partly as a working visitor on a farm through Farm Helpers in New Zealand (FHiNZ, 16 Aspen Way, Palmerston North; tel/fax 06-355 0448; www.fhinz.co.nz) where she led horse treks in Kawakawa, Northland, She was smitten not just with the country because at last report she was applying for permanent residency in order to marry her partner who is a New Zealand Maori.

After leaving his legal practice to take a round-the-world trip, **John Taylor** and his wife **Lavinia** would never have anticipated that they would find themselves working in the West Australian wheatbelt. Instead of continuing their travels to see the world, John and Lavinia stayed on, spending five years in Australia altogether. But they faced a problem common to many couples. John enjoyed the self-sufficiency of life in Western Australia and could quite happily have stayed for good. With its vast landscapes and ample agricultural work he could envisage a rewarding working life there. Lavinia however missed England, especially its social mores. There were some aspects of life in Australia to which she simply couldn't reconcile herself so in the end they both returned to their roots.

Having been tempted by an alternative way of life on the other side of the world, they faced a decision that is more difficult for a couple than a single person, and even more so for a family. Nevertheless a conscious decision to emigrate is a momentous one and marks the most conclusive kind of life change prompted by a gap year. For some individuals putting their work on hold is a catalyst for much needed larger changes in their lives.

## Joining the Expat Community

In every major city of the world you'll find an international community of expat teachers, medics, aid workers, journalists, diplomats, anthropologists, business people, missionaries and not a few eccentrics suspended between two cultures. So it is difficult to feel completely stranded abroad. You may particularly value the support and assistance of the expat community if you don't speak much of the local language or if you need their help to find work.

**Dan Boothby** had read Arabic as an undergraduate and had lived in Syria as a student. Later he decided to leave his job as an awards co-ordinator with the British Academy of Film and Television Arts (BAFTA) to move to Cairo where a good friend lived whom he hoped would introduce him to the local social scene. He was already in possession of a TEFL Certificate and planned to use teaching to support himself while he worked on a novel.

He found it almost alarmingly easy to find work:

> *I taught one-to-one lessons to several people and got about 5 hours a week work and charged £10 an hour. Frankly this was much more than I was worth but if you charge less than the market rate then it is felt that you are an amateur. I didn't feel too guilty charging that amount to tutor the Georgian Ambassador since he probably passed the bill onto his government.*
>
> *I got a lot of students through friends that I made who were teaching at the international schools. The kids at these schools are often in need of extra tuition towards exam times when their parents realise that they've been mucking about all year and are close to failing. The problem is that the kids tend to be very uninterested and so it is difficult to make them concentrate. But I enjoyed one-to-ones. One could build up a large group of students and earn a decent wage but equally teach less hours and have more time – one of the reasons for getting out of England.*

Overall he didn't enjoy teaching and in retrospect he wishes that he had tried to break into local journalism as there were plenty of opportunities in local English language magazines. Yet he time away from London allowed Dan to read incessantly about the theory of fiction alongside pursuing his own literary endeavours.

> *It was a very easy life but I felt penned in by a cultural divide. I had little contact with Egyptians and it's very difficult for European men to meet Egyptian women. It was rather frustrating for a single man.*

Still, the constant round of ex-pat parties meant that Dan wasn't short of company and he travelled extensively in his spare time. Dan took some savings with him but wishes that he had had more (who doesn't?). He lived very cheaply on a houseboat divided into flats, one of which he rented for £30 per month containing a study, bedroom and kitchen. He also paid a nightwatchman-cum-concierge (known locally as a *boab*) an extra £10 per month. His main contact with Egyptians tended to be talking to taxi drivers and, not surprisingly, he caught himself cynically wondering what they wanted from him when they were friendly.

Turning 30 in Egypt was a disturbing experience for Dan and he began to wonder whether he had exhausted the pleasures of drinking beer on a boat. He felt he had to return to London to take up some professional challenges:

*It was a very easy life in Cairo and it gave me time to think. I decided that I quite like the rat race and I returned to London more mellow and confident. But I am a serial 'sabbaticalist' until I find out what I want to do longterm... After London, the chaos of Cairo was initially appealing but I finally decided that living there resembled an open prison because of the cultural divide.*

Of course you may try to function outside the expat scene and concentrate your energies on meeting and befriending the locals, as **Glen Williams** did in Madrid:

*Madrid is a crazy place. During the gaps in my teaching timetable (10-2 and 4-7) I pretend to study Spanish (I'm no natural) and just wander the back streets. I suppose I should try to be more cultural and learn to play an instrument, write poetry or look at paintings, but I never get myself in gear. I think most people teach English here as a means to live in Spain and learn the Spanish language and culture. But there is a real problem that you end up living in an English enclave, teaching English all day and socialising with English teachers. You have to make a big effort to get out of this rut. I am lucky to live with Spanish people (who do not want to practise their English!).*

## Staying On

Making the decision to take a career break abroad can be the prelude to an adventure that might take you in unexpected directions and last far longer than intended. Some people simply don't come home. The longer you stay away, the more difficult it will be to re-integrate (see section on 'Reverse Culture Shock' at the end of this book).

Every individual will have to weigh up the gains and losses of staying or returning. The majority will have too many attachments and obligations back home to contemplate a permanent move. Sometimes the intention of eventually moving home disappears almost imperceptibly as it very gradually transpires that a career and the future are being built abroad. There's an irresistible attraction about living in a place you come to as an adult. You have more freedom to invent yourself and shed inhibitions. Away from family, school friends, college peers and work colleagues, individuals can start afresh without the burdens of old baggage. While inevitably some of these feelings can be ascribed to fantasy, they can become a compelling rationale for emigration, whether by design or default.

**Some post-gap year changes of direction can be dramatic in the extreme:**

Philippa Vernon-Powell had been a very high profile businesswoman and consultant in London earning up to £200,000 a year. In her late 30s, she decided to do an eight-month volunteer stint in Mexico with Outreach International at a shelter for street children in the resort of Puerta Vallarta, which turned her life around. She returned to London and within a short time had raised £17,000 to buy beds, a washing machine, books and sports equipment for the struggling shelter. She has now set up her own street children rehabilitation project in Puerta Vallarta, New Life Mexico, and is staying on to run it (www.newlifemexico.com).

Alienation from the materialistic values of the west often afflicts career gappers who have spent time in a developing country. Some find it impossible to slot easily back into what they have come to view as pleasure-seeking ways. **Kate Ledward** knew that accountancy was not her dream ticket to a happy life even before she went to Africa. Having become aware that her previous trips to Tanzania and Kenya had not satisfied her curiosity about Africa, she decided she needed to return. She stumbled across the charity *SPW* and was impressed with their methodology in partnering each overseas volunteer with a local volunteer and then sending the mixed nationality group into rural villages. Not only were the Ugandans perhaps the most hospitable, happy and friendly people Kate had ever met, the country was also breathtakingly beautiful.

> *When I returned to the UK, I was not able to settle. Having spent a further eighteen long months back in the Financial Services sector, and indeed studying for Financial Planning exams, I kept my passion for the work I did in Uganda alive by volunteering on an organic farm at weekends and taking a short community course in organic growing. Now clear of the gloomy debts from university, I am free to return to one of my dreams come true, and am flying back to my beloved Africa to explore a path that I am now more certain than ever is the one I wish to follow.*

# Travel and Adventure

Traditionally, the gap year between school and higher education is associated with a period of travel, time spent working abroad or a combination of the two. Many new graduates also head off travelling immediately after finishing their courses and before settling into a career. But why can't you have the same adventures at the age of 35 or 55?

Possibly travelling and/or working abroad held no appeal when you were younger. Perhaps a shortage of funds, a lack of confidence or a reluctance to interrupt vocational training and career progression were factors. As a more mature traveller you might have a clearer idea about which countries and cultures you want to visit. Arguably, travel is wasted on the young. There is a tendency these days for very young students to travel rather indiscriminately to far-flung corners of the globe, to places they are not really interested in just to meet up with other travellers, to eat, drink and socialise in exactly the way they would at home but without as many inhibitions. At just eighteen, travellers are more likely to follow the crowd (and the party) than those who are 28, 38 or beyond.

Whatever age you are, nothing can compare with the joy of the open road. The sense of possibility, adventure and even danger can bring feelings of exhilaration unavailable in the workplace. When travelling in developing countries, you can shed – at least temporarily – the clutter and accoutrements of modern life in the western world, for a time to live more simply.

Another of the less trumpeted pleasures of independent travel is the feeling of being free and unfettered. Anyone who has been working in a big organisation or even operating within a family where the other members tend to dictate the rules (e.g. on holidays the man usually takes charge of the map) may have forgotten the unalloyed pleasure of exercising choice of activities and destinations from an infinite number of possibilities.

Almost anyone who has had some experience of independent travel catches the bug and longs to see more and spend a longer time abroad. It might stem from a personal passion like learning languages or saving the rainforest or a fascination left over from childhood with an exotic destination like Madagascar or Patagonia. Cheap air travel has opened up parts of the globe once reserved for the affluent. Today there's little surprise (but usually some envy) when you tell your colleagues that you are planning to go trekking in the hinterland of Rio de Janeiro or diving in the Philippines. Inside many an office worker lurks a secret Indiana Jones longing for a challenge.

Some people take time out from work to embark on a particular journey they have long set their hearts on following. These journeys range from straightforward backpacking to expeditions using specially acquired equipment to an organised adventure trip in which you pay a specialist to help you, which might range from mountain trekking to long distance motorbiking. Options include white water rafting, hot air ballooning, mountain climbing, off-road driving, scuba diving and sailing, perhaps even around the world.

Older travellers taking a gap year may be in a position to travel in greater comfort than would have been possible in their student days, while others may choose to revert to their youth and go backpacking and hostelling. It is possible for people of any age with time at their disposal to stitch together a journey on foot, bicycle, campervan or public transport to almost anywhere in the world and on any budget. Independent travel allows you to get closer to the street and to be less detached from the indigenous people than on conventional holidays and organised tours. Many older travellers are surprised to discover (or re-discover) the joys of backpacking, something they may have fallen into viewing with distaste simply out of prejudice. For example backpackers' hostels in Australia provide not only comfortable accommodation but a ready-made social life for travellers of any age, and are far more convivial than checking into a more upmarket and more solitary accommodation.

For many, travel represents escape and discovery. By immersing yourself in the unknown it is temporarily possible to disorient yourself and undergo a process of detachment from banal and tedious routines and responsibilities that hem in the lives of all adults. At a more practical level, an extended break gives an almost unique period (post-education) to explore in depth other regions and cultures of the world. In the nineteenth century, many individuals never travelled more than ten miles to the next town.

**Having awarded himself several career breaks over the years, Mike Bleazard was lucky enough to become pair-bonded in his mid-thirties with Jane O'Beirne who shared his commitment to stepping out of the rat race every so often because she had done so a few years before she met him:**

When Jane got together with Mike, she was discontented with the solicitor's office where she worked. After one particularly frustrating day at work, she blurted out 'Shall we take off round the world?' Mike nodded his assent and seven months later they did. They were both in the fortunate position of being able to save money quite handily in that period of planning – Jane by moving into the flat that Mike owned so that she saved everything she would have spent on rent and Mike by getting a staggeringly well paid contract (£50 an hour) turning techie-speak into human language. They were each able to budget £7,000 for the six-month trip on top of round-the-world airfares plus they had the rent of £800 a month coming in from Mike's flat. They did not want to rough it for six months but intended to intersperse periods of spartan travel with short bursts of luxury. They looked into doing some voluntary work but the (very expensive) schemes that they came across didn't grab them.

Their initial destination was southern Africa to see the solar eclipse that took place in early December 2002. They headed to Cape Town for Christmas to meet up with friends from Cambridge who turned out to be planning to get married secretly so Mike and Jane were invited to act as best man and maid of honour. They then flew to the Seychelles from Nairobi (losing one of their cameras to a corrupt airport official). Most of the African leg of their trip had been pre-arranged whereas once they moved on to Australia they could improvise a bit more. Yet they realised that much of the time they spent driving the Great Ocean Road (for example) was spent planning the next leg of their journey to New Zealand and they decided to try to concentrate more on the present moment. Their most treasured possession that they never let out of their sight was a gadget capable of storing 12,000 digital pictures (a collection that they delighted in promising to show to families and friends in its entirety).

In retrospect they were glad that they had done the trip in the order that they did: starting with the strangeness of Africa, relaxing into the familiarity of Anglo culture in Australia and New Zealand and finally entering the most challenging phase, travelling around South America with minimal Spanish. They noticed that the average age of travellers met in Chile, Argentina and Brazil was higher than it had been earlier in their trip and they came to the conclusion that adults on gap years are better equipped and more committed to leaving the beaten track than gap year students and other young backpackers who congregate in Cape Town, Kathmandu and Sydney.

Patagonia was firmly on their itinerary but because they were a little apprehensive about venturing into the tail end of the continent at the tail end of the season, so they tried to pre-arrange their trip. They attempted to do so through a well-meaning agent in Santiago, though none of the arrangements they made with him came off. For instance they arrived at a 10,000-strong penguin colony near Punta Arenas to find just four lonely penguins, since five days before the colony had decided to swim off.

With hindsight, they would have done better making arrangements after arrival in Patagonia for visiting national parks, going trekking and finding accommodation. It wasn't until near the end of their trip that they shared a Zen moment in a bus station in southern Chile: they realised that they had absolutely no idea where they would end up that day. They opened their guidebook, liked the sound of a volcano in the vicinity and proceeded to find out if any bus was going that way, but not until after they had retired for a coffee. They felt more free than they had perhaps in their whole lives. As the months had passed, so had their anxiety about mapping out what was to come.

From the plane between Santiago and Punta Arenas they had seen an astonishingly beautiful mountain. A Chilean passenger informed them that this was Mount Fitzroy and they resolved to return by land. After many hours on a bus over unmade roads and crossing the border into Argentina, Mike and Jane were exhilarated to have the chance to hike to the base of Mount Fitzroy and look up its sheer vertical rock walls on which they had looked down from the aeroplane.

## Combining Travel and Work

If on an adult gap year, you wish to work or volunteer abroad (topics that are covered in other chapters), you will have more skills and maturity to bring to a foreign employer or project. Some older travellers consider it self-indulgent simply to travel. For London lawyer **Polly Botsford,** for example, it was important to work and not only travel. Because she thinks that 'you can get jaded very quickly and then end up a mechanical tourist,' she decided to divide her six-month gap equally between travelling and working. Through *Outreach International* Polly arranged to work for an NGO in Cambodia that campaigns against the illegal trafficking of children and young girls.

Likewise **Daniel Smith** aspired to more than just travel in his four-month break from his job in publishing: 'I had long wanted to go to India but didn't just want to go backpacking or bum around in Goa. I looked at lots of different work opportunities but the one offered by *i-to-i* was the one that immediately grabbed me.' Daniel was placed in the publishing arm of an enterprising arts charity in Calcutta where he found the work he was given very rewarding.

Interestingly, quite a few career gappers who have combined volunteering and travel end up enjoying the volunteering more. **Jackie Smith** and her husband Peter took a six-month sabbatical in India and Southeast Asia after many years of working, part volunteering through *MondoChallenge* and part travelling:

> *Since our return in April 2006 we both agree that staying in a small rural village and living with the principal of a local school for two and a half months was the highlight of our six months away. It was fantastic being part of the community if only for a short time. People got to know us and included us in local festivals such as Diwali, which included an impressively-run bingo competition on the field opposite our school as well as lots of food, drink and blessings. I do think that if we travelled again we might do a longer volunteer placement and perhaps even less time being a 'tourist' – maybe even something like VSO. While the world is a huge place and there is always something new to see, we felt that you really can't beat meeting local people, getting to know them and their way of life and sharing stories. It is the only real way to get anywhere near understanding a place and making some sort of connection.*

# TRAVEL CHOICES

People travelling on a gap year later in life will be looking for a unique travel experience, one that is different from their annual holidays in Jersey or Provence. Independent travel allows travellers to make their own way over long distances and is, by most definitions, distinct from tourism which can be roughly defined as a trip abroad in which itinerary and accommodation are booked in advance. Yet a growing number of tour operators is now bridging that gulf by providing challenging adventure holidays on foot or by vehicle over difficult terrain, or by catering to people who want to donate their time and labour to a specific cause like conservation or teaching (see the *Directory of Specialist Programmes*). These packages attempt to introduce travellers to a more authentic experience of countries like Peru or Thailand. Such trips might include a variety of experiences like jungle trekking and cookery lessons as well as free-time sightseeing.

## Organised Travel

Heading into the wild blue yonder is a daunting prospect for most adults taking a break unless they are hardened independent travellers from away back. In many cases it will make sense for a solo traveller to consider joining some kind of structured programme, whether an organised trek in the Himalayas, an overland expedition through East Africa or an adventure trip through South America possibly combined with Spanish lessons and/or a volunteer placement. Environmentally and culturally sensitive tour operators design trips to introduce westerners to a region, country or culture by employing expert guides who can share their insights and knowledge. These trips address a growing market of people who want a trip that's organised for them without losing the experience of adventure and discovery that comes from independent travel. As this book tries to demonstrate, the choice of worthy small and large companies organising short and long trips is quite staggering. For someone in the early stages of thinking about a gap year, the range of possibilities can be overwhelming.

A possible starting place is one of the annual winter travel shows like the *Daily Telegraph Adventure Travel Show* held every January at Olympia, or *Destinations* at Earl's Court in London or the National Exhibition Centre in Birmingham. Both of these are widely publicised in the travel press. A new show joined the calendar in 2006 called *One Life Live* encouraging people to consider major life changes. One of the four zones was devoted to taking a sabbatical to travel or volunteer and many relevant companies exhibited.

When **Paul Carroll** reached his late 20s, he came to the conclusion that there was something seriously wrong with the work-life balance in his pressurised IT job. So he took himself off to the *Destinations* show in Earl's Court:

> *There I saw lots of companies, but few offering specialist programmes for trekking, backpacking and generally challenging itineraries. VentureCo was one, and White Peak Expeditions another. I took a VentureCo brochure that happened to be labelled 'Career Gap'. Later I sifted through all the brochures I had collected from the show and from the Internet and eventually chose VentureCo. I was very impressed as they are very careful with their selection of individuals through a series of interviews.*

Paul went on to book a four-month expedition to Patagonia with VentureCo (see Directory entry). Afterwards he travelled independently for several more months in South America and experienced nature like he had never imagined: 'glaciers, volcanoes, mountain ranges, condors, wild cats, rainforest, jungle, pampas, salt lakes, geysers, etc...' This proved a useful half-way house between going it alone and having a trip completely pre-arranged.

Another way of achieving this balance is to create an itinerary with the help of a specialist travel agent like STA Travel which is familiar with the options suited to the longer-term traveller. Such agents will know for example about hop-on hop-off transport aimed primarily at backpackers in which, typically, you travel in a group of up to 20 on an adapted bus which travels on more off-the-beaten-track routes than conventional bus tours. Passengers are free to get off at any stop, stay as long as they like and resume their journey when they're ready and the next one passes through within a time limit, normally of between two and six months.

Many tour operators in the UK, North America and Australasia can organise a tailor-made itinerary in their area of expertise whether an overland trip through Central Asia or trekking in the Andes. You're not obliged to join a group of strangers if that's not your style since people travelling with a partner, friend or group of friends can be catered for. If solo travel does not appeal, as it often does not for novice travellers or women travelling alone, organised group travel offers many advantages. It can become an excellent way of meeting new people and sharing experiences rather than facing the potential loneliness and anxiety of solitary, independent travel. Many appealing alternatives to the conventional coach tour for OAPs exist around the world; for example in the USA consider the escorted trips aimed at people 18-38 offered by Trekamerica (0870 444 8735; www.trekamerica.co.uk) or by Green Tortoise in San Francisco (800-867-8647; www.greentortoise.com) which uses vehicles converted to sleep about 35 people that make interesting detours and stopovers. On Green Tortoise trips, which place more emphasis on outdoor activities like hiking and canoeing than sightseeing, about a third of clients are aged 25-35 and 6% are older.

Overlanding by motorbike appeals to some, possibly more to mid-life males than other groups. Specialist companies like Globebusters (www.globebusters.com) and Kudu Expeditions (www.kuduexpeditions.com) offer up to four-month motorcycle journeys through Africa and America which are accessible to anyone who can afford them.

## Independent Travel

The clear alternative is to travel completely independently in as basic or as luxurious a style as you choose. Students do not have the monopoly on backpacking. There is no reason why at an older age you shouldn't aim for something more than relaxation and predictability. If you decide to take the independent route, it's a good idea to map out a plan or itinerary in advance because you will probably want to make at least some flight bookings, while retaining the pleasure of following your nose. Many round-the-world tickets cost less than £1,000 and allow you to hop through different countries and continents at your own pace.

So give yourself some flexibility to head off on a magical mystery tour. You may meet locals who take you off the beaten track to visit a deserted beach or waterfall overlooked by the guidebooks, or you may find that some entirely unforeseen opportunity presents itself en route. Travel plans should be as fluid and flexible as possible, provided you know how you're going to get home.

Inspiration can come from someone met in the pub, from the travel section of your local bookshop, television documentaries or from the travel pages of papers like the *Independent* or glossy travel magazines like *Wanderlust*. The worthy organisation Tourism Concern published a book in 2006 called *The Ethical Travel Guide* which describes 300 places in 60 countries which are guaranteed not to be tourist traps.

Americans might consult the classic *Vagabonding: An Uncommon Guide to the Art of Long-Term World Travel* by veteran shoestring expeditioner Rolf Potts. The author defines 'Vagabonding' like the adult gap year of this book, i.e. taking time off from your normal life to discover and experience the world on your own terms. He also maintains a links-laden website http://vagablogging.net. The author argues persuasively that time is a more precious commodity for travellers than money, and liberates you from having to over-organise your itinerary in advance.

Many people are anxious about the language barrier when contemplating travel within or beyond Europe. With a phrase book and a lack of inhibition about playing charades, this perceived hindrance usually melts away.

## Getting it Out of your System

For the now defunct e-magazine she ran, *Just Traveling*, Debra Fuccio (herself a serial gapper from the US) interviewed inveterate traveller **Michael McHugh** (http://jt-interviews.blogspot.com). Michael has found that the few times he has travelled with lots of money, he has enjoyed the experience far less than when he was living on the edge:

> *Let's face it, as Americans we all live pretty cushy lives. Too much of everything. When I travel I love to pare everything down to the bare necessities. The first big trip I took through Europe, I had no extra cash at all. I was terrified every time I went to a cash machine it would laugh at me. I walked everywhere, slept at the beach, showered in McDonalds sinks and then went to art museums all day. It certainly isn't for everyone, but I was in the process of deconstructing this over-fed, over-stimulated suburban persona, trying to find what was really important. It's the old cliché of 'finding yourself' but it really happens. You take away all the cultural characteristics of your home country/family/friends and you're left with YOU.*
>
> *In Europe I was the poorest person in town; in Cambodia, I was the richest. People earn in a month what we would spend on lunch, which creates a totally different mindset. People treat you differently and you become very suspicious of people's motives. It is the opposite of liberating. Some people would love this feeling of being superior to the locals, but I hated it.*

As Michael has got older he no longer craves travel in the way that he did and thinks that his 'travel for the sake of travel' period is over:

> *I've been to lots of countries and have a pretty good idea of the way people live around the world. I've seen rich, poor, cold, hot, friendly, unwelcoming, peaceful, war-torn, optimistic and hopeless. So I don't get the same buzz from it that I used to. In other ways it is just part of who I am. I'm always exploring New York and talking to the people from other places. The next time I go somewhere on a big trip it will be for a purpose. Working in Africa or India. Trying to change the world a little bit instead of just looking at it.*

# PLANES, TRAINS AND AUTOMOBILES

There follow some general guidelines for finding bargains in train, coach, car, ship and air travel. More detailed information on specific destinations can be found in travel guides from Lonely Planet and Rough Guides. The amount of travel information on the Internet is staggering and this chapter cannot hope to tap its resources. There are websites on everything from sleeping in airports (the fabulous www.sleepinginairports.net) to sharing lifts across the USA and Canada (www.erideshare.com). Many sites have pages of intriguing links; to name just one, try www.budgettravel.com.

## Booking Flights

For longhaul flights, especially to Asia, Australasia and most recently Latin America, discounted tickets are available in plenty and there should never be any need to pay the official full fare. Scheduled airfares as laid down by IATA, the airlines' cartel, are primarily designed for airline accountants and businessmen on expense accounts and should be avoided.

The days of the bucket shop are long gone. Now high street travel agents and mainstream Internet travel agents can offer exceptional deals. But the very lowest fares are still found by doing some careful shopping around on the telephone and Internet. Even if you choose not to book online and want the reassurance of dealing with a human being, the web can still be a great source of information about prices and options.

Discount agents advertise in London weeklies like *TNT* and *Time Out,* as well as in the travel pages of newspapers like the Saturday *Independent*. Phone a few outfits and pick the best price. Those with access to the Internet should start by checking relevant websites, for example www.cheapflights.co.uk which has links to other useful sources of travel information. Viewers can log onto their destination and then see a list of prices offered by a variety of airlines and agents. Increasingly, it is possible to book tickets on the Internet, though this is too impersonal for some, who prefer the personal touch available from face-to-face or at least voice-to-voice contact.

The cheapest flights are probably available from airlines like Aeroflot or Biman Bangladesh which are considered dubious by cautious and conservative types. East European carriers (like Tarom) and Asian carriers (like Eva Airways) are often worth investigating for low fares. Try to overcome your reluctance, since flying with them is guaranteed to be more interesting than flying on Air Canada or British Airways. When Sarah Spiller fell in love with Sri Lanka after joining a turtle conservation project and persuaded her husband that they should buy a holiday house there, she made several trips on Sri Lanka Airlines and feels that she is already on holiday the minute she steps aboard. The travel agency Eastways (020-7247 2424;http://www.aeroflotonline.com) has the franchise for discounting tickets for Aeroflot, the Russian airline which has flights from London to Beijing or Seoul from about £420 return.

The price of round-the-world (RTW) tickets has remained fairly consistent over the past few years. Check www.roundtheworldflights.com (0870 442 4842) for ideas or its sister site www.globalvillageflights.com (0870 422 4848). Another recommended agent is Travel Nation in Hove, Sussex (0845 344 4225; www.travel-nation.co.uk). RTW fares start at £830-£860 plus taxes and most have a maximum validity of one year. Taxes have doubled over the past two years and for a RTW fare are usually in the range of £200-£350. The cheapest fares involve one or more gaps which you must cover overland. An example of a good RTW fare available through Travelmood (see below) is £745 plus tax departing from London in the low season (April-June) with stops in Hong Kong, Auckland and LA. For an extra £100, Sydney can be added on the routes offered by Virgin Atlantic and Air New Zealand. For not much more you should be able to book one of the most popular RTW routes such as London – Bangkok – surface to Singapore – Perth – surface to Sydney – Christchurch – surface to Auckland – Fiji – LA – surface to New York – London.

Some of the principal agencies specialising in longhaul travel are listed here. All of these offer a wide choice of fares including RTW. Telephone bookings are possible, though these agencies are often so busy that it can be difficult to get through. Although STA specialise in deals for students and under-26s, they can also assist older travellers planning a gap year.

*STA Travel* have about 65 branches in the UK and more than 450 worldwide. Offer low cost flights, accommodation, insurance, car hire, round-the-world tickets, overland travel, adventure tours, ski, and gap year travel. For bookings and enquiries call STA Travel on 08701 630026 or log on at www.statravel.co.uk to find fares and check availability. You can request a quote by email.

*Trailfinders Ltd,* 194 Kensington High St, London W8 7RG (0845 058 5858 worldwide; 0845 050 5940 Europe); www.trailfinders.com. Also more than a dozen branches in UK cities plus Dublin and five in Australia.

*Flight Centre* – branches around the UK (0870 499 0040; www.flightcentre.co.uk).

*Journey Latin America,* 12-13 Heathfield Terrace, Chiswick, London W4 4JE (020-8747 3108; www.journeylatinamerica.co.uk). A fully-bonded agency which specialises in travel to and around all of Latin America. Consistently offers the lowest fares and the most expertise. One of the best flight deals at the time of writing was on Iberia to Rio or Caracas for about £550.

*Marco Polo Travel* 24A Park St, Bristol BS1 5JA (0117-929 4123; www.marcopolotravel.co.uk). Discounted airfares worldwide.

*North South Travel,* Moulsham Mill Centre, Parkway, Chelmsford, Essex CM2 7PX (01245 608291; www.northsouthtravel.co.uk). Discount travel agency that donates all its profits to projects in the developing world.

*Quest Travel* – Kingston, York and Brighton offices (0870 444 5552; www.questtravel.com).

*South American Experience Ltd*, 47 Causton St, Pimlico, London SW1P 4AT (020-7976 5511; www.southamericanexperience.co.uk). Latin American specialist with good customer service.

*Travelbag,* 3-5 High St, Alton, Hants. GU34 1TL (0870 814 4440; www.travelbag.co.uk). Originally Australia & New Zealand specialist, now owned by ebookers.

*Travelmood,* London office: 214 Edgware Road, London W2 1DH (08700 664566; www.travelmood.com). Branches in Islington, Guildford, Leeds, Liverpool and Dundee.

When purchasing a discounted fare, you should be aware of whether or not the ticket is refundable and whether the date can be changed and if so at what cost. **Roger Blake** was pleased with the round-the-world ticket he bought from STA for £940 that took in Johannesburg, Australia and South America. But once he embarked he wanted to stay in Africa longer than he had anticipated and wanted to alter the onward flight dates:

> *That is the biggest problem of having an air ticket. I had planned for six months in Africa but I've already spent five months in only three countries. I have been into the British Airways office here in Kampala to try my verbal skills but have been told the 12-month period of validity is non-negotiable. A lesson for me and a warning to future world travellers, to check before they buy whether or not the ticket is refundable/extendable.*

Jen Moon is another adult gapper who found it difficult to predict how long she and her two young daughters would want to stay in any one place on their four-month adventure in 2006:

> *Dividing the time was the hardest bit as I didn't know what to expect. In fact dates changed three times before I finally paid and three dates changed during the trip. Thank God for Trailfinders and unfixed dates.*

Similarly, 28 year old **Tara Leaver** splashed out on an ambitious RTW route with the One World Alliance (British Airways, Air New Zealand, etc.) for about £1,300 including Central America, South America, Easter Island, Tahiti, New Zealand, Australia and South East Asia. Apart from her first month (April 2006) which she pre-arranged in Costa Rica, she didn't want to over-plan for the rest of her year off. Some of these deals impose mileage limits (e.g. 28,000 miles) so you will have to make some careful calculations.

In the US, check the discount flight listings in the back of the travel sections of the *New York Times* and *Los Angeles Times*. Discounted tickets are available online from Air Treks in San Francisco (1-877-247-8735; www.AirTreks.com) which specialises in multi-stop and round-the-world fares. By far the cheapest airfares from the US are available to people who are flexible about departure dates and destinations, and are prepared to travel on a standby basis. The passenger chooses a block of possible dates (up to a four-day 'window') and preferred destinations. The company then tries to match these requirements with empty airline seats being released at knock-down prices. Air-Tech at 588 Broadway, Suite 1007, New York, NY 10012 (212-219-7000; www.airtech.com). The transatlantic fares being advertised at the time of writing were $159 one way from the east coast and $249 from the west coast, excluding tax, a registration fee of $29, a FedEx delivery charge of $18+ and a fuel surcharge of up to €50 when departing from Europe. Discounted fares of $250 return between the US and Mexico or the Caribbean are also available.

From the UK to Europe it is generally cheaper to fly on an off-peak no-frills flight out of Stansted, Luton or regional airport than it is by rail or bus. Almost all bookings are made online and telephone bookings attract a higher fare. Airlines like *Easyjet* (0905 821 0905; www.easyjet.com), *Ryanair* (0871 246 0000; www.ryanair.com), *BMIbaby* (0871 224 0224; www.bmibaby.com), Jet2 based at Leeds Airport (0871 226 1737; www.jet2.com), and Thomsonfly (www.thomsonfly.com) connect the UK with a large range of European cities and beyond. No-frills flying has been available in North America for some time, especially through Southwest Airlines based in Dallas (www.southwest.com). Normally the cheapest advance purchase coast-to-coast fares in the US are about $200 though Southwest were advertising a fare of $150 including taxes between Philadelphia and Los Angeles (autumn 2006). Meanwhile this style of flying has spread to the continent and discount airlines have proliferated like Air Berlin and Germanwings in Germany and Wizz Air in Poland at www.wizzair.com. To check which discount airlines operate to which European destinations, log on to www.flycheapo.com. The idea has spread to Australia with Richard Branson's Virgin Blue (www.virginblue.com.au) and to Canada with airlines like CanJet and WestJet.

An unusual way of locating cheap flights is available from Adventurair (PO Box 757, Maidenhead, SL6 7XD; 01293 405777; www.rideguide.com) who produce *The Ride Guide* on CD-ROM (£11.99/$16.99) which gives details of companies operating cargo planes, aircraft deliveries and private planes. Any of these may have seats available for bargain prices.

## Rail and Coach

One of the classic gap year experiences is to InterRail around Europe (www.interrail.net), an experience which is readily available to people over 26, albeit at a higher price than it is to young travellers. It may sound a little tame compared to round-the-world flights or Himalayan treks, but it can provide an amazing taste of the delights of Europe. For the InterRail ticket, you must choose how many zones you intend to cover and bear in mind that seat reservations will cost extra; current prices for the over-26s are £215 for 16 days in one zone, £295 for 22 days in two zones and £405 for a month anywhere in Europe. These are the prices if bought in the UK; prices in euros bought on the continent are lower. Anyone intending to do some concentrated travelling by train should contact a specialist operator like Rail Europe (08705 848848; www.raileurope.co.uk) or Rail Choice (0870 165 7300; www.railchoice.co.uk) who sell a large range of European and international rail passes.

Within Europe, consult the *Thomas Cook European Rail Timetable* whereas the bible for rail travellers outside Europe is the *Thomas Cook Overseas Timetable* (£11.50 each). The *Overseas Timetable*, published each May, is valuable for coach as well as train travellers since there are many areas of the world from Nepal to Papua New Guinea where public road transport is the only way to get around short of flying. Except where smooth air-conditioned buses provide an alternative to third class rail travel, coach travel is generally less expensive than trains.

Eurolines is the group name for 32 independent coach operators serving 500 destinations in all European countries from Ireland to Romania. Promotional prices start at £30 return for London-Amsterdam if booked 7 days in advance. Bookings can be made online at www.nationalexpress.com/eurolines or by phoning 08705 808080.

For smaller independent coach operators, check advertisements in London magazines like *TNT*. For example Capital Express (57 Princedale Road, Holland Park, London W11 4NP; 020-7243 0488; capitalexpressuk.com) runs daily between London and Prague or Brno; fares start at £63 return.

One of the most interesting revolutions in youth travel has been the explosion of backpackers' bus services which are hop-on hop-off coach services following prescribed routes. These can be found (among others) in New Zealand, Australia, Ireland, Scotland and England. For example travel in Europe within the whole operating season (May to October) on Busabout (258 Vauxhall Bridge Road, London SW1V 1BS; 020-7950 1661; www.busabout.com) costs £575 though many cheaper options are available.

## Great Railway Journeys

Undertaking one of the great rail journeys of the world is something that might easily appeal to people taking a gap year at any age. Anyone who has read any of the abundant literature of rail travel like Paul Theroux's *Great Railway Bazaar* and Eric Newby's *The Big Red Train Ride* about the Trans-Siberian may have had their appetite whetted and want to take a longer-than-usual holiday to travel by train between Moscow and Beijing or on the Trans-Canada from Toronto to Vancouver. Some lesser known routes might also appeal such as the Blue Train of South Africa, the Eastern & Oriental Express of Malaysia or the Sierra Madre Express of Mexico.

You can either plan a rail journey independently or via a specialist agency like*Great Rail Journeys* (01904 521900; www.greatrail.com). Specialist travel agents can arrange the Trans-Siberian trip for you, for instance the excellent travel company *Regent Holidays* (0870 499 0911; www.regent-holidays.co.uk) which pioneered tourism in Cuba, Eastern Europe and Central Asia. For lesser known routes such as the Silk Route Railway through Kazakhstan and China, you will have to put it together yourself, possibly with the help of the very useful website www.seat61.com which has links to specialist booking agencies. If you are already in China, you can simply organise the ticket and visas yourself as **Barry O'Leary** did:

> *I had discovered that if you book the Trans-Siberian on your own and don't pay for an agency to rip you off and organise everything yourself it's actually really cheap. Sure you have some hassle getting visas for China, Mongolia and Russia but isn't that all part of the fun? The total cost to get from Beijing to Moscow with 3 visas was only about £250, not bad for 6 days on a train and some tasty meat and celery stuff.*

Alternatively you can use a Chinese agency such as Monkey Business located in Beijing's Red House Hotel (www.monkeyshrine.com). For detailed advice, see the *Trans-Siberian Handbook* published by Trailblazer at £12.99 or *The Trans-Siberian Railway (2006)* from Lonely Planet (£14.99).

## Cars

If you are considering taking your own vehicle, contact your local AA or RAC office for information about International Driving Permits, motor insurance, green cards (international motor insurance card), etc. Members of motoring organisations should ask for free information on driving and services provided by affiliated organisations in other countries. Although plenty of sources (especially the motoring organisations that sell them) recommend obtaining an International Driving Permit (IDP) for £5.50, your national licence is sufficient for short stays in most countries. Check the RAC web page www.rac.co.uk/web/travelservices/travelling for the list of countries (like Albania and Japan) in which an IDP is required.

In some countries like Australia and the USA you might decide to buy a cheap car or camper van after arrival and hope that it lasts long enough for you to see the country. Buy a standard model for ease of finding spares. Some travellers have even managed to sell a vehicle at the end of their trip.

An underrated alternative to hitch-hiking is to use a lift-sharing agency of which there are dozens of outlets across Europe, especially in Germany, where there are Citynetz offices in most of the major cities. For a varying fee (usually about £10-£20 plus a share of the petrol) they will try to find a driver going to your chosen destination. The Quebec website www.allostop.com has links to ride-sharing schemes around Europe. The Backpackers Ultimate Guide (bug.com) runs Bugride, an online lift-sharing exchange in Europe and Australia. The websites www.hitchhikers.org and http://europe.bugride.com list long-distance rides within Europe, for example a random check revealed seats in a car going from Leipzig to Amsterdam (for a share of the expenses of €40) and London to Barcelona (free) at the time of writing. Here are some details of European agencies:

*France:* Allostop, 30 rue Pierre Sémard, 75009 Paris (1-53 20 42 42 or 8-25 80 36 66; www.allostop.net or http://pcb.ecritel.fr/allostop/welcome.html). Prices are set according to distance of journey, e.g. €5 for less than 150km, €16 for up to 400km, up to €90 for a journey of 3000km plus a small registration fee on a sliding scale. Prices are a little lower if the journey avoids toll motorways.

*Belgium:* Taxistop/Eurostop, 28 rue Fossé-aux-Loups, 1000 Brussels (+32 70-22 22 92; fax +32 2-223 22 32). Also has offices in Ghent and Ottignies (www.taxistop.be). The admin fee charged to passengers by Taxistop is 80 cents per 100km (minimum €6.20, maximum €20). In addition passengers pay drivers €3 per 100km.

*Germany:* Citynetz-Mitzfahrzentrale – www.citynetz-mitzfahrzentrale.de. Website gives addresses, phone numbers and emails of offices around Germany. Prices work out at approximately 6 Eurocents per kilometre.

Matches can seldom be made straightaway, so this system is of interest to those who can plan ahead.

## Driving Expeditions

Anyone planning to take a vehicle off the beaten track will need to be pragmatic and able to rise to various challenges. Diesel is more easily obtained than petrol and, in general, a diesel engine is more reliable and requires less maintenance. Taking your own vehicle is an expensive way to travel but the freedom it offers is worthwhile if you have the resources. In some parts of the world, it is unwise to leave your car or van unattended; losing your means of transport as well as all the contents in one fell swoop would represent a truly horrifying disaster. In countries where robbery is commonplace, it may be necessary to hire watchmen to guard the vehicle including by night while you sleep in a neighbouring hotel. For example, in Egypt 'boabs' or apartment building concierges/doormen often double as guards and charge a dollar or two a night.

Crossing borders with your own vehicle is often fraught with difficulties and expense. For example, **Rachel Pooley** and **Charlie Stanley-Evans**, whose experiences of driving a Land Rover through Africa are recounted in the next section, found themselves being charged extra 'costs' by border officials. This was particularly bad in Romania, Bulgaria, Turkey, Syria and Egypt (but not Jordan). Crossing into Egypt by ferry from Jordan they were asked to pay a staggering £200 because the Land Rover had an engine over 2000cc. Exercising some ingenuity, they claimed to constitute a 'group' because, as Rachel claimed, she was pregnant with twins; but this ploy did not succeed and their budget took a mighty hit. In your project budget, allow for these unforeseen levies. Red tape in Egypt was also onerous and they spent two weeks in Cairo organising the paperwork to ship the vehicle to Kenya.

Other problems include poor roads, difficulty interpreting road signs in an alien script and suicidal driving styles. Entering Cairo, a huge sprawling city choked with traffic, Rachel and Charlie were stumped by an inability to read the Arabic road signs or ask for directions. Sometimes it may also be difficult to buy petrol. It is crucial to carry plenty of spare supplies. Syria and Jordan are countries with almost no campsites where they were once forced to pitch their tent on a roundabout in Aleppo, after asking permission from the local police. The discomfort of staying in the middle of a Syrian Piccadilly Circus was aggravated by the absence of public toilets for women.

## Desert Driving

Motorists must be sure to be suitably equipped for journeys across inhospitable terrain – modern folklore is laced with stories of skeletons being discovered a few miles from broken-down cars in desert regions. The first essential when planning a journey off the beaten track is to ensure your vehicle is fit for the task. It should be mechanically sound, and suitable for the roads you intend to use. Always seek local advice preferably from a motoring organisation or the police on whether your vehicle is fit for the journey you plan to make. You should notify a responsible person of your intended route and ensure that you let them know when you arrive safely at your destination.

At least two spare wheels are advisable; the heat on desert roads can melt the bitumen which then sticks to tyres. Punctures are commonplace on unsealed roads so make sure you know how to change a tyre (and that the wheel nuts are not jammed) before you leave civilisation. Petrol stations are thin on the ground and potentially low on fuel supplies so substantial supplies of fuel and water should be carried, not least in case you need to help out a less well-prepared motorist. The standard calculation of the amount of water needed is 10 litres per person per day. A selection of spare parts such as a fan belt and electrical fittings is also advisable, as well as shovel, axe and tow rope. In an emergency, crawl under the vehicle for shade and drink the radiator water, provided it has no chemical additives. If possible, do not exert unnecessarily, reduce your salt intake, increase your sugar intake and keep a fire going so that the smoke might be spotted. Never leave your vehicle in the event of a breakdown since you have a much better chance of being rescued.

One of the hazards on unsealed (or newly surfaced) roads is of flying stones hitting the windscreen. Some drivers take the precaution of placing their fingers on the windscreen whenever they meet an oncoming vehicle, which absorbs the shock of the impact and reduces the risk of shattering. If the windscreen breaks, however, use gloves or a cloth to punch out a hole to see through. It is a good idea to carry a plastic windscreen for emergency use.

## Useful Contacts for Land Rover Drivers

Scores of off-road driving centres can be found throughout the UK. For a list of them consult the website www.aidventures.co.uk or the British Off-Road Driving Association (www.borda.org.uk/members.html).

*Rough Tracks and Country Lanes*, 47 Pomphlett Rd, Plymstock, Plymouth, Devon PL9 7BT; 07870 324090 or 01752 519050; nickrundle@roughtracksandcountrylanes.com; www.roughtracksandcountrylanes.com). 1-day course costs £150, 2 days for £275 and 3 days for £350; plus £150 per day if vehicle is also hired.

*Explore Off Road,* Snape Lane, Crewe, CW2 5QN; 01270 820192; www.exploreoffroad.com.

*Keith Gott Land Rover Specialists,* Greenwood Farm, Old Odiham Road, Alton, Hampshire GU34 4BW; 01420 544330; www.keithgott.co.uk. Specialist dealer that services and customises Land Rovers for range of clients including the Foreign Office and the National Trust. The company can equip a vehicle for any journey, for example by extending water and fuel tanks, and by providing roof racks, tents and showers.

*Brownchurch Ltd,* Bickley Road, Leyton, London E10 7AQ; 020-8556 0011; www.brownchurch.co.uk. Markets overland equipment and heavy-duty roof racks for Land Rovers. Full list of items with prices available on their website.

*Land Rover* – www.landrover.com/gb. The company website is an online catalogue with extensive information about the current models, used vehicles and how to find dealers around the UK and globally, which might be useful if you needed to find spare parts on a journey. Click on the Adventures – Land Rover Experience link to find nine centres where you can do half or full-day off-road training courses (normal price £150-£250). Land Rover run occasional expeditions in remote places of the UK and abroad (e.g. Namibia) for Land Rover owners who dream of an off-road expedition but want the assurance of having a guide and technical support.

## DESIGNING YOUR OWN ADVENTURE

Hitting the road can take many forms. At the most basic you can walk. Walking one of the world's best or lesser known long distance footpaths, whether the spine of Corsica or the Southern Alps of New Zealand, would be a worthy ambition for a gap year and a means of getting to grips with the landscapes and people of one region. Closer to home many grown-ups take up the challenge of a long distance path like the Pennine Way and are amazed, despite the fact that it is a household name, that they have it virtually to themselves. Unless you plan to take a 'gap decade' you are unlikely to want to emulate the project of Briton Karl Bushby who is attempting to walk 36,000 miles around the world. In 2006, his deportation from Russia on suspicion of espionage was overturned, allowing him to resume his mighty trek at roughly the half-way point.

If you want to cover more distance, you can plan to travel by public transport or take your own vehicle whether van, bicycle, motorbike or boat, which allows you the freedom to go wherever the whim takes you. One Dutch woman is at the moment journeying to the south pole in a tractor (www.tractortractor.org). The drawback is that you become dependent on a piece of machinery that might prove difficult to protect and maintain in remote areas of the world. However, a vehicle offers autonomy and allows you to chart your own course.

Each of the tales from the road profiled in this chapter illustrates some of the choices available if you are contemplating a gap year to travel the world. These individuals chose different means of travel through different regions. Each has a unique story to recount and each represents just one of the thousands of journeys that travellers take every year in which they hope to experience adventure and a measure of self-discovery too. Beyond the picket fence and the privet hedge lie the excitement and challenges of travel.

## Into the Heart of Africa

**Rachel Pooley** aged 24 and **Charlie Stanley-Evans** aged 28 both decided to leave their jobs in London and drive to Cape Town. Rachel had been working for a mental health charity and Charlie had been employed in the wine trade. Together they felt an urge to travel and so planned a long-distance trip by road. Initially, Rachel's father felt she should be thinking about settling into a career, but neither had commitments and they wanted to see Africa. They were bored with London and wanted change. Charlie made a good profit from the sale of his flat, so he had capital to put into the expedition.

For £18,500, Rachel and Charlie bought an old MOD Defender TDI/ long wheel chassis from a specialist dealer, Keith Gott (address above) who then built a new body and new engine to allow them to sleep in the vehicle and on the roof. Brownchurch Ltd. supplied a roof rack with tent, which could be put up in half a minute on wooden boards and could be stored at the front of the rack. Other important supplies included jerry cans for water, which could be warmed in the sun during the day to supply water for a shower. Looking back on their hugely ambitious journey, one practical mistake they identified was not taking a fridge for food and drinks. But they do not regret their decision to take neither a phone nor a camcorder because it forced them to take a closer look at what they were seeing.

They spent three months planning what to take and trying to anticipate all their requirements for day-to-day life in the tropics and also for emergencies. To prepare themselves they took an off-road driving course and learnt motor maintenance, all about air and oil filters and how to change tyres. They took 500lbs of spare parts including special air snorkel attachments to keep out dust and water.

Leaving in April, their trip took them through Europe and to Turkey on the threshold of Asia and its more alien cultures. They travelled on through Syria and Jordan to Egypt where they shipped the Land Rover to Kenya with P&O, which they had booked in advance because it was impossible (as it is now) to travel through Sudan. Picking up the jeep in Kenya they then took it through safari game parks and into neighbouring Tanzania.

Without the vehicle, their experience of Africa would have been wholly different. It enabled them to escape the well-worn routes covered by crowds of other tourists and to take their own safari into fascinating places like the Tsavo West National Park. They slept either in the Land Rover or on the roof. At other times they could use campsites with loos and showers.

In Malawi they accidentally fell into buying a six-month lease on a backpacker's hotel, the Mwaya Beach Lodge on the edge of Lake Malawi. This was the highlight of their journey through Africa but wholly unplanned. Despite the difficulties of supplying the lodge with food, dealing with difficult guests, and managing the staff of nine people, it taught them skills they could use back home in Britain. They built a house for themselves with brick and thatch for £200 together with a garden. 'We were tempted to stay long-term and buy the lodge, which had potential. It was a heavenly place and we enjoyed the work but the life of ex-pats in Africa is a little strange. We met too many who were stoned or drunk,' says Rachel.

From Malawi they headed south through Zimbabwe and into the Kruger National Park in South Africa, Namibia and onto Cape Town. In general their African adventure was hugely rewarding:

*We learnt a lot about each other and other people. It makes us appreciate life more now. We are less concerned about work and fussier about the work we choose to do. The mentality in Africa is very different because there's no concept of planning ahead. Each day is a new challenge.*

In retrospect they see the Land Rover as crucial to their experience of Africa. They still own it and use it as a rather sturdy car in the English countryside and are now thinking of making a similar trip in Europe or the Americas.

Of course other means of transport can be equally exciting in Africa, even public transport. **Mark Tanner** is a New Zealander in his late 20s who thinks that 'it's a shame more people don't take time out from the job'. He aims to take off about every year in three from office life where he works as a product marketing manager. Most recently, he took six months off to teach English in Khartoum through the *Sudan Volunteer Programme* (see entry) followed by a very ambitious paddling expedition. Along with a Canadian friend, Mark became the first man to paddle from the source of the Blue Nile to the Mediterranean Sea, a journey that took just short of five months and covered 5,000 kilometres. An account of their epic journey complete with descriptions of terrifying rapids, crocodile attacks and hostile locals can be found at www.niletrip.com. For Mark, volunteering in Sudan was a useful precursor to the rafting adventure:

*I guess you could say the time in Sudan was a gap year for grown-ups. Teaching was a breeze compared to the paddle, but it prepared me for many of the cultural challenges during the paddle. Also having taught at the University of Khartoum helped give me creditability with officials during the paddle.*

## Travelling by Bicycle

One of the most rewarding and accessible ways of travelling is by bicycle. You remain in control of your own route and can veer off the beaten track to take the back roads while still maintaining a healthy mileage each day. Cycle touring represents freedom. It is a cheap and clean form of transport. For improving physical fitness, you can't improve on a bike journey. A bicycle allows the rider to stop to appreciate the views or sights along the route. Due to their speed and relative quietness, cyclists have a much better chance than other road users of seeing animals and birds. It can often provide a peg for interacting with the local population both in areas where cyclists abound and in areas where cyclists are a rarity and have novelty value. Enormous pleasure can be derived from the knowledge that you are crossing a landscape under your own steam. Walking achieves the same end but cycling allows you to travel much further in the same time.

Provided you take the right equipment it's possible to be very versatile, either taking roads or mere tracks. You can also skip regions that hold no interest for you by putting your bike on a train or bus. It is not unknown for trucks to stop and offer a lift to a cyclist, especially one labouring up a mountain. Bear in mind that you don't need to be an experienced cyclist to use a bicycle for a long distance journey. Everyone can obtain a bike and find a pace that is comfortable. An average target in relatively benign terrain might be 50 miles a day which might seem daunting to a novice, but is manageable for most reasonably fit people. By comparison experienced and super-fit cyclists can cover twice that.

Let us imagine that in your youth you were a keen (not necessarily avid) cyclist. You remember with great fondness your cycling holidays in the Cotswolds, round the Ring of Kerry or along the Loire Valley. Perhaps your dedication to cycling survived into your working life and you have used your trusty machine on and off for commuting to work. The arrival of children has inevitably cramped your cycling style and if you're lucky you have got your money's worth out of the bicycle rack you bought at Halfords in a fit of enthusiasm. Come to think of it you haven't been on a decent long ride for a decade and certainly not taken your bicycle abroad. It is an astonishing statistic that the British own 21 million bicycles (more than they do cars), the majority of which are gently rusting in garages and sheds.

A gap year might provide a chance to resurrect an interest in this most wholesome of pastimes. The National Cycle Network in the UK (www.sustrans.org.uk) covers an estimated 10,000 miles of designated cycle routes, many of them along disused railway lines and canal towpaths. But you needn't confine your aspirations to the UK. With a large scale map and a comfortable bicycle with a good gear range, you can enjoy cycling almost anywhere.

**Ambrose Marsh is a Canadian physician who enjoyed a couple of extended cycling trips around Europe in the 1970s. As his 50th birthday approached, his wife Leah asked him what he would most like to do.**

He thought about it for a while and decided that he would like to do some travelling on his own followed by an adult cycling trip in an interesting part of the world. She cheerfully agreed to look after their two young children while he cycled from Madrid to Bilboa and explored the Basque country. He sent a round robin e-mail to his address book, inviting friends to join him on his 'birthday-boy-designed perfect celebration'.

He wrote to his friends 'Spain seems a spot to go. I have been once but there are many places in Spain I haven't seen and I love tapas and dark red wine. Did I mention mountains? I had dreamt of a long cycle ride from Istanbul to Beijing but I didn't do enough planning, the geo-political situation has made it virtually impossible and I couldn't afford all the maps anyway. I now plan to cycle with whichever friends wish to and can join me. I am thinking rural central Spain, small hotels. Personal bests will not be officially recorded but all paces will be tolerated. I am well aware of new babies, new jobs and new conferences that may complicate our already full lives. I don't know, it sounds like it could be fun.'

And it was. After the spirit-sapping climb north from Madrid airport, the small group had a marvellous time following the network of minor roads. They were helped in their route finding by the book *Cycle Touring in Spain* by Harry Dowdell (Cicerone Press, £14) but still managed to get into various scrapes and have adventures. One of his companions had a shiny new bicycle with such high-tech pedals that she sometimes couldn't loosen them before falling over and on one occasion cut her leg quite seriously. The moral is, always get to know your machine thoroughly before setting off on a long cycle ride.

**Tom Moreton** aged 28 and his friend Paul Beaton aged 30 departed from Newcastle to cycle to Istanbul. Tom had set up a web design business precisely so that he could be self-employed and take time out to travel for extended periods. Whereas his mother was very encouraging about this trip, some of his contemporaries remained unconvinced that it was a good idea to leave his home and business for four months. Neither Tom nor Paul had much experience of cycling over distances or steep terrain but they decided that their bicycles provided the best way of seeing Europe. They took 119 days to travel via Norway, Sweden, Germany, Poland, the Czech Republic, Slovakia, Austria, Slovenia, Croatia, Hungary, Romania and Bulgaria to Turkey.

With the help of country-specific maps on which camping grounds were marked, they could plan their route each day, choosing minor roads whenever possible. Occasionally it was not possible to reach a campsite or hostel by nightfall, though this was of minimal concern in Norway and Sweden where you are legally allowed to pitch a tent as long as it is not within 100 metres of a house. Occasionally they were forced into a hotel and at the other extreme to camp illegally in a lay-by. The technical problems they encountered were remarkably few: a spoke, a buckled wheel and a broken gear changer. In Prague it was difficult to find repairs for some damaged ball bearings. On one occasion in Bulgaria they accidentally found that they had filtered onto a motorway which was not very pleasant, especially when they received a hostile reception from a group of prostitutes. Roads in Turkey were very narrow without hard shoulders. But at no point on their journey did they feel endangered by the conditions.

Their equipment did not require a huge investment. They chose hybrid mountain bike frames made by Trek which cost £200 each. These bikes are made for touring rather than for travelling on rough terrain. After researching tents, they plumped for one produced by Mountain Brand, which cost £80 and is used by the World Health Organization. For storage Tom and Paul used a Canadian-made pannier system known as PanPack, which sits on the back of the bike and converts into a backpack. They found that this item of luggage had too many straps to remove with ease, so they tended to leave them on the bikes and felt that they were not sufficiently waterproof. In retrospect they wish they had taken a pair of rubberised panniers produced by Ortlieb of Germany. They took a small tool kit, spare inner tubes, puncture repair kits and spare brake cables.

Tom believes his trip has made him more relaxed about money and work and given him more perspective about what he values in life. An immediate physical change for Paul was that he lost two stone.

An even more ambitious cycling journey in the opposite direction was undertaken by teacher **Sally Haiselden** between finishing her contract at an international school in the Sudan before Christmas and returning to Cambridge in the summer. Almost from her arrival in Africa more than two years before, Sally had been harbouring thoughts of cycling home. Her friends and acquaintances had provided her with lots of reasons not to do it: 'But there are snakes and scorpions,' 'What about water?', 'It is a long way!', 'You will be tired', 'But you are a woman. You are alone'. She says, 'It's not as though I had not thought about the risks but such talk made me more stubborn and determined.'

In 200 days, she cycled a truly impressive 8,855.27 kilometres through Sudan, Egypt, Jordan, Syria, Turkey, Bulgaria and along the Danube to Germany, Holland and home. At times she became addicted to the self-indulgent lifestyle of being without stress, responsibility, schedule or appointments. Some news from home made her realise how lucky she was to have the time, money and particularly the health to be able to do what she wanted. A year or so on, she had once again embraced stress, responsibility and strict timetables since she was teaching a lively year five class at a Cambridge primary school. Having posted an entertaining diary of her adventures on the Internet, at last report she was hoping to turn her experiences into a book, which would be the icing on the cake of a marvellously enriching gap year.

It seems that owners of web design businesses are drawn to long distance cycling since another one in that line of work, **Edward Genochio** from Devon, gave up his business in February 2004 to cycle to Shanghai and as of mid-2006 is en route home again. Ed covered the 20,500 kilometre distance in less than 11 months following a new route across the Gobi Desert. His unsupported expedition back again has seen him crossing a 4,000 metre high passes in wintry Tibet and meeting all sorts of weird and wonderful types; his entertaining website is recommended (www.2wheels.org.uk).

Keen cyclists can benefit from joining the *Cyclists' Touring Club,* Parklands, Railton Rd, Guildford, Surrey GU2 9JX (0870 873 0060; www.ctc.org.uk) which provides free technical, legal and touring information to members; membership costs £33.

## BACKPACKING – TRAVELLING BY YOUR WITS

The purest form of travelling is by hitching rides or on public transport cheek by jowl with the local people. Many dream of indulging their wanderlust, following their noses, crossing a country by any means possible. By creating your own route and using your wits to find your way, you'll find yourself obliged to interact with local people rather than being cocooned in a foreign run tour.

Yet you will seldom be entirely isolated. Almost everywhere in the world from Baluchistan to Patagonia, you'll encounter other travellers and expats. Often you will find yourself inside an informal community of travellers who stay in the same hostels, travel on the same ferries and swap travellers' tales. This camaraderie of the road often provides a welcome grapevine and support system far from home. But sometimes it is a depressing reminder of how small the world has become for privileged westerners.

Travelling in a loosely structured way allows you to explore features of a country that might not be signposted in a guide. You are more likely to learn where the locals shop, eat and socialise if you have the courage to keep your nose out of a guidebook. Of course guidebooks can be very useful and reassuring for novice travellers. But they are sometimes bestowed with more authority than they deserve. Often, two or three years might have elapsed between your arrival and when the guide was researched. Urban life is especially fluid and city listings quickly go out of date.

Spontaneity will bring dividends. You will be more open to chances of integrating with local communities if your itinerary hasn't been pre-programmed by books and other travellers. When engaging with local people, always follow the golden rule of trusting your instincts. It may be stating the obvious, but you should never accept an invitation to go somewhere or participate in an activity that makes you feel uncomfortable or threatened. Even if you run the risk of offending a 'host', you need to keep your internal compass functioning. Bear in mind that foreigners may be viewed as easy targets for some form of exploitation, principally financial. If you feel that an offer sounds too good to be true then it is likely to turn out to be just that.

Don't lose sight of why you're backpacking. Often, it will be hard work and occasionally gruelling. Travelling in reasonable comfort is exhausting enough. Sightseeing is often a pleasure but it is taxing too, so give yourself plenty of time out for relaxation, whether reading in cafés, writing a letter on a tropical veranda, strolling in foothills or lounging on a sunny beach. Occasionally, it's a good idea to splash out on a comfortable hotel, particularly if you are feeling under the weather. Clean sheets, air-conditioning and a laundry service are reviving treats after several weeks on the road and are usually worth the extra expense.

While juggling bus or train timetables and the need to find suitable accommodation, try not to rush. The slow pace of life as a traveller, especially in the developing world, is something to be savoured not bemoaned. Dawdling allows you to appreciate different experiences and sensations in places to which you may never have the chance to return. Dashing hither and yon should be left to the very young who, in the words of the veteran traveller and writer Dervla Murphy, '...seem to cover too much ground too quickly, sampling everywhere and becoming familiar with nowhere... it would be good if the young became more discriminating, allowing themselves time to travel seriously in a limited area that they had chosen because of its particular appeal to them, as individuals.' This is something that more mature travellers on a gap year can aim to achieve. Remember that your sabbatical is designed precisely to give you the time you normally lack on a conventional holiday from work.

Once you have been carrying your pack for a couple of weeks, caught the right buses, met a few other travellers, you will probably laugh at your pre-travelling misconceptions of danger and risk. The economy end of independent travel is a burgeoning market worldwide, especially in Australasia, Latin America and Africa and you will soon find a bewildering choice of destinations with suitable facilities. If you are trying to capture the essence of travel and want to make a distinctive break from your annual holiday then open-ended backpacking guarantees a chance to find your own adventure.

At the same time that it offers the romance of travel, backpacking is undeniably arduous and uncertain. Sleeping on crowded trains or hiking through mosquito-infested jungles may hold little appeal. For some, pitching a tent on Dartmoor in a drizzling mist and bedding down in a soggy sleeping bag require plenty of courage and daring. People past their thirties may decide that they don't want to rough it any more or to replicate student life, and will travel accordingly. They may have little interest in experiencing foreign cultures at a grassroots level and may prefer to concentrate on some other aspect, such as making a study of the art and architecture, history or language of a foreign culture. (See the chapter *New Skills and New Projects.*)

## Pre-Nuptial Travels in Africa

After his engagement, **Nick McNulty** decided at the age of 28 to be brave and leave his job as a manager in a West London Health Authority to travel through Africa, because it represented what he thought of as his last opportunity to follow a whimsical dream. African wildlife and its intrinsic mystery had always appealed to him. It made sense to head off before he became settled with a new family. Nick backpacked across the length of Africa the old-fashioned way by hitching rides with new friends or on local transport, like a nineteenth-century explorer now aided by maps, banking, modern transport and the occasional support of the British Council's various libraries across the African continent.

Nick McNulty attributes many of his best experiences to his own 'bumbling naïveté', without which he believes he wouldn't have seen so much. By underplanning his trip and moving with a greater degree of spontaneity, Nick enjoyed being able to avoid the mass of tourists. On his journey he made friends with Ahmed with whom he travelled from Algeria to Benin. Nick stayed first with

Ahmed's family and then with a brother in a Ghanaian slum, unusual experiences which he attributes to his backpacking style of travel. Nick also found rides with a couple of German wheeler-dealers driving a Mercedes across Africa to sell in Nigeria. 'I found myself on what was less the hippy-trail and more the route of would-be entrepreneurs. Many Africans I met were also pursuing money-making schemes.'

In Kenya he met up with his fiancée, Anna, who took a shorter break from the BBC to meet him. Together they continued the journey into Tanzania and Madagascar. Eventually a glimpse of the lights of Cape Town clustering round the massive form of Table Mountain felt like a homecoming to Nick. The trip did not seriously change the dynamic of his career as he returned to the NHS in a similar role, but the experience has had a lasting impression: 'The trip was great. It has been one of the best things I've done in my life with the exception of marrying my wife and becoming a parent.' Anna believes the trip was a wonderful time for them to spend together before their marriage. For her part the travels inspired Anna to produce a series on post-colonial Africa for the BBC's World Service.

Like any trip, theirs was not trouble-free. On the border crossing between Algeria and Niger, Nick sat on the border with his two German travelling companions for six days because the border had been closed. Waiting for the guards to resolve the problem, they had to cope with a shortage of food and with boredom, which was eased by playing repeated games of chess amid the Sahara's unending dust and rubble. On another occasion Nick had some money stolen and an accidentally unpaid credit card bill at home forced him to survive on $100 for two weeks. In Benin a policeman confiscated his passport leaving him feeling very vulnerable to the possibility of corruption.

Nick's gap year illustrates that it's possible to travel in a leisurely way across a vast continent of different terrain and climates in quite a spontaneous and loosely planned fashion. Because relying on your wits and travelling solo requires courage and self-confidence, it's arguable that this option delivers the greatest rewards.

## ADVENTURE TRAVEL

A gap year is an ideal time to indulge a taste for adventure. Some will consider one of the classic overland journeys across continents or will want to pit themselves against the elements on the high seas (see section on *Sailing* below). But staying put and going native can provide the backdrop for any number of adventures.

While staying in the town of Kratie in Cambodia for six months of her gap year, **Hannah Stevens** was more willing than most to experiment with new experiences:

> *I took a few days off work to travel with three friends up to Ratanakiri in the North East of Cambodia. We went trekking through the rubber plantations on an elephant to a hidden waterfall that was directly out of 'The Jungle Book'. In fact I'm pretty sure I heard Baloo singing in the distance! The whole thing was absolutely phenomenal, and I had to keep reminding myself that this is where I live! It certainly made me smile! Sometimes, I can't quite work out how I've ended up here in such a glorious place, with wonderful people and a rich culture.*
>
> *On one journey, I found myself volunteering to sample the local cui-*

*sine, fried tarantulas! The head was absolutely hideous and popped in my mouth, drowning my tastebuds in brain fluid; but the legs and body were fairly acceptable, somewhat crunchy, but certainly edible. I spent the following four hours of the journey picking leg hair out of my teeth, and doing fairly repulsive burps! I think I'll pass next time! With the rainy season come crickets! Swarms of noisy, ugly, flying cockroaches. But, unlike six months ago, I don't squeal and flap, but catch and eat them! Chop off their legs, rip out their guts, stick a peanut up their bum, and deep fry them. Genuinely delicious, and it keeps us occupied. Coming soon to a dinner party near you!*

Like tarantulas and crickets, the thrill of risk-taking may be an acquired taste but it is one which can bring enormous satisfaction. When long-time Religious Education teacher, **Nigel Hollington,** set off to join a Greenforce conservation project in Zambia, he knew that he would be expected to handle rodents, and decided to confront his phobia head on. He packed an extra-strong pair of gardening gloves for the purpose and did not shirk when the moment came. His year off included a succession of minor triumphs such as this, which he found extraordinarily satisfying.

Pushing yourself to the edge of danger can hold a special appeal. More conventional challenges like bungy-jumping, white water rafting, parasailing and various other adrenalin sports are tempting to many independent travellers (but make sure your insurance policy will cover them).

## Overland Journeys

Venturing across vast continents, dark or otherwise, can be a daunting prospect for an independent traveller. An alternative is to make the journey with one of the numerous established overland tour operators, most of which charge between £100 and £150 a week plus a food kitty of about £50 a week. The longer the trip the lower the weekly cost, for example Oasis Overland trips (www.oasisoverland.co.uk) start at £70 per week plus £30 a week local payment (for food and camping fees) on 30-week trips and go up to around £150 a week plus kitty for shorter South American trips A number of adventure tour operators follow a huge number of routes through all the continents of the world. Whereas some overland routes are fraught with difficulty, others are comfortable and almost routine.

The old hippy overland route to India and Nepal has been problematical for many years though not impossible if travelling from Iran to Pakistan, bypassing Afghanistan which is completely off-limits. The situation in Sudan means that it is not feasible to travel overland from Egypt to Kenya, though various routes penetrate the rest of the continent.

Petrol-heads might be tempted by the poor man's/woman's variation on the Paris-Dakar Rally. Teams that enter the Plymouth-Banjul Challenge (www.plymouth-banjul.co.uk) must travel to the capital of the Gambia in an old banger that costs less than £100 (preferably a Lada).

## Overland Tour Operators

A selection of overland companies is listed here. Others may be found on the Overland Expedition Resources website www.go-overland.com. Many overland companies advertise in the glossy adventure travel magazine *Wanderlust* (01753 620426; www.wanderlust.co.uk).

*Absolute Africa,* 41 Swanscombe Road, Chiswick, London W4 2HL (020-8742 0226; www.absoluteafrica.com). Adventure camping safaris in Africa.

*Acacia Adventure Holidays,* Lower Ground Floor, 23A Craven Terrace, London W2 3QH (020-7706 4700; www.acacia-africa.com). Africa specialist with over 200 tours lasting from 3 to 70 days. A free 112-page colour brochure provides detailed tour information.



*Adventure Overland,* 9 Ridge Road, Mitcham, Surrey CR4 2ET 106 (020-8640 8105; www.adventureoverland.com). Specialises in Central Asia, including Turkmenistan, Uzbekistan and Tajikistan. The Grand Adventure Overland lasts 42 days. They can also put together a tailor-made itinerary.

*Africa's Best Overland Safaris,* 93 Leyland Rd, Penwortham, Lancashire PR1 9QJ (01772 741600; www.overlandsafaris.co.uk). Tours of South Africa, Namibia, Botswana, Zambia and Zimbabwe.

*Bukima Adventure Travel,* 43A Riffel Road, London NW2 4PB (0870 757 2230; www.bukima.com). Have introduced specialist tours to Africa, Egypt and South America for the over-40s as well as a programme of other tours open to all.

*Dragoman Overland Expeditions,* Operations Department, Camp Green, Kenton

Road, Debenham, Suffolk IP14 6LA (0870 499 4475; www.dragoman.com). Expeditions to Africa, Asia, South and Central America. Adventure journeys off the beaten track often without western infrastructure. Travellers are carried in a specially adapted vehicle which is a cross between a jeep, minibus and army truck.

*Economic Expeditions,* 020-8969 1948; www.economicexpeditions.com). Africa specialist.

*Exodus,* Grange Mills, Weir Road, London SW12 0NE (0870 240 5550; www.exodus.co.uk). One of the leading adventure travel companies in the UK, organising adrenalin-fuelled activities graded according to difficulty to give you guidance about physical endurance. In addition to overland expeditions, Exodus offer trekking holidays, cycling holidays, multi-activity holidays and trips in Europe lasting from 1-24 weeks. More than 500 tours in 90 countries.

*Explore Worldwide Ltd,* Nelson House, 55 Victoria Road, Farnborough, Hampshire GU14 7PA (0870 333 4002; www.explore.co.uk). Europe's largest small group adventure tour operator. These exploratory tours are a safe and social introduction for those planning an extended journey to the country or region.

*Guerba Expeditions,* Wessex House, 40 Station Road, Westbury, Wilts. BA13 3JN (01373 826611; www.guerba.co.uk). Originally an Africa specialist, now runs trips to other continents as well.

*Imaginative Traveller,* 1 Betts Avenue, Martlesham Heath, Suffolk IP5 7RH (0800 316 2717; www.imaginative-traveller.com). Runs small group adventures around the globe, some of which are based on voluntary work. Ring them to request a brochure on your chosen continent or region. Trips last up to a month.

*Intrepid Travel,* 76 Upper St, Islington, London N1 0NU (0800 917 6456; www.intrepidtravel.com). Small group adventure tour operator with trips to Asia, the Middle East, Latin America and Europe.

*Journey Latin America,* 12-13 Heathfield Terrace, Chiswick, London W4 4JE (020-8747 3108; www.JourneyLatinAmerica.co.uk). A fully-bonded agency which specialises in travel to and around all of Latin America. Runs dozens of escorted tours throughout the continent using private or public transport, and also offers range of multi-activity adventure trips.

*Ke Adventure Travel,* 32 Lake Road, Keswick, Cumbria, CA12 5DQ (017687 73966; www.keadventure.com). Organises adventure trips on bike or by foot around the world from the Himalayas to Brazil. Most trips last two to four weeks.

*Kumuka Expeditions,* 40 Earl's Court Road, London W8 6EJ (020-7937 8855/0800 389 2328; www.kumuka.com). Itineraries through Africa and Latin America including the 'Andean Adventure' which takes groups from Quito, Ecuador to Santiago, Chile over 56 days (£1,350 plus $1,365 local payment).

*Oasis Overland Ltd,* The Marsh, Henstridge, Somerset BA8 0TF (01963 363400; www.oasisoverland.co.uk). Africa, the Middle East and South America.

*Tucan Travel,* London Office, 316 Uxbridge Road, Acton, London W3 9QP (020-8896 1600; Brochure request 0800 804 8415; UKsales@tucantravel.com; www.tucantravel.com / www.budgetexpeditions.com). Open age group adventure tours and independent travel throughout Latin America, Cuba and Antarctica. Budget Expeditions is their youth brand which takes participants to Europe, Egypt and South America. Sample price of the latter is £950 for 49 days travelling between Rio and Santiago via Patagonia plus local fund of $500.



*World Expeditions,* 3 Northfields Prospect, Putney Bridge Road, London SW18 1PE (020-8870 2600; www.worldexpeditions.com). Long established adventure travel company with large choice of journeys on all continents including the Arctic and Antarctic. Trips can take up to 30 days. Adventures to suit all ages and fitness levels.

Collectively these companies employ large numbers of competent expedition staff including leaders and cooks, though most companies require a longer commitment than would be available on a career break. See 'Overland Tour Leaders' in earlier section *Working in Tourism.*

## Charity Challenges

A large and growing number of charities in the UK offer adventurous group travel to individuals who are prepared to undertake some serious fundraising on their behalf. These are energetically marketed so are often advertised in the travel advertisements of the *Independent* and other broadsheets. Household names like Oxfam, the Youth Hostels Association and the Children's Society organise sponsored trips, as do many more obscure good causes. Joining one of the trips organised by the specialist Charity Challenge allows you to raise money for the charity of your choice; contact *Charity Challenge,* 7th Floor, Northway House, 1379 High Road, London N20 9LP (020-8557 0000; www.charitychallenge.com). Note that experienced tour leaders and medics may be needed for these trips and offered subsidised or free places.

Charity trips seldom last longer than a fortnight so are perhaps not of central interest to people on a career break. But the chance to participate in a group activity which at the same time funds a good cause is welcomed by some, especially those who don't relish the prospect of taking an adventurous trip on their own. Cycling, trekking, canoeing, rafting, mountaineering, all are on offer in most corners of the world. These trips have proved particularly popular among women in middle life who lack the confidence to undertake an adventurous trip on their own and who often find it easier to justify a trip abroad if it is for a good cause as well as for their own pleasure.

Some charities mount a series of 'challenges'. For example Cancer Research

UK runs regular fundraising treks to Patagonia, China and Kilimanjaro (0870 850 8735; www.cancerresearchuk.org/treks). The minimum fundraising targets are normally £4,000 which includes the cost of the trips themselves.

While these events have proved a popular way of raising money for a favourite charity, some critics have argued that it is an inefficient way of raising money for worthy causes. As much as half of the money raised by each sponsored traveller goes towards paying for their holiday (flight, accommodation, etc.), something which family, friends and colleagues who support the fundraising might come to resent. One solution is to simply pay that portion out of your pocket and fund-raise the rest. Charity challenges do appear to achieve the dual goals of raising money and raising awareness of the charity's purpose and achievements by engendering a sense of occasion. Of course anyone undertaking a challenging trip can use it to raise money for a good cause.

## Expeditions

One romantic idea for people planning a break from the daily grind is to join an expedition venturing into the more remote and unspoiled parts of the world from Tierra del Fuego to Irian Jaya. It would be very jolly if you could be invited to join a party of latter-day explorers in exchange for some menial duty such as portering or cooking. However expedition organisers and leaders nowadays demand that participants have some specialist skills or expertise to contribute beyond mere eagerness. For example an advert for people needed on an Arctic expedition included among its volunteer requirements a post-doctoral archaeologist, an electronics officer for proton magneto-meter maintenance and an antenna theorist. One suspects that they weren't inundated with applications.

The *Royal Geographical Society* (1 Kensington Gore, London SW7 2AR) encourages and assists many British expeditions. The Expedition Advisory Centre at the RGS published a booklet *Joining an Expedition* in 2001 listing about 60 organisations that regularly arrange expeditions; this can now be read free online (www.rgs.org.uk). The EAC also hosts a weekend 'Explore' seminar every November on 'Planning a Small Expedition', which covers fundraising and budgeting for expeditions as well as issues of safety and logistics. If you want personal advice on mounting an expedition, you can make an appointment to visit the EAC (020-7591 3030/3033; eac@rgs.org). The Society's historic map room is open to the public daily from 11am to 5pm. The Expedition Advisory Centre has generously put online most of the grant-giving organisations listed in its publication *The Expedition Handbook* (which can be bought for £16.99). Although many grants are ring-fenced (e.g. must live within eight miles of Exmouth Town Hall) it is certainly worth checking and applying as widely as possible.

*Raleigh International* (www.raleighinternational.org) is the longest established and most experienced expedition organisation, having run hundreds of three-month expeditions overseas. Their aim is to enable people to reach their full potential through challenging community, environmental and adventure projects as part of an overseas expedition. Building schools/clinics in Namibia or collecting scientific data in Costa Rica are examples of projects undertaken in Raleigh International's five expedition countries (Ghana, Nicaragua and Malaysian Borneo are the other three).

Raleigh employ a considerable number of staff aged 25 to 70 to organise expedition logistics for the groups of young Raleigh volunteers. Each year ten three-month expeditions are staffed with a team of self-funding volunteers from diverse working backgrounds who take on roles such as project manager, accountant, doctor, nurse, engineer, photographer, builder, trek leader and communications expert. Not all of the 40 roles on an expedition require specialist knowledge. The main requirement is an affinity with youth development, a positive attitude and a willingness to fund-raise approximately £1,500 to cover all expenses except flights (can be substantially reduced by claiming on gift-aid). Selection takes place through written applications and an assessment weekend that simulates potential team challenges through physical exercises and problem solving. Volunteers must know how to swim and speak English. Former expedition staff acknowledge that the expeditions are hard work but the experience is unique, rewarding and contributes to career development. This is something that is officially acknowledged by some employers (such as the Ministry of Defence) who sponsor their employees to participate as 'Commercial Venturers'.

Going on an expedition is a great way to test yourself, which is something **Jane Belfourd** would probably agree with since she almost stepped on a giant boa constrictor when she was on a Raleigh expedition in Costa Rica. **Alasdair Taylor** (age 26) traded the comfort of his city life as a management consultant in London for three months in the wilds of Patagonia and the chance to get his hands really dirty. As part of a 40-strong volunteer staff team on a 2004 Raleigh International expedition in southern Chile, Alasdair led groups of eleven 17-25 year olds from around the world on a mission to build footpaths in Queulat National Park and then took them on to Colonia to collect moraine samples to be used to calculate what drives the world's climate:

> *I am covered in mud, it's raining and I am looking up at an amazing hanging glacier with three waterfalls pounding down from it into the laguna below. Around me is my team of wet, mud-splattered people, all still smiling. This is a far cry from my work in the UK! And I mustn't complain about the weather – we were unexpectedly blessed with endless sunshine for the first month or more. I came to Chile for the extremes that it offers, weather certainly being one of them. I actually expected life on expedition to be more uncomfortable than it is. There have been far fewer crises than one would anticipate on an expedition this large (we are 170 people in total) and doing such a range of activities. One of the self-improvements I will cherish is my newly found ability to sleep on any floor, the fact that I can now be almost pleasant in the morning and an appreciation of the finer things in life!*

*World Challenge Expeditions* (08704 873 173; leaderinfo@world-challenge.co.uk) takes on several hundred expedition leaders to supervise school expeditions to developing countries. Trips take place in the summer and the minimum commitment is four weeks. Applicants must be at least 24, have a MLTB (Mountain Leader Training) and some experience of working with young people and preferably of travelling in the Third World. Expenses are covered and a stipend can be negotiated. Leadership training courses take place in Derbyshire.

The *Brathay Exploration Group* (Brathay Hall, Ambleside, Cumbria LA22 0HP; 015394 33942; www.brathayexploration.org.uk) has organised hundreds of expeditions since its inception in 1947. Each year it sends out 10-15 new teams to far-flung parts of the globe. *Outward Bound* (www.outwardbound-uk.org/global/expedition.html) organises expeditions to the jungles, mountains and tropical islands of Sabah in the Malaysian part of Borneo, South Africa, Romania and Slovakia. Expeditions, which are open to anyone over 15 with plenty of participants in their 20s, help with projects relating to wildlife such as turtle breeding or the orang-utan sanctuary, helping with research of marine life, insects and plants. The participation fee (excluding flights) starts at £1,700.

Every other year *XCL Ltd* (Reaseheath, Nantwich, Cheshire CW5 6DF; 01270 625825; enquiries@xcl.info) runs two or three-week expeditions for approximately 50 adults from diverse backgrounds. Ethiopia is the destination for 2007. Previous expedition destinations have included seldom-visited Guyana in South America, Uganda in Africa, and Sikkim in India. Community projects include teaching in indigenous communities, running business workshops, conservation work, sports development and basic construction work. Preparation takes place at two residential training weekends; the cost is £2,100.

Those with a specialised project might discover that targeted funds are available from trusts and charities. However many, like the *Mount Everest Foundation* (www.mef.org.uk/mefguide.htm), are earmarked for high level expeditions undertaking first ascents, new routes and scientific research on mountains, which are beyond the capabilities of all but the most serious climbers.

*Wilderness Medical Training* (The Coach House, Thorny Bank, Garth Row Kendal, Cumbria UK LA8 9AW; 01539 823183; www.wildernessmedicaltraining.co.uk) puts on courses in expedition medicine for lay people as well as doctors. Their foundation course is called 'Far From Help' which teaches the use of prescription medicines. Courses last 2-7 days and cost £220-£795.

## SAILING

Sailing is a versatile sport that can form the basis of an adventurous gap year. Learning to sail the oceans is a perfect way to fill a gap in your career. It is possible for experienced sailors to charter a boat with or without crew, or act as crew for someone else with a boat, for short or long crossings. The pleasures of open-ended island hopping in the Aegean, Caribbean or South Pacific are easily imagined though difficult to realise. Sailing represents the ultimate freedom to chart your own course and, for some, a chance to stretch mental and physical limits by sailing around the world in a yacht race.

On a sailing adventure you are bound to see dolphins, whales, flying fish and rare birds. You get in touch with nature by seeing and feeling the rhythms of the sea. You learn about sailing, meteorology, navigation. But there are also drawbacks. You will probably suffer from seasickness at the beginning. You will have to deal with a panoply of adverse weather conditions and probably experience terror at least once, especially when you move into the path of a supertanker. You have to get up in the middle of the night to take the watch. Every little task is made more difficult by the constant movement of the boat. It may be that there will be no wind for days at a stretch. But if you are prepared to cope with all this, a sailing trip can be exhilarating in the extreme.

In the context of a career break, sailing is a truly escapist activity. Out at sea you have no choice but to stop thinking about work and home because the daily tasks will require all your concentration. Long distance sailing allows you to suspend your life while simultaneously demanding an intense and unique form of communal living.

**Having finished her accountancy exams, Jennie Sanders wasn't sure what she was aiming for next and suddenly felt as though all she had ahead was a lifetime of work:**

*I had often seen adverts for sailing courses in the back pages of sailing magazines and thought how much I would like to do one. I knew that my employer PricewaterhouseCoopers invest a great deal in training up new graduates and are understandably eager to hang on to them once they are qualified. The company is also keen to promote flexible working policies, and career breaks are one option they offer to staff who have worked for them for at least four years. So I followed up one of the ads and booked on a 3½-month course with Flying Fish in order to indulge my passion for sailing (I had been sailing with my family since the age of ten) and qualify as a professional skipper.*

*The first month in North Wales was fairly windy and wet, but with Australia to look forward to, no one seemed to mind too much. We spent most of the first month learning (or refreshing) the basics and doing classroom work including chart work. No sailing experience was required; in fact one participant hadn't even been on a ferry before. Whereas some of the grown-up trainees found it strange going back to a classroom, living in shared accommodation (on the boats at very close quarters) and being told when to be where, I found it relaxing not to have to think about what to do next.*

*Soon we were all off to Sydney where we were installed in an apartment right on the beachfront in Manly – amazing. Sailing consisted of day sailing on Sydney harbour and some longer passages including night sailing up and down the east coast of Australia, as well as some racing. We took it in turns to be skipper, in order to get in the necessary practice to pass the Yachtmaster exams.*

*The course was expensive [the current price is £9,650], but by using my savings, working for a couple of months whilst I was away, and making the most of a six-month interest-free loan when I returned, I managed to do virtually everything I wanted to whilst I was away. Following the course I got a sailing job in a marina in Sydney (a far cry from sitting in front of a computer in an office in London!). Originally I had applied to my employer for a six-month unpaid break but decided to extend it to nine months since I was having such a good time. This allowed me to travel up the East Coast of Australia on to Fiji for a couple of weeks and then return to the UK to do some more sailing, including to the Scilly Isles and Ireland, as well as taking my final Yachtmaster exam.*

*After passing the exam, I decided that I couldn't put off the return to work any longer. PricewaterhouseCoopers had agreed to keep my job open (although they didn't guarantee it would be in exactly the same department) but it was felt that my technical knowledge at work might get too out of date if I stayed away for a year or more. When I was quizzed by one of my bosses as to what I had got out of the course, I was able to stress that the forward planning, organisation and people managing involved in being a skipper would be of potential benefit at work. In fact a few months after my return, I was promoted to manager. The return to work was more difficult than I had anticipated, for instance finding people who had previously been junior to me promoted ahead of me and also working to tight deadlines didn't come easily again.*

> *I never worried that my career break would harm my career. I am now a corporate tax manager with six people working under me. As well as having improved my work skills, I now race in a very competitive sportsboat class, which I do every Sunday nine months of the year. It gives me something to look forward to all week, and keeps me active and refreshed so that I am able to do my job better. I hope to take another career break when I can, but next time I'll use it to sail round the world.*

To judge whether sailing might be an idea to pursue for your own career break, dip into the wealth of sailing literature, including a classic like Joshua Slocum's *Sailing Alone* or a light-hearted account of sailing with small children in *One Summer's Grace* by Libby Purves about sailing around the British Isles with her husband Paul Heiney and their two children aged three and five. If you are committed enough to go after an advanced qualification like the Yachtmaster which might lead to a career change, see the section on Sail Training in the chapter *New Skills and New Projects*.

## Crewing on Yachts

In every marina and harbour, people are planning and preparing for long trips. There may be requests for crew posted on harbour notice boards, in yacht clubs or chandlery shops from Marina Bay in Gibraltar to Rushcutter's Bay in Sydney. The most straightforward (and usually the most successful) method is to head for the nearest yacht marina and ask captains directly. The harbour water supply or dinghy dock is usually a good place to meet yachties.

People who display a reasonable level of common sense, vigour and amiability, and take the trouble to observe yachting etiquette should find it possible to persuade a yachtsman that they will be an asset to his crew. As one skipper comments, 'A beginner ceases to be a passenger if he or she can tie half a dozen knots and hitches, knows how to read the lights of various kinds of ships and boats at night, and isn't permanently seasick.' Obviously, it is much easier to become a crew member if you have some experience. But there are opportunities for people who lack experience at sea, and it is unwise to exaggerate your skills. Once you have worked on one yacht it will be much easier to get on the next one. The yachting world is a small one. It is a good idea to buy a log book in which you can enter all relevant experience and voyages, and be sure to ask the captains of boats you have been on for a letter of reference.

Inexperienced crew are never paid and most skippers will expect a contribution towards expenses; at least US$25 a day is standard for food, drink, fuel, harbour fees, etc. but not airfares to join the yacht or visa fees. The more experience you have, the more favourable arrangements you will be able to negotiate. Also, your chances are better of having a financial contribution reduced or even waived if you are prepared to crew on unpopular routes, for example crossing the Atlantic west to east is much tougher than vice versa. If you demonstrate to a skipper that you take safety seriously enough to have learned a little about the procedures and if you are clean and sober, sensible and polite, you are probably well on your way to filling a crewing vacancy. Offshore sailing is a risky business and you should be sure that the skipper to whom you have entrusted your life is a veteran sailor. A well-used but well-kept boat is a good sign. A good starting place for novice crew might be to get to grips with a good yachting book such as *RYA Competent Crew* which contains invaluable information on technical sea terms and the basics of navigation.

Even better would be to sign up for a sailing course. The first level, Competent Crew, can be reached in a five-day course at any Royal Yachting Association recognised centre for £300-£450+. Complete beginners living in or around London who fancy the idea of sailing and just want a taster weekend should contact Capital Sailing based in London's Docklands (08700 272669; www.capitalsailing.com). The owner wants to make it possible for people to become qualified sailors more gradually instead of quitting their jobs and committing many thousands of pounds all at once. If you are planning your trip a long way in advance, scour the classified columns of*Yachting Monthly, Yachting World* or *Practical Boat Owner*, though advertisers are likely to require a substantial payment or contribution towards expenses on your part. Increasingly skippers use the Internet to find paying crew. Sites that promise to match crew with captains include www.floatplan.com/crew.htm which carries details of actual vacancies, for example 'UK – GREECE – Delivery crew required immediately for three-masted Schooner for voyage from UK to Greece. These are paid positions. Contact Reliance Yacht Management at crew@reliance-yachts.com' or 'EL SALVADOR – PANAMA – Looking for crew for a 53' ketch leaving El Salvador for Panama. 3 months cruise to explore the Costa Rican and Panama coasts. Share expenses for food and fuels. This should be a fun leisurely cruise.' A certain number of listings contain a lonely hearts element: 'Mexico and Beyond – Attractive fit slender female crew member wanted for Mexico, South Pacific and beyond. Seeking a smart, stable woman, who loves adventure, cruising, has a sense of humour and a good heart. Romance a possibility, but as we will be short-handed most of the time, the passion for sailing and a life of adventure is the crucial element.'

## Useful Crewing Contacts

Crewing agencies in Britain, France, Denmark, the West Indies, the United States and elsewhere match yacht captains and crew. These are mostly of use to experienced sailors. In the UK the *Cruising Association* (CA House, 1 Northey St, Limehouse Basin, London E14 8BT; 020-7537 2828; office@cruising.org.uk; www.cruising.org.uk/cahouse/crewing.shtml) runs a crewing service to put skippers in touch with unpaid crew. Meetings are held on the first Wednesday of the month at 7pm between February and May for this purpose. They claim to offer a variety of sailing (including two or three week cruises to the Mediterranean and transatlantic passages) to suit virtually every level of experience. The fee to non-members for this service is £25.

Among the largest crewing registers in the UK is the *Global Crew Network* (23 Old Mill Gardens, Berkhamsted, Herts. HP4 2NZ; 0870 910 1888; www.globalcrewnetwork.com) which specialises in crew recruitment for Tall Ships, traditional boats and luxury yachts worldwide. Another matching service is operated by *Crewseekers* (Crew Introduction Agency, Hawthorn House, Hawthorn Lane, Sarisbury Green, Southampton, Hants. SO31 7BD; tel/fax 01489 578319; info@crewseekers.co.uk). Their membership charges are £60 for six months, £85 for a year; joint members may be added for an extra £15. Their web pages (www.crewseekers.co.uk) are updated daily showing the latest boats worldwide requiring crew. New members may also register online. Alternatives include:

*Crew Network Worldwide* – www.crewnetwork.com. Crewing offices in Antibes, Palma de Mallorca, Fort Lauderdale and Auckland.

*Reliance Yacht Management,* First Floor Suite, 127 Lynchford Road, Farnborough, Hampshire, GU14 6ET (01252 378239; info@reliance-yachts.com). Registration fee of £35.

Concentrations of crewing agencies can be found in other yachting capitals too such as Antibes and Fort Lauderdale. The main crewing agencies in Antibes are housed in La Galerie du Port, 8 boulevard d'Aguillon, 06600 Antibes. For example try contacting Peter Insull's Crew Agency (+33 4-93 34 64 64; www.insull.com).

A number of crewing agencies are located in Fort Lauderdale, the yachting capital of Florida. The following list of crewing agencies is partly courtesy of the web page of Floyd Creamer who runs Floyd's Hostel and Crew House (954-462-0631; www.floydshostel.com). You must normally sign up at these agencies in person.

*Carole Manto Inc.,* 412 SE 17th St (954-523-2500; info@carolemanto.com)

*Crew Unlimited,* 2067 South Federal Highway (954-462-4624/fax 954-523-6712)

*Crew Finders,* 404-408 SE 17th St (954-522-2739; www.crewfinders.com). Also has summer office in Newport, Rhode Island (2 Dean Avenue, Suite 5; 401-849-5227)

*D & R Woods International,* 500 SE 15th Street, Suite 102 (954-524-0065;)

*Elite Crew International,* 714 SE 17th St (954-522-4840; www.elitecrewintl.com)

*Palm Beach Crew,* 4220 Broadway, West Palm Beach, FL 33407 (561-863-0082; www.yachtcrew.com)

See also *Working on Yachts & Superyachts* by Jennifer Errico, from Vacation Work at £10.99.

## Racing the Oceans

Sailors with the prospect of an extended career break might want to consider participating in one or more legs of a round-the-world race. This will require a huge commitment of time and money. A round-the-world race can be brutally demanding where you live from watch to watch, with no more than three hours at any one stretch to sleep, eat and wash. For all of the romance of sailing, it remains a dangerous and strenuous sport, wherein lies part of its enormous appeal. The lure of the sea draws many to try their luck. The boat becomes a sealed world of its own.

Whereas some yacht races like the Volvo Ocean Race (formerly the Whitbread Round the World Race) are open only to professional sailors, others cater to novices as well as more experienced yachtsmen and women. However, if you're drawn to the notion of joining the crew of a racing boat, there are other opportunities such as the Challenge and Clipper races described below. It is possible to join a crew for one leg of a race or for an entire race. The costs are very steep but previous crew members see this as part of the general challenge.

**Humphrey Walters** lectures on inspirational leadership after deciding a few years ago to join the 'Global Challenge', the notoriously gruelling round-the-world yacht race which involves racing the 'wrong' way around the world (i.e. against the prevailing winds, currents and tides). His primary motivation was to increase his knowledge of team building and leadership. 'I wanted to know what makes the difference between average and high performance teams and the critical actions needed in hostile and unpredictable conditions.' Such a learning experience, he hoped, could be applied to developing his business. Humphrey also wanted to learn how to step away from his responsibilities and to delegate to others in the company. It would be a chance to re-focus and re-energise himself. However, he wanted to do something dramatic during a career break, to embark on a project with a purpose.

Sailing around the world proved to be as informative as he had hoped at the outset:

> *It was astonishing what I learned. Leadership is only one element in a successful organisation. I found that the most important thing is 'followership', how people follow a leader. Leaders can go through anything provided they know they are supported. Great leadership is born from great followership. Otherwise the leader won't take the risk.*

The environment of a yacht produced uncertainty, instability, turbulence and complexity, all features of the business world. What many have discovered before, the effectiveness of each team to work together, is what matters ultimately. The age of participants ranged from 21 to 60 and included many nationalities and professional backgrounds. *Ocean Rover's* team included an unemployed person, a student, doctor and scientist. Without the race, these individuals' paths would probably never have crossed but soon they had become an 'aquatic Coronation Street'. All were struck by how narrow one's life can become without realising it and how easy it is to experience life within a limited circle of professional colleagues and old friends and neighbours.

Because the conditions of the race were particularly demanding, an outstanding level of co-operation was necessary. Speed of progress is about a third as fast as in the opposite direction. Travelling against the winds produces waves of 45 degrees, so that every crew member had to be tethered to the boat while on deck. Shifts were exhausting too, with everyone working three hours on and three hours off. Their three hours off had to include eating and sleeping. Crews lose track of the normal calendar in a perpetual rhythm of working on deck and attending to the body's most basic physical needs. It was a dangerous journey. Humphrey seriously believed that the boat would sink the night that it was hit six times in a row by huge waves and knocked down.

Humphrey Walters is now an energetic advocate of taking a career break to test yourself. He sees many people in their thirties avoiding the opportunity to take on a major challenge outside work:

> *People around 35 and up should go on a career break. They need to find experiences which will allow them to find out that they can do things they never realised they could do and stretch themselves to limits they never thought possible. You are likely to come back notched up a gear in terms of your confidence, the way you operate and your ability to handle difficulty. It doesn't need to be yachting. You've just got to keep yourself in a learning environment especially nowadays in the competitive economy. It took me three times as long as a 25 year old to learn new skills and I'm not stupid.*

For more insights into what can be gained from this kind of career break, look at his book *Global Challenge: Leadership Lessons From The World's Toughest Race* by Humphrey Walters et al (published by the Book Guild; price £24.50).

The other not inconsiderable challenge is that participants must raise £28,750 to take part in the 2008/9 *Global Challenge* (less for just one leg) which means that people have to make great personal sacrifices to raise the funds to participate. But there are much more accessible organisations which offer the same advantages. For example the Jubilee Sailing Trust operates two tall ships the *Lord Nelson* and the *Tenacious* which are crewed by disabled and able-bodied volunteers on short voyages costing from £500.

Ocean rowing is another way of pushing yourself to the limit. The next Atlantic Rowing Race will start in November 2007 and is promoted by Woodvale Events Ltd (Pridhamsleigh Farm, Near Ashburton, Buckfastleigh, Devon TQ13 7JJ (01364 644432; www.woodvale-events.com).

## Sailing Contacts

*Challenge Business International,* Meridians House, 7 Ocean Way, Ocean Village, Southampton SO14 3TJ (023 8071 5300; www.challengebusiness.com). Founded by Chay Blyth, Challenge promotes high profile yacht races and other events to benefit sponsors, participants, fans and the media. These include the gruelling Global Challenge (described above) and the Challenge Transat in which 72ft yachts sail from Southampton to Boston and back again, explicitly aimed at amateur or novice sailors since full training is provided. A crossing in one direction costs £4,750. The website www.up4transat.co.uk kicks off with a rallying cry: 'Get less sleep; Feel more stress; Work longer hours; Have the time of your life.' In describing what past participants have experienced: 'From their work-a-day lives on land where days run together in predictable sameness, they are suddenly thrust into an existence that could not be more different from the norm... It's exhausting beyond explanation, but exhilarating beyond measure.'

*Clipper Round the World Yacht Race,* Clipper Ventures plc, Unit 1 A, Granary & Bakery, Royal Clarence Yard, Weevil Lane, Gosport PO12 1FX (023 9252 6000; www.clipper-ventures.co.uk). Race balances short sprints and long tactical races. The company is looking for people from all ages and walks of life including those without sailing experience. The shortest leg is just six weeks. A berth for the whole ten months costs £28,500 and a single leg costs from £6,350 (£2,950 for the compulsory 19-day training plus £3,250-£4,160).

*Flying Fish* – see Directory entry.

*Global Challenge Crew Volunteer Team* – see Challenge Business above.

*International Academy* – see Directory entry.

*Jubilee Sailing Trust,* Hazel Road, Woolston, Southampton, SO19 7GB (023-8044 9108; www.jst.org.uk). The JST was created in 1978 to provide an environment which promotes the integration of physically disabled and able-bodied people on board two square-rigged tall ships the *Lord Nelson* and the *Tenacious*. Anyone can join the crew on short voyages lasting between four and 15 days at a cost of £499 to £1,250.

*Plas Menai National Watersports Centre,* Caernarfon, Gwynedd, Wales LL55 1UE (01248 670964; www.plasmenai.co.uk).

*Royal Yachting Association,* RYA House, Ensign Way, Hamble, Southampton, SO31 4YA (0845 345 0400 or 023 8060 4100; www.rya.org.uk). As the governing body for sailing and motor boating in the UK, the RYA is the best starting place for any information about courses at every level for sailing or power boating.

*The Tall Ships People,* Moorside, South Zeal Village, Okehampton, Devon EX20 2JX (tel/fax 01837 840919; www.tallshipspeople.com). Offer berths for the annual Tall Ships Race (formerly the Cutty Sark Race) run by the charitable organisation Sail Training International and for other maritime events and races. The full daily cost of a berth is £60-£80. Although at least half the places are reserved for people 18-25, many older people are accepted too.

*UK Sailing Academy,* West Cowes, Isle of Wight PO31 7PQ (01983 294941; www.uksa.org). £4,795 for Instructor training, £8,950 for Professional Crew & Skipper training, and £875 for Jump Start (2 weeks in UK).

# SPECIAL INTEREST HOLIDAYS

According to a BBC survey, swimming with dolphins was ranked top of the list of 50 things to do before you die. Many other dream trips on the list involve contact with wildlife, including whales and sharks, elephants, tigers and camels (see page 332 for a case study of a Scottish gent who spent time in Africa looking after lion cubs). Many wildlife charities and placement agencies listed in the Directory arrange for untrained volunteers to work with rangers and conservationists, and these are among the most popular ways to spend a grown-up gap year.

## Skiing and Snowboarding

Just as life at sea or in the bush becomes an obsession for some, spending time on the snow slopes is the ambition of a whole community of initiates. Many were introduced to skiing or snowboarding at a young age and have returned to the mountains at every opportunity. But snatched holiday weeks do not satisfy the craving and taking a whole season out to ski can constitute a fantastic gap year at any age.

A handful of companies specialise in running intensive instructors' courses; see chapter *New Skills and New Projects.* If you merely want to spend a season skiing, you might consider the arrangement offered by a company like Alpine Elements (1 Risborough St, London SE1 0HF; 08700 111360; info@alpineelements.co.uk) which specialises in renting out affordable accommodation to skiers and snowboarders for between one and six months in a selection of resorts including Whistler in Canada and five resorts in France. The starting price for shared accommodation for the whole season is £1,850.

Two other companies offering long-term accommodation are Seasonaires ('Derwood', Todds Green, Stevenage, Herts. SG1 2JE; 0870 068 4545; www.seasonaires.com) with options in Les Arcs, Trois Vallées and Chamonix (France), Mammoth and Breckenridge (USA), Whistler and Fernie (Canada) and Wanaka (New Zealand); and Mountain Life which has properties only in Whistler (62 Farleigh Road, Addlestone, Surrey KT15 3HR; 0845 838 2269; www.mountain-life.co.uk). Accommodation in the British Columbia resort of Whistler costs from £400-£725 a month; the longer you stay, the cheaper the rent. Be warned that most people who want to spend a whole season in a ski resort are young party animals. To offset the expense of skiing, it may be possible to pick up work in ski resorts (see the chapter on Working Abroad).

## Adventure Sports

Sailing and skiing are only two sporting activities among many that can form the basis of an adventure trip. Many tour operators specialise in delivering extraordinary experiences rafting, trekking, cycling, mountaineering or diving to name just a few. As well as checking adverts in the magazine *Wanderlust*, check the searchable listings of the Association of Independent Tour Operators (AITO, www.aito.co.uk).

The travel-quest site (www.travel-quest.co.uk) is a free online directory of specialist tour operators including activity and adventure holiday providers. It provides company profiles, website access, brochure request, etc. and gives information on activities from heli-skiing to hot air ballooning around the world. Also check Action-Outdoors (www.action-outdoors.co.uk; 0845 890 0362) which offers hundreds of activity and sports holidays in a range of destinations.

Operators in the field of adventure sports holidays often make a pitch for older people fed up with every-day routines and conventional holidays. The following publicity from the rafting company Water by Nature (www.waterbynature.com) is typical and hard to resist:

> *Take a break from your modern, hectic work schedule. All too often now we are so caught up in the hustle and bustle of life that we forget the important things: good friends, lots of fun, a bit of sunshine and great food. A river journey for those who have yet to experience it offers complete escapism from your regular life – no hassles and no stress! If you need a real holiday, we have the perfect solution.*

After his expedition with *Raleigh International* in Sabah (Malaysia) came to an end, **Matt Heywood** relished the prospect of realising huge ambitions for the rest of his gap year, before returning to work as an engineer:

> *I intend to take my PADI Open Water diving course in Borneo, then do a six-day expedition up the East Ridge of Mount Kinabalu. I will then spend three weeks doing a lap of Sabah by bicycle. Following that I intend to get as many adrenaline fixes as possible as I mountain bike, climb and raft my way around Canada, USA, Central America and New Zealand. I may try to use my Raleigh experience to gain temporary employment as a mountain bike guide. The final part to my dream year is to use my Raleigh experience to gain managerial employment within Holden, Ford of Australia (however my girlfriend still needs a little convincing).*

Another ambition that some people have is to learn to fly, whether as a paraglider, hang glider or Microlight pilot, for example at Airways Airsports in Derbyshire (01335 344308; www.airways-airsports.com) with a sister airport in Ontur, Spain.

## Birdwatching Holidays

Anyone who pursues birdwatching as a hobby should be aware that trips organised by specialist ornithological tour operators are often over-subscribed. This has been attributed to the gathering anxiety in the developed world that unspoiled natural environments are being whittled away and species lost at an alarming rate. The media has in recent years made people in the developed world aware of all the threats to unspoiled natural environments, creating a feeling of urgency that these precious places should be visited before it is too late.

The Reverend **Brian Blackshaw** fitted in two birdwatching holidays during his 14-week sabbatical from his parish duties. He greatly enjoyed his trip with the eco-tourism operator Company of Whales (www.companyofwhales.co.uk) from England across the Bay of Biscay to the Picos Mountains of northern Spain on which the group saw more than 104 species, including the exceedingly rare middle-spotted woodpecker. In the latter part of his sabbatical, Brian went to Scotland with Speyside Wildlife (www.speysidewildlife.co.uk) and felt mentally and spiritually renewed by his time spent in wilderness landscapes, away from the telephone and the pressures of work in a busy Hertfordshire parish.

# Taking the Family

## ADJUSTING THE WORK/LIFE BALANCE

Taking a sabbatical to spend more time with family is one of the major reasons that people take time out from work. Paid maternity leave can be viewed as a statutory career break. Proposed new family-friendly legislation due to come into force from April 2007 would increase the entitlement to parental leave in addition to the two weeks' statutory paid paternity leave.

Once they return to full-time work, many parents harbour feelings of loss and guilt at the relatively small amount of time they can spend with their tiny children and resent being forced to delegate too much of the responsibility for rearing a child to a nanny or nursery. Obviously childcare is essential for anyone who wants to maintain and pursue a career, but any parents in a position to step off the professional treadmill for a time to spend time with their children might be tempted to read this chapter.

Many parents decide to take a break from work to enjoy an expedition together or a family project. An extended family break allows the (increasingly rare) chance for a collection of individuals, sometimes with widely differing interests, to operate as a single unit. It affords a rare unbroken opportunity to experience unadulterated family life, undistracted by phones, meetings, deadlines, work and the demands of a social calendar.

A number of family odysseys have been turned into books. One of these is *Across America with the Boys* in which the travel journalist **Matthew Collins** describes his trans-America drive with his two sons aged three and nearly-five (of which more below). His motivation was the impending start of school by his elder son Charlie and the opportunity to give some space at home to his wife who was beginning a demanding new job. 'I was also fed up with the children's overpriced nursery and I hated handing them over during the day to other people,' says Matthew.

Many parents now work long hours and often feel as if they are missing out on much of their offspring's childhood. It is a motivating factor in some parents' decisions to take time out from work to participate in a collective family activity. It might mean experimenting with living in a foreign country for several months, or it can involve a family adventure like overlanding, sailing or cycling.

Children will undoubtedly make a gap year more complicated, whatever their ages. In the first place, you will have more expenses and responsibilities than when you were childless (though if you are paying for full-time childcare, the saving of taking them out will be colossal). Certain things like doing a round-the-world yacht race or spending time at a meditation centre in India will probably be out of the question unless you have a long-suffering partner willing to hold the fort during your absence. Sometimes a break away from family life as well as a job can be to the benefit of everyone, though you must make it clear to the children (and your partner!) that they are not being abandoned permanently.

This chapter is for those who have decided to spend a large chunk of time with their families on the road. Do not underestimate the number of people who will raise objections to a sabbatical *en famille* on grounds of risk to career, risk to health, irresponsibility to children's education, expense, etc. Mostly they are just envious. **Jen Moon** courageously decided to follow a promise she had made to herself that on her 40th birthday, she would be doing something completely different. As a single mother of two daughters aged nine and eleven, she faced even more opposition and describes the school yard reaction: 'Although other parents at the girls' school kept saying how they wished they could do it, all the while they were looking at me as if I belonged in a mental home'. An account and assessment of her trip is included later in this chapter.

A sample objection is raised by someone on the www.bootsnall.com 'Travelling with Children' messageboard (March 2006) in reply to several families planning round-the-world trips with small children, though it seems clear that the killjoy did not himself have children. In any case it is best to be prepared for such negative attitudes:

> *You do know the kids are not going to get much out of the experience. I always wonder about adults with small children who want to satisfy their travelling jones [desires] without taking into consideration the comfort of the children. Just do a favor and don't put them in danger like the Canadian woman I met while trekking in Nepal who had her 6 month old baby on her back at 5,000 meters because she always dreamed of seeing the Himalayas. Small children should be in their neighborhood playing with their friends instead of being taken to museums, enduring long flights and*

tucantravel
latinamerica • cuba • antarctica
TRAVEL
take the adventure of a lifetime!
www.tucantravel.com
reservations & info: 020 8896 1600
brochures (24hrs): 0800 804 8415

destinations worldwide
BUDGET
Bexpeditions
for 18 to 35's
MORE adventure!
why pay more?
when you can go with
Budget Expeditions!
best vehicles • best equipment
best destinations • best prices • best meals
Most people dream of seeing what the world has to offer. Whether you just want one week holiday in Europe or a six month expedition through South America, there is definitely a trip of a lifetime for you when you travel with BEX!
Reservations & Info 020 8896 1600
Brochures (24Hrs) 0800 804 8435
www.budgetexpeditions.com

*car rides, and essentially being treated as an extra set of luggage when their parents have a travel agenda to satisfy. Sorry if this comes across as harsh and I am sure you will disagree, but I can't stand it when adults who have had children put their needs before the needs of their children.*

## Maternity Leave

Maternity leave is the most common reason for female employees to take time out from work and it is now an accepted feature of modern working life. New mothers are paid at least 90% of their salary for the first six weeks after a birth and then £108.85 (from 2006) per week for the next 20 weeks. When that period is up, mothers are entitled to take a further 26 weeks of unpaid leave and still be guaranteed that their jobs will remain open for them (provided they have worked for that employer for a continuous 26 weeks before taking maternity leave). Provision has been substantially enhanced by the current Labour government and is indicative of its emphasis on improving the work-life balance. Significantly, a junior health minister, Yvette Cooper, set an example a few years ago by claiming her full entitlement to maternity leave and became the first government minister to do so. For more detailed advice, consult the admirably clear DTI website (www.dti.gov.uk) or the national arbitration service, ACAS (see below).

For working mothers, a career break is a physical necessity in the period shortly before birth and in the baby's young life afterwards. Now that maternity leave of up to six months is a commonly accepted feature of employment, companies have adopted strategies and set aside resources to cope with these temporary absences. The degree of generosity beyond the legal requirements varies among companies depending on such criteria as how eager a company is to encourage a female employee to return to her old job instead of remaining at home. For many years research found that British companies lagged behind their American counterparts in the area of childcare and flexible working hours, though British companies are catching up. The annual lists of the 50 or 100 best companies to work for produced by the *Financial Times* and the *Sunday Times* invariably include companies that are the most family-friendly and allow flexible working hours. Many allow mothers to take career breaks for child-rearing ranging from six months to five years.

In order to motivate new mothers to return to work many top companies pay bonuses on return to work following maternity leave. For example IBM gives workers with more than five years of service who return to their jobs after maternity leave a 25% rise in salary for the next two years. Also, returning mothers may go part-time for two years with a guarantee of full-time employment afterwards.

Additional maternity leave (i.e. unpaid leave after the paid leave) is a statutory entitlement for qualifying employees. The obligation to pay salary ends after the initial mandatory period of 26 weeks though some companies do continue to pay some kind of retainer.

Booklets by the arbitration service ACAS on employment protection and rights are available from Jobcentres and via the Department of Trade and Industry (DTI) website www.dti.gov.uk. Alternatively you can seek advice from the national helpline for Working Parents 08457 474747 or the TIGER website (Tailored Interactive Guidance on Employment Rights) www.tiger.gov.uk. Other useful resources include:

*Working Families,* 1-3 Berry St, London EC1V 0AA – 020-7253 7243 – (www.workingfamilies.org.uk). Lobby group, formerly Parents at Work and New Ways to Work.

*Work Foundation* – sponsors a website www.employersforwork-lifebalance.org.uk which includes case studies of companies that are innovating in this field.

## Paternity Leave

Increasingly fathers are taking time out to help cope with the arrival of a new baby. For the first time in the UK, paid paternity leave of two weeks following the birth of a baby was introduced in 2003 and is now paid at the same rate as maternity leave, i.e. £108.85 per week. Naturally, a two-week absence from work hardly qualifies as a gap year, but it indicates a growing acceptance that many fathers want to take time off from work to help with children or even become the proverbial 'house husband' for a period of time.

The government's new benefits for parents proved controversial with business (especially small business) at first though are now accepted practice. In fact many new dads do not take up the entitlement because of the relatively low wage, preferring to take time out of their annual leave after the birth of their babies. Proposed new legislation as part of the Work and Families Bill due to come into force from April 2007 would give fathers up to 26 weeks unpaid leave. A further proposal is for statutory maternity pay to become transferable to the father if the mother decides not to take up her full entitlement.

Mothers with their own careers now expect their male partners to contribute more time to child-raising. An increasing number of fathers positively wish to do so, providing they can come to an arrangement with their employers.

## Parental Leave and Taking Time out for Dependants

In emergencies and for limited periods of time, both parents and people with dependants are entitled to formal employment leave. Parents can take leave provided they are named on the birth certificate or have legal 'parental responsibility', which covers adoption. The proviso is that there needs to be at least one year's service with the employer. Continued payment of salary is left to the employer's discretion.

The care of children can form the motivation of a formal career break negotiated with an employer beyond the maximum four weeks allowable by law. You might want to spend time with a child coping with prolonged illness or recovering from one. Alternatively, a child might need extra coaching to prepare for an examination or a sporting event.

On a less happy note, a career break might be required to care for an elderly parent or sick partner. At some point in our lives we are all likely to suffer from illness with varying degrees of severity and dependency. This is most likely to affect the ageing parents of people in work. Formal career breaks are sanctioned by some organisations, for example some NHS Trusts, to take into account the possibility that an employee may need to take time out to care for a relative.

In more than a few cases, the death of an elderly parent is a trigger for someone to decide to take a gap year, especially if they have been heavily responsible for the care of their parents and unable to get away. The death of **Sarah Spiller's** father marked a turning point in her life. Planning a volunteer trip abroad provided a distraction not only to Sarah but also to her mother who was enthusiastic on Sarah's behalf. Because Sarah had inherited some money from her father, she didn't need to worry about the financing of the trip. Her husband was also supportive of her idea to go away and do something different. She settled on Sri Lanka which had bewitched her on a previous visit and a turtle protection scheme through *Teaching & Projects Abroad* where she helped escort the turtles safely to their breeding ground, worked in a hatchery for turtle eggs and helped show visiting parties of Sri Lankan children round so as to instill the conservation message in them.

Similarly, teacher **Nigel Hollington** (then age 50) was spurred to action by the death of his father which freed him from some of his filial responsibilities. His mother is well looked after in sheltered accommodation but, at her age, he was reluctant to go away for long periods of time at a stretch. So he decided to divide up the year out he had been granted by his headteacher into chunks and do a variety of things and come home in between.

## Getting Everybody on Board

In almost all cases, the idea of a gap year is the grand design of one person in a family who tends to be the prime mover, the one to initiate and orchestrate the break and who is prepared to bear the responsibility for uprooting the rest of the family. Whereas one parent might be enthusiastic about putting their professional life on hold, this may not be so welcome or manageable for the other. As 'the Dad' wrote in the **De Jager Family** blog in February 2006 (http://blogs.bootsnall.com/Dejags) several months before he and his wife and children aged one and four set off on their round-the-world trip: 'Well my wife's enthusiasm, courage and drive have finally paid off; she has drawn me out of the well called home renovating and into the world of travel, and I finally got down to the business of planning the first leg of our trip'. Unless the family is deeply dysfunctional, the motivating adult must get everybody on his or her side. Sometimes the instigator's enthusiasm is sufficient to carry all before it, but it is essential that the following partner should not bury his or her reservations since this can escalate quite quickly into resentment.

The **Grant** family embarked on a remarkable journey, to become the first to encircle the globe in a horse-drawn caravan, described in sometimes painful detail in David Grant's book *The Seven Year Hitch: A Family Odyssey*. On the tenth page of his narrative after the family has had a trial run with a caravan in Ireland and before the Big Trip begins in earnest, he writes:

> *Unnoticed by me, Kate was beginning to have reservations but she did not say anything. She did not want to be the wet blanket who spoiled the fun. She had enjoyed Ireland as much as anyone but I think she foresaw, even then, that a prolonged sojourn in the confines of a caravan might not suit her. In her words, 'I really did have doubts about David and me travelling in such close confinement. The children I didn't doubt at all. Children are very adaptable, curious about new ideas and concepts. But I thought it was a trifle unfair to expect them at ages five, seven and nine to appreciate what our proposed wee doddle round the world would really mean.'*
>
> *I was in no mood or state to notice. Fired by all I had learned during our travels, I was as eager to go as a horse in a starting-stall.*

By page 39 Kate has found the trip unbearable and flies home to her father's house. She rejoins the family at intervals and is with them as they trudge to their final destination, Halifax in Canada, seven years after setting off. The index is telling; of the several headings under David Grant, we can look up 'tensions of journey' not to mention 'horse collar accident' and 'sued for assault'.

Loved ones cannot always be expected to share our dreams, passions and grand schemes. If there is a great discrepancy in what partners want out of a gap year, accommodations must be reached, perhaps dividing the allotted time into two phases; the first an overland trip to the Andes or a sojourn in a Hebridean bothy for her sake, the second a cycling tour or cookery course in Tuscany for his.

If children are part of the picture, further compromises will be necessary. Children seldom welcome change and upheaval, especially as they get older. Whatever their ages, the children should be included in the planning and preparations, and their preferences taken into account. They could be allowed to choose the odd treat destination like a theme park or a safari or even be given a chunk of the itinerary to arrange.

## Travelling During Parental Leave

The vast majority of parents stay at home to enjoy their new infant. But there are circumstances in which it might be appropriate to combine statutory parental leave with a more adventurous career break. Perhaps one set of grandparents lives a long way away and the family could think of spending a few months in rented accommodation in a different place or country. A sabbatical abroad might appeal to a two-parent family with one or more older children, where the parents are more relaxed about having an infant, and want to take full advantage of their parental leave.

Overlanding through Africa or volunteering for a jungle expedition probably won't be possible, but babies are remarkably portable, even if a new sleep-deprived parent weighed down by the paraphernalia of nappies and buggies might find this hard to believe. Infants under two fly for next to nothing: up to 10% of the adult fare to Australia, though just the tax in other cases. Parenthood is a universal experience which will open many doors – or at least conversations – with people the world over who may surprise you with how generously they try to smooth your way.

## The Ideal Age

After children reach school age, disrupting their education becomes an issue. Some families prefer to take off just before their children start school declaring that this is the blessed age of innocence. In Matthew Collins's experience, ages three to four is a perfect period to take children away for a long trip. Before that you will have to contend with nappies and toddler problems. After they start school they begin to lose some of their innocence. Matthew noticed that his two sons were less sweetly innocent aged five and seven when they crossed Canada (see below).

**Looking back at the American trip, Matthew Collins believes that it was one of the best things he has ever done:**
*A glorious experience, I'm so glad I did it. At the age of three and four, the boys were so fresh. They had a pre-school innocence. Here was an opportunity to spend a large chunk of time with the children, watching their personalities develop. It was a time to enjoy my kids and they enabled me to appreciate new places through their eyes.*

Matthew remembers that the children never got bored in the United States and there was no VCR for them in the motor home. 'One of the great things about travelling with kids is that you spend so much time talking. We talked about everything. The stimulation was so great for the children.' One tactic to avert any irritation with confinement on the road was to keep the driving light, reserving the heavy duty driving for the evening. The advantage of driving through the hot and humid southern states was that the boys had a siesta during the afternoons giving Matthew some time to catch up with chores or just to enjoy a period of silence. The family also enjoyed stopping in the campgrounds mostly equipped with swimming pools.

The other significant advantage of travelling with children was that they were fearless about talking to anyone and acted as an icebreaker between adults. Once they approached a Hell's Angel and asked why he had so many horrible tattoos. Instead of a hostile response, the tough biker was won over by their naïve charm.

**Libby Purves** is another parent-cum-author who travelled with her children at roughly the same age. She looks back in wonder on the summer that she and her husband took their two children (aged three and five) on an adventurous and sometimes dangerous cruise around the British Isles recounted in her book *One Summer's Grace* (which could serve as a subtitle for any number of gap years *en famille)*. The edition now available includes an Afterword written a decade after the trip: 'We are now sometimes filled with shocked dismay at the smallness and vulnerability of the children we took through 1,700 miles of unforgiving seaways. Frankly, we look at other people's five- and three-year-olds now and think that we must have been barking mad. But I don't know.' The positive outcomes she identifies include a store of memories they can all still share, a lasting sense of unity in adversity and a penchant for pursuing Grand Projects despite the risks, since after all 'you'll be a long time dead'.

Her warts-and-all account of the cruise includes the low as well as the high points. She describes how the children's moods swung wildly and on occasions they were overcome with rage or homesickness or anxiety that they would never see their friends and family at home again. The parents patiently tried to explain that 14 weeks might seem like a very long time but they would all return to their normal lives afterwards. Libby Purves writes: 'As we set off northward from Puffin Island Sound, crew morale was low, pulled down by this insistent infant undercurrent of discontent...Alone of the crew, I was relishing the whole adventure. I felt rather guilty about this because I had originated the whole thing, set the dates, organised the finance and the empty house for it, and effectively dragged my whole family off to sea. I realised that, as the only happy human being on board, I had a duty to improve our lot.' And for the most part she was successful.

## Taking the Children out of School

Once the children are in school, you will have to obtain the permission of the Local Education Authority to take them out of school for more than ten days; the school office should have the form. Permission will be granted only if the authorities can be reassured that the child's education will not be damaged (see section below on Schooling). Try to avoid taking them away when they are scheduled to do special exams; in the UK, children sit Standard Assessment Tests (SATs) in the summer terms of years two, six and nine. Although an obvious time to take the children away is between finishing one school and starting another, it might make it harder for them to re-enter normal school life when all their peers have already made the transition.

An increasing number of parents are refusing to be deterred from taking the break they crave. They are finding ways that will be beneficial for their children while at the same time allowing them to spend a substantial amount of time together during the formative years of childhood. If there's a guaranteed way of maximising that ever elusive 'quality time,' a sabbatical expedition surely is one solution. Parents report that taking the kids away from television and videos teaches them to entertain themselves with reading, drawing and writing.

Transplanting teenagers from their natural habitat can be more problematic even if you are happy to interrupt their preparations for GCSEs, AS Levels and A levels. Most well adjusted adolescents will resent being removed from their social network and forced to spend more time with their parents and siblings than they would at home. If possible, try to give adolescents as much freedom as possible. One way of placating them might be to make sure they are allowed to spend plenty of time in Internet cafés so that they can maintain contact with their friends at home. You might consider arranging the exclusive use of a laptop for them.

Outsiders will often exclaim over the educational benefit of travel with children. But children have a way of subverting expectations and are more likely to remember the street urchin pestering them to buy a flower than the great Buddhist temple, or the time a wave knocked them over rather than the sea creatures on the beach. A career break with children should be organised at a time when the parents will most appreciate it, not the children. It doesn't matter if you go when they are too young to remember anything. It does matter that you communicate enthusiasm and demonstrate a zeal for travel, for nature, for history, for whatever it is you are zealous about, which they will emulate and someday apply to their own interests (you hope).

# TRAVELLING WITH YOUR KIDS

The best opportunity for a joint family enterprise is an adventurous expedition abroad. This may involve backpacking in a developing country, sailing or off-road driving. For some parents a travel adventure is an ideal time for the family to spend a concentrated period of time together, finding ways to live harmoniously while also discovering new cultures and seeing some of the great natural and constructed wonders of the world.

## Resisting the Doom Merchants

As mentioned, taking children on an extended trip overseas is not universally admired. While a few friends and family may question the legitimacy and wisdom of taking a sabbatical as an individual or in a couple, taking children abroad can be a source of friction. It may be deemed irresponsible, selfish, risky or unfair to uproot the children. Questions will be asked, perhaps with the best intentions. Will it be safe to take young children to extreme climates? How will their education suffer? Will they catch malaria or hepatitis? Won't it be very disruptive?

Every family sets its own priorities, rules and patterns of behaviour and they need not be dissuaded from a jointly desired project by the criticisms of outsiders. While some parents believe that keeping to a routine in the familiar environment of home is the best policy for keeping kids contented and attentive at school, others – especially those who have done some serious travelling in the past – concentrate on the positive potential of a Big Trip together.

Steps can be taken to minimise the unsettling effects of travel on children. Obviously they should carry a couple of their most beloved objects. A small photograph album of their friends and favourite places at home can serve to remind them that their old life still exists and can also be of interest to people met on the road. Whenever possible a routine should be established so that certainties such as a bedtime story are maintained. The key to minimising stress and fractiousness is to avoid constant movement. If possible, base yourself in one place long enough for the children to create a temporary network of familiar faces, if only the waiter or the greengrocer's son. And when you all need a break from each other, ask in your lodgings or contact a local student organisation about hiring a babysitter.

Cultural differences can result in incidents that can sometimes be upsetting, sometimes amusing. In many parts of Asia, children are considered almost public property. Local babies may be used to being prodded and cooed over and passed from hand to hand, but your western children may not be so keen on these little acts of idolatry. Older children may well enjoy the attention and like to be in the photographs of umpteen Oriental matrons but may balk when they are squashed up beside the shy daughter to be in a photo. Be prepared to rescue your child from any situation that is making him or her uncomfortable.

Cultural clashes will be less apparent in Europe, though some parents have commented on the German penchant for intervention. While accompanying her children to a playground in Germany, Alison Hobbs, wife of a university physicist on sabbatical, was taken aback to be offered some money by a stranger in order to buy shoes for her (cheerfully shoeless) baby. Still on the subject of shoes, another mother was berated in German for wearing flip flops while balancing a two year old on her shoulders on a popular climb to the Dikteon Cave on Crete where Zeus was born.

## The Incalculable Benefits

A family adventure can provide an educational stimulus that will exceed anything available in a classroom. Instead of merely looking at photographs of the Amazon or the Taj Mahal in a book from the school library, children can actually experience its beauty and scale, and glimpse the civilisation out of which it emerged. In terms of the geography field trip, driving across Europe or sailing round the Caribbean certainly outclasses a visit to the local wood. The world becomes a classroom for both parent and child. Just don't harbour inflated ideas of how rapt your children will be by the Himalayas or the Pyramids. From the time an infant is 24 hours old, parents learn that generalisations and advice about childcare are sometimes helpful, sometimes useless, depending on their child's nature. So the experiences of other parents on gap years may be of very limited use. While some will enthuse wildly about how their children learned Swahili/took up birdwatching/wrote poetry, you may be stuck with the kids for whom the highlight was the size of the billiard table in a faded old colonial hotel or how they mastered the art of building card houses. Your moment to enthuse wildly might come unexpectedly when you realise what little trojans your sturdy capable longsuffering children turned out to be, cheerfully wielding their chopsticks or stoically carrying their luggage through crowded sweltering bus stations.

**Single parents might be even more reluctant than other parents to contemplate a gap year with children. Jen Moon is an exception.** Convinced that it would be a wonderful learning experience for the children, she was determined to take nine year old Sarah and eleven year old Lisa on a big trip in 2006. She successfully negotiated with her employer for a four-month break (which she decided in the end was just long enough) and also with the school. After years of saving by working at two jobs and writing a book about working on yachts (*Working on Yachts & Superyachts*, available from www.vacationwork.co.uk), she decided that her dream was affordable. Such a trip is inevitably expensive but she begrudged none of it: 'Seeing how happy I feel having achieved the dream and seeing how incredibly the children have come on, it would in my eyes be worth double what I paid. It's lovely to be home and I feel far more contented in my life having done what I did.' When asked about the high points, she says that out of 120 days at least 108 had high points. That conclusion with the benefit of hindsight displays a more confident attitude than she felt in the planning stages:

*One of the low points was the stress before actually going. It was incredibly tough, knowing that, as I was a single parent, the kids would have no one should something happen to me. I found that very scary.*

The trip to Australia, New Zealand and America was a resounding success for all three of them. However Jen admits to odd moments of loneliness, especially when the young gappers headed off clubbing or wherever their fancy took them. She was surprised to encounter relatively few travellers in her age bracket, which is squarely between all the school and college-leavers and the retired folks. The kids would also have liked to meet more travelling kids.

With hindsight Jen would have stretched the budget to get a bigger camper van and two laptops. The children both did lots of homework during the trip and wrote journals, so that competition for laptop space was always intense and one or other was invariably behind.

But the experience was overwhelmingly positive:

*The rewards have been immense, not least of all spending concentrated quality time with the kids. Both of them have had their maths level improve significantly (Sarah by three grades), their geography means so much more to them and both generally feel 'special' in that they have done something that most kids never even dream of doing. That makes them have a sort of inner confidence that many of my friends and family back home have noticed and approved of as it is not a brash precociousness.*

An extended family trip can be educational in another sense for fathers, many of whom have had less contact with young children than their partners. Author Helena Drysdale says that travelling around Europe in a motor home, while researching a book on tribal peoples, was instructive for her husband Richard. 'Having been working since their birth, he was aghast at how little time children left him to do his own thing. Like most men, he had no idea what bringing up children day in, day out, really means.' Be prepared to experience occasional feelings of loss when you recall your travels pre-children. Some of the old carefree magic may be missing to be replaced by what might seem at times relentless domesticity. But parenthood at home or abroad encompasses highs and lows, and the lows always pass.

## Crossing the Sahara

The **Allans** of Paisley in Scotland undertook what might appear to be a heroic enterprise. Norman was a self-employed businessman and Judy was at home raising and educating the children when they decided to take their five children all under 11 overland across the Sahara to Zimbabwe where Judy had grown up. There they planned to work with a Christian charity called Youth With A Mission (01582 463216; www.ywam-england.com) which supports missionaries by organising building projects and working with children.

As all parents know, caring for young children at home is very time-consuming and tiring. To undertake all these chores on the road might seem, frankly, intimidating. Nevertheless, the Allans managed to achieve the trip without serious problems partly because of their ability to solve detailed logistical problems by sensible planning.

The most serious problem they encountered occurred long before they reached the wilds of Africa. Their Land Rover broke down on the notoriously Darwinian Peripherique, the orbital ring road around Paris, and they didn't trust it to carry them through Africa. Later in Gibraltar, they ditched the Land Rover in favour of a Toyota Land Cruiser, which they discovered to be more comfortable and spacious. They usually slept in the vehicle unless they were staying for three days or more in one spot. Then they would pitch a large tent. In North Africa there was no threat from wild animals, but in Zimbabwe, they were compelled to sleep in the vehicle and on the roof. Animals in southern Africa do pose a danger especially as they are often well camouflaged. Surprisingly, the wild buffalo presented one of the greatest hazards and not big cats as one might assume from umpteen television documentaries.

The principal difficulty they faced is one that other travellers complain of too: crossing borders. Bored and poorly paid border guards frequently ask for money. Crossing into Niger was particularly problematic and sometimes they encountered arbitrary roadblocks set up to extort money. One occasion was memorably menacing when the guards took their kettles. Judy and Norman's strategy was to refuse politely but firmly to pay any money but offered medicine or food instead. Travelling with the children helped ease their way because kids are very popular in Africa. Travelling with a young child in unlikely circumstances has been known to give travellers something akin to diplomatic immunity.

Despite their young age, the children learned to work together and to work hard. The boys learned to pitch the tent to help their parents with the task of setting up camp. The major challenge within the family was to keep the children occupied during the long hours of hot and dusty travel. Within the constraints of travel, they tried to keep to a daily routine, being on the road by eleven each morning. For the girls, Judy brought dolls and clothes and toy utensils, while for the boys she took toy figures, animals, cars and some Lego. She also brought board games and cards. Another helpful tool was a batch of story tapes including traditional fairy tales.

Averting boredom among the children was a challenge but maintaining their good health required much vigilance. Before leaving they were inoculated and began taking anti-malaria medication. The two youngest children took quinine in syrup form but they hated the taste so much that Judy was not sure whether they were receiving enough dosage to protect them. This was the reason why most of the family avoided driving through Equatorial Africa where malaria is most prevalent.

The youngest child was still in nappies and Judy felt compelled to take disposables. She knew of some people who travelled with washable nappies and put them in water filled tupperware boxes, hoping the constant movement of a vehicle would act to imitate a washing machine, but she felt it was simply impractical.

For medical supplies, the Allans took the excellent kits sold by MASTA (see 'Useful Contacts' listings near the end of the *Nuts and Bolts* chapter), which include a spoon that shows you how to measure out the right amounts of rehydration salts (one level teaspoon of salt and two tablespoons of sugar to a litre of water). Additionally, the kit included supplies for an emergency, which were in fact needed on the trip. The family doctor also supplied some basic antibiotics to take with them.

The main precaution the family took was to follow advice about food. They ate only canned or dried food from their stores towed in a trailer, and they always used purification tablets for water. The diet of canned chicken, beef, tuna, lentils and spaghetti might have become monotonous but it did the trick and none of them suffered serious stomach problems. Following the advice of *The Sahara Handbook*, only once did they eat meat, when they knew it had been slaughtered that day. The other exceptions to the strict regime of dried and canned food were fruit they had peeled themselves and local bread and porridge.

## Working and Volunteering Abroad

Volunteering to work for a charity abroad is much trickier to organise for a family than an individual or couple. Companies that place volunteers in overseas conservation projects or as English teachers are simply not equipped to find housing for families. One organisation that does place families is VSO. However, VSO stresses that it can only place families in certain circumstances, for example if there are more requests for assistance than there are volunteers. In this case VSO can provide additional support for partners and/or dependant children, which would include housing and insurance. It stresses that each case is considered on its own merits and taking a partner and children may reduce the range of placement options. Sometimes it's possible for a parent to take children unsupported by VSO at additional cost to the family.

Two-parent families have the option of letting one parent take a paid or voluntary job while the other looks after the children. But what about single parents who want a break from home routines? Having spent long periods of her life living in Barcelona, Orlando and Australia, **Jacqueline Edwards** wanted to live abroad with her two-year old son Corey after studying aromatherapy and massage. Ingeniously, she inserted notices in vegetarian and vegan magazines throughout Europe, and received a number of offers including an offer of a free house in Austria in exchange for helping to look after rescued animals, from an elderly couple near Paris and a natural therapies retreat centre west of Madrid. She chose to accept a live-in position as a cook/cleaner in Spain, though she returned home prematurely.

**Jacqueline Edwards thinks that it is always a gamble when you decide to leave the comfort and security of your home environment to look for a new life abroad. She explains the special problems she encountered as the single mother of a young child:**
*I felt that my son was too young (he was two) and still at an age when he needed my full attention, which severely limited my work options.*

*Being a single parent meant spending 24 hours a day, every day with my son (who is borderline hyperactive) which I found exhausting. I didn't have the support network that I have in England with grandparents, family, friends, etc. to help with childcare and, as we were in a strange environment with a different language. I didn't feel comfortable leaving him with strangers. I moved around a lot, looking for a suitable place to live and this is very unsettling for a child of his age. He was too young to understand that he still had a home and family in England whom he would see again one day.*

*In general it was not a very positive experience for either of us. Having said that, we're back here in Spain again. Last year I met a family who were looking for an au pair (through an ad in a Spanish magazine) and we kept in touch. So I came here to look after their son and live in their house in exchange for room, board and a small wage. It seemed the ideal solution but unfortunately it wasn't. Living in someone else's house is always difficult but when you are bringing a small, active child with you the problems can multiply. We were all very optimistic because we had lots of things in common and similar lifestyles. But we hadn't considered such issues as whether the children would get on; they didn't and spent a lot of time fighting which put a lot of strain on all of us. Living as an au pair is fine for an 18 year old but when you are a single mother aged 30 used to lots of freedom, it is almost impossible. So I moved out into a rented flat and continue to work for the family. I am earning the same wage as before so will have to look for another way of earning. I'm thinking of teaching English to children and doing massages in the evenings after my son has gone to bed.*

Living and working on an organic farm, as described in the section about the international organisation WWOOF in the chapter 'Doing Something Worthwhile', is something that families can do. For example one of the highlights of the **Whitlock Family's** one year round-the-world tour (as recounted in the 'Personal Case Histories' at the end of the book) was their short stay at an organic farm in Hungary which they arranged through WWOOF (Worldwide Opportunities on Organic Farms). Because of his interest in habitats and conservation projects, Nick Whitlock was especially looking forward to living and working alongside local people and fellow travellers on WWOOF farms. The family arranged to stay on a goat farm in a remote area about 25km from Kaposvar where they picked fruit and helped in the kitchen and where 10 year old Tom helped look after the herd of goats, meanwhile all staying in an idyllic old farmhouse.

Opportunities like this are also open to solo parents, especially on communities. For example in South Africa, the travelling Rawlins family (www.rawlins.ws) met two British women, each travelling with her 11-year old offspring and working at the eco-community near Durban called Absolute Elsewhere (PO Box 807, Richmond 3780, Kwazulu-Natal; 031-209 6006).

## Red Tape

Children of British nationals now need their own passports (unless they are already included on a parent's current passport). Always check that every member of the family has a current passport with enough validity to last for the whole trip plus a safety margin of six months which is demanded by some countries. Be aware that if a child is included on a parent's passport and that parent had to return (say, for a family emergency), the child could not travel separately with the other parent unless they were also included in that parent's passport. Note that some countries (like Canada) have signed up to the Hague Convention on International Child Abduction to discourage unauthorised removal of children across borders, and a lone parent travelling with children can be asked to show a letter of permission from the absent parent.

## Accommodation

If travelling with young children, take it slowly, allowing plenty of fun and relaxing interludes between the days of travel and sightseeing. Try to find accommodation which is not only child-friendly but where your children are likely to meet other children. Animals are always popular so you might try to stay on a farm or a campsite in the bush. Self-catering accommodation means that you don't have to worry about your little tearaways terrorising other diners in the hotel restaurant or other eating establishments. Out of season, villas in Italy and Spain can be vastly more affordable than during the school holidays.

Campsites and youth hostels are venues where children often feel most at home. Nature Friends International (www.nfhouse.org) with headquarters in Vienna run a network of 1,000 mountain, forest and city hostels, mostly on the continent, which welcome parents and children. This would be one way of keeping costs down in an expensive country like Switzerland. Many have their own playgrounds and most are very inexpensive.

Agritourism is another appealing option where you spend a week or more on a working farm. One possibility for finding addresses of farms which might welcome families is to obtain one of the guides from ECEAT (European Centre for Eco-Agro Tourism, Postbox 10899, 1001 EW Amsterdam, Netherlands; www.eceat.nl). They publish separate English-language *Green Holiday Guides* for Britain & Ireland, Bulgaria, Poland and Spain & Portugal and other countries in Dutch- or German language versions for €10-€15.

Renting a cottage or house for a few months and staying in one place is often a better way to organise a long family break (see the section on home exchanges in the chapter *Nuts and Bolts*). Everyone enjoys the chance to get to know (and to become known in) a new community but children especially like the security that familiarity imparts and the chance to develop relationships with local children or adults and perhaps even go to school.

## Children's Health

As mentioned earlier, attention to hygiene and care about what children eat and drink in developing countries is critically important. Children tend to be conservative eaters so may be more content than adults with safe foods like peanut butter and packet soups brought from home. But children get thirsty and care will have to be taken about purifying water in some countries. Purifying tablets and iodine make the water taste unpleasant, so it is a good idea to travel with a supply of lemons (if available) to make the water more palatable.

General information on obtaining health advice can be found in the chapter on *Nuts and Bolts*. Most GPs nowadays have computer access to detailed information for patients heading for the tropics and will be able to advise on the recommended and necessary immunisations (including the correct dosage for children) for specific destinations. Malaria poses such a serious risk in some parts of the world that they are best avoided, and it would make sense to choose a route that minimises exposure to risk. Parents of children travelling through a malarial zone will soon come to dread the pill-taking ritual, since chloroquine is exceedingly bitter and most children find it difficult to swallow pills whole. Practising on something more palatable before departure might help. Mechanical precautions against malaria are easier to manage (e.g. wrist and ankle bands soaked in DEET); younger children might enjoy the experience of sleeping under a tent of mosquito netting.

Among the items in your medical kit, carry a disinfectant like Mercurochrome to treat even minor cuts and scrapes. In tropical climates, even minor wounds attract flies and can easily go septic. And be very disciplined in applying sunblock at frequent intervals.

## Books and Resources

*Across America With The Boys* by Matthew Collins (MATCH Publishing; £6.99, via www.matthewcollins.co.uk). A former presenter of the BBC's *Travel Show*, Matthew Collins decided to cross the United States in a motor home for three months before his sons began school. The book recounts their adventures from Florida to LA and the impact it had on their relationships.

*Across Canada With the Boys and Three Grannies* by Matthew Collins (MATCH Publishing; £7.99, via www.matthewcollins.co.uk). Recounts the experience of travelling with two 'grannies' found through adverts and one blood relative granny and how three generations reacted to the same journey.

*The Seven Year Hitch: A Family Odyssey* by David R. Grant (Pocket Books, 2000; £7.99). The highlights of this epic journey by horse drawn caravan seem few and far between, especially as the father and three children struggle to find enough to eat and keep warm as they cross Kazakhstan and then get bogged down in Mongolia. Hard to imagine anyone wanting to emulate this trip.

*Treasure Islands: Sailing The South Seas in the Wake of Fanny and Robert Louis Stevenson* by Pamela Stephenson (wife of Billy Connelly) about her gap year adventures sailing in the South Seas (Headline Books, 2005).

*The Sahara Handbook* by Simon Glen (Roger Lascelles, 1990). Now out of print but second hand copies should be available via www.abebooks.co.uk or amazon. Invaluable practical asset for the Allan family as they drove across one of the world's most barren landscapes.

*Are We Nearly There Yet?* by Sheila Hayman (Hodder & Stoughton, 2003; second-hand from amazon). Amusing book about travelling with children.

*Live and Work Abroad* by Huw Francis and Michelyne Callan (Vacation-Work, 2001; £11.95). Subtitled a 'Guide for Modern Nomads' this book has a chapter on 'Children and the Move'. Vacation-Work also publish a *Live and Work* series for a number of countries in Europe and worldwide.

*Family Travel: The Farther You Go, the Closer You Get* edited by Laura Manske (Travelers' Tales, 1999; £10.99). Hard-to-find collection of 45 tales narrating the joys and trials of families finding their way abroad. The contributors include well known personalities like Michael Crichton and Tim Parks.

*One Summer's Grace* by Libby Purves (Coronet Books, 1997; £8.99). In the summer of 1988, Libby Purves and her husband Paul Heiney sailed with their children aged three and five on a voyage around the coastline of Britain.

*Let's Move Overseas* by Beverly D. Roman (BR Anchor Publishing, 2000; second-hand via amazon). This US publication is aimed at children aged 8-12 to help them cope with the transition to a new home overseas with the use of games and exercises.

*Cadogan Take The Kids Series* (www.cadoganguides.com). Destinations include England, Ireland and France.

*Travel Abroad with Children* by Sam Gore-Lyons (Arrow, 2003).

*Travel With Children* by Maureen Wheeler & Cathy Lanigan (Lonely Planet Publications, 2002; £8.99). Guide for parents planning to go travelling with children aged three months to 14 years. Practical advice includes information on health and travelling during pregnancy.

*Your Child's Health Abroad* by Dr. Jane Wilson-Howarth and Dr. Matthew Ellis (Bradt Travel Guides, 1998; £10.95). Aims to help adventurous parents travel confidently with their kids, and explains how to diagnose any health problems.

As usual the web contains a wealth of useful and useless information. Start with www.travelwithyourkids.com which has advice and suggestions from longtime expats and real parents on how to travel internationally (or just long distances) with your children. Try also www.travelforkids.com which lists kid-friendly sites worldwide. As mentioned earlier family blogs on the internet can be both inspiring and instructive. Bootsnall.com includes a travel forum about travelling with children which is worth surfing. The Fleming family published their Family Tale of a Global Adventure online at www.rfleming.net after completing a round-the-world trip with their two daughters aged eight and four.

## SCHOOLING

Most parents will feel anxious about removing their children from formal education for an extended period. Some lucky parents have managed to enrol their children in a school abroad which can be very worthwhile even for a relatively short time. The usual problem is language but most children would prefer to spend time interacting with children over a language barrier than being cooped up with their family. Sports, games, music, smiles and many other pleasures are still accessible to them.

In countries where English is spoken, it can be a wonderful eye-opener for children to experience a different school environment for a few months. Even if the school is ghastly, the children will learn to appreciate their old school instead of taking it for granted. People travelling on a tourist visa will not usually be permitted to put their children in the state education system free of charge but it is worth investigating the possibility both beforehand and locally. If one of the parents has a special visa (e.g. work permit, academic visitor visa), it may well be possible. If the children's visas are to be added to a parental visa, make sure they go on the one which has the permission to work/reside.

**Lindsay and Nick Whitlock** decided to spend an inheritance of £25,000 on something that would change their lives as a family for the better. They were not unduly worried about the schooling that Thomas aged ten and Esther aged four would miss. With the benefit of hindsight on their year-long travels, their confidence was justified. It turned out that the academic disruption was less an issue than the social disruption:

> *Although both our children missed a year of school, and Tom even missed his SATs, this, offset against the experience they had gained, does not seem to have had a long-term effect. In fact, we never sought official permission from the LEA, although I wrote to Thomas' headmaster, who was happy to give his full support! As a teacher myself, I felt that I would be able to provide a 'skeleton' curriculum as we travelled. This was not possible as I had envisaged it, as the conditions during the trip meant that it was impossible, and, even when we did do 'travel school' it was generally*

*met with resistance by the children. However, my children are resourceful and have developed an immense ability to overcome difficulties, and catching up has posed no problem for either of them.*

*On our return, my son had grown unused to communicating with his peers. While he was brimming with enthusiasm and confidence talking to adults, and could happily entertain a hostel full of backpackers with eloquent travelling tales, he found it very hard to relate to others of his age group for whom the most interesting event of the year was (perhaps) Jade winning Big Brother. He quickly gained a reputation at his new school, where he tried so hard to settle in, for being a bit freaky. Fortunately, in some ways, circumstances forced us to move again four months after returning to the UK, and he had adjusted enough to cope better second time around.*

*For our daughter Esther, aged 5 on return, the adjustment was easiest. She had missed her 'reception' year at school, and, having shown no interest in being taught formally by me, was therefore behind academically. However she is a naturally sociable child, who had, if anything, developed quite exceptional social skills in play with children everywhere, language no obstacle, and she quickly fitted in and caught up. Now, at nearly seven, she's doing very well at school, and in all areas of her life.*

## Home Schooling

If you decide to take the children on a trip abroad, their formal education need not be completely suspended. Several sources of help are available from organisations that produce courses and reading material for parents who want to teach their children themselves. Not all children are susceptible to being taught formal lessons by their parents, and the project may not succeed with stubborn, wilful or rebellious children. But 'lessons' can be disguised: a child may be keen to keep a diary of the trip while being loath to do an exercise from a text book.

As mentioned earlier, **Jen Moon's** daughters did plenty of homework while they were on the road, mainly thanks to their mother's determination to keep them at it. Nine year old Sarah wrote in her journal after a 'really looonnnggg walk' to see giant redwoods in southern California: 'Although it was pouring with rain and it was really cold mum started to give Sarah a geology lesson! It just goes to show we do homework whatever the weather! I was glad to get home and have my nice hot chocolate.' Writing a journal is of course an education in itself. Jen was fascinated to notice the progress they made, from the rough efforts at the beginning, especially of nine year old Sarah when she could barely write, to the 'very accomplished, laugh-out-loud, work' at the end. Much of the daily accounts concerned food, but the educational benefits often shine through, as in this extract from 11 year old Lisa's journal, written in their campervan in northern New South Wales:

*We walked down onto the beach where we splashed in the sea. Suddenly mum spotted something sparkly in the sand, it was called phosphorescence, it was so amazing. There were little sparks everywhere. It was so weird, like stars in the sand. It was really magical, almost fiction. We had a splash in the water, the sparkles were in the water too and it all got in my hair. Sadly we got cold so we had to go back. We had been there nearly two hours. It felt like twenty minutes! It had been a strange night that I will remember forever.*

The value of ticking curriculum boxes palls in comparison.

**Bonny Havenhand** was 13 when her parents decided to leave their comfortable ocean-side house in Newcastle New South Wales and spend a year in Siem Reap, Cambodia (see Personal Case Histories). Carrying on his publishing business remotely, her dad Bryan took on the role of home tutor which, he learned, requires serious commitment:

> *Home schooling is hard work and takes a lot more time than originally anticipated! Everything seems to be done with minimum effort, but maybe that's all you get from a 13 year old. Bonny's going OK with it, but needs a lot of help with maths, so I've had to relearn fractions, algebra, the Pythagorean Theorem, etc. etc. She is keeping up with her schoolwork and is half way through her second term's work. Not, I might fairly add, without a great deal of hassling and patience from me. I'm not wanting to take anything away from her as she has spurts where she does a lot by herself without being hassled.*

Bonny's school in Australia sent material on a regular basis. As soon as it was returned it was marked and new work would be sent. This worked well until someone at home in charge of forwarding the post failed to do so which caused problems. Bonny was not just on the receiving end of education. Despite her young age, she started teaching English to the local kids each afternoon for an hour and the numbers grew so much that her father had to step in to lend a hand.

The Education Act in the UK makes specific provision for home schooling, stating that parents are responsible for their children's education, 'either by regular attendance at school or otherwise.' Children who are registered as being home schooled do not, by contrast with children who attend schools, need permission from the local education authority before departing.

A wealth of online courses and educational CD-ROMs is now available, though these materials can be expensive. Numerous options for online and open learning allow a child to study accredited courses and to acquire qualifications. Virtual schools have sprung up all over and mean that your child can study from a syllabus that suits him or her without having to be physically present. Usually, a child will be assigned to a teacher who monitors progress via e-mail or less usually by fax, phone or the ordinary postal service. A good starting point for information about correspondence courses is to contact the Open and Distance Learning Quality Council, which maintains a database of all accredited correspondence courses.

The Home Education Advisory Service (HEAS) and Education Otherwise have good reputations for helping parents take on the formidable task of creating their own school. The HEAS Advice line can put you in touch with other subscribers who live abroad who might be able to offer practical advice. Many western countries have a support group address. Often these subscribers are members of the diplomatic service or work in the military. Some families may prefer to follow the British curriculum for Key Stages 1, 2, 3, GCSE, AS or A2 level by taking the syllabuses and textbooks with them. HEAS publishes a leaflet called 'Examinations and Qualifications' giving information about the different options available for taking formal qualifications.

## Home Schooling Resources

The two principal organisations in the field are Education Otherwise and HEAS:

*Education Otherwise*, PO Box 325, King's Lynn, Norfolk PE34 3XW (0870 7300074; enquiries@education-otherwise.org; www.education-otherwise.org). UK-based membership organisation which provides support and information for families whose children are being educated outside school and for those who wish to uphold the freedom of families to take responsibility for the education of their children. It takes its name from the Education Act which states that parents are responsible for their children's education, 'either by regular attendance at school or otherwise.' The organisation also publishes a number of titles like 'School Is Not Compulsory' which explains your rights and duties and shares the experiences of home-educating families. This is included in the membership pack (initial annual membership costs £25). Other titles explain how to teach children at different stages of their education.

*Home Education Advisory Service (HEAS),* PO Box 98, Welwyn Garden, Herts AL8 6AN (01707 371854; enquiries@heas.org.uk; www.heas.org.uk). National organisation providing information, advice and support for home educating families. Subscription to HEAS is open to home educating families. Annual subscription is £13.50 (£19 overseas) and includes a quarterly bulletin, access to the Advice Line for curriculum information and a regional list of subscribers. The service produces several publications like the 'Introductory Pack', the 'Home Education Handbook,' and the 'Big Book of Resource Ideas' for information on books, CDs, websites and clubs for most school subjects. Leaflets are available too covering exams, special educational needs and home education overseas.

Resources for long distance learning include:

*Open and Distance Learning Quality Council* – 020-7612 7090 (www.odlqc.org.uk). This body provides accreditation for all kinds of distance learning centres, acting as a reliable initial point of enquiry.

*University of Cambridge Local Exam Syndicates,* CIE (Cambridge International Examinations) Department, Syndicate Buildings, 1 Hills Road, Cambridge CB1 2EU (01223 553554; international@ucles.org.uk). This examination board sets the International GCSE (IGCSE) among many others. You can contact them for information about the syllabus, the location of examination centres abroad, past exam papers and suggested book lists to accompany the relevant syllabuses.

*International Centre for Distance Learning (ICDL)* – www-icdl.open.ac.uk. Database of 5,000 UK courses and programmes taught by distance learning, mainly post-secondary.

*Open Learning Centre International,* 24 King Street, Carmarthen, Wales SA31 1BS (0800 393743; www.olci.info). The Centre was founded in 1983 to offer a service of flexible training, personal development and education for industry, commerce, public organisations and individuals throughout the world. A huge range of subjects to study is on offer in addition to all the basic subjects from the usual to the more esoteric like Swahili and Thai. The courses have one level of difficulty and the company suggests that candidates should be aged twelve years and up. Each course takes approximately 100 hours to complete but this will vary according to ability.

*Worldwide Education Service (WES),* Waverley House, Penton, Carlisle,

Cumbria CA6 5QU; 01228 577123; www.weshome.demon.co.uk. WES supplies tutorial-based courses for children aged 4-13. All courses are based on the National Curriculum of England and Wales. WES Home School families live in more than 100 countries on every continent, or are travelling between them.

*Nisai Satellite School,* Milton Road, Harrow, Middlesex HA1 1XB; 020-8424 8475; http://nisaisatelliteschool.com. Offers distance learning courses for overseas pupils designed to provide them with education to UK National Curriculum standards. Courses may be followed via the Internet and e-mail leading to British International GCSE examinations and qualifications.

*Schoolfriend* – 020 7435 6868; www.schoolfriend.com. This website (accessible by subscription only) was set up to help children aged 4-13 practise online what they have learned at school. While not directly intended as a resource for distance learning, it can be used as an additional tool by parents teaching their children while they travel. Subscription charges starts at £32.50 for 3 months.

Exam revision sites proliferate on the web. For example the BBC has very good 'Bitesize' sites for Key Stages 2, 3 and GCSE (www.bbc.co.uk/schools/gcsebitesize).

*National Curriculum* – www.nc.uk.net. Information about the National Curriculum for England subject by subject. For the Scottish curriculum visit www.ltscotland.com. For Northern Ireland visit www.ccea.org.uk.

## Other Useful Resources

*British Council,* 10 Spring Gardens, London, SW1A 2BN (Switchboard 020-7930 8466 or Enquiries 0161-957 7755; www.britishcouncil.org). The British Council is a body funded by the British Government to promote British cultural, scientific and educational exchange with the international community. It runs 225 libraries and information centres worldwide where British newspapers can be read and reference material accessed, which could assist your children's education abroad. The Council also administers British accredited exams at their centres, which span the globe, operating in nearly 250 cities and towns in 110 countries.

*Dorling Kindersley* – www.dk.com. Publisher of illustrated guides on huge range of educational subjects. Parents can search for maths and other books appropriate to Key Stage 1 or 2.

*Usborne Publishing,* Usborne House, 83-85 Saffron Hill, London EC1N 8RT (020-7430 2800; www.usborne.com). International publisher of children's books, specialising in well-researched and produced reference books directed to young readers. The publisher's titles range from language learning to *World of Shakespeare*. Many of the reference books are Internet-linked, taking readers to specific multi-media websites.

*Tigerchild* (www.tigerchild.com) aims to be a balanced source of information on raising and educating children. Resource links accessible after free registration include 46 that are relevant to travel such as 'Books for Travelling with Kids' and 'Childhood Travel Vaccines'.

# New Skills and New Projects

Stepping back from the daily responsibilities of a career offers the unrivalled luxury of being able to enjoy time to pursue personal interests. Time is a precious commodity in the developed world and in short supply. Away from the hurly-burly of professional obligations, individuals can take stock of their lives and re-evaluate their personal ambitions. At least that's what they hope.

Having time for yourself allows you to define yourself as an individual rather than as a worker. Anyone who takes time off can use it, as many of the interviewees for this book have done, to develop new or under-used skills or simply to live in a manner of their own choosing. Literally and figuratively, it's a time to climb mountains, to set yourself challenges and learn how to accomplish them beyond the confining arena of the conventional workplace. All those avenues and byways for which a working schedule does not normally leave time can be explored, and opportunities grasped to participate in an activity for the sheer pleasure of it. Pursuing a new activity also expands your social horizons. It can prove remarkably stimulating to link up with a group of people totally unconnected with your professional experience.

Those whose working lives began immediately after finishing their education may never have deviated from the pre-ordained path of working life. Dutifully they proceed along their career path, assuming that most options are closed to them, that they will not have the chance to pursue other interests or hobbies in depth. But a career break can change all that, giving people a chance to take up further education, retrain or expand their skills.

The choices for further education are immense, ranging from weekly courses run by the local authority to a full-time university degree course. The Open University described later in this chapter is one of the most successful institutions to come out of the 1960s, enabling students to take degrees without having to become residential students.

A career break gives you time to stretch yourself in formal adult education or in learning new skills in or out of a classroom. Studies may be wholly for pleasure or they may be applicable to your career. Learning a foreign language often satisfies both requirements. Improving your knowledge of a language will give you access to a different culture while also enhancing your professional profile. Qualifying in TEFL (Teaching English as a Foreign Language) is popular and is discussed in the chapter 'Working and Living Abroad'.

Exploration of an entirely new field expands horizons and sometimes even prompts an unplanned-for career change. If you've only known one area of work then taking a career break might allow you to glimpse other professional worlds.

## CREATING YOUR OWN PROJECT

A career break for study or leisure involves a serious commitment of money and time so should be used well. It deserves careful planning so that the time doesn't leak away. Many people will use the time to create their own project, to fulfil an ambition or simply to indulge a passion. You might have a generalised desire to see the world, as described in the chapter *Travel & Adventure*. On the other hand you may want to take the chance to fulfil a specific ambition such as perfect your watercolour technique, learn to parachute, join an archaeological dig, trace your family roots, row across the Pacific, concentrate on getting fit, write poetry or a book, make a pilgrimage, study circus skills or help to protect an endangered species. In those moments of disgruntlement at work, each person is likely to have a private fantasy of an alternative life, even if it involves just three months away.

It is not essential to go abroad to satisfy one's curiosity about different worlds or fulfil long-held ambitions outside one's sphere of employment. Among the favourite alternatives to the pressures of the corporate world are working on the land or in the country, e.g. gardening and animal care. Hadlow College in Kent offers a range of courses suitable for people who want a complete change; horticulture, equine studies, animal care, etc. can be studied full- or part-time (01732 853236; www.hadlow.ac.uk). The Royal Horticultural Society offers a range of gardening courses for interest and career advancement (www.rhs.org.uk). The English Gardening School is run by the Chelsea Physic Garden (66 Royal Hospital Road, London SW3 4HS; 020-7352 4347; www.EnglishGardeningSchool.co.uk) and is a good place to turn a hobby into a job. One year diploma courses are available in Garden Design (£7,550), Practical Horticulture, Plants and Plantsmanship and Botanical Painting (all for £4,550).

Domestic circumstances may make leaving home impossible or undesirable but that need not rule out a gap year. **Mike Bleazard** wanted to see how much fun he could have by staying in his home environment of Cambridge pursuing a personal project that he would never have had the time to pursue while working.

**As a self-employed computer geek, Mike Bleazard had saved up enough pennies to take three months away from work, this time to pursue a new idea which he had developed with a friend.**
They wanted to design and self-publish a series of themed walking tours of Cambridge and distribute them in pamphlet form through local shops and via their website (www.shortcutguides.co.uk). It proved to be great fun to research and design them, one on the old colleges, two on modern architecture, another on churches, with the possibility of adding one on punting. His aim was to break even though of course it will not be unwelcome if his venture ends up making a profit. By printing them in bulk, the production cost is just 13 pence plus a penny to the Ordnance Survey (for permission to adapt their map) while they retail at £1.20.

He ended up working harder than he did when he was in employment but found that he enjoyed the experience intensely. Through the project he met people from many different worlds, from architects to publicans. Not everyone was wildly enthusiastic about his take on the sights, for instance a senior member of St. John's College strenuously objected to his description of the statue of King John in the gatehouse as 'effeminate'.

## Using a Gap Year to Develop your Career

One practical way of taking a gap year without creating too much distance between yourself and your work is to create a project that enhances your professional skills. Some bodies have established schemes whereby employees are temporarily assigned to another organisation to learn from a different environment. But you could also initiate such an exchange.

Often individuals will take a career break to pursue a particular goal within their own field. This is well-established among university academics who (in theory if not always in practice) are given a break from their teaching duties one term in seven (the meaning of the word sabbatical) in order to engage in full-time research. This time enables specialists to concentrate on their field and be productive, often resulting in an article or book. Some other employers have taken over the idea of sabbatical; for example newspapers like the *Financial Times* bestow paid or unpaid leave on their columnists who want to write a book. School teachers, lawyers, doctors and other professionals occasionally organise an attachment to a different institution to work on a particular academic project.

For many years Jonathan Ashley-Smith was Head of Conservation at the Victoria and Albert Museum and is also a world authority on the care of bronzes. He was actively encouraged by the director of the museum to take a gap year following 18 years as department head in charge of 50 people. At the time he resisted the suggestion that he had become bored and cynical in his job, but now acknowledges the truth of it. Jonathan decided to use his break to write a book outlining a new theory of conservation called Risk Assessment For Objects Conservation, which promotes a more flexible attitude among museums over the loan of objects for exhibitions. This is a topic that often causes friction between museum directors and conservation departments. After his 'sabbatical-with-a-purpose' he returned to work 'utterly invigorated with lots of brilliant ideas for research and more books.'

After working in the same London law firm for five years, **Sara Ellis-Owen** was a valued member of staff. She came to a point where she felt she needed time out from work and from London, and so asked for unpaid leave for three months. She also asked the *pro bono* department (meaning working for the public good) whether they would be able to support her once she had found a short-term legal placement abroad in a developing country. They generously agreed to pay for her flight to Belize and her placement fees to the Edinburgh-based charity *Challenges Worldwide* with whom she had fixed up a legal placement in Belize City.

She wanted to make the most of her time off and use her legal skills in a different way. She had to choose between a placement reviewing the Fire Act (whilst living in the fire station!) or a placement reviewing the laws of Belize to determine their compliance with the UN Convention on the Rights of the Child. She chose the latter because it sounded interesting and completely different from what she had done before. She was working with an NGO that advocated for the rights of all children in Belize:

> *Within a day of arriving I got stuck in, printing off all the relevant legislation, reviewing each in turn, highlighting the gaps and suggesting improvements. In order to form a view, I had to get up to speed with the 49 separate Articles of the 700-page Convention, a daunting task. I remember thinking on my first day that this was such a big task that I might not get to finish it within three months. Once I was comfortable with the Convention, I met with various people in the community (Police, Family Court, Department of Human Services and Community Rehabilitation Department) all of whom had strong views on the shortcomings of the law. I discovered interesting gaps in the outdated laws, for instance Belize law permits the use of corporal punishment in schools and the laws are slanted heavily in favour of girls (in terms of protection from violence and abuse). The most challenging part of my day was keeping up the motivation and not to become swamped by the wealth of information.*
>
> *Although my placement was relatively short, I found myself able to accomplish a great deal and benefit the National Committee for Families and Children (NCFC) as well as myself. I hope that my report will be used by the various NGOs to push for much needed changes in the law. It was a slight shock to the system coming back to a busy environment in London, but I felt refreshed after my break and my perspective on life was different – I refused to get stressed.*

*Challenges Worldwide* is experienced at placing volunteers in professionally relevant positions abroad from which they can gain new skills and different areas of expertise. Similarly *Outreach International* aims to match skills to placement. For example Helen Balazs, an orthotic technician in her early 30s, went to Cambodia for three months to train landmine victims and disabled young people to become commercial artists. It is often true that a change is as good as a rest.

Some career-breakers who join volunteer projects in the developing world without much thought come back fired up to pursue international development more seriously. The Charities Advisory Trust (www.charitiesadvisorytrust.co.uk/development) runs a four-week residential summer course in Mysore, India which can serve as a taster of career-level work in development. It includes sessions led by Indian activists and visits and two work placements with local

NGOs. The course fee of about £1,000 covers accommodation, food and transport within India.

A logical next step could be formal studies in international development. Some of the most well established courses in the field are taught at the International Development Department of the University of Birmingham (Edgbaston, Birmingham B15 2TT; 0121-414 5038; www.idd.bham.ac.uk) where several MSc programmes in development are on offer which include overseas study visits.

# ADULT EDUCATION

A prevailing theme of this book is that the modern economy demands an unprecedented degree of adaptability. While this can be stressful and even frightening, it also presents opportunities for reinvigoration and stimulation. Lifelong education has been one of the watchwords of the Labour government and can provide an exciting chance to move in a different direction, whether purely for pleasure, self-improvement or a combination.

The choices available in adult or continuing education are vast. It is possible to study any subject you can think of from Mandarin to massage, computing to archaeology. Are you interested in a part-time or full-time course? Do you want a vocational degree? Or are you keen to study a subject for pleasure? Think about what it is you want to achieve by further study during a career break. You might want to take your undergraduate studies a stage further by gaining an MA, MSc or even a PhD. During the past ten years the numbers attending postgraduate courses in the UK has quadrupled (including students from overseas). Most mature students prefer to study at their local university or college. Some elite institutions cater particularly for the needs of mature students. For example Birkbeck College is a member of London University and specialises in teaching mature students. While it is possible to take a full-time postgraduate degree, most teaching takes place in the evenings so that mature students can continue working during the day. It is possible to enrol in first or higher degrees in the arts, sciences or social sciences. Most course details can be found on the college website (www.bbk.ac.uk) or you can write to the Registry, Birkbeck College, University of London, Malet St, Bloomsbury, London WC1E 7HX (enquiries 0845 601 0174).

Ruskin College in Oxford specialises in providing educational opportunities for adults who want a second chance in education. For a variety of financial, personal or social reasons some adults have never had access to higher education. Ruskin seeks to redress this shortfall and has established a strong reputation for the quality of its adult education. The average age of students is 35 with a range from 22 to 74. Interestingly dyslexic students make up as much as 20% of the total student body. Courses are residential although it's possible to take shorter courses too. For information call 01865 310713, check the website www.ruskin.ac.uk or write to Ruskin College, Walton Street, Oxford OX1 2HE. A special residential programme called Ransackers is aimed at people over 55 who have never benefitted from higher education and who have a topic that they want to explore for a term. Full funding is available in association with Better Government for Older People and the Esme Fairburn Trust (details from Liz Mathews on 01865 517820; lmathews@ruskin.ac.uk).

According to UCAS (Universities and Colleges Admissions Service), the number of applicants over 25 years of age who are applying to universities and colleges keeps rising, so you are bound to find a peer group wherever you enrol.

A lack of confidence inhibits many older potential students. Many mature students feel an extra burden of stress because often they have given up a lot to return to education and stand to lose more than a 19 year old who drifts on from school. Most institutes of higher education have a mature student guidance officer who will be able to offer reassurance and practical advice on funding (see section on 'Financial Support' below).

## Lifelong Learning

Those who turned their backs on further or higher education at an earlier stage are now being encouraged to go back to college to acquire new skills and knowledge and an analytical training. A gap year might be the time, whatever your age, to pick up qualifications you never had the chance to study before or which you fluffed while being distracted by more entertaining youthful pursuits. The traditional notion of narrow windows of time for learning is becoming redundant. In an age of rapid technological innovation the concept of lifelong learning is becoming an orthodoxy which has ramifications for all areas of study.

By definition, formal adult education courses award certificates and degrees. This type of education can be roughly divided between further education, which takes place in local further education and tertiary colleges mainly offering vocational courses, and higher education which encompasses undergraduate and postgraduate study leading to a degree. Higher education includes degrees, Higher National Diplomas (HNDs) and Certificates, and Diplomas of Higher Education. It is possible to migrate from one to the other, as demonstrated in the case study later in this chapter of Sandra Murray, who took her first tentative steps back into education at her local college but continued her course at university in Edinburgh and went on to do an MBA.

Increasingly, universities run recreational courses for adults through departments variously called Continuing Education, Extra Mural departments or Short Course Units. These courses do not offer the same academic challenges as the degree programmes, but they do give adult learners access to the same academic resources like tutors and libraries without subjecting the students to the same pressure or commitments in terms of time and cost. If you already have a degree and professional qualifications you may not want to study towards another degree. If you want to study for pleasure, there may be little justification in putting yourself through another round of exams. Studying during an adult gap year should be pleasurable as well as enlightening, a period ideally free of anxiety and stress.

## Useful Contacts for Adult Education

*Adult Residential Colleges Association (ARCA),* 6 Bath Road, Felixstowe, Suffolk IP11 7JW (01394 27816; www.arca.uk.net).

*City & Guilds,* Customer Services Enquiries Unit, 1 Giltspur St, London EC1A 9DD (020-7294 2800; www.city-and-guilds.co.uk). Set up in the 19th century to provide technical training for a variety of trades, C&G is now a leading provider of vocational qualifications in the UK suitable for anyone wishing to improve their skills or to retrain before returning to work. Subjects for study include agriculture, catering, clothing, construction, education, electronics, furniture, healthcare, IT, retail and distribution, sport and tourism.

*Floodlight* directories produced by the Association of London Government list courses in London and are sold by newsagents and bookshops, or are available online in a searchable database of courses (www.floodlight.co.uk).

*Part-time Floodlight in London* appears in early July; *Summertime Floodlight* is published before Easter and *Full-time Floodlight* comes out in the early autumn.

*National Institute of Adult Continuing Education (NIACE),* Renaissance House, 20 Princess Road West, Leicester LE1 6TP (0116 204 4200; www.niace.org.uk). Leading organisation for adult learning; publishes a range of booklets on topics related to lifelong learning and co-ordinates Adult Learners' Week.

*UCAS (Universities & Colleges Admissions Service)* – 0870 1122211; www.ucas.com/guides/MatureGuide.pdf. Publishes *Mature Guide* which can be read online.

*University of the Third Age* – www.u3a.org.uk. Promotes lifelong learning mainly among retired people.

*Second Chances* (available from Trotman, 2005; £22.46). National guide to adult education and training opportunities.

### Business Studies and the MBA

Mature students often consider embarking on a business degree to facilitate a career change or improve their prospects. Using a gap year to obtain a Master of Business Administration (MBA) is not uncommon among employees working in any form of financial or commercial administration. In recent years it has become almost *de rigeur* for advancement in certain professions like management consultancy. It's a trend that has taken its lead from the United States where this field of study was pioneered. Some of the major American business schools like Harvard, Columbia and Wharton in Philadelphia are prestigious and expensive. But European business schools are catching up: the London Business School and INSEAD in Paris were ranked in the top ten business schools worldwide by the *Financial Times* in their 2006 MBA Survey.

The MBA is an ideal degree for individuals who have spent some years in work following graduation. It offers the chance to study abroad in the US or France, for example, while gaining a degree that is highly valued in business. Effectively, it almost guarantees a significant lift in professional salary and opportunities. Students tend to be aged between 26 and 35. Holders of MBAs are some of the best-paid employees in the workforce which is just as well since fees for one year's MBA study can easily rise to £20,000.

The *Association of MBAs (AMBA)* (www.mba.org.uk) runs a scheme with NatWest for financial assistance to prospective students wishing to take MBA courses. To qualify you must have a Bachelor's degree or suitable professional qualification plus two years' relevant work experience, or non-graduates must have five years' experience in industry or commerce. It is possible to obtain two-thirds of present gross salary plus tuition fees for every year of the course. Preferential interest rates apply.

## OPEN LEARNING

Distance learning is often now referred to as open learning, replacing the old description of 'correspondence course'. It is a concept of keen interest to individuals who want to embark on adult education without leaving home. By definition, the concept allows any student to study from home with the assistance of the Internet supplemented by text and audio-visual materials. Tutorial help is provided by e-mail, post, telephone and occasionally in face-to-face meetings. One-week residential courses are usually built in to the programme.

Many of the same qualifications are available by open learning as by attending courses on college campuses. Realistically, most adults in their 30s, 40s or 50s do not have the freedom (nor the inclination) to leave their comfortable homes to live in student digs or residential halls for extended periods. Parents at home caring for young children often find this a valuable option.

Flexibility is at the heart of open and distance learning, giving students the ability to learn at their own pace and in their own time from anywhere in the country or indeed the world. Computer skills are now compulsory. Course materials can be quite expensive although this can be mitigated by access to a good local library and the huge resources now available online. Generally speaking, distance courses are much cheaper than full-time residential ones. Learning any subject, especially practical ones, from books can be a challenge, as can disciplining yourself to stick to a self-imposed timetable. Be wary of extravagant claims by distance learning course providers since an element of practice may be considered essential for certain areas of endeavour (e.g. learning to teach English).

## The Open University and Other Providers

The Open University was established to teach mature students including those individuals without any formal qualifications. Now considered a great success, the OU has established a reputation for the quality of its teaching and research. All of this is a tremendous resource for aspirational adult students.

The large range of courses range from short modules to PhDs. It is possible to construct your own degree programme by choosing from the 160 single nine-month courses or signing up for one of the 30 two-year diplomas listed in the *Undergraduate Prospectus*. Courses can be spread over many years with breaks and students can begin studying at any level appropriate for them. Most work is undertaken by distance learning, using interactive learning, audio-visual and printed materials, CD-ROMs, television and radio programmes on the BBC, and personal contact with tutors. Open2.net is the online learning portal from the Open University and the BBC.

Aside from first and higher degrees, Open University students can study a variety of non-degree courses like computing, health and social welfare, management, the history of ideas and art history, among many others; log on to www.open.ac.uk/courses to conduct a search. Most courses from the undergraduate programmes are available too without proceeding to a full degree. For further detailed information contact your nearest OU regional centre. To find the nearest centre call the Course Information and Advice Centre on 01908 653231.

Alternatives to the Open University take the form of specialist correspondence colleges, viz. the *Open College of the Arts, National Extension College* and *Open Learning Centre.* For information on accredited colleges, contact the *Open and Distance Learning Quality Council* (all listed below).

The Internet has revolutionised distance learning. To take just one example, Birkbeck College, the adult education arm of London University, has been running virtual screenwriting workshops for a number of years. One day a week ten students log on for a two-hour tutorial. One tutor claims that online learning gives students greater confidence to speak up and the students make great efforts to meet up socially.

People considering doing a distance course with a private institute should try to ascertain how widely recognised the qualification or 'diploma' will be. Certain fields attract the occasional cowboy operators, for example in the booming field of Teaching English as a Foreign Language (TEFL), a few companies in the field (often operating from a Post Office Box number) have a definite credibility gap. Try to find out if there is an accreditation council in the field and if so whether the institute is a member. Ask to be put in touch with past students and seek the opinion of respectable organisations or prospective employers in the field.

## Useful Open Learning Contacts

*The Open University,* Student Enquiry Service, PO Box 197, Milton Keynes MK7 6BJ (0870870 333 4340; www.open.ac.uk).

*Association of British Correspondence Colleges (ABCC)* – 020-8544 9559 (www.homestudy.org.uk). A trade association representing correspondence colleges, offering advice and information for prospective students. Standards are regulated and a common code of ethics applied.

*Learndirect* – 0800 100 900 (www.learndirect-advice.co.uk). Government information service on education at all levels including Distance, Open and Flexible Learning.

*Open College of the Arts (OCA),* Registration Department, Freepost SF10678, Barnsley, Yorkshire S75 1BR (freephone 0800 731 2116; www.oca-uk.com). OCA offers home-study courses in art and design supported by tutors who are practising artists. There are 45 courses in painting, sculpture, textiles, interior design, photography, garden design, dance, music and singing. Students can begin their course at any time of the year. Most courses cost £499 and include either distance tuition, mostly by post, or five hours of face-to-face tuition.

*Open and Distance Learning Quality Council (ODLQC)* – 020-7612 7090 (www.odlqc.org.uk). Grants accreditation to private colleges offering distance learning. Accredited colleges range from the Kevala Centre in Devon which teaches alternative therapies like Indian head massage to the Horticultural Correspondence College.

*Open Learning Centre International,* 24 King St, Carmarthen SA31 1BS (0800 393743; www.olci.info). Offers flexible education and training programmes to individuals throughout the world. Continuous start dates.

*RDI (Resource Development International),* Midland Management Centre, 1A Brandon Lane, Coventry CV3 3RD (024 765 15700; www.rdi.co.uk). Distance learning in Accounting, Finance, Management, Marketing, IT, Business Administration and Law via key partners such as the Universities of Sunderland, Leicester and Northumbria.

*University of London External Programme* – 020-7862 8398; www.londonexternal.ac.uk). 100 different degrees and diplomas are delivered externally to students in more than 140 countries.

## Financial Support for Returning to Education

Finding financial support for further education is undeniably difficult. At a time when the government has tripled student fees in England overnight and expects undergraduates to take out huge loans to fund themselves through college, it will be difficult to find financial aid as a mature or postgraduate student. The 1960s, 70s and 80, can now be viewed as a golden age for higher education in which studying was seen as an entitlement rather than a privilege.

Mature students over 21 and under 54 are eligible to apply for a means-tested student loan. People over 19 who missed out on education when young and want to study full-time for GCSEs, NVQs or A levels may be eligible for the new means-test Adult Learning Grant of up to £30 a week. Full-time students who have dependent children may be eligible for a Childcare Grant and, depending on the household income, a Parents' Learning Allowance. Further information is available from the DfES Student Support Information Line (0800 731 9133) or check the website www.direct.gov.uk which includes information about routes into higher education for mature students.

If you need help funding a training course, in anything from feng shui to TEFL teaching to ski instructing abroad, you may be eligible for a Career Development Loan. CDLs are bank loans covering up to 80% of the cost of a vocational course lasting less than two years followed by up to a year's practical experience. The Department for Education and Skills (DfES) pays the interest until a month after your course finishes whereupon you must begin repayments at a favourable rate of interest. Write for details to Freepost, Career Development Loans (0800 585505; www.lifelonglearning.co.uk/cdl). Note that long-term unemployed people over 25 may be eligible for Job Seeker's Allowance even though they are doing a full-time training course (www.jobcentreplus.gov.uk). Some colleges are entitled to offer special dispensation to mature students. For example people over the age of 30 may be given tax relief by some UK colleges. Learner Support Funds (www.support4learning.org.uk) may help with part of the fees and for books and travel.

Sometimes access bursaries are made available to eligible students. Colleges can make discretionary child care grants of up to £1,000 to help parents pay for care while they study. Similarly, colleges also run hardship funds from their respective social service departments. Some colleges are entitled to offer special dispensation to mature students, e.g. giving them tax relief.

The alternative source for funding is to contact various charitable trusts, which make specific educational grants. When applying to a college or a university, enquire about the availability of financial support. In addition to running hardship funds for the most needy students, many educational institutions award scholarships and bursaries so it is always worth asking how to qualify for additional support. Sometimes paid research or teaching assistant positions are available in higher education which can partially offset the costs of your own study.

In order to encourage recruitment into nursing and teaching, the government has implemented a programme of inducements. For anyone considering an MBA course, special loans are available through the Association of MBAs at preferential rates provided you meet certain qualifying standards.

## Books and Publications

Many education reference books are expensive and best consulted at your local public or university library. Most local authority or careers (Connexions) libraries will contain a well-stocked section dedicated to further, higher and adult education.

*Prospects* (www.prospects.ac.uk) is the graduate careers web portal in the UK. Search 'Mature' to access information for students over 21.

*PICKUP National Training Directory* published by Guildford Educational Services Ltd. (01252 337500; www.gesvt.com/data/pickup/pickup.htm). Comprehensive easy-to-search directory of vocational short-term training courses throughout the UK, with a predominance of IT, language and management courses. Sold as a CD-ROM (£155+VAT) so try to consult it at your local careers office or library.

*A Guide to Courses and Careers in Art, Craft and Design: Creative Futures* from the National Society for Education in Art and Design (01249 714825; www.nsead.org). £7.50. If interested in pursuing an art course, also consult the annually updated *Progression to Art & Design* from UCAS.

*Choosing Your Degree Course and University* by Brian Heap (Trotman, 2006; £21.99). Trotman publishes a huge range of educational and careers literature; its catalogue can be accessed on its website www.trotman.co.uk.

*Directory of Vocational and Further Education* (Pearson Education). Updated annually. Comprehensive guide to vocational courses, further education and sixth form colleges in the UK. £90 (held in libraries).

*The Big Guide 2007*, UCAS (www.ucasbooks.co.uk); £29.50 with CD-ROM. This annual publication provides information about all degree and HND courses at public universities and colleges.

*Mature Students' Directory* (Trotman; £15.99). A guide aimed at people over the age of 21 hoping to enter higher education.

## LEARNING FOR PLEASURE

Sometimes individuals need time to relax and shake off years of stress. A gap year can provide the leisure time to extend your knowledge of a favoured subject purely at a recreational level. Perhaps you have discovered an activity while on holiday like riding, diving, art or cookery which you want to pursue in more depth. A career break presents an ideal opportunity to immerse yourself for several months in a new interest.

Everyone has interests over the course of their lives that go into hibernation at certain periods. Sometimes your interests move on and change, but more often a shortage of time is to blame. Perhaps while at school or college you had a passion for football, art, photography, an allotment garden, chess, human rights campaigning, Thai cookery, mountaineering, creative writing, playing in an orchestra, pigeon racing or singing in a choir. Gradually this commitment may have dwindled as work has taken up more time and energy. This deficit may have been exacerbated by the onset of parenthood.

But it is never too late to revive an old interest or introduce yourself to a new one. Throughout the UK literally hundreds of subjects can be studied in evening classes, for weekends or for longer periods. These courses tend to be listed under the rubric of 'adult education' and are often organised by the local education authority. Normally they are offered at an introductory level though advice can usually be offered about where to pursue an interest to a higher level. Courses are usually part-time or take place outside regular working hours but there is never enough time to sign up for the courses you fancy. The bad news in 2006 is that current British government policy favours 14-19 education and education for employment, at the expense of adult education. As a result fees have risen sharply which has led to the cancellation of many courses.

**Fiona Carroll** felt she had been neglecting her own life in favour of her job as a project manager for a software company in Switzerland and decided finally to take a full year's break to spend time with her family in Ireland and also to take painting courses in Switzerland. She believes her old company would have kept the job open for her but she wanted a change to decrease the amount of time she spent at work and obtain a better balance between her job and her private life. 'I didn't want to travel. I just wanted to be.' Remaining at home gave her the opportunity to pursue her love of art. She started taking lessons in painting near her home, which she is able to continue still by working a four-day week. She takes every Tuesday off which she describes as 'wonderful'.

**Brian Blackshaw had been Vicar of Cheshunt in Hertfordshire for eight years, working in a very large and challenging parish, when he investigated the possibility of a sabbatical:**
The Church of England is an employer that allows its hard-working staff to take occasional sabbaticals and Brian's application for a three-month sabbatical was accepted when he was aged about 60. Such sabbaticals are not uncommon in the Church though only after at least ten years of service. In the past, when C of E sabbaticals tended to be longer, recipients were expected to pursue formal studies or do some writing. But three months is too short a time for that and, although it is necessary to demonstrate that one's time off will be spent in something worthwhile, a degree of latitude is given for pursuing personal interests.

Brian had been studying Italian on and off and one of his ambitions was to deepen his knowledge of the Italian language and culture. He had visited Florence before and had been encouraged to return by a Polish friend who loved the city. Like almost everybody else, he began his search on the Internet and his Google search for the British Council led him to the British Institute of Florence (see Directory entry) whose programmes sounded ideal. So he rented an apartment in Florence and attended intensive Italian language classes for four hours a day. On arrival he noticed that the Institute also had places on a Baroque and Mannerist art course so he enrolled in that as well. This involved a one-hour lecture a day with some eminent art historians, both British and Italian, and visits to the Uffizi Gallery and other Florentine galleries as well as to Rome. He considered the standard of teaching to be superb and describes his art course as a joy. He felt that this intensive and enlightened exposure to some of the most magnificent examples of Renaissance art allowed him to break into a circle of knowledge which he had long found intimidating and from which he had felt excluded. He feels that many people are deterred by a perception of how difficult something will be, but that given the right circumstances it is possible to prick the bubble and enter the charmed circle.

He enjoyed the company of the 15 or 20 other people on his courses although most were much younger, including several post-A level students, some interested in pursuing art history at university, and a sprinkling of more mature people including a couple of Americans temporarily resident in Florence. He was delighted with the facilities at the British Institute and now feels that he could make it a base for any future sojourns in Florence.

Altogether Brian was off work for 14 weeks and three days and felt that he made good use of his time. In addition to his month in Italy, he joined two birdwatching trips, one to the Picos Mountains of northern Spain and the other to Speyside, visited friends in Switzerland and his eldest daughter in America. He also luxuriated in having enough leisure time to read an average of two books a week. But the highlight remained his time in Florence when he felt in some ways he rediscovered his humanity. In his busy parish, 180 funerals must be conducted a year plus hospitals and prisons visited and countless other duties fulfilled. With the Church of England financially stretched, the vicar's workload can be gruelling, and time off all the more necessary.

## Recreational Courses Abroad

A gap year allows you to contemplate studying something that interests you in a foreign country, like African drumming, flamenco dancing or skiing. Specialist travel companies can arrange special interest courses. For example the Association of Independent Tour Operators (AITO, 133A St Margaret's Road, Twickenham, Middlesex TW1 1RJ; www.aito.co.uk) lists a number of upmarket tour operators that can arrange watercolour courses in Italy, wine appreciation in Chile, birdwatching in China, and so on.

The American counterpart is the *Specialty Travel Index* (305 San Anselmo Ave, San Anselmo, CA 94960; www.specialtytravel.com) which is a useful source of information about 400 specialist tour operators. Their website is searchable by destination and activity or you can purchase the twice-yearly directory for $10 ($25 abroad). Cultural tours and special interest programmes tend to be fairly upmarket and it is usually much cheaper to sign up with a local organisation abroad, something which is becoming easier with the help of the Internet.

To take just two examples, someone who has always had a fascination with China might consider the new range of short or semester-long courses offered in Suzhou near Shanghai by the Boland School (www.boland-china.com/culture) which includes the predictable (Chinese language and cookery) as well as the more obscure (calligraphy, music and martial arts).

Thousands of miles away in Central America Art Workshops in Guatemala in Antigua (www.artguat.org) offers a variety of eight-day workshops in the fields of photography, weaving, fibre arts, watercolours, painting, mixed media, collage and creative writing. Prices are around $1,650.

## Cookery Courses

Cookery is an important hobby for many and a passion for a few. Pursuing an interest in food in a foreign country can be one of the most satisfying courses to build into a career break. Furthermore a catering certificate opens up many appealing employment options in ski resorts, private villas or private yachts for those who are looking for a change of direction.

Private certificate and diploma courses are expensive, especially if you splash out on one of the household names like Cordon Bleu or Tante Marie. Here is a selection of courses in the UK and Europe:

*Ashburton Cookery School,* 76 East St, Ashburton, Devon TQ13 7AX (01364 652784; www.ashburtoncookeryschool.co.uk). Specialist and diploma cookery courses of varying durations. 1-day courses cover choice of Bakery, Italian, French, Moorish, Thai, Express Dinner Parties, etc. 2-day courses cover for example Chef Skills, Beginners, Italian, Thai or Vegetarian. Also 5-day 'Pressure Cooks' course originally designed for chalet hosts and boat crew and 4-week Basic Cookery Diploma course. From £115 for 1-day course to about £2,000 for 4-week diploma course.

*Ballymaloe Cookery School,* Shanagarry, Midelton, Co. Cork, Ireland (21-46 46 785; www.cookingisfun.ie). Situated on organic farm by the coast with access to excellent ingredients. 12-week Certificate in Cookery course plus range of short courses. €8,375 for Certificate course excluding accommodation.

*Cookery at the Grange,* The Grange, Whatley, Frome, Somerset BA11 3JU (tel/fax: 01373 836579; www.cookeryatthegrange.co.uk). 4-week course costs £2,650-£3,090.

*Le Cordon Bleu Culinary Institute*, 114 Marylebone Lane, London W1V 2HH (020-7935 3503; www.cordonbleu.net) Also branches in Paris and 15 countries. 10-week course costs £4,427.

*Edinburgh School of Food & Wine,* The Coach House, Newliston, Edinburgh EH29 9EB (0131-333 5001; www.esfw.com). Diploma and Certificate courses last 6 months, 3 months, 4 months, 2 weeks, 1 week and 1 day.

*Food of Course Cookery School,* Middle Farm House, Sutton, Shepton Mallet, Somerset BA4 6QF (01749 860116; www.foodofcourse.co.uk). 4-week Foundation Cookery Course among others.

*Gables School of Cookery,* Bristol Road, Falfield, Glos. GL12 8DF (01454 260444; www.thegablesschoolofcookery.com). Specialists in training chalet hosts and yacht cooks. £2,395 inclusive for 4-week course.

*Kilbury Manor Cookery Courses,* Colston Road, Buckfastleigh, Devon TQ11 0LN (01364 644079; www.kilbury.co.uk). Tailor-made courses for beginners to advanced.

*Leiths School of Food and Wine,* 21 St. Albans Grove, London W8 5BP (020-7229 0177; www.leiths.com). Basic Certificate course lasts 4 weeks full-time in September. Beginners' Certificate 10 weeks October-December.

*Malaca Instituto,* Calle Cortada 6, Cerrado de Calderón, 29018 Málaga, Spain (+34 952-29 3242; www.MalacaInstituto.com). Recreational cookery with Spanish language course. About €700 for 2 weeks plus registration fee of €65.

*The Murray School of Cookery,* Glenbervie House, Holt Pound, Farnham, Surrey GU10 4LE (tel/fax: 01420 23049; www.cookeryschool.net). £1,500 for a 4-week course.

*The Orchards School of Cookery,* The Orchards, Salford Priors, Nr Evesham, Worcestershire WR11 8UU (tel/fax: 01789 490 259; www.orchardscookery.co.uk). 5 days to 2 weeks, year round.

*Rosie Davies,* Penny's Mill, Nunney, Frome, Somerset BA11 4NP (01373 836210; www.rosiedavies.co.uk). 4-week Certificate course for £2,700 including accommodation.

*Tante Marie School of Cookery,* Woodham House, Carlton Road, Woking, Surrey GU21 4HF (01483 726957; www.tantemarie.co.uk). UK's largest independent cookery school.

*La Varenne,* Château du Feÿ, 89300 Villecien, France (+33 3-86 63 18 34; www.lavarenne.com). Courses popular with Americans.

*La Vieille Forge,* 4 Rue de Burguet, Berlou, 34360 Herault, France (+33 4-67 89 48 63; www.lavieilleforge.com). Short courses in the Languedoc region of France.

*Walnut Grove Cookery School,* Le Hunaudiere, 53400 Livre la Touche, Mayenne, France (+33 2-43 98 50 02; www.walnutgrovecookery.com). 5-day gourmet cookery course from £925. Located in the Loire Valley.

### Creative Writing

The working world is full of aspiring writers of fiction, poetry, travel journalism, plays and so on. A career break allows the leisure to pursue this aspiration a little more seriously. A course in creative writing might provide a useful fillip in this direction. You can't learn to write well without practice and without bouncing your attempts off a critical audience. Evening classes are available in most centres of population.

The *Arvon Foundation* (42a Buckingham Palace Road, London SW1W 0RE; www.arvonfoundation.org) runs five-day writing courses at its several locations in rural Britain (West Yorkshire, Devon, Inverness-shire and Shropshire). Courses are open to anyone keen to try their hand at writing poetry, fiction, stage drama or TV and radio scripts. The course tutors are professional writers, some of whom are well known from newspapers and bookstands. The current cost is £475 inclusive of accommodation, food and tuition. Grants are available to those unable to afford the full cost (see their website).

Other courses, some abroad, are advertised in the literary pages of the quality press and on the website www.author-network.com/courses.html. For example writing courses are offered between March and October on the Greek island of Skyros at the holistic holiday centre mentioned below in the section on *Retreats*. Past courses have been tutored by extremely well known authors like Margaret Drabble and Sue Townsend, author of the Adrian Mole series.

## LEARNING A LANGUAGE

A gap year is an ideal opportunity to brush up on a barely-remembered GCSE (or perhaps even O level) language or start from scratch with a new language. Most current and future employers will view this as a commendably constructive allocation of time, and anyone with competence in another language has an advantage in many job hunts. Many older people might have in the back of their minds the possibility of buying property abroad or even retiring permanently and therefore have a straightforward motive in mastering a language.

Knowledge of a foreign language connects you to another culture and makes friendships with local people possible. Increasingly, UK residents are buying second homes in France, Spain, Italy, etc. Since the opening of the Channel Tunnel there has been a psychological shift in the British attitude to the continent and much of the nation is falling in love with aspects of foreign cultures.

British professionals are often put to shame by the linguistic superiority of their counterparts on the continent and feel that they were poorly taught at school with too much emphasis placed on grammar and literature. Even with a GCSE and A level in a language, many Britons arrive in France, Germany or Italy still tongue-tied through lack of confidence and a serious linguistic deficiency.

## Language Learning in the UK

Britons are notoriously slow to learn foreign languages. Yet the spirit is willing if a recent statistic is true claiming that 7% of the UK population are studying a language at any one time. Evening language classes offered by local authorities usually follow the academic year and are aimed at hobby learners. Intensive courses offered privately are much more expensive.

After stepping down from the post of Director General of the CBI and before becoming the country's pensions guru, **Adair Turner** spent many months writing a book about the future of capitalism from his home in London. But he also exploited the time he took away from formal employment to improve his meagre French, which he felt was a serious gap in his education. Each week a tutor would visit him at home to develop his conversational ability:

> *I suspect that most people 15 years after leaving full-time education are aware that there are some things that they could have done but the choices they made or the education they were given didn't develop that. In my case it was languages. I made the right choices in education except that I wasn't taught languages very well. I wanted to fill that in.*

If you are really dedicated, consider using a self-study programme with books and tapes (which start at £30), distance learning course or broadcast language course, though discipline is required to make progress. Although many people have been turning to the web to teach them a language, many conventional teach-yourself courses are still on the market, for example from OUP (www.askoxford.com/languages), Berlitz (020-7518 8300), the BBC (08700 100222), Linguaphone (0800 282417; www.linguaphone.co.uk) and Audioforum (www.audioforum.com). All of them offer deluxe courses with refinements such as interactive videos and of course these cost more. Linguaphone recommends half an hour of study a day for three months to master the basics of a language. **Polly Botsford,** a lawyer in her early 30s, thinks that learning the language is the key to understanding a foreign country because that is the only way to communicate with the people. Although she made some progress in learning Khmer after joining her volunteer project in Cambodia, she regrets that she didn't study the language before leaving home:

*It is arrogant to arrive somewhere and expect to hear and speak only English. I read quite a few books and talked to a lot of people, which is part of the fun and the build-up. For me the low point in Cambodia was a constant sense of frustration that I could not properly understand people. Often I felt like a complete uncultured idiot for not conversing with people in their native tongue. It has been the bane of my life that I cannot traverse linguistic borders.*

If you are interested in an obscure language and don't know where to study it, contact the National Centre for Languages (CILT, 020-7379 5101; www.cilt.org.uk) which has a certain amount of documentation on courses, especially in London.

Hold out a carrot to yourself of a trip to a country where your target language is spoken. Even if you don't make much headway with the course at home, take the tapes and books with you since you will have more incentive to learn once you are immersed in a language.

Useful contacts in the UK include:

*Alliance Française,* 1 Dorset Square, London NW1 6PU (020-7723 6439; www.alliancefrancaise.org.uk). Sponsored by the French government, the Alliance manages 13 teaching centres throughout the UK including Bristol, Glasgow and Manchester. Contact the website for details of your nearest teaching centre and French clubs. Sample cost would be £240 for 30 hours of tuition over two weeks.

*Institut Français Language Centre,* 14 Cromwell Place, London SW7 2JR (020-7581 2701; www.institut-francais.org.uk). Also in Edinburgh. The Institute is the official French government centre of language and culture in London. Like the Alliance Française, it offers business French, classes for beginners and advanced speakers and private tuition. Classes are graded in difficulty from numbers one to eight.

*Instituto Cervantes* (Spanish Cultural Institute), 102 Eaton Square, London SW1W 9AN (020-7235 0359; www.cervantes.es). Also in Manchester and Leeds. Non-profit cultural organisation now the largest worldwide Spanish teaching organisation.

*Italian Cultural Institute,* 39 Belgrave Square, London SW1X 8NX (020-7823 1887; www.icilondon.esteri.it/IIC_Londra).

*CILT (Centre for Information on Language Teaching),* 20 Bedfordbury, London WC2N 4LB (020-7379 5101; www.cilt.org.uk). The government's National Centre for Languages.

*Goethe-Institut,* 50 Princes Gate, London SW7 2PH (020-7596 4004; german@london.goethe.org; www.goethe.de). Centres also in Glasgow (0141-332 2555) and Manchester (0161-237 1077).

## Learning a Language Abroad

A more enjoyable and successful way of learning a language is by doing it on location. While studying French or German at secondary school, you normally have two hours of classes a week, which works out at about 80 hours a year. While doing an eight-week intensive course, you might have 240 hours, the equivalent of three years of school instruction plus you will be speaking the language outside the classroom, so progress is normally much quicker. To give a very rough idea of the cost, a typical intensive French language course in a major European city might charge about €2,000 for eight weeks of 20 lessons per week; accommodation would be in addition.

Numerous British and international agencies represent a range of language schools abroad offering in-country language courses. The agents are very familiar with differences between schools, qualifications, locations, etc. and what is most suitable for clients. *CESA Languages Abroad, Caledonia, Cactus Language* and *Language Courses Abroad* (see Directory entries), among some others listed below, all have wide-ranging programmes abroad in Europe and beyond. These agencies also provide a useful back-up service if the course does not fulfil your requirements in any way.

In her late middle years **Pamela Tincknell** began to toy with the idea of spending more time in Spain. Like so many others Pamela has always hated the dark and gloomy British winter and fancied the idea of the Costa del Sol. She had been taking the regulation holidays in Spain since the 1960s and had dabbled in beginner Spanish evening classes but decided that the time had come to extend her linguistic aspirations. A chronic hoarder, Pamela fished out a cutting from a Sunday supplement she had squirreled away as many as 20 years earlier which was about language courses abroad. To her surprise she found that the company featured, CESA (see Directory entry), was still going strong and so she requested their brochure.

She knew that she wanted to be on the coast rather than inland and chose the civilised resort town of Nerja. She joined a fortnight-long course at the Escuela de Idiomas Nerja (www.idnerja.es) designed for the over-50s, consisting of three hours of language tuition a day plus plenty of excursions. That experience hooked her and she began to consider spending an entire year learning Spanish. She is thoroughly convinced that going off-season was a good move, not only because of the lovely weather but because the winter attracts older people, including what Pamela calls 'lifers'. Pamela recommends a small resort for an initial language course but now feels that she has outgrown living near an expat enclave and has grown tired of waiters who reply in English to questions in Spanish.

**David Storey** is another satisfied CESA customer. Because his job as a long-distance lorry driver takes him frequently to France, he wanted to improve his French, so signed up for a three-month course in Bordeaux last September:

> *I obviously improved my French but also I found the whole experience of meeting new people and noting the cultural differences to be very rewarding. I had taken up the course out of a desire to improve my French, which since A-level had not been practised and just barely remembered. In my work for an international freight company I had travelled extensively throughout Europe working with many colleagues for whom English was not their first language. As I was reliant on people speaking my language I began to regret my inability to speak a second language myself so I decided to pick up again with my long neglected French.*
>
> *I found that many of the French people I met were very welcoming and friendly and were generally impressed that I was trying to speak their language. Whilst in Bordeaux I played at two small squash clubs and was welcomed, which was a great opportunity to chat and mingle. Also there was some good dressing room banter on the subject of football and I found myself on more than one occasion having to defend the football merits of Peter Crouch. I recommend going to watch the local football team in Bordeaux as well. The Saturday evening kick-off times really foster a family atmosphere.*

*I stayed in the home of a local man and found the experience to be delightful and informative in itself. For one thing his apartment was very near the school in a very beautiful part of the Centreville and he even invited me to spend time at his coastal home at Lacanau, which is a surfers' paradise, and in winter a wonderfully peaceful retreat from the madness of the city. It was a great introduction to the French 'esprit', as he would share his philosophies and outlook on life. As for Bordeaux it's a fantastic city, with the Centreville being just the right size to retain a friendly and intimate atmosphere. I certainly plan to go back there next winter and settle a few squash match grudges.*

Of course it is not necessary to book a language course via a mediating agency as **Annabel Iglehart** from Edinburgh discovered in her gap year after university when she signed up with a major Spanish language school with many branches:

*After working in a variety of jobs at home, I went to Salamanca to do a three-month intensive Spanish language course with Mester. I planned and paid for my course and accommodation directly through Mester and this saved me a lot of money; it was by far the most economical way to organise the trip. The course was fantastic. The classes were fast-paced and the teachers excellent. I lived with a Spanish family for a while and then moved to a flat with other students. I met loads of people with whom I am still in touch.*

Literally thousands of language schools around the world would like your business, so care needs to be taken in choosing one that suits individual needs. Possible sources of language school addresses on the web are www.languageschoolsguide.com (part of www.goabroad.com), www.language-schools-directory.com and http://language.shawguides.com. After considering the obvious factors like price and location when choosing a language school, also try to find out the average age and likely nationalities of your fellow learners, how experienced and qualified the staff are, whether there will be any one-to-one tuition and whether the course concentrates on oral or written skills, whether extracurricular activities and excursions are included in the fee, and generally as much as you can. One key factor is whether or not a school prepares its students for exams. If they do and you are there only for the fun of it, you may find that lessons are not suitable.

Whereas some language schools run purely recreational courses, others offer some kind of qualification. Some schools are instantly recognised such as the Alliance Française and the Goethe Institute. At the other end of the spectrum, some schools offer nothing more than a certificate outlining the period of study and perhaps the level of language reached or work covered in the course, which may be of limited value if you ever need to show proof of language attainment.

However the majority of adult learners are there not to gain a diploma but to have fun and learn more about a foreign culture to which they have been attracted. Recreational language courses are offered by virtually every school. Some programmes are more structured than others, so students need to look for flexible courses which allow them to progress at their own rate.

A recent innovation is language lessons on the street; instead of simulating a shopping situation in the classroom, instructors take their clients to the shops so that the language can be used in real situations. The company Languages Out There (www.languagesoutthere.com) operates in Spain, Germany, Italy and the Czech Republic, and you may come across the system elsewhere. For instance Español Andando in Buenos Aires (www.espanol-andando.com.ar) offers Spanish tuition in this 'fun, budget and unconventional way'.

Many people agree that the fastest way to improve fluency is to have one-to-one lessons, though of course these are more expensive than group classes. Usually a combination of the two works best.

**Retirement can provide the perfect catalyst for planning new language learning departures, as was the case for Ed McFadd from southern California:**

*After thirty-eight years as a teacher and school principal, I retired on my sixtieth birthday and married a lovely woman two days later. Retirement was to be a new adventure but my only real expectation was to get my ageing sack of flesh back into some sort of fit condition and possibly study French. In preparation for a vacation we had taken in France a couple of years previously, I had bought some language learning tapes, which I listened to on my suburban commute. Turned out I rather enjoyed my reacquaintance with the language after three and a half decades. Even though I retained only a few rudimentary lessons from back then, the attraction was still there.*

*With all the time available to me I joined a local walking group, the YMCA fitness programme and enrolled in the French 1 evening programme at the University of California. I am now carrying around 35 fewer pounds and am able to get by in French. I have taken every course I could reasonably drive or take a bus to, joined a couple of French clubs, and even started my own. And, of course, I have joined the Alliance Française. I cannot say it has been easy, but with persistence it is possible.*

*The most recent highlight of my studies has been a three-week sojourn at a private language school in Montreal. I chose the winter in part because it was less expensive and also because I enjoy the change in seasons. Further, I stayed in a host family setting which was a treasured experience and I continue to correspond with the host as well as some other students from the school. I have continued my French back at home with a force intensified through my studies in Montreal, though I am still quite busy with the varied pursuits of a retiree – including petanque!*

*I highly recommend both the school (LSC Montreal) and the adventure. One quickly learns the routines of a new city, getting around, shopping, museums, restaurants. What is so inviting is to practise your language skills with everyone and anyone willing to suffer your mauling of their mother tongue. I am always amazed at the graciousness of the native speakers.*

*It doesn't seem to take much money to study a language. The internet is an inexhaustible source of information, references and programmes. The critical factor is to identify what it is you care about, want to do or want to learn, make a few forays into the thing and see what happens. I never ever thought I would be in Montreal in January studying French, and yet it was a highlight of my life. Studying with the younger generation as well as a few more mature students, walking about one of North America's premier cities in mid-winter, making new friends and learning to speak French all combined to reaffirm my decision to stick with this hobby. I'm now working part-time for just a few months to add funds to my next venture – six months in France in 2008. My wife, who is retiring in a few weeks, will join me in Europe so that we can enjoy our time together as I continue my studies. This is the best time of my life!*

Staying with a host family is obviously much better for language progress. Another possibility is to forgo structured lessons and simply live with a family. Several agencies arrange paying guest stays which are designed for people wishing to learn or improve language skills in the context of family life. Try *En Famille Overseas* (La Maison Jaune, avenue du Stade, 34210 Siran, France; tel/fax +33 4-68 91 49 90 or in UK: 01206 546741; www.enfamilleoverseas.co.uk) which specialises in France but also arranges homestays with or without language tuition in Germany, Italy and Spain. *EIL*, a non-profit cultural and educational organisation, offers short-term language exchange homestay programmes in a range of countries (287 Worcester Road, Malvern, Worcestershire WR14 1AB; 0800 018 4015 or 01684 562577; www.eiluk.org). The current administrative fee for making the arrangement is £400 for four weeks, £600 for stays lasting 8 or more weeks.

Of course you may prefer the most informal route of all, which is simply to use a phrasebook and interact with the locals. Several years ago 30-something Mike Bleazard and his partner Jane took six months off to travel around the world. They were especially looking forward to the last leg of their travels since South America was the first completely non-English speaking region they visited. In preparation they had bought some 'Learn Spanish in no time at all' tapes and struggled through the first 90 minutes of lessons in six weeks. Once they landed of course they noticed a decided improvement, if only in motivation:

*After seven weeks in Chile, we can now order a beer, a bus ticket and ask for a double room with private bathroom – fluently. We still can't understand a word that anyone says back to us. So we've taken to just nodding sagely and saying 'si' when anyone replies – which has got us into all kinds of trouble.*

Their linguistic skills continued to fall short when it came to planning their trip to Patagonia from Chile's capital:

*Because of our inadequate Spanish, we were advised by an official at the Tourist Information Office in Santiago to see Jorge, Santiago's Mr Fix-It for gringos travelling to Patagonia. So we spent six hours with Jorge arranging an action-packed three weeks. Arrived in Punta Arenas and soon found that the plan was a complete disaster and no one spoke English. Intensive two-day training course in Spanish unravelling mess with helpful locals. Sign language proved particularly useful.*

## Useful Addresses for Learning a Language Abroad

The following companies represent language schools worldwide. Note that other key players (CESA, Caledonia, Cactus and Language Courses Abroad) all have more detailed entries in the 'Directory of Specialist Programmes'.

*Amerispan,* PO Box 58129, Philadelphia, PA 19102, USA (800-879-6640 or 215-751-1100; www.amerispan.com). Specialist Spanish-language travel organisation with great expertise in arranging language courses, voluntary placements and internships throughout South and Central America. Now offers other languages worldwide.

*Dialog-Sprachkurse International GmbH,* Eisenbahnstr. 41, 79098 Freiburg, Germany (+49 0761-28 64 70/6; info@dialog.de). International language group offering courses in Freiburg, Nice and Costa Rica.

*Don Quijote,* 2-4 Stoneleigh Park Road, Epsom, Surrey KT19 0QT (020-8786 8081; www.donquijote.org). Spanish specialist with courses in Spain (including Tenerife) and Latin America.

*EF International Language Schools,* Dudley House, 36-38 Southampton Street, London WC2E 7HF (0800 068 3385; www.ef.com). Foreign language courses at privately owned and EF schools in France, Germany, Italy, Spain, Ecuador, China and Russia.

*EIL Cultural & Educational Travel,* 287 Worcester Road, Malvern, Worcestershire, WR14 1AB (0800 018 4015; www.eiluk.org). Non-profit cultural and educational organisation. Short-term homestays in more than 20 countries.

*Eurointerns*, Gaztambide, 26, 2º – B, 28015 Madrid, Spain (34-667 838 136; www.eurointerns.com) finds internships for about 100 candidates (average age 25) in Spanish and Belgian firms for practical language enhancement and work experience. Basic internship placement lasting 2-6 months costs €690.

*Gap Year for Growns-ups,* Zurich House, Meadow Road, Tunbridge Wells TN1 2YG; (01892 701881; www.gapyearforgrownups.co.uk/Learn-a-Language). Spanish or Portuguese language courses integrated with volunteer placements in Latin America. Also programme to learn Mandarin in China.

*IALC (International Association of Language Centres),* Lombard House, 12/17 Upper Bridge St, Canterbury, Kent CT1 2NF (01227 769007; www.ialc.org). Language school association with more than 90 members in 22 countries. Small group and individual courses for adults in the official language or languages of the country, with cultural activities and accommodation if required.

*IST Plus,* Rosedale House, Rosedale Road, Richmond, Surrey TW9 2SZ (020-8939 9057; info@istplus.com/ www.istplus.com). Language study abroad programmes (French, German, Spanish, Italian) in 23 destinations across Europe and Latin America for all ages.

*Journey Latin America,* 12-13 Heathfield Terrace, Chiswick, London W4 4JE (020-8747 3108; www.JourneyLatinAmerica.co.uk). Specialist travel agency and tour operator arranges Spanish and Portuguese courses throughout South and Central America. Courses offered at all levels from beginner to advanced, lasting one to four weeks. All programmes offer the opportunity to stay with a family. Prices range from £188 for one week in Antigua (Guatemala) to £1,079 for four weeks in Rio.

*Lanacos,* 64 London Road, Dunton Green, Sevenoaks, Kent TN13 2UG (01732 462309; www.lanacos.com). Language agency run by linguists, offering courses in 200 destinations. From about £400 for a fortnight in Granada to £2,500 for 12 weeks in Paris.

*OISE Intensive Language Schools,* Binsey Lane, Oxford OX2 0EY (01865 258333; info@oise.com/ www.oise.com). One of Europe's leading language training organisations that offers small class tuition of French in Paris, German in Heidelberg and Spanish in Madrid. Residential courses of any duration from one week to one year.

*S.I.B.S. Ltd,* Beech House, Commercial Road, Uffculme, Devon EX15 3EB (01884 841330; www.sibs.co.uk). Language consultancy which arranges language courses abroad for clients.

*Twin Languages Abroad,* 2nd Floor, 67-71 Lewisham High St, London SE13 5JX (020-8297 0505; languagesabroad@twinuk.com; www.twinlanguagesabroad.com). French, Italian, German, Portuguese, Spanish, Russian and Greek.

*Vis-à-vis,* 2-4 Stoneleigh Park Road, Epsom KT19 0QT (020-8786 8021; www.visavis.org). French courses, all levels. Schools in France, Belgium and Canada.

## Language Courses for North Americans

At a time when broad-minded Americans may find themselves wanting to try to dispel accusations of insularity and supremacy, going abroad in a gap year to learn or improve a foreign language may have special appeal. Programmes that combine structured study of a language or culture with volunteering are arguably a paradigm of the kind of foreign travel experience that can more than justify taking time out from work. Many organisations both international and local can arrange such placements, often in conjunction with a homestay to maximise exposure to the language. One of the cheapest options for Americans who want to study French is to head for Québec in Canada, for instance Language Studies Canada in Montréal (www.lsc-canada.com) mentioned above.

As in the UK, agents in the US and Canada make it easier for North Americans to find and book a suitable language course. An effective search engine for locating courses is provided by the Institute of International Education on www.iiepassport.org which makes it easy to search by country and programme. Other recommended sites include www.worldwide.edu, www.languagesabroad.com and www.studyabroad.com.

Here are some language course providers and agents of possible interest to North American grown-ups planning to spend time abroad learning a language.

*Bridge-Linguatec Language Study Abroad,* 915 S. Colorado Blvd., Denver, CO 80246 (800-724-4210; www.bridgeabroad.com). Language training company with cultural immersion programmes in Europe and Latin America.

*Center for Cultural Interchange,* 746 N. Lasalle Drive, Chicago, IL 60610 (312-944-2544; www.cci-exchange.com). CCI offers language school programmess for adults in co-operation with language schools in Costa Rica, Ecuador, France, Germany, Italy, Japan, Mexico, Peru, and Spain.

*Center for Study Abroad,* No. 93, 325 Washington Avenue South, Kent, WA

98032 (206-726-1498; www.centerforstudyabroad.com). Short and long courses in Europe and the Far East.

*Eduvacations,* 1431 21st St NW, Ste. 302, Washington, DC 20036 (202-857-8384; www.eduvacations.com). Travel company specialising in customised language courses combined with sports, art instruction, etc. throughout Europe, Latin America, the Caribbean, Russia, etc.

*Language Liaison,* PO Box 1772, Pacific Palisades, CA 90272 (1-800-284-4448; www.languageliaison.com). Total immersion language/culture study programmes and leisure learning courses.

*Language Link,* PO Box 3006, Peoria, IL 61612-3006. 800-552-2051; www.langlink.com). Represents Spanish language schools in Spain and Latin America.

*Language Studies International (LSI),* www.lsi.edu. Language courses available in France, Spain, Germany, Switzerland and Costa Rica.

*Lingua Service Worldwide,* 75 Prospect St, Suite 4, Huntingdon, NY 11743 (1-800-394-5327; www.linguaserviceworldwide.com).

*National Registration Center for Study Abroad,* PO Box 1393, Milwaukee, WI 53201 (414-278-0631; www.nrsca.com). 125 language schools and universities in 43 countries. Many include options to participate in volunteer work or career-focused internships.

*Summer Stays International,* 620 SW 5th Ave, Suite 625, Portland, OR 97204 (503-274-1776; www.summerstays.org). Non-profit organisation offering full immersion language and culture courses for adults.

## SPORT AND LEADERSHIP COURSES

Few better ways exist of shaking out the cobwebs than to learn to sail, climb or lead trekkers during a gap year later in life. It is often difficult to master a sport or make significant improvements if you can only dabble in it during your free time and brief holidays. Concentrating over an extended period may allow you to gain useful qualifications for future use, such as a PADI diving certificate, a Yachtmaster sailing qualification or a Mountain Leadership course. Longer courses leading to a National Vocational Qualification (NVQ) are available in adventure tourism and expedition leadership which might be of interest if you are considering changing professional direction.

If you would like to do a sports course with a view to working abroad, you might be interested in courses offered by *Flying Fish* (www.flyingfishonline.com; see Directory entry) or one of the other training specialists. A gap year with Flying Fish starts with a course leading to a qualification as a sail, surf or wind-surf instructor, yacht skipper, divemaster or dive instructor, ski or snowboard instructor, or even as galley chefs. A typical three-month course involves three or four weeks of sports training in Cowes on the Isle of Wight, followed by a work experience placement (eight weeks on average) in the UK, Australia or Greece. Trainees can seek advice from a Flying Fish careers adviser to find paid work too. The topic of Sailing including Crewing on Yachts is covered in the chapter Travel & Adventure.

### Sail & Dive Training

Several training organisations specialise in preparing people for undertaking some serious sailing or watersports. For example one of the longest established recognised centres is *Plas Menai National Watersports Centre* in North Wales (between Snowdonia and the sea). As well as offering courses in sailing, kayaking and mountain sports at all levels, it also runs a fast track instructor training programme which would suit career breakers who are attracted by the worldwide employment opportunities for qualified yacht skippers and outdoor instructors. Plas Menai offers a 17-week Professional Yachtmaster course as well as 4 to 26-week dinghy, windsurfing, kayaking and mountain instructor courses. The RYA Yachtmaster qualifies you to charter a yacht from almost anywhere in the world or enter the yachting industry.



Another leader in the field is the *UK Sailing Academy* whose range of water-sports courses extends to three and four months and which offers an on-site careers service used by more than 700 companies looking to recruit instructors. UKSA is also mentioned in the chapter on 'Travel & Adventure; course details are available from UKSA (West Cowes, Isle of Wight PO31 7PQ; 01983 294941; www.uksa.org). If you would like to do a watersports course abroad, see the entries for *Flying Fish, Nonstop Adventure* and the *International Academy* in the Directory.

Diving in an exotic location is another option that may appeal. A random sampling of possibilities includes:

*Dive Indeep Co. Ltd,* 162/8 Chaweng Beach Road, Koh Samui, Suratthani 84320, Thailand (+66 772 30155; www.diveindeep.com). PADI Scuba Diving Courses from beginner through Dive Master.

*PJ Scuba*, Mermaids Group, 75/124 Moo 12, Jomtien Beach Road Nongprue, Banglamung, Chonburi 20260, Thailand (www.learn-in-asia.com). Internship programme Learn in Asia Dive Internships Co. Ltd

*EcoSea Dive & Adventure Cambodia,* Ekareach St, Town Center, Sihanoukville, Cambodia (+855 12 654 104; Dive@EcoSea.com). PADI Divemaster training.

*Itime Experience Ltd,* 105 Ladbroke Grove, London W11 1PG (0845 355 1183; www.itimeexperience.com). Surfing, windsurfing and kitesurfing courses in Margarita (Venezuela) and the Dominican Republic in the Caribbean. Optional Spanish courses also available.

*Scuba World Philippines* www.scubaworld.co.ph. Dive centres throughout the Philippines with scuba career training programmes.

*Subway Watersports,* Brick Bay, Roatan, Bay Islands, Honduras, Central America (www.subwaywatersports.com/Courses/internship.htm). Internship working in a dive shop while training towards a professional PADI Divemaster. Cost approximately $1000 for 4 weeks; $1400 for 6 weeks; $1700 for 8 weeks.

*Ticket to Ride Ltd,* Ramsford Farm, Roundhurst, Haslemere, Surrey GU27 3BN (www.ttride.co.uk). New venture that teaches teams of 20 to surf along the coast of South Africa. 3-month trip costs from £4,850 + VAT.

## Snow Sports

A handful of UK companies specialises in running intensive courses for aspiring ski and snowboard instructors, many of them for pre- and post-university gap year students. As in the case of many of the gap year agencies, some have recently started to target older clients; for example the *Basecamp Group* launched a course geared towards 'sabbatical' clients two years ago which is going strong. (Last year they had more than 30 career-break clients, mostly from the IT, financial, legal and medical professions.) *Nonstop Ski & Snowboard* markets to career breakers more than the gap year market and claims that 50% of their clients are on sabbatical breaks or looking for a career change or time out. On one of their recent 11-week courses 30 of the 56 participants were over 25, so older clients can be confident that they will be in like-minded company. A further attraction for older ski trainees is that the accommodation is in houses rather than a hostel.

The following organisations offer snow sports training for recreation or for qualifications. Most have entries in the Directory chapter:

*British Association of Snowsport Instructors (BASI),* Glenmore, Aviemore, Inverness-shire PH22 1QU (01479 861717; www.basi.org.uk). BASI runs training and grading courses throughout the year in alpine skiing, snowboarding, Telemark, Nordic and Adaptive. The most junior instructor's qualification is a Grade III which is awarded by BASI after a five-day foundation course following a two-week training course on the continent or in Scotland. Courses take place throughout the season and also on the glacier in the summer.

*Basecamp Group,* Unit 30, Baseline Business Studios, Whitchurch Road, London W11 4AT (tel/fax: 020-7243 6222; www.basecampgroup.com). Ski & Snowboard Instructor Courses in France (Meribel and Val d'Isère) and Canada (Whistler, Banff and Kicking Horse). See Directory entry.

*International Academy,* King's Place, 12-42 Wood St, Kingston upon Thames, Surrey KT1 1JY(0870 060 1381; www.theinternationalacademy.com). Recently taken over by Crystal Holidays and targetting the 18-24 market more than older skiers. Ski/snowboard training and ski/snowboard instructors' courses in resorts in the USA, Canada and New Zealand.

*Nonstop Ski & Snowboard,* Shakespeare House, 168 Lavender Hill, London SW11 5TF (0870 241 8070; www.nonstopski.com/ www.nonstopsnowboard.com). Ski and Snowboard Instructor Courses in the Canadian Rockies (Fernie, Banff and Red Mountain). £2,950 for 3-week course, from £6,450 for 11-week courses includes flights, accommodation, most meals, lift pass and all tuition.

*Peak Leaders,* Mansfield, Strathmiglo, Fife KY14 7QE, Scotland (01337 860755; www.peakleaders.com). Time out and gap year ski and snowboard instructor courses in New Zealand, Argentina, Switzerland and Canada. £6,500 for 10/12 weeks.

*Ski-Exp-Air,* 770 Colonel Jones, Ste. Foy, Québec GIX 3K9, Canada (418-654-9071; www.ski-exp-air.com). Ski and snowboard school located in Québec City serving an international clientele, including career-breakers, leading to instructor certification. 3-month course costs C$13,300-C$15,900 (£6,475-£7,740).

*Ski Le Gap,* 220 Wheeler St, Mont Tremblant, Quebec J8E 1V3, Canada (819-429-6599; www.skilegap.com). Ski and Snowboard instructor's programme designed for gap year students from UK though older trainees are accepted if they are passionate about skiing.

**At age 32, Mike Kindred was 'bored to death with the 9 to 5 lifestyle':**
*I needed to feel alive again and the plan was to take a season out of work and be a ski bum for a year. Whilst looking through a ski magazine I came across an ad for Peak Leaders which caught my eye. So why bum in France for a year when I could go to Canada and become a ski instructor? Without a doubt it was the best decision I have ever made. I made some great friends who I will always stay in touch with, from traveling around South America, teaching skiing at the same hill, sailing around the Greek islands or just meeting up in London for drinks and to reminisce about the 9 weeks we spent together. I came away with my level 2 ski instructor, avalanche awareness, back country training (which was the highlight of the trip for me), first aid and the most memorable 9 weeks of my life. It is now November and the start of my second season teaching in Canada. I am now a level 3 CSIA ski instructor and a Level 1 CASI snowboard instructor (yes, the dark side). So for the next five months I'll be sliding down a hill on a tray or I'll have two planks strapped to my feet. I feel so lucky to be part of such a wonderful sport.*

## Adventure Training

Experience or training in adventure sports can open many doors. Even if a career change is not on the agenda, leadership training can be put to good use during vacation time. The website www.bluedome.co.uk has thorough information about useful outdoor qualifications including the Walking Group Leader and Mountain Leader Award assessed by Outward Bound among others (www.outwardbound-uk.org). A new all-round adventure instructor course lasting six weeks has been developed by Mountain Water Experience, Courtlands, Nr Kingsbridge, South Devon TQ7 4BN (01548 550675; www.mountainwaterexperience.co.uk).

*World Challenge Expeditions* (Black Arrow House, 2 Chandos Road, London NW10 6NF; 08704 873 173; leaderinfo@world-challenge.co.uk) takes on more than 400 overseas expedition leaders for at least a month of the summer to lead groups of young people to places like Bolivia, Zambia and Borneo. Leaders, who must be over 24 and have the MLTB (Mountain Leader Training) have their expenses covered for the duration of the expedition. Training courses are organised through WCE's Leadership and Development Centre in the Peaks (Manchester Road, Buxton, Derbyshire SK17 6ST; 01298 767900).

Opportunities exist closer to home as well. For example *PGL Travel* (recruitment@pgl.co.uk) offers training and work opportunities to people who want to work in the outdoors either in the UK or France especially as kayak, canoeing and sailing instructors. The long established charity *HF Holidays* (www.hfholidays.co.uk/leadersinfo) owns 17 country house hotels in scenic locations around the British Isles where guests enjoy a walking and social programme. Voluntary walks leaders are chosen after assessment courses held in the spring; ring 01768 890091 in Cumbria for details.

The following organisations offer sports training for recreation or for qualifications:

*Adventure Vocations,* Marine Drive, PO Box 36, Diamond Harbour, New Zealand (+64 3-329 3389). UK office: 35 Chester St, Edinburgh EH3 7EN (0131-226 402); www.adventurevocations.com. 9-10 week career-break courses in outdoor or snow instructor training and raft guiding; the latter cots £4,800.

*Exp-Air-Guide,* 770 Colonel Jones, Ste. Foy, Québec GIX 3K9, Canada (418-654-9071; www.exp-air-guide.com). Outdoor Adventure Guiding school which takes clients to the rivers and lakes surrounding Québec City to teach techniques for organising a wilderness trip. Course includes fast water and sea kayaking, canoe-camping and trekking. C$17,900 (£8,700) for 3-month course.

*Outward Bound Trust,* Hackthorpe Hall, Hackthorpe, Penrith, Cumbria CA10 2HX (01931 740010; instructorenquiries@outwardbound-uk.org). Trainee instructors over the age of 21 accepted to help deliver outdoor education programme to groups of young people.

*Water by Nature Rafting Ltd.,* The Trainers Office, Windy Hollow, Sheepdrove, Lambourne, Berkshire RG17 7XA (01488 72293; www.waterbynature.com). Whitewater raft and kayak guide training in Morocco and Turkey. 2 months in each country or short course in Turkey lasts 2 weeks.

## TRAINING FOR A CAREER CHANGE

Adult education or re-training is not only a means to equip yourself for better prospects within your first chosen career, it also offers a viable way of changing course or moving sideways into a related field. Changing career after many years in one profession is, to be honest, difficult. Are you too old to start again at the bottom of the ladder or are some of your skills transferable? Can you afford the financial risk of committing to training and expecting a potentially reduced salary for several years?

The whole concept of 'finding your vocation' has become dated, and many people at age 35 or 45 are no longer satisfied with what they chose after school or college. Should we be surprised by this? Expectations change, working scenarios shift. What may have seemed desirable and glamorous at 23 now may seem hollow and meaningless, which is why so many professionals with dizzying incomes choose to give it up for something simpler and more fulfilling. Nothing in life is static so why should we assume that once we embark on working life we will still be performing the same role, albeit with greater responsibility and reward, by middle age or by retirement? However daunting a step, a career change may be the only way to obtain a longed-for change in lifestyle or to regain a sense of purpose and pride in one's work. If a career has brought disappointment and unhappiness, the time comes to move on. For further information on changing career see *Back To Normal or a Change for Life*?.

Formal qualifications allied to a particular occupation can give you a leg up into a new job. You may have decided to return to education following redundancy or frustration with your current situation. It may have become apparent that your job was leading nowhere and now it appears essential to gain new qualifications in order to resolve the situation. You might also have discovered a new passion to which you want to dedicate a year or two's study. A period of study can lead in unexpected directions too. Another benefit is that academic study will provide an exciting new challenge at a time when you might be feeling under-motivated and frustrated.

**When Sandra Murray from Edinburgh, mother of four, started to re-evaluate her life, she asked herself if this was where she wanted to be until she retired, and the answer was no:**
*My daughter suggested I get the prospectus for a local college, pointed me towards the Travel and Tourism course which interested me and I enrolled. When my classes commenced, I was not only one of the oldest in the class, I was also computer-illiterate. The first assignment I submitted was hand-written. I can honestly say those first few weeks in college were among the most stressful of my life. Not only was I returning to education after many years at home bringing up children, I also had to work with a computer which, quite frankly, petrified me. However over the first term I found the classes interesting, gained confidence with a computer and submitted work that was actually being passed by the exam board.*

*Towards the end of the two years at the local college, our class was given the opportunity to attend an open day at a university. From the original college class of 25 students, only two of us applied to complete our studies at university. Again, this was quite a daunting experience. But through hard work and determination, I secured an Honours BA (second-class upper division) in Tourism Management.*

After the course Sandra fixed up a three-month volunteering placement with a small NGO in Bangladesh through the Edinburgh charity *Challenges Worldwide* (see Directory entry). Returning from this rewarding adventure, she embarked on a one-year postgraduate MBA course in Hospitality Management. She now looks back over the past five years and thinks to herself how easily life could have passed her by. Not only has she proved that she is educationally competent, but she is now able to apply for positions within a working environment which at one time would have been completely beyond her reach.

Today many of us are managing our own 'portfolio' careers, a term used by the sociologist Charles Handy who argues that insecurity can be viewed as freedom. For **Elaine Hernen,** an MA in new media studies offered a crucial opportunity to steer her professional life in a new direction. Disillusionment at work had coincided for her with the end of her marriage and she decided to achieve a clean break with the past. She spotted an ad for the University of Westminster's one-year MA course in Hyper Media and suddenly felt an urgent desire to obtain a place on it, though funding was a worry. In an imaginative move, Elaine decided to contact the Musicians' Union to suggest that she undertake research for them in return for funding and they agreed. The course proved to be exactly right for Elaine in her search for a new career and a life change:

> *I had always been involved in multi-media: super-8 performance, mixing theatre with film, journalism and recording music. The MA changed me and took me back to my old self and also created a new self. You never know what your thing or vocation might be until it is invented. Maybe you need to invent it yourself. It's never too late to change, to do something radically different and get away with it, however tough and scary it may seem.*

Opportunities abound for obtaining vocational training in a large range of careers like teaching, nursing, journalism, computing, outdoor education, accountancy, law and design. A period of study during a gap year can offer you the time to earn new qualifications and to forge new contacts. Naturally, it doesn't commit you to a complete change of career. The break in itself might put professional dissatisfaction in context. By examining other careers you might actually decide that your chosen career is indeed what you should continue to do albeit with certain changes or by looking for a new employer. You might be confusing job frustration with a difficult working environment or boss.

**Thirty-three year old management consultant Roger Coles took a Yachtmaster course with Flying Fish. He loved it so much that he has changed career and is now working as a full-time sailing instructor for a sailing school in Poole:**

*I had been dissatisfied with my career for a few years. I wanted something more exciting and engaging, something that allowed me to wake up every morning and think 'yes – another day at work'. I've been into sailing since I was young and began to wonder whether it might be possible to make a living out of my hobby. But I also wanted to do something that allowed me to transfer some of my skills from my career as a Management Trainer. So I decided that Yachting Instructor might be the right role for me. I knew the pay wouldn't be great compared to what I was used to, but this was more about the lifestyle than money. I found that Flying Fish provided just the right training course, and their emphasis on travel and adventure would also give me an opportunity to sail in Australia which I had always dreamed about. They also gave me lots of advice about the kinds of jobs that I would be eligible for, and how best to approach potential employers.*

*So I made the decision to go for it, reminding myself during moments of panic that if it didn't work out, I could always go back to what I was doing before I handed in my notice and left my job in the city for a new life. The training was at times pretty hard, and I had to apply myself, but it did help having had previous yachting experience. Sometimes it seemed like a holiday, sometimes I had to treat it like a job. At all times I knew it was an investment in me, both in terms of retraining for a new career and also giving me the opportunity to get off the merry-go-round of life and take an objective look at it.*

*I'm pleased to say I passed all my qualifications and was fortunate enough to be offered a full time, year round contract as an instructor with Sail UK Yachting and Racing. I now spend two weeks out of three on the water, training people towards RYA qualifications. It's a completely different experience of work to what I was used to. I work every day, morning to night with my crew of students, but often it just doesn't seem like work. People often ask me if I would ever go back to my old life. The answer is no. I might move back into doing work that is of a similar nature, but it will be in an environment of my choosing – probably a yacht!*

# Spiritual Development

Stress may not kill you, but it can shorten your life and stifle your inner existence. Unfortunately, modern lifestyles don't allow much time for harmonising our minds and bodies or listening to our inner voices. The usual remedy of a relaxing holiday in the sun is often insufficient to recharge the batteries for the increasing strains to which people in full-time employment are constantly subjected.

Small wonder then, that there is a growing trend among people of all types to take time out from their careers to 'find themselves'. Some prefer to be guided in the ways of self improvement while others just seek the opportunity for the time and space to do their own thing. The growing demand for soul therapy, spiritual growth, personal development, or whatever you want to call it, has created a bewildering variety of options for the path to nirvana. As a measure of the rising demand an increasing number of commercial travel companies are offering alternative holidays and spiritual enlightenment packages. The possibilities given here are intended to represent the more traditional and less commercialised possibilities, many of which you can arrange independently.

## WHAT IS A RETREAT?

The main point about a retreat is that it springs from a conscious decision to step out of your normal daily life, away from ego and daily responsibilities to go on an inner spiritual journey. This does not necessarily mean having spiritual experiences (though many people do), but it is about refreshing yourself, reordering your priorities and making contact with your deeper self.

### What Kinds of Retreat Are There?

The range of options that might once have been limited to convents, monasteries or ashrams is now much wider and can take you as near or as far from home as you wish. Retreats can involve anything from Buddhism to gardening and from communing with nature to timetabled lectures and seminars in a French convent or American religious foundation.

Many people's idea of a retreat is probably one where you stay in a convent or monastery for a period of reflection and meditation. This has long been practised by Christians, especially Roman Catholics, as well as Buddhists and other religious groups. But you don't have to be a devout adherent of the particular religion to take part. Ignatian retreats, based on the spiritual exercises of the founder of the Jesuits, can last 30 days (though shorter durations are also common). These are directed retreats on a one-to-one basis during which passages from the Gospels are chosen for daily contemplation and discussion. Seekers are led to review their lives in the light of the Gospels. Despite their religious origins, Ignatian spiritual retreats are available to anyone, religious or not. For further information contact *The Retreat Association* (address below).

Among the best known Christian retreat communities in the UK are Ampleforth Abbey, home to Benedictine monks (www.ampleforth.org.uk), the Iona Community mentioned below and Mirfield an Anglican monastic community in West Yorkshire (www.mirfield.org.uk). In France, the Taizé Community (www.taize.fr/en) invites adults over 30 and families with children to make Sunday-to-Sunday visits between March and October. Visitors may camp or stay in Taizé accommodation (prices €12-€25 a day) and participate in the three services a day plus Bible study.

Short retreats can be arranged in countless places. To take just one example *L'Ermitage Sainte Thérèse* is a convent in Lisieux, France, where a full board stay of five days and return coach travel from London costs £229. Mass is said daily and the teachings of St. Theresa form the focus of the retreat. For details contact Tangney Tours (see below).

## Secular Retreats

A retreat does not have to be bound to the belief system of a particular religion like Buddhism or Catholicism; it can be totally secular as in mind-body-spirit retreats which deal with awareness and self-discovery. A considerable revival of interest in Celtic spirituality has taken place in recent years. Celtic retreats tend to focus on a sense of God present everywhere in the natural world.

## Buddhist Centres

Buddhism has wide appeal to westerners and many Buddhist centres in Europe welcome individuals interested in learning the fundamentals. The *Throssel Hole Buddhist Abbey* in Northumberland offers introductory weekend retreats as well as longer guided Zen retreats. Guests make a voluntary contribution towards their keep which includes vegetarian meals. The association *Buddhafield* organises camping retreats in beautiful locations that cost about £50 for a weekend, £160 for ten days.

Other Buddhist centres in the UK that welcome guests include the *Losang Dragpa Buddhist Centre* in West Yorkshire where the maximum stay is one week (two weeks for non-UK residents), the *Madhyamaka Centre* also in Yorkshire which accepts visitors for a week or longer, and the *Manjushri Mahayana Buddist Centre* in Cumbria with no limit on length of stay.

Sunnier climes can be even more life-enhancing and the *Guhyaloka Buddhist Centre* in the mountains near Alicante in Spain is a peaceful place for a break. This full-time community dedicated to study, meditation and work welcomes male visitors who want to spend a summer or winter retreat. Guests choose between a solitary retreat in one of the small chalets dotted around the nearby valley or a working retreat.

With the dramatic rise in tourism to Thailand, Sri Lanka and other Buddhist countries over the past decade, more and more Buddhist centres welcome western seekers for short or longer stays.

## Ashrams

The trend for foreigners to stay in ashrams or Gandhian communities in India and Nepal has been growing ever since the 1960s. Ashrams offer teaching in *hatha* yoga, mantra, meditation, study of the scriptures or possibly a combination. Ashrams vary greatly: rich and poor, modern and urbanised, humble and rustic. A few are even located in caves. Each ashram has a guru (leader) or ashram-in-charge whose personal style is crucial in determining the atmosphere of the ashram and whether or not you will find it sympathetic. Some have a fixed price for a stay; others request donations.

## Yoga

Yoga can give you a whole new outlook on life as it works equally on the mind, body and spirit. Although many people use yoga simply as a way of staying fit instead of reaping its metaphysical benefits, others get interested in the spiritual aspect and want to explore more deeply. The obvious answer is to take a career break and book a place on a spiritual retreat at an ashram in India. Others get interested after they have travelled in a country where it is practised. Since discovering Sri Lanka on a turtle conservation project with *Teaching & Projects Abroad*, **Sarah Spiller** became very interested in Buddhism and yoga. Practising both in Sri Lanka and London, she (almost) mastered standing on her head and will have plenty of opportunities to develop her practice since she has bought a holiday house in Sri Lanka.

Yoga teacher Ruth White of the *Ruth White Yoga Centre* in London has been running an annual yoga retreat (one to three weeks) in spring on the Aegean island of Lesbos for many years. The syllabus is validated by the yoga governing body in the UK, the British Wheel of Yoga.

## How Much Does it Cost?

The price of spiritual therapy can be very reasonable, but then a monastery or convent offers no frills or distractions. A typical charge for a week's full board is £200-£250. Commercially organised alternative holidays start at around £325 per week. Some organisations, particularly Buddhist ones, make no specified charge at all, but expect a voluntary contribution and help with the domestic chores. The time you can spend in such an arrangement should be negotiated with individual establishments. If you stay for several weeks and work for your keep you will still normally be expected to make a token contribution of, say, £30-£40 per week.

# COMMUNITIES

Many communities (previously referred to as communes) welcome foreign visitors who share their values. Sometimes a small charge is made for a short stay or the opportunity given to work in exchange for hospitality. The details and possible fees must be established on a case-by-case basis.

**Rob Abblett** from Leicester is someone who has taken dozens of breaks on communities around the world:

> *I've visited, worked and had many varied experiences on over 30 communes around the world. I like them because they are so varied and full of interesting people, usually with alternative ideas, beliefs, but also because I almost always find someone that I can really connect with, for sometimes I need to be with like-minded folk.*

Before arranging a longish stay in a community, consider whether or not you will find such an environment congenial. Some are very radical or esoteric in their practices so find out as much as you can before planning to stay for any period of time. Most communards are non-smoking vegetarians and living conditions may be primitive by some people's standards.

Shorter stays in more distant places can be readily arranged. Many communities are engaged in special projects which may coincide with your interests. For example the long-established *Corrymeela Community* in County Antrim works for reconciliation between Protestants and Catholics in Northern Ireland.

Many well-known communes in the world welcome visitors. For example *Stifelsen Stjärnsund* is located amongst the forests, lakes and hills of central Sweden. Founded in 1984, the community aims to encourage personal, social and spiritual development in an ecologically sustainable environment. It operates an international working guest programme throughout the year, but is at its busiest between May and September when most of the community's courses are offered. Carpenters, builders, trained gardeners and cooks are especially welcome. First-time working guests pay SEK500 (about £38) for their first week of work and if the arrangement suits both sides it can be continued with a negotiable contribution according to hours worked and length of stay. Enquiries should be made well in advance of a proposed summer visit.

In Denmark the *Svanholm Community* consists of 120 people including lots of children. Numbers are swelled in the summer when more volunteers (EU nationals only) arrive to help with the harvest of the organic produce. Guests work 30-40 hours a week for food, lodging and (if no other income is available) pocket money.

One of the most famous utopian communities is *Auroville* near Pondicherry in the South Indian state of Tamil Nadu, whose ambition is nothing less than 'to realise human unity'. Volunteers participate in a variety of activities to reclaim land and produce food and are charged anything from $5 to $20+ a day for board and lodging according to their contribution.

## Contacts and Resources

*Diggers and Dreamers: The Guide to Communal Living* published by Edge of Time, BCM Edge, London WC1N 3XX (0800 083 0451; www.edgeoftime.co.uk). The 2006/7 edition (£6.50) contains an updated listing of communities in the UK.

*Eurotopia: Directory of Intentional Communities and Ecovillages in Europe,* (www.eurotopia.de). English version provides a comprehensive listing of 336 international communities in 23 countries (mainly Europe and the UK). It can be ordered from Edge of Time for £12.50.

*Communities,* 138 Twin Oaks Road, Louisa, VA 23093, USA (540-894-5798; http://directory.ic.org). Publish *Communities Directory: A Guide to Co-operative Living* (2005); price US$24 plus $4 US postage or $8 overseas by surface post. It lists about 600 communities in the US and about 100 abroad including 'eco-villages, rural land trusts, co-housing groups, kibbutzim, student co-ops, organic farms, monasteries, urban artist collectives, rural communes and Catholic Worker houses'. Much of the information is available on their website.

*Global Ecovillage Network (GEN),* based at ZEGG Community in Germany and at Findhorn in Scotland (info@gen-europe.org/ www.gen-europe.org). GEN functions as the umbrella organisation for a wide range of intentional communities and eco-villages all over the world, many of whom welcome guests and volunteers. (US contact: ecovillage@thefarm.org; Australiasia information: http://genoa.ecovillage.org).

*Auroville,* Bharat Nivas, Tamil Nadu 605101, India (+91 413-622121; www.auroville.org)

*Stifelsen Stjärnsund,* Bruksallén 16, 77071 Stjärnsund, Sweden (+46 225-80001; www.frid.nu). Community that welcomes working guests.

*Svanholm Community,* Visitors Group, Svanholm Allé 2, 4050 Skibby, Denmark (+45 4756 6670; www.svanholm.dk).

# RELIGIOUS PILGRIMAGES

There are as many kinds of pilgrimages as there are faiths. Catholics, Protestants, Muslims, Hindus and others all have their sacred shrines to which their followers make pilgrimages. Whether it is to Lourdes, Knock or Mecca (the latter strictly only for Muslims on the Haj), Canterbury or Varanasi, the experience of being a pilgrim may clear a path to God or constitute a voyage of the inner self towards some kind of healing integration.

## Santiago de Compostela

Probably the most publicised pilgrimage in western Europe takes place along a 500-mile route (*El Camino de Santiago*) through France and northern Spain to the purported grave of St. James the Apostle (Sant Iago to the Spanish). The name 'Compostela' comes from *campus stellae* (field of stars) named after a hermit who was attracted to the site of Sant Iago's resting place by starry visions which reputedly preceded the rediscovery of his bones. A popular place of pilgrimage since the 9th century, it fell out of favour in recent, more secular times but was revived and was given a spectacular boost in 1994 when the pope visited.

Pilgrims to Santiago are not all Catholic and many are not even religious, as the experience is individual and meaningful for those of all faiths or none. About a third of pilgrims are Spanish and the rest are foreigners. The true pilgrim covers the entire route on foot which is a gruelling lesson in humility and blisters and takes at least three weeks. But many people content themselves with doing just a section of the route or cover some of it by car or public transport which serves some of the towns en route.

Pilgrims can sleep out under the stars or stay in pilgrim hostels, many of which are in historic old buildings where cheap or even free simple accommodation is provided in dormitories. If you walk the route in autumn you may be able to sustain yourself in authentic pilgrim style on the bounty of nature garnered en route: walnuts, figs, chestnuts, apples and mushrooms are just part of the fare that can be picked wild. A classic modern account of the pilgrimage from Paris to Santiago *The Pilgrimage to Santiago* by Edwin Mullins is essential reading (see below).

### India

Many Westerners are attracted by Eastern faiths, particularly in India where the Hindu religion dominates. Among the most sacred Hindu shrines are the cave at Amarnath in (terrorist-affected) Kashmir, the all-year shrines at Ayodhya, Gaya and Varanasi in Uttar Pradesh and the summer-only shrine at Badrinath. You can also visit Dwarka in Gujarat all year round. Kurukshetra in Haryana is a popular destination for viewing eclipses of the sun or moon and Gangasagar Mela in West Bengal can be visited in January or February. In Sri Lanka, April is the favourite time of year for climbing Adam's Peak which can easily be done in a day.

Although these sites are sacred to Hindus, westerners are seldom prohibited from making a pilgrimage alongside believers just for the spectacle and sense of occasion. The more serious seeker after enlightenment may want to find a teacher (guru) or holy man (saddhu) in the vicinity of a temple or shrine. Saddhus are often rather alarming in appearance: unwashed, ash-smeared, unshaven with matted dreadlocked hair, wearing only a loincloth and with coloured markings on their forehead and bodies. However, there are plenty of bogus ones so if they seem too keen to get their hands on your money or even your body, you should make excuses and leave. Genuine saddhus should be approached with respect and courtesy. Under no circumstances touch them as you will defile their purity.

## SPIRITUAL TOURISM

Travel companies are never slow to exploit a demand and the hunger for spiritual enlightenment has already produced packaged products. One route to self-improvement might be with *Skyros*. Skyros offers a variety of courses for a self-improvement sabbatical. People over 21, preferably with experience of nursing, catering or maintenance, may be eligible to become 'work scholars' at the holistic holiday centre on the Greek island of Skyros in the northern Aegean. In exchange for basic duties, work scholars are given full board and accommodation and a weekly allowance of £50. The minimum stay is three months from April or July. The main perk is that workers are allowed to participate in the multitude of courses and workshops on offer including windsurfing, music, ikon painting, feng shui and yoga. Details are available from *Skyros*, 92 Prince of Wales Road, London NW5 3NE (020-7267 4424; www.skyros.com). Skyros also has centres in Havana (Cuba) and in Ko Samet (Thailand) where the courses include an introduction to Thai culture, meditation and herbal massage.

Religious organisations have often been canny when it comes to free enterprise. In the Middle Ages this usually took the form of selling indulgences. Nowadays you can go on a religious holiday which may or may not contribute to remission of your sins. The ecumenical Christian *Iona Community* maintains a resident community on the Isle of Iona in the Hebrides. Visitors can share in the common life, at the Abbey or in the more modern MacLeod Centre, with a week's programme costing £224 per person. There is an access fund for those on low incomes. The Iona community also accepts volunteers to help with many different duties, normally for periods of at least six weeks. The season runs from March to October. Details of all the above are available on their website www.iona.org.uk.

If your requirements are for something older than Christianity, then you can search for enlightenment amongst the oldest sciences of ancient civilisations, which are mainly of the holistic and herbal medicine variety. These include *ayurveda* from India, *reiki* and *tui na* (a healing art of Chinese massage). Many other healing techniques can be used to minister to the mind-body-spirit. *Neal's Yard Agency* (the 'Travel Agent for Inner Journeys') mails enquirers a free brochure of such healing holidays published quarterly.

*Cortijo Romero* has been organising year-round, personal development holistic and creative holidays in Spain for more than a dozen years and offers a choice from holistic massage to the joy of communal singing. Many courses revolve around unlocking your hidden potential and finding your true self.

Emotional and even physical healing can come from sources other than retreats and holistic treatment. You could take a leaf out of St. Francis of Assisi's book and find your ideal retreat communing with creatures. There are many who swear that swimming with dolphins is a cure-all especially for the emotionally dysfunctional and those suffering from depression. While you could test this claim by trying to arrange a sabbatical in a dolphinarium, most prefer to swim with dolphins in the wild, though even this has been arousing controversy. How the dolphins feel after charming the demons from humans is not recorded, though studies have shown that too much human interaction interferes with the ability of dolphins and their offspring to fend for themselves in the wild.

Living and working among less privileged people often has a spiritual dimension. Those who think that this might be their route to inner harmony should consider some of the voluntary opportunities canvassed throughout this book. **Nicholas Carbis**, a potter and deacon of the Russian Orthodox Church in Devon, spent six weeks at the Kitezh Community for orphans in western Russia through the *Ecologia Trust* (see Directory entry) and describes how the experience fed his inner self:

> *When I first arrived at Kitezh it was like a beautiful painting, peaceful under a blanket of snow. I walked through the frost-hard compacted snow to share in the meditation exercises as the red sun crept through*

*the silhouetted forest. Together connecting with natural energy that warmed the circle of figures, flying without leaving the ground. Afterwards I would jog to the church to say some prayers, and I would pass the children in their circle preparing for the day. I have a picture of the Church alive with angels, waiting for the Easter procession lit by candles under paper wigwams. I would like to render down my thoughts of my time at Kitezh by giving two illustrations: while standing in the church of the monastery of Optina Pustyn, looking up at the beautiful icons and listening to the most lovely voices singing, I had a deep feeling of reverence. Later I had the same feeling of reverence standing in the middle of Kitezh, looking up at the most beautiful starlit night, listening to the nightingales sing. Life in Russia is hard, and the Community of Kitezh is burdened with many pressures. However, I believe it is the way Kitezh incorporates beauty and reverence into everyday life that enables people to have hope.*

## Religious Retreats

*Buddhafield Retreats,* Trevince House, Hittisleigh, Exeter, Devon EX6 6LP (0870 738 9144; www.buddhafield.com). Meditation and Buddhism taught at festivals, fairs and other events, as well as retreats in Devon and Somerset.

*Guhyaloka Buddhist Retreat Centre,* Finca El Morer, Sella, Alicante 03579, Spain (+34 647 240791; www.guhyaloka.com). Summer or winter retreats for men only at a centre in a remote valley of Spain.

*Iona Community,* Iona Abbey or MacLeod Centre, Isle of Iona, Argyll PA76 6SN (01681 700404; ionacomm@iona.org.uk; www.iona.org.uk). £237 per person for a one-week stay but 130 volunteer positions available.

*Kagyu Samye Ling Tibetan Centre* – 01387 373232; admin@samyeling.org; www.samyeling.org). Tibetan monastery retreat near the River Esk in the Scottish borders. Weekend workshops cost £60. Volunteers with maintenance skills sometimes needed.

*Losang Dragpa Buddhist Centre,* Dobroyd Castle, Pexwood Road, Todmorden, West Yorks. OL14 7JJ (01706 812247 ext 201; www.losangdragpa.com). Working volunteers pay £40 per week.

*Madhyamaka Buddhist Centre,* Kilnwick Percy Hall, Pocklington, York YO42 1UF (01759 304832; info@madhyamaka.org).

*Manjushri Mahayana Buddhist Centre,* Conishead Priory, Ulverston, Cumbria LA12 9QQ (01229 584029; www.manjushri.org.uk)

*Tara Buddhist Centre,* Ashe Hall, Ash Lane, Etwall, Derbyshire DE65 6HT (01283 732338; www.taracentre.org.uk). Working visitors are charged £5 a day.

*Throssel Hole Buddhist Abbey,* Carrshield, Hexham, Northumberland NE47 8AL (01434 345204; www.throssel.org.uk).

## Alternative Holidays and Travel Companies

*Circle of Light Spiritual Holidays & Retreats,* Strawberry Cottage, 3 Loring Road, Salcombe, Devon TQ8 8BL (0845 456 1007; info@spiritualholidays.com; www.spiritualholidays.com). Organises spiritual journeys to Tibet, Nepal, Peru, etc. Also organises Wellbeing Weekend Retreats in the UK (www.wellbeingretreats.com).

*Cortijo Romero:* 23 Cottage Offices, Latimer Park, Latimer, Chesham, Bucks. HP5 1TU (01494 765775; www.cortijo-romero.co.uk). Centre located in southern Spain offering interesting range of personal development courses; typical cost £440 per week.

*Neal's Yard Agency* – see below.

*Pilgrim Adventure,* Culver Park, Tenby, Pembs. SA70 7ED (01834 844212; www.pilgrim-adventure.org.uk). Christian walking pilgrimages around the British Isles, e.g. to the Hebrides, Scillies, etc. Walking through mountains, island hopping, traditional music and seashore worship.

*Retreats Beyond Dover,* c/o St. Etheldreda's Church, 14 Ely Place, London EC1N 6RY (020-7379 7273; www.retreats.dircon.co.uk). Organises time-out-with-God retreats in Spain, France and Italy.

*Pax Travel Ltd,* 152-156 Kentish Town Road, London NW1 9QB (020-7485 3003; www.paxtravel.co.uk). Organises pilgrimages for individuals to Rome, Santiago, Malta, Mexico, etc.

*Skyros,* 92 Prince of Wales Road, London NW5 3NE (020-7267 4424; www.skyros.com).

*Tangney Tours Pilgrimages,* Pilgrim House, Station Court, Borough Green, Kent TN15 8AF (01732 886666; www.tangney-tours.com). Organises retreats and stays in convents and monasteries including the Convent of St. Thérèse mentioned above.

## Contacts and Publications

*The Good Retreat Guide* by Stafford Whiteaker (Rider Press, 2004; £12.99). According to the description on amazon.com, the book explains what a retreat is and the difference between the various types: religious, non-religious, group, individual and those with a special theme. Over 500 places are listed, Buddhist, Christian and New Age, ranging from cottages to castles, in Britain, Ireland, Spain and France.

*Crossroads Retreats,* 0870 225 0315; www.crossroadsretreats.co.uk. A charity founded in 2004 to allow participants to consider key questions and face difficult decisions with professional guidance and coaching. Weekend retreats held several times a year in Oxford and Bedford.

*The Retreat Association,* The Central Hall, 256 Bermondsey St, London SE1 3UJ (0845 456 1429; info@retreats.org.uk). Group of Christian retreat centres which publishes *Retreats,* an up-to-date guide to 200 retreats mostly in England, Scotland and Ireland. The 2004 edition is available from Christian Bookshops including SPCK, Wesley Owen and St. Paul's Media for £5 or direct for £6 including postage. You do not have to be a committed Christian, but must respect the rules.

*The Retreat Company*, The Manor House, Kings Norton, Leics. LE7 9BA (0116 259 9211; www.theretreatcompany.com). One-stop resource for all those seeking to take a retreat of any kind, at home or abroad. Holistic professionals and staff offer unbiased advice and support. Maintain a directory of holidays, getaways and courses that promote personal transformation and a healthy work/life balance.

*Neal's Yard Agency,* BCM Neal's Yard, London WC1N 3XX (tel/fax 0870 444 2702; www.nealsyardagency.com). Gives information and advice on holistic and alternative holidays in the UK, Mediterranean and Asia. Free quarterly *Holiday & Events Guide* and publisher of *Places to Be,* a directory of alternative holidays mainly in the UK for £8 (including postage).

*The Pilgrimage to Santiago* by Edwin Mullins (Signal Books, Oxford; £9.99). An illustrated reprint of the 1974 classic account of the pilgrim route starting from the Rue St. Jacques in Paris. Described as 'an amalgam of history, geography, religion and archaeology, fact and fiction'.

*British Wheel of Yoga,* 25 Jermyn St, Sleaford, Lincolnshire NG34 7RU (01529 306851; www.bwy.org.uk). Primarily deals with Yoga Centres in the UK but can help provide contacts for studying at yoga centres in India. Membership (£22) includes a subscription to the quarterly magazine *Spectrum* which deals with yoga issues worldwide.

*Ruth White Yoga Centre*, Church Farm House, Spring Close Lane, Cheam, Surrey SM3 8PU (01993 831032; www.ruthwhiteyoga.com). Yoga retreats in Greece and elsewhere: £524 for one week, £913 for two weeks (excluding flights).

# Back to Normal or a Change for Life?

The thrill of a grand project or adventure during a gap year will ultimately run its course. Eventually the time off that has been negotiated will come to an end. With luck you will be anticipating many pleasures on re-entry. If you have been abroad for an extended period, you may have escaped homesickness but you might still be longing for a pint of bitter, a bacon sandwich, Radio 4's 'Today' programme or green fields. These and many other compensations should help to alleviate the post-travel blues.

In some cases the prospect of returning to a former career is too dismal to contemplate. If the choice to take a career break has been of value it should have taught you that everyone has the ability to determine his or her own course. There is nothing shameful in changing direction in mid-life if you have discovered that your heart lies elsewhere. By the same token there is nothing shameful about returning to your old employer if that is what you choose to do. After all, that is what the majority of teachers, nurses, managers, computer geeks, etc. who take a gap year do.

# RETURNING TO WORK

Returning to work after a career break, particularly one lasting a year or more, necessitates a period of adjustment that is bound to be challenging. Your time away should have energised you and given you inspiration to make changes in your personal life and in the way you work. In all probability, the experiences you had while your career was on hold will not only have enhanced your appreciation of life and added to your professional versatility, but also equipped you with new skills.

These skills may not seem to have an obvious application in your department or office, but your experiences are bound to have boosted your self-confidence, improved your ability to think on your feet, handle a crisis or persevere in the face of setbacks. If you have helped to build a medical centre in the Andes, taught English as a foreign language, trekked in the Himalayas or made a temporary home in a foreign city, you will have pushed yourself in difficult circumstances beyond the safety of your daily routine. To take just one example, computer training firm Happy Computers (www.happy.co.uk/jobs) believe that TEFL teachers make good IT trainers even if they lack an IT background.

Coping successfully with upheaval in leaving your job, town and friends behind should be valued in a society and economy in which willingness to change is often expected and usually rewarded. It is your job to sell this positive angle to your current and prospective employers.

Some people use a career break to sample alternative lifestyles, particularly if they aren't happy with the direction their professional lives are taking. In some cases people discover a new or better vocation. In others, the fantasy idly entertained while commuting to work may prove impractical or unsuitable. Their gap year may have brought about a process of disillusionment, which is not a bad thing in itself, since no one wants to build a future on illusions. It is always worth getting such things out of your system if you can. The result might be that an unrealistic ambition can now be put aside, leaving you to move on and rededicate yourself to your profession.

**After six months of travelling round-the-world, Jane O'Beirne and her partner Mike Bleazard flew home from Rio, mildly dreading the prospect of re-establishing themselves.**

Jane had wrestled with the idea of making her career break into a career change. While on the road she had considered many alternatives to the law, from care work to opening a pasta restaurant. After a couple of months of combing the ads in the newspaper it became clear that without going back to do extensive retraining (e.g. in physiotherapy), she would be eligible to apply only for relatively lowly administrative or care jobs paying a third of what she had earned as a solicitor. So she enlisted with a legal temp agency near Cambridge and enjoyed a series of locums of short duration, which is an efficient way of sampling the working environments of potential permanent employers. Jane soon found full-time employment in the probate department of a small laid-back law firm where hours were civilised, pressures few and where 'billable hours' were not the motive force.

Mike was also faced with having to find another job on his return. He had kept in touch with various potential employers by e-mail. However while he was away, many high-level IT businesses had been forced to batten down the hatches in the current economic climate, and he could see no way in. He could have walked into a contract in London but was determined to find a job within cycling distance of home. After a few months he did so and was content to be once again earning a steady income since he and Jane have now got an infant son.

At a more private level, a gap year can act simply as a time for personal development. Priorities change with age. The successful career that seemed such a glittering prize in your youth may not seem so important in later life. Some careers begin to feel insatiable in their demands, in which case returning to work may require careful deliberation. How are you going to avoid the problems that plagued you before the gap? It may be a question of working fewer hours to spend more time with family. You may now want more time to enjoy interests outside work or it may simply be a desire to take on less managerial responsibility to alleviate levels of stress. Before you return to work, evaluate the aspects of your working life that you might like to change. Have your career goals shifted?

## Returning to Your Old Job

It is advisable to keep up some contact with a workplace during a career break and to demonstrate your ongoing commitment to return, to allay understandable doubts on the part of your employer that you will actually return from your adventure. Keeping yourself informed of staff and organisational changes will also prove beneficial on your return. Particularly in fields where change occurs at a rapid pace, efforts to remain abreast of changes will assist the process of returning to work. After volunteering on an orangutan project in Borneo, **Jake Brumby** returned to his job in project and account management for a website development company:

> *It took me one month to get back up to speed at work. I was not very productive at first. It is important to remember the things you discovered about yourself and keep these alive. You can easily slip back into old/bad habits.*

Some organisations that offer formal career breaks stress the importance for absent staff of keeping informed of any changes to the organisation and their old department. Employees will probably want to stay in touch by e-mail with colleagues or other freelancers in the field. Lots of companies and organisations produce staff newsletters which you should make an effort to obtain so that a connection to the workplace is maintained during the absence and helps the process of readjustment.

Likewise, the Training & Development Agency for Schools (www.tda.gov.uk/Recruit.aspx) produces a termly magazine and information about free refresher or 'returner' courses for teachers taking a professional break. Details of the Returning to Teach Programme are available on 0845 6000 993 or by emailing info@returning2teach.co.uk.

Returning to work is bound to be a shock to the system even if you have been away for only a few months. Rarely do absentees return to find that their bosses or colleagues harbour any resentment, though your return to work may unsettle new working relationships or fiefdoms that have developed during the break. In your absence, you may have gained a new line manager or managing director who has made significant changes to a corporate culture. Old colleagues may have left and new technology introduced. Adapting to change is the principal challenge to returning to the workplace. Former travelling routines like commuting by train will have to be revived and tolerated. Freelancers will have to re-learn the discipline of organising their time according to the requirements of clients.

Sometimes individuals expect to be treated like conquering heroes but are in fact given a rather matter-of-fact or even frosty reception. A jocular 'you lucky bastard' can disguise a modicum of resentment and jealousy. These feelings are not inevitable but they may surface as they did when **Ceri Evans** returned from a spell of living in Barcelona to take up her old job as a senior counsellor in a sexual health clinic. She hadn't expected to encounter hostility but that is what she sensed among some colleagues in her department.

The period of adjustment may be painful at first though it is bound to get easier. In all likelihood, the office or department has continued to function smoothly without you, as any organisation must. On your return you may even be a little irritated to see how well others have coped in your absence.

## JOB-HUNTING AFTER A GAP YEAR

If you need to look for a new job after a gap year, the technique will be the same as for any job search. The difference is that a career break means an interlude from formal work and therefore a gap on your CV, which will not necessarily be viewed in a positive light. However if the candidate can demonstrate that he or she has developed and acquired new skills as a result of the experience, a gap year can be seen as a strength and an advantage.

If you have volunteered in a relevant field, you may find your employability much improved. For example **Phillip Elcombe** from Folkestone had finished a media degree but had not been able to find the kind of work he wanted in the UK. With the help of the volunteer travel agency *i-to-i*, he joined a privately owned and funded radio station in Accra, Ghana which airs a variety of programmes including news, talk shows, music and interviews with celebrities and politicians. Volunteers were expected to take a lot of initiative, bringing new ideas, styles of reporting and giving a fresh perspective on local issues. He concluded at the end of his stint as a volunteer that his future career prospects had definitely been improved:

> *If you are passionate about what you have done and can show how your experiences as a volunteer have benefited you, then it always stands you in good stead. One of my co-volunteers in Ghana had an interview in London just after she got back, took her photos from the project with her and the employer was so impressed by the qualities she could offer from her experience in volunteering that she got the job.*

Leaving a chronological gap on your CV will inevitably attract attention so don't try to hide the fact that you've taken a gap year. There is no need to apologise or feel defensive about it. The time spent away will almost certainly have recharged your batteries and enhanced your employment prospects (unless you just sat at home and watched television). It might have also provided the impetus to attempt a step change.

After more than five years working as an engineer for Jaguar in the Midlands, **Matt Heywood** was ready for a long break. He also wanted to figure out whether to pursue a career in management on his return to normal paid life. Having chickened out of *Raleigh International* before university he now was impressed with what he learned from their website and thought that becoming a staff member on a three-month Raleigh expedition to build a school in Borneo would give him a competitive edge on his CV:

> *Whilst on expedition I have realised that there is a lot of satisfaction to be gained from developing people, not just products. As a result, I will be applying for managerial positions when I return to employment.*

Career advisors and human resources people often say that a good CV can include some life experiences that may not relate directly to a job application. Often these unrelated activities demonstrate social skills, initiative and breadth of interests. This is partly why students are urged to fill their time at college with a range of activities outside their formal degree studies.

## The Older Job-Seeker

With the recent proposals to raise the state pension age to 68, we can all expect to work longer than our parents' generation did mainly because we are living longer. From October 2006, it will be illegal for employers to discriminate on the basis of age, in line with EU legislation, which reinforces the idea that the average working life will be extended. Rachel Krys of the Employers Forum on Age (www.efa.org.uk), which campaigns for diversity of ages in the workforce, teased out a relevant implication of these changes in a press release (May 2006):

> *As the Government makes these changes we must consider the impact they will have on employers and employees. Given our ageing population, raising the pension age should come as no surprise. It does mean that flexible working practices, career breaks, part time working and job sharing can no longer be the preserve of the most enlightened employer – they have to become a reality for everyone in order to make working for longer palatable.*

If our working lives are being extended why should a career break in our 40s or 50s present a problem for employers, particularly when skills are in short supply? Furthermore a longer working life will save businesses millions in training and recruitment costs.

A return to work for women after raising a family may necessitate retraining or learning new skills. The *Women Returner's Network (WRN),* Chelmsford College, Moulsham St, Chelmsford CM2 0JQ; (01245 263796; www.women-returners.co.uk) is a charity dedicated to helping women return to work after a career break. It runs both a telephone helpline and a website that lists numerous handy resources such as training courses, sources of funding and contacts for government agencies and also allows women to register for information updates. The 24-page WRN Workbook can be downloaded from their website with hundreds of useful links. The charity finds that the major issues are childcare costs, loss of confidence and lack of skills. By going back to work part-time, many women lose out on training opportunities open to full-time staff.

## Changing Employment Practices

As described in the first chapter of this book, the government and many companies are increasingly interested in promoting the work-life balance. This shift is bound to strengthen the application of someone who has taken a career break. For promoting a healthy work-life balance, experts identify the importance of flexible working, including flexi-time, part-time work, job-sharing, shift-swapping, working from home and team-based self-rostering. Companies that favour work-life balance and family-friendly policies are enjoying reduced absenteeism and better employee retention. Winner of the 'Best Boss 2006' competition, Bruce Draper of Geotechnical Instruments in Leamington Spa, claims that staff turnover was running at a third each year before he introduced flexible working which brought that figure down to about zero.

If you are returning to the workplace after a break you might want to adjust your working life to suit new priorities, of which childcare is the most obvious example. One popular measure is the adoption of a shorter working week. Some companies have gone so far as to reduce the working week to four days, leaving an extra day for administration or domestic life. **Fiona Carroll**, a project manager in a software company located in Switzerland, asked for a four-day week when she found her new job after a career break. Her weekly pay is reduced by a fifth but she now has an extra day to devote to her outside interests. Subtle changes in work can dramatically improve one's quality of life, but you may need to be proactive in persuading an employer to grant flexibility.

Working life can be very demanding and so it pays for employers to encourage loyalty and create a supportive, friendly working environment. A positive experience at work is guaranteed to improve loyalty and performance. Obviously, only a few companies can be pioneers, but in a competitive environment for recruitment, those employers that lag behind will lose the most talented staff to their rivals. Beyond certain resistant professional niches, change seems more rapid in sectors like IT and financial services. Employers are being prodded by competition to liberalise their policies on a range of issues from maternity leave to flexible working. Returning from a gap year need not be an intimidating experience. The public sector is similarly keen to promote flexible working and to recruit staff who might bring valuable skills from elsewhere. In tandem with the government's support for work-life balance, organisations like the NHS, Britain's largest employer, are eagerly introducing employment policies that earn staff loyalty, particularly as the costs of training staff in areas like nursing are so high.

## Useful Books and Contacts

The annually updated *What Color is Your Parachute?* by Richard Nelson Bolles (Ten Speed Press, $17.95) has become a classic in the job-search and career-change market. Its sensible and supportive advice encourages readers to evaluate their own personalities and strengths, and then to apply these insights to the job hunt.

A more conservative approach is taken by *The Which? Guide to Changing Careers* by Sue Bennett (£10.99). It is a practical guide to tackling the challenge of finding a new career, giving advice on job-hunting, self-employment, retraining, financial issues and how to turn what may seem to be a predicament into an opportunity. The book aims to help identify what you have to offer, and then target suitable openings.

Changing Direction (www.changingdirection.com) is an organisation dedicated to helping people to approach the workplace after a career break, especially women. The coach who runs the company, Diana Wolfin, has also written a book *Back to Work – A Guide for Women Returners* (Robson Books, 2004).

As well as exploiting the resources of Job Centre Plus (the government job-finding service), you might be able to benefit from returning to the careers service of your old university. Institutions have different policies but they are usually happy for an alumnus to make use of their resources. An increasingly popular source of help is to consult a private career counsellor or life coach.

## Useful Websites

The ease with which recruitment websites can be updated and personalised makes them invaluable tools in providing up-to-date information which can be quickly sorted according to preference. These specialist sites allow the user to search updated listings, build and post an online CV and obtain e-mail alerts. National newspapers like the *Guardian* and *The Times* have also made a big pitch for the jobs market, with entire sub-sections of their websites dedicated to this area.

The Internet offers a bewildering array of job-finding resources. Everywhere you look on the Internet potentially useful links can be found. Be aware that many seem to offer more than they can deliver and you may find that the number and range of jobs posted are disappointing. A surprising number of company home pages feature an icon you can click to find out about jobs with that company. Here is a brief selection of potentially useful sites.

*www.rec.uk.com* – The Recruitment & Employment Confederation is the professional body representing recruitment agencies in the UK. Search the website for agencies in your field.

*www.brookstreet.co.uk* – Brook Street is a UK-wide employment agency. Type in your postcode and the site will point you to the nearest office. There's also advice on compiling a CV, interview techniques, etc.

*www.cityjobs.com* – Contains thousands of jobs on behalf of clients who specialise in the finance, IT, accountancy and legal sectors.

*http://jobs.guardian.co.uk* – Guardian Unlimited runs impressive job listings online. Particularly strong on public service, charity and media jobs, the site also incorporates a special section for graduates.

*www.JobsGoPublic.com* – A site aimed at public sector workers looking for employment in a range of fields from museums and libraries to nursing and midwifery.

*www.manpower.co.uk* – Manpower is one of the UK's largest recruitment chains. On the site you can find current job listings, online training courses and office addresses. The address of the international site is www.manpower.com.

*www.monster.co.uk* – Lists thousands of jobs worldwide and publishes advice on job hunting and preparing a CV.

*www.opportunities.co.uk* – Comprehensive listings for career opportunities in the public sector.

*www.prospects.ac.uk* – UK's official career site for graduates maintained by the Higher Education Careers Services Unit, Prospects House, Booth St E, Manchester M13 9EP. Publishes huge amount of information for graduates and students in the UK. Links to 'Jobs Abroad'.

*www.realworldmagazine.com* – Mainly aimed at new graduates though information of use to 'mature graduates'. It carries articles about various professional fields including interviews with employees and advice on how to get hired.

*www.recruit-online.co.uk* – SAT UK Recruitment Guide aims to provide comprehensive guide to online UK jobsites, recruitment agencies and consultants.

*www.stepstone.co.uk* – Stepstone describes itself as the leading European jobs portal and carries thousands of searchable job vacancies in Europe and the UK. The site also offers career advice and tips on how to market yourself.

*www.workthing.com* – A free job site providing a searchable database of vacancies, editorial advice, information on training courses and employment news.

## Specialist Agencies

*Blue Arrow Personnel Services* – www.bluearrow.co.uk. Major employment agency which aims to place all kinds of people from students to late returners. Blue Arrow recommends that people who want a gradual return to the working world should consider taking temporary work which allows flexibility and an opportunity to try different jobs and employers.

*Merrow Language Recruitment,* 100 New Kings Road, London SW6 4LX (0845 226 4748; www.merrow.co.uk). Deals with senior bilingual and multilingual secretarial positions in Europe.

*Prospect Management Services Ltd,* 3rd Floor, Charles House, 7 Leicester Place, London WC2H 7BY (020-7439 1919; www.prospectmsl.com). Agency specialising in the new media and digital technology sector which is seeking to take account of larger professional and personal goals.

*Thirty Plus Recruitment,* 92-93 Great Russell Street, London WC1B 3PS (020-7323 4155; www.thirtyplus-recruitment.com). Agency that places people in administrative, secretarial and accounting jobs in Greater London up to retirement age. In the past they have found work for house husbands, carers and mothers returning to work.

*Forties People,* 11-13 Dowgate Hill, London, EC4R 2ST (020-7329 4044; www.fortiespeople.net). Specialises in clerical and secretarial work for more mature candidates in London and Watford.

*Wiseowls* – www.wiseowls.co.uk. London-based non-profit organisation providing an employment agency, educational website, and Business Start Up Initiative assistance aimed at people over 45.

# CHANGING DIRECTION

A year spent away from professional life may be the prelude to larger more permanent changes. You may have had an inkling that your old job was going nowhere or was causing dissatisfaction. A gap year may act as a stepping stone to leaving for good even if that was not the original plan. Another scenario is that a break spent in another activity may have been so rewarding that it compels a re-evaluation of one's career path, which had once been taken for granted.

The charms of office life may have palled with distance. A career breaker met by the *Daily Telegraph* journalist Rosemary Behan (herself on a gap year in 2006) reported her motives for taking off to rough it in China: 'I had bosses who made David Brent look competent. This has taught me that I have many options in life, and my time could be better used. I am going back to work as a freelance consultant, because I'm sick of working around people who sit behind a desk for eight hours a day, eat Mars bars for lunch and don't even have time to look in the mirror to see how ill they look.'

Some career breaks are consciously taken at the outset as a way of forcing the pace, as a springboard for changing career. You may literally be returning to the first rung of a ladder. Of course skills learned in a former occupation will never leave you, even though you may be starting afresh in a new field. In some cases, it will mean modifying a previous experience, for example applying a medical or legal qualification to a manufacturing, business or commercial service.

Changing direction in life is often fraught with anxiety. However, taking a risk is sometimes necessary before reaching a certain goal. Cultural commentator Michael Bracewell, writing in the *Guardian* of a widely-held sense of entrapment in office life puts it well: 'Whatever might lie beyond the office, from goat farming in Snowdonia to having that one idea which will make you worth more than Ikea, there is always that membrane of fear which keeps the bulk of us at our desks.'

**Clodagh O'Brien's** gap half-year in South-east Asia changed his outlook permanently:

> *Before I left I worked in London as a science journalist. I now work as Communications Officer for a charity that provides services to people affected by acquired brain injury (www.headway.ie). I found that my experiences in Asia, especially after visiting Cambodia, made me want to give back something to society while still remaining involved in science. I think the trip opened my eyes to the huge array of obstacles that people in third world countries face and made me realise I eventually want to work in a disadvantaged country to make life easier for those living in awful conditions*

## A New Career in Development?

Some career breakers return from their travels or volunteer work in far-flung impoverished countries all fired up to carry on working in the field of international aid and development. They dream of living in exotic places, helping poor people to improve their lives, and getting paid for it. Working in development aid or disaster relief offers all these things. However, while many dream of such a career, only a chosen few actually manage to get a foothold in what has become a highly competitive and increasingly professional business.

**Till Bruckner** has a great deal of experience in pursuing this trail, having travelled the world after university funded by working in a bread factory in Wales, picking flowers in Cornwall and so on. Over the past few years, he has gradually gained enough relevant experience with NGOs, in Sudan for example, to land contracts with aid agencies that saw him in 2006 with a budget of $900,000 on a contract to design a project for refugees in Georgia. Here he debunks some of the myths:

> *To understand why a few succeed where so many fail, it is best to look at what kind of people agencies like CARE, Oxfam and Save the Children do* ***not*** *need. These fall into three categories – heroes, unskilled idealists, and people with skills that are available locally.*
>
> *To take the first one, agencies do not need heroes. Many people believe that development work is in some way heroic, with western aid workers battling desert storms to get medicine to a relief camp in the nick of time. The truth is far more prosaic. The vast majority of relief and development work done by foreigners involves answering emails, writing reports and attending boring meetings. The last thing a truck driver in a sandstorm needs is a foreigner giving smart advice, and the nightmare of every agency boss is an employee who jeopardises a whole programme by disregarding tight security restrictions. If you want to do heroic stuff, become a freelance journalist instead.*

*Secondly, agencies do not need unskilled idealists. Posters of aid agencies sometimes show good white people spoon-feeding starving African babies. In the real world, this never happens. Even if you offer to work for free, it makes much more sense for an agency to create much needed employment by paying a local to do unskilled work. If you are an idealist and want to help poor people, get in touch with an agency in your home country and offer your services as a fundraising volunteer there. Alternatively, if you are in a poor country, just walk into an orphanage or nature park and ask if they can use some unpaid help.*

*The third group that agencies do not need is people with skills that are available locally. Aid agencies exist to help poor people. Therefore, they will always hire car mechanics, forklift drivers, secretaries and translators from inside the poor countries where they operate. Taking on a foreigner – even without any pay – to drive a truck in an African country makes no sense. It is far better to lift one more local person out of unemployment and poverty by giving him or her a job.*

So what sort of people are aid agencies looking for? The best way to find out is to look at some of the websites listed below and see what skills are in demand. Generally speaking, agencies hire people with considerable technical skills and a few years of professional experience, including doctors, logisticians, accountants, and microfinance specialists. Most advertised vacancies will draw dozens, if not hundreds, of applications from qualified and experienced people. With no prior experience, unless you are a doctor and willing to work for free, it is nearly impossible to find a job this way. Most people working in development today originally started off far more informally. For example many are former US Peace Corps volunteers or hardcore travellers who somehow got a foot in the door while they were in a developing country. The majority began their careers as unpaid interns or volunteers, proved that they were capable of doing a good job, and then after half a year or so started moving up the ladder and into administrative or managerial positions. However, even becoming an unpaid volunteer can be difficult. Volunteers create costs by taking up the time of their supervisors, and by requiring office space and computer access.

**Till Bruckner goes on to share his insights into the job hunt:**
So how do you find an organisation that suits you and convince it to give you a chance? Here's a step-by-step guide:

- *Think about what you can offer.* One skill that is severely in demand in most countries is the ability to write coherent texts in flawless English. Development organisations produce an amazing amount of paperwork, much of which is produced by local staff with shaky English and then has to be corrected or re-written by a native speaker. If you have good writing and editing skills, and you volunteer to subject yourself to the tedium of proof-reading documents for half a year, there should be demand for your services. Alternatively, you could offer to teach English for free for a few hours a week, or give a course in writing skills. Also, think about special skills that you can offer. Maybe you could revamp an agency's computer system or layout publicity materials for free? If you are unsure about what agencies are looking for, just drop in on one, or take part in a training course for relief and development workers.

- *Identify organisations you want to work for.* In every poor country, there is some website directory listing most of the agencies working there with their activities in detail. If you cannot find this website, just ring the local office of any agency and ask them where to find the directory. Look for organisations whose work interests you. Do they work with children, farmers, refugees, or with the environment? Make a shortlist and then get the email address of the 'country director'. If necessary, phone the organisation to get it. An email to a general address is likely to get lost.
- *Write a short email* to the country director of each organisation you have chosen. State that you are interested in helping his/her work, and write precisely identifying which problem you are proposing to solve for him/her, e.g. proof-reading, training staff in specific software skills, language lessons, etc. If you have a professional-looking CV, attach it to your email. Make clear that you expect little or no pay, but that in return, you would appreciate being able to learn about how international development works. Ask for a chance to meet and discuss your possible contribution. If you are already in your target country, you have a huge advantage. If not, state in your email that you will be visiting the country during a certain week in the future, and ask for an interview date then. Once you get a couple of positive replies, pack your bags and go! People are unlikely to take you on without having met you in person. Without a lot of initiative, you will never get a foot in the door.
- *Be professional at the interview.* If you get an interview, treat it like any job interview. Dress smart-casual (no tie). Have a copy of your CV with you. Make sure that you know in detail what the organisation does. Also remember that development aid has become big business. The person interviewing you is probably on a very good salary. If you save him/her time and money, it is perfectly acceptable to ask for what you will get in return, e.g. participation in training and workshops, remuneration for transport expenses or even free accommodation. If the country director seems hesitant to commit to taking you on for a long time, offer to start by doing a week of free work with no strings attached. Once you have a foot in the door, it becomes easy to walk in. As elsewhere, most people are hired through word of mouth, and if you are good at getting things done, word will spread. Working part-time for two or three organisations at once can accelerate this process.

Welcome to one of the most exhilarating, frustrating and challenging careers in the world!

People returning from conservation projects abroad often have the same impulse to change direction as happened to **Richard Nimmo** in his early 30s:

> *While working in sales and marketing for a radio station, I realised that I needed a break from my hectic and pressurised work life. I also had a strong desire to take some time to see and work in a new environment, challenge myself, as well as make a positive contribution through a con-*

*servation project. I volunteered on Blue Ventures Marine Conservation programme in Madagascar and then spent a further month travelling around the country. Living and working in a remote community with volunteers from many countries and local people gave me a huge sense of achievement as we all contributed to a successful and award-winning marine project. My return to London was a shock to my system and I found the priorities of western commercial society quite distasteful at times after living amongst poverty in Madagascar. I have definitely not returned to my old lifestyle. Working and living in Madagascar was a wonderful experience that has given me a new focus and an impetus to work in a new sector. My career has changed and I hope to continue working to achieve conservation goals.*

## Useful Websites for Development Work

Till Bruckner has provided this annotated list of resources on the web:

www.sussex.ac.uk/cdec/careers_path.php?carpath=15&carsection=4 – great place to start
www.idealist.org – good for beginners
www.reliefweb.int/vacancies/index.html – lots of vacancies for professionals, good for checking out what is in demand
www.comminit.com/vacancies.html – based in Victoria, Canada. Also information on relief training courses.
www.bond.org.uk/classifieds/internationaldevelopmentjobs.html – BOND stands for British Overseas NGOs for Development
www.wse.org.uk/vacsearch.htm – loads of vacancies and links
www.charityjob.co.uk/seekers.htm – strong on admin jobs
www.jobsincharities.co.uk – jobs in UK
www.oneworld.net – not as useful as some.
www.dotorgjobs.com – primarily of interest to Americans
www.interaction.org – job and volunteer newsletters for paying subscribers
www.eldis.org/news/jobs.htm – based in Brighton, useful links
www.coop4coop.org – no job vacancies, only list of agencies.
www.aidworkers.net – info for relief workers
www.bioforce.asso.fr – French organisation that provides relief training

## Unexpectedly Detained

A gap year may have an unavoidably life-changing effect, especially one which involves exposure to new cultures, lifestyles, ways of working and a different set of values. According to the 19th century aphorist and Harvard professor, Oliver Wendell Holmes, 'a mind that is stretched by a new experience can never go back to its old dimensions'. London lawyer **Polly Botsford** never doubted that her gap year as a volunteer for an NGO in Cambodia would be enjoyable but she had firmly resisted the notion that it would change her. She now cheerfully acknowledges that she was wrong and it did precisely that.

In some cases the changes which a gap have brought about may be more than just psychological. Bachelors may have found partners, women may have found motherhood and so on. Or the reverse may have happened. An earlier relationship may not have survived a separation or diverging goals and you now find yourself free to form new attachments whether to new lovers, new cultures or new pursuits. Perhaps you have fallen under the spell of Paris, Sydney, Rio or the African veld and have lost the urge to return to your roots (see section 'Staying On' in the chapter *Working and Living Abroad*).

The downside of an open-ended career break is the absence of security. Venturing through the game parks of Africa or learning to scuba dive on the Great Barrier reef is certainly more appealing to some if they know that they can return to normality by having a job to return to. For others, a clean break is the goal and any commitments back home would negate the mystique and catharsis of leaving old responsibilities behind.

Even when there is no intention of veering away from a known profession, events can dictate otherwise. **Rachel Pooley** decided not to go back to her former career working for a mental health charity on returning from a trans-Africa Land Rover trip with her partner Charlie. Having accidentally found themselves running a backpacking lodge on the edge of Lake Malawi, they learned to value work differently. Their experience of running the lodge without electricity or running water and managing the staff made them more practical and self-reliant. They are now much less preoccupied with a traditional career and are much choosier about the work they want to do. Malawi and the ubiquitous tragedy of AIDS taught them to appreciate life more and to approach the challenge of each day as it arrives. The opportunity to be self-employed and to run their own business, albeit for just six months, made the idea of returning home to work in a big organisation much less appealing. Their break encouraged them to explore different ways of working and to hold out against opportunities that didn't feel right for them.

## Becoming Self-Employed

For some people, being an employee suits their lifestyle and aspirations. They enjoy being part of a team in which the major decisions are taken by the boss. They feel that their contribution is sufficiently valued and financially rewarded and they appreciate being able to leave professional worries in the office at 5.30pm every day and during four weeks of paid holiday. Whereas many employees feel that this leaves enough free time to pursue outside interests, others feel constrained by this regimen.

One means of taking greater control of your working life is to become self-employed which, in the eyes of the tax office, is the same thing as setting up a business, even though you simply want to deliver a service or product yourself without the worry and hassle of employing other people. Being a self-employed freelancer or consultant can be an economically efficient way of working because many expenses like office equipment and business travel can be set against tax.

Before deciding, it is advisable to speak to an accountant who specialises in working with the self-employed. Assess how your income is likely to change and whether you can expect to meet all your financial obligations. Above all, you will have maximum freedom to set your own working hours and holidays. The obvious drawback is that your income will vary, for example there may be seasonal variations in the demand for your work and there will be no perks traditionally provided by an employer like free telephone and envelopes and Christmas parties, let alone contributions to pensions, paid holidays and company cars.

When long term employment with one company is declining and employment is increasingly available on short-term contracts only, it makes good sense to sell your skills and experience as a contractor, flexibly moving from one project to another. It will certainly provide variety and the stimulus of frequent change.

A useful reference book here is *The Which? Guide to Working from Home* by

Lynn Brittney. While not solely concerned with self-employment, the guide suggests all kinds of economic activity that can be conducted from home, many of which are concerned with self-employed activities like running a playgroup or bed and breakfast through to practising complementary therapies. This guide provides you with all the hints and tips you might need if you are to make a success of it.

## REVERSE CULTURE SHOCK

Before worrying about re-adjusting to the working world, you should be prepared for a certain level of disorientation on a personal level. Not everybody can be as upbeat as Barbara Schick, an Austrian photographer whose gap year was spent in Brazil travelling and volunteering: 'It was beautiful to be away for half a year but just as beautiful to come back home to friends and work' though she goes on to confess that a year on, she is ready to leave again for a while.

Coming home from a stay away can engender reverse culture shock, especially if your gap year has included extended travels in the developing world. You may feel suffocated by the commercialism all around. Life at home may seem dull and routine at first, while the outlook of your colleagues, friends and family can strike you as limited and parochial. You may find it difficult to bridge the gulf between you and your stay-at-home colleagues who (understandably) may feel a little threatened or belittled by your experiences.

**Joni Hillman** vividly recalls her case of reverse culture shock after returning from being a volunteer in India:

> *Reverse culture shock is always much worse than the acclimatisation process you go through when you first arrive in a foreign country because you're just not prepared to feel different about your old life. I think being aware that it might be difficult to return home is the key. Give yourself time, or throw yourself into something. I moved house and started my Masters within 10 days of arriving home. If you have seen horrific poverty or had conflict experiences it can sometimes be really difficult to engage in a conversation with your oldest friends about seemingly trivial things like Eastenders! It can also be difficult to sum up your experiences in a couple of sentences, which is generally all people have got time for when they ask 'How was it?'. Keeping a diary is a good idea because it can help you digest your experiences into manageable chunks for other people. And remember that they are invariably jealous of the wonderful experiences you have been gutsy enough to go out and find, while they waste their lives in offices.*

The process of shaking up your life is undoubtedly risky. The experience may leave you out of step with your social and professional circle at home. Even if you know that you are perfectly capable of settling back into your old life, you may not be willing, because too many of your views and values have changed to be comfortable. On the other hand you don't really have a choice and will simply have to stop looking agog at your Starbuck's bill and telling everyone that this would pay for a week's travelling in India or a fortnight in Laos.

As **Jenna Bonistalli** found when she returned to New York after seven months of travel plus volunteering in the Himalayas and Rajasthan, it was difficult to think about the expenses she would be taking on again (car, apartment, health insurance) which all seemed plainly ridiculous in contrast with her experiences in 2006:

*Yet that's the way of life here and you sort of have to play the game in order to survive. I have certain moments where I catch myself and really put my own situation into perspective with what I have seen and understood elsewhere. It's funny though, in some ways surviving in America, particularly a young person who plans to work in service, non-profit related fields, is a very overwhelming task with different challenges, but difficult ones.*

This telling extract describes re-entry to normal life. It is taken from the final chapter 'An English Alien' of Nigel Barley's *The Innocent Anthropologist,* a superbly amusing account of the author's time spent researching the Dowayo tribe of the Cameroons, (Penguin, 1983):

*It is positively insulting how well the world functions without one. While the traveller has been away questioning his most basic assumptions, life has continued sweetly unruffled. Friends continue to collect matching French saucepans. The acacia at the foot of the lawn continues to come along nicely. The returning anthropologist does not expect a hero's welcome, but the casualness of some friends seems excessive. An hour after my arrival, I was phoned by one friend who merely remarked tersely, 'Look, I don't know where you've been but you left a pullover at my place nearly two years ago. When are you coming to collect it?' In vain one feels that such questions are beneath the concern of a returning prophet.*

As Nigel Barley sees it, the sight of groaning supermarket shelves induces either revulsion or crippling indecisiveness. Polite conversation may seem temporarily impossible. But most returned field workers end up feeling overwhelming gratitude for having been born a Westerner. Generally the feelings of displacement and restlessness pass soon enough when the reverse culture shock wears off and you begin to feel reintegrated.

While at times it will seem that time has stood still during your absence, at others you may feel that you have missed important events while away: children are born, friends get married, couples part, neighbours move away, governments are voted out, radio presenters retire. Despite modern telecommunications making it much easier to keep abreast of these changes, there may be a feeling of alienation from your past.

One aspect that **Marcelle Salerno** found most difficult after one of her many adventures during her gap years was the naïve generalisations some of her fellow Americans were prone to make:

*Already I find it difficult to speak to people when they discuss 'world news' if I know they haven't seen anything of the world first-hand. After living with Muslims for a month in Morocco I see the current political issues differently. After living with tribal Africans for 6 months I see race in a whole different light.*

Apart from social unease, you might have more immediate practical worries such as where you will live. If you have a house or flat to return to, that should be no trouble, assuming the tenants or housesitters have looked after it adequately. But if you gave up your rented or mortgaged accommodation to take a career break, finding a place to live will be of primary concern. You can only camp out with friends for so long, though you will probably be welcome to stay longer with parents or siblings at least to provide a base while you're house hunting. Depending on how much privacy you have and to what extent you feel yourself to be imposing, this arrangement will probably spur you on to find a place of your own as briskly as possible. Casting yourself at the mercy of your parents again can be viewed in a positive light as thirty-something **Lucy Bailey** did after four wonderful months working at two different game lodges in Kenya with *The Leap* though finding a stimulating job proved impossible in the short-term:

> *I ended up going to live with my parents in Derbyshire (who I get on with fantastically and which was actually a really lovely opportunity to be with them for a little while and get to know them again!) for a few months and did some temping to keep the wolf from the door before moving back down to London. I was a secretary for a company that made bespoke generators located on an industrial estate on the outskirts of a really grim ex-mining town in rural Derbyshire! There was nothing to do at lunchtime apart from drive to the local gravel pit where I'd sit in my car eating my ham butties, smoking cigarettes and watching the giant rats scuttle in and out of the piles of burnt out clothes and abandoned broken toilets. It was easily one of the worst jobs I've ever had, but certainly had comedy value, which is fortunate seeing as I do some comedy writing and performing and it's provided a great deal of material!*

If you have been away for a long time, consider throwing a party to let everyone know that you're home and available for a continuation of your former social life. But don't expect to slot back seamlessly. In some cases your interests and priorities may have changed and be prepared for it to take time before you find the common ground with friends and family. The physical trappings of your life may have changed too. The well-loved garden of a home you rented to strangers may have declined beyond recognition and years of hard work lost.

On the other hand, you may find that nothing much has changed at all which can be equally alienating in its way. From having returned to her job in the law after six months spent in Cambodia, Japan and South America, **Polly Botsford** passes on what she learned about re-entry:

> *You just have to be realistic. If you think things are going to be different, then you are going to get very depressed. Time stands still – or so it seems. Your flat will look the same, your wardrobe will not have been revamped, and the tube strikes will still be going on. But in fact, much will have changed and happened without you, it just takes a bit longer to see the subtleties. If possible, plan to come back in the summer (always a little kinder). Get every photo into an album (or onto a web page if that is how you are doing it) within a month or you'll never do it. Don't rely on staying in touch with fellow travellers as a way of keeping the experience alive. You have to move on. If you do develop fantastic new friendships then that's great but you can't force them.*

While change may be somewhat surprising and even shocking, it cannot negate or diminish the extraordinary phase of life you will have enjoyed during your gap year.

# Personal Case Histories

## Debbie Risborough

**Although Debbie Risborough at age 38 was enjoying her job as accountant for a small friendly company, she was bored and decided she wanted to travel and try something completely different. Like everyone in this position, the idea of abandoning everything to get on a plane left her nerves in tatters, especially with her mother treating her as though she had gone mad and would never return. The year out was to be funded initially by savings though she knew eventually she would have to make use of the £4,000 credit limit on each of her four credit cards and her overdraft facility of £1,400.**

*In total I was away about 14 months. I decided to do voluntary work as I am not a very good tourist and I also needed things to be planned upfront so that I would not worry about what would happen next. I made a list of all the countries that I wanted to visit and looked for voluntary work in them. Three months was a good length of time in most countries as tourist visas last that long. My trip included India for six weeks (three weeks with Indian Volunteers for Community Service and three weeks travelling); South Africa for three months with Sneewitje Creche; Australia for one month of holiday (since I had nothing planned, a month was enough for me); Fiji (nine weeks with Greenforce on a marine expedition and about 10 days travelling); Argentina for three months teaching English with Travellers Worldwide while taking a Spanish course at the University of Buenos Aires; and finally two months of holiday in Canada where I liked it so much I stayed on until my ticket was due to expire.*

*The India stay was quite a short time as I wasn't sure how I would cope with the change in culture. I chose the Greenforce expedition because I had always wanted to learn to dive and that was an opportunity to do that. The Travellers programme in Argentina seemed good value for money. In fact Argentina turned out to be the high point as everything just worked and I loved it all. The low point was the last few weeks of the Greenforce placement: the weather was not good, I was stuck on an island with 15 18 year olds for company (it really didn't matter how nice they all were) and I knew I had another three weeks to go!*

*In general the reality far exceeded my expectations as I didn't really know what to expect so was really nervous. The only part of the trip I had built up in advance was the Fiji expedition so it was not surprising that reality kicked in here. I am still amazed that I managed to effectively travel around the world on my own and nothing bad happened. I didn't lose anything, get anything stolen or have any nasty stories to tell. I am truly thankful for that.*

*When I returned I was totally amazed at how life continued. When I got back I was on a mission to work in the NGO field and temp in the meantime. I managed to get a temporary job after 10 days back in the UK and obtained a year's contract with an NGO in Sudan within four months by consulting the website of MANGO which matches accountants with overseas aid agencies. The job was as Finance Officer for Concern Worldwide in Darfur which progressed to Country Accountant due to a vacancy; so I am still using my accountancy qualification but in a field that I am really interested in. During that year in Sudan, I managed to get married to a Sudanese national and am now pregnant and back in the UK to have the baby.*

*When I came back from my travels I needed to take out a loan for £10,000 to pay everything off. All in all I think I probably spent about £16,000 which was quite expensive but it was worth every penny. The biggest expenses were the plane ticket (£1,772), the Greenforce expedition (£2,750) and the Travellers Worldwide fee (£1,710).*

*My future plans are to start a business buying handicrafts from third world projects and selling to the UK market and in 2008 to sail around the world the wrong way with the Global Challenge. Luckily my husband is supportive of all this and I just have to work out how it can be done with no money and family responsibilities!*

*In general my gap year was a mental breakthrough for me. I managed to get out of the need for working for money, the necessity of earning a living and craving for stability with partner, house, etc. I actually went out and did something that I really wanted to do. That gave me the inspiration to do other things that I really wanted to do. I may not now have a house or the latest car but I have managed to find a life partner and I have not regretted the trip one bit. On the contrary, I feel that I did the right thing at the right time and learnt a lot of useful skills, which I am putting into use all the time.*

## Neil Munro

**After 28 years as a lecturer in Scotland, Neil Munro was reeling from a family act of betrayal and ensuing legal frustrations that had resulted in a nervous breakdown and end to his marriage. An advertisement for 'Year Out Volunteer Placements' caught his eye in a geographic magazine in a doctor's waiting room, so he made contact with *Travellers Worldwide* and was soon signed up for a placement at Antelope Park in Zimbabwe. His four-month stay there turned out to be therapeutic as well as enjoyable:**

*A reasonably seasoned traveler, I set off happily enough. But illusions that I had overcome my traumas were soon shattered. Faced with X-ray apparatus and metal detectors at the airport, I froze, speechless and trembling violently. A kindly lady official soothed me with motherly support, but my vulnerable condition was confirmed.*

*Antelope Park covers 3,000 acres of mixed vegetation, some woodland but mostly savannah grassland and spiky acacia bushes, where significant numbers of impala, zebra and wildebeest roam, along with eight giraffes and a family of warthogs. The lion breeding programme at Antelope Park is designed to achieve the release of lions into the wild and has approval from the WWF. Funding is by tourists who pay for activities such as 'Walking with Lions', cub viewing, game viewing, swimming with elephants, horse riding, etc.*

*To develop familiarity with the bush, the cubs (which have been bred in captivity to guarantee a strong gene pool) are walked free from about six weeks to 18 months old. During these walks they usually stay close to their human companions, viewing humans as senior members of their pride, while soaking up the feel of the bush. These encounters generate mutual interest with the occasional stalk and chase by the larger cubs which, being well fed, are easily outrun but sometimes kicked by zebra. Learning can be hard!*

*I was to be working with two of these cubs, Casper and Cleo. After a fascinating lesson on working with lion cubs, we were joined by some volunteers for my first lion walk, an incredible experience. I also learned that because Caspar and Cleo had had a sadly traumatic start to life they were the only cubs not to have bonded with any humans, neither guides nor volunteers. This meant that they would not walk normally with the volunteers and my first walks with them were painful indeed. The cubs had to be harried and chased to walk any distance and at every opportunity would scamper off in different directions, seeking the prickliest areas, then making plaintive calls to each other. Everyone involved became frustrated and before long the volunteers would give up, put down cushions and sit reading while Caspar and Cleo lay re-united under a shady bush.*

*Unlike the other volunteers, I have children and I think that is why I found the cubs' dependence on and devotion to each other so endearing. Seeing their insecurities as a challenge and wanting to help them, I began to lie with them, keeping my hand as near their noses as possible so they would get used to my smell. I also sat with them in the evenings when Caspar, realising that my legs were softer and warmer than the ground, began to sleep on top of them. Sitting in the dark under an African sky bright with stars with a lion cub on one's bare legs is a wonderful experience. Cleo would lie alongside me and let me stroke her but she was never as affectionate as Caspar.*

*Normal lion cubs just eat, sleep and play hunting games of ambushing, stalking, tripping and attacking. But Caspar and Cleo had never played so it was particularly rewarding when they began to do so. At last they had thrown off their insecurities to find walking and playing fun. Rehabilitation seemed complete and as the days went by, along with other volunteers, we explored extensively, finding some wonderful trees for the cubs to climb. I also helped the cubs overcome their fear of, and to drink from, the lake; a simple thing but their trust delighted me. Life was good for us all.*

*Soon bottle feeding Caspar and Cleo ended and it was time to move them to a main enclosure to continue their development. As we strolled across the lawns and footbridge for the last time I was reminded of my feelings when I walked my daughter up the aisle to be married, the same tearful pride filling my heart.*

*Some days later, having walked Caspar and Cleo, I was returning to camp with one of the volunteers who had become a friend, chatting about music. Spontaneously I found myself talking about my childhood and family, topics I had been unable to speak about for some three years due to my brother's betrayal. I realised that, just like Caspar and Cleo, I had recovered from my traumas – our mutual healing had initiated three new beginnings.*

*The parting, when it came, was emotional but subdued, my sadness mellowed by my recovery, a need to return home and by my sense of achievement in ridding Caspar and Cleo of their insecurities. Overall my placement was the most incredible experience of my life – a beautiful park, delightful people and wonderful animals. I will remember it all with gratitude and joy for the rest of my life. I have returned a restored individual, but not just restored, also mellowed, contented and optimistic.*

## Stephanie Metcalfe

**Like many people whose spouses are offered a transfer abroad, 33 year old Stephanie Metcalfe found herself giving up her job as a social worker in England in order to move to Helsinki with her husband for six months:**

*We had talked before about the possibility of living and working abroad at some stage in the future and we decided this was too good an opportunity to miss, even though it meant losing quite a lot of my income. It is not an easy decision to take time out from your career and I think that seeing me do it made several people re-think their own situations and consider doing the same thing. It was hard for my family to understand why I would give up a 'good job' in England and take a low paid, unqualified job abroad. However, at the end of the day the decision was for my husband and me to make and my family have seen how it has improved our quality of life so now they are less negative about the experience.*

*Financing the time away was difficult and we had to cut back a lot on our usual level of spending and be very careful about managing our money. My husband was still getting his normal wage but I worked as a live-out au pair and my salary was more like pocket money. However, we had already decided that it would be worth it so we could have the experience of living in another country.*

*I studied Finnish at university while I was in Finland and I would definitely recommend this to anyone living in a foreign country. It helps you to feel more at home when you can understand some of the things you hear and read around you and really it's only polite to make an effort to speak the language of the country you are in. It's also a great way to make friends from all over the world.*

*The experience gave me the opportunity to step outside my everyday life in the UK and gain a fresh perspective. Being in a different country makes you stop and question lots of things that you take for granted and it has given me the time and the space to reflect on my life and what my plans for the future are. I also feel very lucky to have had a nannying job that I enjoyed so much arranged through Snow Au Pairs (www.snowaupairs.com). I would have been happy to stay longer, maybe one or two years.*

## Bryan Havenhand

**Bryan Havenhand from Australia spent the whole of 2005 in Cambodia with his wife Anna and 13 year old daughter Bonny. Anna found work as a language teacher after arrival in Siem Reap and her wages covered all local living expenses including the rent of a comfortable house. They had a fascinating year, though not without its challenges:**

*My wife Anna wanted to teach English overseas and had completed a CELTA to this end. (A native German speaker, she ended up mostly teaching German instead to tour guides at Angkor Wat in Cambodia.) Our daughter was in the early years of high school so if we were to go, this was the time. I took the idea on as a bit of an adventure. The family (siblings and parents) were not overwhelmed by the idea and both sets of parents were opposed to it. They did not say this outright, but constantly stressed the negative side of things. It was seen as dangerous, more so because of the spread of bird flu in Cambodia and nearby countries. It was seen as somewhat irresponsible taking our 13 year old daughter as well. Our friends thought it was a great idea and especially encouraged our daughter who was not looking forward to it as she thought she would miss her friends badly.*

*The year out was self-funded although my wife earned up to US$700 per month which well and truly covered our basic costs in Cambodia including the rental of our house. We did not travel much (our daughter didn't want to travel around the country at all) though we went once to Thailand, once to Laos just before we left and two short trips around northern Cambodia. I also did some English teaching that came along plus I taught quite a few local kids (as did our daughter for a while). Otherwise I was still working on my business (a small publishing company called Global Exchange), attempting to help home school our daughter, run the household (we did have a housekeeper) and generally keep things on an even keel.*

*The highlights were the people who lived around us (we had much more contact with the locals than with other expats), the Angkor temple complex, people we met in villages and locals we befriended. We were also lucky to have quite a number of friends from both Australia and Germany visit us during the year. For me the hardest part was the constant heat (for much of the year it would be 35 degrees Celsius at 6.30am and it would only get hotter from there). I also had problems with the monotony, the barking dogs at night and the early morning (4.30am) chanting from nearby wats. Sometimes I got little sleep.*

*It was definitely worth the effort and I think it has given our daughter a useful perspective on life that she wouldn't have otherwise got from simply travelling to a place. She dropped her Paris Hilton look-a-like friends not long after she came back and took up with some new friends who have a healthier outlook on life. When our daughter has finished high school we might just do it again.*

## Alefiya Rajkotwala

**While working as a manager in technology consulting, Alefiya found out about her employer Accenture's partnership with VSO:**

*I have always been interested in the development sector. For a long time I had wanted to experience it for myself; to live, work and learn alongside people whose world I only glimpsed through the media. However, I was struggling to fit it in with my chosen career of technology consulting and Accenture's Business Partnership programme with VSO was the perfect answer.*

*The application process was surprisingly simple. I was able to give plenty of notice to Accenture, received the required support and approval easily and the VSO assessment and pre-departure process was intense but straightforward. In January 2005, I left to start my VSO placement in Kigali, Rwanda. My placement duration was nine months and I was employed at the Secrétariat National de l'Enseignment Catholique (SNEC) which is the central Catholic body of education.*

*The Catholic Church of Rwanda owns and manages over 70 per cent of the education institutions in the country including primary, secondary and tertiary. I was an Organisational Advisor to the education arm of the church. This included setting up management procedures in the central office where I worked and also liaising with the schools all over the country to help with their planning and financial management. In addition to working downstream within the church hierarchy, I was also working at a partner level with the Ministry of Education at both the national and provincial level.*

*I had never worked in education, let alone in a different country and culture, working in a second language and spending day and night learning about people in the organisation, the history, the politics, in addition to trying to actually do some real work such as changing communication methods, etc. Like any project in Accenture, I learnt quickly that the ideas of management and efficiency apply everywhere.*

*Overall, Rwanda was an incredible experience both professionally and personally. Every stereotype I had arrived with was challenged - the inside workings of the Catholic Church, an African government, and a country with a violent past. Personally, my eyes just opened up to a whole new understanding of the real cycles of poverty, the good and bad consequences of foreign aid and how the human spirit seems to be strong enough to survive anything.*

## Nick Leader

**Retired from college administration, 68 year old Nick wanted to do something tangible to help the developing world in a field that he had some experience in.**

*I had travelled extensively through Third World countries recruiting the sons and daughters of wealthy parents for a foundation course and university degree in the UK. I thought that it was now time to try to do something for the ordinary students, however modest this might be.*

*I was attracted to the People & Places programme in Cape Town as it seemed to offer an opportunity to do some practical work in an area that I was familiar with. Most of my family and friends thought I was fairly brave to go to a black township school and live locally with a township family rather than in 'White' Cape Town. 'Rather you than me' was the standard refrain, 'but we want to hear all about it when you get back.'*

*People & Places working with Saga were just starting up in South Africa and my brief seemed ideal, which was to investigate the problems that the school was having and to suggest worthwhile projects for future volunteers. The highlight of the experience was being the only white face amongst 1,400 teaching staff and pupils and (I hope) being accepted as a useful additional pair of hands. Once I had written my report, I could volunteer classroom teaching, exam invigilation and marking, lend out my instant coffee and discuss cricket and football scores. I soon realised that I would not be able to solve any of the major problems facing the school (high absenteeism, high crime rates, poor school administration, lost hours of teaching, low staff morale, use of English as the medium of instruction when Xhosa was the first language, etc.).*

*Volunteers go out as idealists and come back as realists. Volunteers get more out of the experience than they can put in. Both true in my case.*

## Rob Evans

**Sometimes the late converts to travel are the most zealous. Rob Evans from South Wales had been to university, moved to London to work in the University of London Computing Centre and turned 28 without ever having left the country.**

*If Derren Brown had come up to me in the street five years ago and said that I would be taking a year off work to travel around south-east Asia, I (and almost everybody that knew me at the time) would have laughed in his face. I hadn't travelled widely. In fact, I hadn't travelled at all. I had not travelled as a child, and did not pick up the habit in university or straight afterwards. The first time I left the country was at age 28 for a conference shortly after starting a new job, and I started to see the attractions of other countries, and soon enough I was hooked.*

*Like many others I started to throw random comments around that maybe someday I would take some time off work to do a bit more travelling, but nobody believed me, and I am not even sure I believed it myself. I had a grand plan for a trip along the Andes but this had to be scaled down to a more realistic month of backpacking around Peru with a couple of friends. After I'd been home for a while I went to a party to welcome home some backpackers I'd met in South America. Earlier that day my landlord had mentioned that he would like to reclaim the flat I was renting as his daughter had found a job nearby, so a couple of choices started to crystallise.*

*On one hand I could make my belated first step onto London's property ladder and scour the suburbs for a grotty flat. On the other I could blow the money I'd been saving for a deposit on doing the thing I'd been threatening and disappear to foreign climes for some time. Given that I was at a party with a large number of people who had been travelling themselves, there was probably only one way this decision was ever going to go.*

*Still unsure of my decision, I made the most of the obstacles that could have scuppered the plans. Thinking that six months would be more than enough time to see a lot of the world, I went to my boss and asked for a year off, hoping to bargain down. I didn't need to (and I am eternally grateful to them for promising to keep my job open for me whilst I was away). One of the benefits of university employment appears to be that I could take a year off quite simply.*

*So now instead of six months to fill, I had twelve. What was I going to do? I decided to see if I could find something useful to fill a few months. A quick search on the web turned up an option that appealed with Trekforce Expeditions: I had already decided I wanted to go to Southeast Asia and they offered a two-month conservation project followed by an optional two months of teaching. I had never taught before and, whilst the thought of it was slightly unnerving, one of the reasons for travelling was to experience something new, so I signed up for the full programme. I felt guilty at the thought of asking others to fund something I wanted to do, when I could afford it myself with the money I had saved. To this end, I did not do any fundraising and just paid the contributions of £3,000 plus flights to Borneo, equipment and vaccinations out of my savings.*

*While waiting for my year off to begin, doubts began to creep in. Was I making the right decision? How much older would I be on an expedition that appeared to be primarily aimed at students spending a gap year either before or after university? As it turned out, I was not the oldest, and there were several others in a similar situation taking an extended break from work. Some of these were the medical staff, also volunteers, but also included a 38 year-old who worked at Heathrow and another 32 year-old working for the Ministry of Defence.*

*Both phases of the expedition were experiences I hope to remember for a very long time. The conservation work involved camping in the rainforest of Borneo for two months working on one of the world's largest biodiversity projects. Accommodation was a hammock slung between a couple of trees, and the whole group had to work as a team to keep the camp in order and get the project work done. The teaching may have been less of a physical challenge, but it was certainly no less of a mental test. Based in a village that has no roads to it, I was teaching English to groups of 11-14 year-olds in classes of up to 39.*

*After the expedition finished, I stayed in Malaysian Borneo for another two months, travelling and researching some trekking information for the owner of a guesthouse, and then travelled for a month each in Peninsular Malaysia, Thailand, Laos, Cambodia and Vietnam before heading back home. The lowest point of the year was probably the time I was ill with suspected dengue fever. This required a five-day stay in hospital and a slightly longer time feeling less than 100%.*

*I learnt that it is easy to fill a year. Take your time and enjoy the view. Throughout the year I bumped into people who had a schedule and were zipping here and there without much chance to spend time in any particular place. The best thing you can do is to be conservative in what you think you can see, then when the boat that only runs once a week in the dry season doesn't have enough passengers to go and you have to wait for the next week's boat, you won't be stressing about it, you can just sit back and enjoy the fact this this is how locals travel. Rigid timetables, even the flexible rigidity as practised by British trains, is very hard to find outside first world countries, and it turns out not to be such a bad thing.*

*Of course, eventually the time came to wean myself back onto British time. Through much of the journey I'd been convinced, and to no small extent afraid, that settling back into work would come all too easily and my adventures in Asia would quickly be nothing but memories. I'm happy that it wasn't as easy as I was expecting. Happy because it means that my attitude to life has changed. Like the stories I hear from most people that take time off, about a month after I came back the post-travel blues started to kick in. My feet weren't so much itching as they felt like a cartoon image of magic boots, pulling me in all directions other than staying in the same place for an indefinite period. Now, two and a half months after returning, the sight of rain on track-side trees as I get the train to south Wales brings back images of freshly-soaked jungle. The freedom of time to myself had been replaced by the necessity to be in the office from morning until early evening, but at least now I can imagine that there is a goal for earning the money – the next trip!*

## Lucy Bailey

**Lucy was fleeing a broken heart in the one way she was sure would work because travel had cheered her up in the past. In her job as account handler for a tiny ad agency whose clients were all travel-based, she had worked on an awareness campaign for the Kenya Tourist Board. The campaign certainly worked on her because it was her first choice of destination:**

*The Internet is a wonderful thing. Virtually everyone has a website these days, so it was easy to get ideas. I sent off for written info as all organisations charged for their service and I wanted proof that they were a professional set-up who would really know what they were doing. The Leap first proposed Malawi to me, but there's no Acacia trees there and therefore no giraffes. I wanted the full-on African experience and was quite sure that I wanted to go to Kenya. It was clear that The Leap had experience here, so this swayed my decision.*

*I was away for four months, predominantly split between Shompole, a boutique eco lodge near the Tanzanian border and Naibor, their luxury semi-permanent tented camp just outside the Masai Mara. I also took time off to explore more of Kenya and was lucky enough to go on two safaris, both with tour guides that I'd met on camp. I really did pack an awful lot into this period and, without wishing to sound ludicrous, have never felt so alive.*

*Leaving Kenya was very hard, as I was just enjoying it so much and didn't want to return to the UK to face my old life. I had the chance to work in paradise for four months in just the most idyllic setting. One particular memory is of canoeing with some friends down the river near the lodge that ran along the floor of the Great Rift Valley and negotiating our way through some mangrove roots that formed an avenue over our heads. We turned a corner in the river to see a hippo sitting right in the water in front of us bathing and taking it easy. Hippos are notoriously dangerous and skittish and can easily kill you, but there was something quite fabulous about seeing it in its natural home and I wasn't frightened at all as I was just in awe. Well, maybe a little bit frightened.*

*I think you have to be a certain sort of person to take time away like this, but I was in such a negative, unhappy place and KNEW that travel and seeing the world had made me feel great in the past, so this was definitely the right country for me to choose to go to recuperate. It's actually quite a hard country to deal with 'properly' as it has so many ecological and social issues, but its beauty, friendliness and wildlife are incredibly rewarding. A very glum girl had left Heathrow in July and a better, shinier version of Lucy returned four months later. Now that's a great investment!*

## Karen Hedges

**Karen Hedges had been working in travel PR for eight years and was beginning to get bored. So at age 28 she decided to quit her job to go freelance and save for travelling and volunteering.**

Karen was looking for something completely different from her normal life, such as planting trees or something practical. She noticed a small ad for Azafady in the *Guardian* and applied for a ten-week placement to begin in January 2003. Azafady's partner NGO works only in the southeast of Madagascar which is the poorest region. Karen and nine other volunteers were taken into a remote village on foot to join an ongoing project. In this case, they were building desks for school children who had been sitting on the floor. Local men carried in the raw materials and the children helped with sanding, etc. The hardest part for Karen was living in a tent for the whole time, though she did adjust. The rest of the group was congenial, mostly British and in her age range (25-35).

While in Madagascar she learned that the growing problem of HIV is not being tackled and she formed the idea of returning to Madagascar at a future date to investigate it. First she had to save up enough money and luckily found well-paid freelance work soon after returning to England. She saved money by flat-sitting when she could or staying with various friends and relations including her grandmother. She also fund-raised for her project and liaised with Azafady to go out under their auspices. She spoke to government ministers and health officials to find out the scale of the problem (an estimated 1% of the 16,000,000 population is affected). She wrote a proposal for a two-year project in developing HIV education and did things like organise a concert for World Aids Day and write and distribute leaflets to boys attending football tournaments. Azafady is now raising funds to implement the programme.

Since then she has been working in Public Relations for Christian Aid and knows that her experiences in Madagascar proved at interview that she was the right person for the job. She has just returned from a PR trip to Recife Brazil, accompanying a journalist who was writing an article about a project to get street children and abused girls off the streets. Karen is finding her new job more fulfilling than the previous ones.

When she decided to take her gap year, she knew she wanted to change jobs but didn't know what she wanted. The career break helped her to choose a new direction, i.e. to work in the charity sector. She is glad that she took her year off later rather than straight out of university because it meant that she could pay for it upfront and not return in debt.

## Diane Ralph

**Diane participated in Cross-Cultural Solutions' Russia programme with her nephew, as part of a six-month break to celebrate her 50th birthday. She volunteered in an orphanage and a home for the elderly, both in Yaroslavl.**

*Nothing prepares you for the poverty of the orphanages like Perokopski or the Elderly placement. However, the warmth that oozes from these places is totally heart-wrenching and an experience I will never forget. Unfortunately, it hasn't completely changed me, maybe you have to do it a few times before you realise that you don't need everything in the shop, even if you can afford it.*

*In January this year I reached the tender age of 50. I had a beautiful home, a brand new car, a really good job and still I wasn't happy. As a birthday treat to myself, I decided to travel and take six months off doing nothing but what I wanted to do. So I packed in my job, sold my car and my elder sister and I went to Hong Kong, Sydney, Ayers Rock, Cairns, Las Vegas and back. I then went to Spain for a couple of weeks before I decided to do some voluntary work.*

*I chose Russia ahead of all the other placements because I have always been fascinated by the secrecy of Russia and thought this was probably the best way of seeing the real side. From being met at the airport to leaving, the translators could not do enough for us. We would never have survived without them. Not only did I meet some really lovely Americans, but the children! It was awful at first because here were we from relatively wealthy backgrounds (compared to them) and they didn't envy us, they didn't ask us for anything, they were happy because we had given our time to play with them. That costs us nothing except our volunteer programme costs and it was worth every penny to see some of the photographs of the kids and their smiles. At the placement with the elderly there is a lovely lady who is referred to as the 'Flower Lady'. She makes flowers from any scrap of paper she can lay her hands on, sweet wrappers, etc. I bought a couple of sheets of wrapping paper which cost about 20p and I made a friend for life. Next time I went to visit, she gave me some flowers she had made from the paper.*

## Jo Hanbury

**As her 30th birthday loomed, Jo Hanbury decided to join VentureCo's 'Patagonia Venture' which consisted of a one-month language course in Cusco, Peru, one month working on the Polylepis tree conservation project in the high Andes and a two-month expedition from Machu Picchu, via Lake Titicaca, the Amazon jungle, Bolivia's Altiplano and Chile's Lake District, to the Patagonian ice-cap in Argentina.**

*After 5 years of number-crunching for a blue chip multi-national company, I decided it was time for a career break. South America was out there, just asking to be explored, but persuading stressed-out friends to quit their jobs and come along too proved an impossible task. Thankfully I found VentureCo, and a ready-made group of like-minded characters all looking for an experience to revitalise our lives.*

*And what an experience it was. I learnt Spanish in the 'Amigos' school in Cusco, where the money we paid for lessons was used to teach under-privileged local children English. I lived with a local Peruvian family, eating and drinking with them, enjoying their incredible hospitality and insane senses of humour, and by the time I left had become an avid supporter of the local football team, CienCiano. The whole of our VentureCo group spent a month up in the Andes, camping in a Quechua village, helping build a community hall, watched by herds of alpacas and the towering glacier-covered mountains. We surveyed high-altitude Andean forest, replanted a hillside with the help of hundreds of villagers, and hiked over stunning countryside, never once coming across other foreigners.*

*After the wonders of the Inca Trail, the expedition started for proper, taking in Bolivia, Chile, and ending at the bottom of Argentina, Tierra del Fuego, the end of the world. On the way, we hiked from snow-covered mountain passes down into steamy mosquito-infested jungle, we drove across vast bright salt-pans, past multi-coloured flamingo-filled lakes. We climbed snow-capped volcanoes, galloped horses in the Atacama desert, hiked for days in the wild beauty of Chilean Patagonia, and ice-climbed on and inside glaciers.*

*Three and a half months of this turned out to be not nearly enough, so once the VentureCo trip was over, I carried on travelling with some of my new-found friends. I then went over to Australia and China. Now I'm finally back in London, with a very different view of the world, a fresh desire to choose the career I really want to have, and albums full of wonderful memories. And after another five years' work I fully intend to do it all again in another part of the world, because somehow I don't think those two-week holidays you get to take twice a year can even begin to compare!*

## Rachael Wood

**After working in media jobs throughout her 20s, Rachael from Kent describes the motivations and rewards of taking a large chunk of time out to travel. In her opinion, travelling makes you hugely employable. You have learnt skills, conquered challenges and are grounded as a person. She now works as marketing manager for the company Gap Year for Grown Ups and says that her new job is one she is passionate about.**

*I have always dreamed of travelling the world. When I was young I made myself a promise that I would see the world by the time I turned 30. After university I chose to concentrate on building a career in media and it seemed that every time my travel bug bubbled to the surface, a promotion was in sight and I squashed it back down with a pay rise and new challenges.*

*With hindsight I realise that I had never done what was expected of people in their mid-20's. Marriage- and mortgage-free, I had subconsciously kept myself free of ties. Turning 29 and seven months into a new job I knew it was now or never. I told a few family and friends and was shocked at the barriers they foresaw filled with negativity – 'what about your career? What about your house and belongings? Pensions? Money? Us?' and the most popular one 'What will you do when you return?'. I realised everyone was voicing all the barriers that I had put in my way myself which had made me put off my trip for eight years.*

*Life is for living and you only get one life. I wanted to make the most of my one-year career break and it was fine-tuned to include all the places I had ever dreamt of visiting, though of course some will have to wait for another time! The plan was South America, New Zealand, Australia and South East Asia. I ended up visiting 16 different countries and was away for 20 months in total.*

*My trip was 'A Trip of Firsts' - First time……hiking on a glacier with crampons, snorkelling on the Great Barrier Reef, whale watching, sleeping under the stars in a hammock, dancing to the beat of the carnival drums in Rio, swimming with dolphins, watching Ayers Rock glow at sunrise, meditating with monks in Thailand, holding a koala bear, playing with orphaned street kids, bush camping, New Year water festivals in Laos, sand boarding down giant sand dunes, full moon parties, travelling to remote islands by fishing boats, 60 hours on a bus with no stop, trekking in snow capped mountains and volcanoes, jungles, tropical islands, waterfalls, remote hill tribe villages, playing with baby elephants…My list and memories are endless, along with the people that I met and the cultures that I experienced…. my world has opened up….I lived my dream.*

## Davide Tassi

**Davide Tassi is an Italian national who speaks six languages including Spanish. At age 33 he was working in the financial corporate world in Luxembourg but becoming dissatisfied with this life and had some ethical concerns about his employment. He had travelled widely and especially liked Latin America so decided to leave his job, possibly for a permanent change (though that was not to be). He had modest savings and lived on $12,000 for 14 months.**

Davide knew that he wanted to go to Ecuador because he had been there before and understood its potential. He then began the laborious task of finding a suitable NGO to which he could give his time. He knew that he did not want to pay high fees to a placement agency and he also knew that he did not want to dig holes or do any other lowly work that local people could do. He was looking for something that could use his specialised business skills, though he knew that success would also depend on retaining a passion for caring.

He was particular about the NGO's philosophy of development since so many of them are not sustainable. Non-profit-making is bad in his view because it means that the NGO may not survive. He became involved with re-structuring the way one NGO worked and then turned his attention to the projects with which the NGO was involved, in this case cocoa marketing. The first step (at least half the battle) was to get people to co-operate and work together, which was difficult to achieve in this case. Of course the logistics are so much more difficult than in Europe with its sophisticated infrastructure.

For one month he moved to an affiliated NGO and worked with indigenous people in Amazonia who were planting cocoa trees (which don't bear a yield for at least three years). He described this month as 'very beautiful' and it was here that he realised that what you give is much less than what you get. Overall he feels that he saw some successes and the contribution he made to assist trade prospects continues.

By October 2005, he was running seriously low on funds and knew that he would have to return to Europe. But before leaving South America, he decided to go to Brazil to learn Portuguese. Through internet searches he came across Iko Poran (see entry). He felt that the $125 fee he paid to Iko Poran plus the required $125 donation to the project was fair. Iko Poran have been in existence only for a couple of years, facilitating the matching of volunteers with projects in Rio. Davide worked with 6 to 12 year olds at the National Circus School which builds the confidence of street kids and potentially allows them to become involved with the Circus, organising shows, etc.

He was sufficiently advanced in his profession not to be worried about slotting back into the workforce and now works in the area of European compliance for Citigroup, a company that despite some bad publicity has more corporate responsibility than some. He believes that more and more companies are looking at the human component as well as the professional skills. He believes that it is easier to talk to the MD of a company than a medicine man. It takes skill and sensitivity to talk to peasant farmers in a language they can understand. He is proud of how he adapted from a pampered European lifestyle to living in a hut.

## Marcelle Salerno

**It is rarer for Americans to take a mature gap year than for Europeans. Undeterred, Marcelle Salerno decided to take five years off to travel on all the continents after her job disappeared:**

*I was 42 years old and had been working for 20 years when I was laid off from my job as an insurance industry executive. I decided to seize the opportunity and change my life. Most people I knew were supportive but said they wouldn't do it (even if they had the money) because of the dangers and loneliness of travelling by yourself; this surprised me. I thought money would be the biggest obstacle. But it wasn't, it was fear.*

*In order to afford it, I downsized. As a middle-aged single woman with no kids it wasn't hard. I sold most of my possessions and the rest I put into storage. I live off savings and investments. I decided on five years because there are five continents and I thought if I budgeted wisely the money might last that long. I plan to spend six months a year on the road.*

*I chose Global Vision International because GVI was one of the few organisations with a marine programme in Africa. I spent ten weeks in the Seychelles doing marine surveys and five weeks in South Africa on a game reserve working on animal behavioural studies. The Seychelles is a very expensive place to visit as a tourist. Volunteering can be a very economic way to visit an expensive or exclusive destination. You won't get the first class amenities but you will get to see the same things the tourists are paying a much higher price to see. I found that while the young people enjoy hanging out and making new friends, older people want to see the sights and do things. On the African Game reserve we were staying in the same Wildlife Park as a 5-star resort. We saw the same animals as the guests who had paid five times what we paid. Now that's a bargain.*

*One of the highlights of my travels so far was when I was 'trapped' in Morocco during Eid Al-Kabeer (which means the Grand Feast). The entire country came to a halt and there was no transport or food available to buy for a couple of days. A local family took me in and I joined them in the ritual slaughter of a lamb for the feast. You don't get to see that on your average tourist bus trip.*

*It is eye-opening for most Americans to discover how the rest of the world views American culture. You can only appreciate these observations when you live with people and remain in an area for an extended period of time. I am pleased to say that I have made a few long-term friendships from both volunteer programmes.*

## Allan and Annabel Westray

**After shortlisting several volunteer-sending organisations, Allan and Annabel Westray finally plumped for MondoChallenge after meeting in person with the helpful and enthusiastic director:**

*I had sold my wine-importing company and wanted a complete break and change from corporate life UK so decided to travel around India with my wife for six weeks before we both went on to work as teachers in a small school near Darjeeling in North India. We stayed at the school for three months and had a wonderful time.*

*Our decision met with lots of encouragement and envy from our family and friends. I was 55 years old and Annabel was 50 so some were surprised that we were having a gap year at this stage of our life, especially our three children who were in their 20's.*

*Initially it was tough getting used to very simple living conditions, such as the lack of water and utilities. But establishing wonderful relationships with the children at our school (age 3 years to 9 years) and their families was a real highlight.*

*It was almost harder returning to a normal UK lifestyle upon our return as we had become accustomed to a very different life, even if only for five months. We also realised how lucky we are and how much we take for granted in the UK. After about two months we had acclimatised again and in most ways reverted to our pre-India lifestyle. The experience was a great success for both of us. We met so many really lovely Indian people who showed us so much kindness and their wonderful sense of humour.*

## Bradwell Jackson

**American Bradwell Jackson's holiday travels throughout his 20s and 30s persuaded him to re-invent himself as a long-term world traveller. His dream is to wander the earth in a happy-go-lucky way, earning and paying as he goes.**

*After reading* Work Your Way Around the World, *I wondered if it was really possible to get a job teaching English so easily. Well I found out that it is. While vacationing in Madagascar, I decided on my last day there to pop into an English school I saw at the bottom of the hill where I was staying. All I wanted to know was what the requirements were to be an Engiish teacher in this school, but an hour after meeting with the owner, he offered me a job! This was the catalyst to 'go for it'.*

*I made the decision to quit my job, leave my home, give away most of my belongings to charity, and sell my car so that I could wander the earth freely. I left for Mexico on the last day of 2005. I was sitting at a metro stop in Mexico City, trying to figure out what school to go to for my first planned job enquiry. After I decided that the particular school I had in mind was too far away, I looked up and saw an English school right across the street. Providence, I thought. I was right. I sauntered on upstairs, cheerfully asked if they needed an English teacher, and about an hour and a half later, I was told when to start my training. It really was that easy.*

*I teach a range of students including some teenage girls. For them I came up with the idea of asking them to talk about a television programme* Rebelde, *which is very popular amongst teens here. I also got them to pull out a teen magazine and tell me about the stars in it. I have also asked my students about popular Spanish songs and asked them to translate them into English for me.*

*Mexico is the first country I have visited on my world wanderings (which may last up to three years) and I can't believe how lucky I've been. The people are top-notch and I certainly must count my blessings. This inspires me to think that I could be just as lucky in the other countries I go to. I have very itchy feet, and I've got to keep moving.*

*The next country I plan to visit is England. My heritage is there, and I am named after a small town in Essex. As of June 2006 I will be going on to France and trying to get a job as an English teacher.*

## The Whitlock Family

**Lindsay Whitlock provides an honest and thoughtful account of her family's round-the-world travels. She was 28 and a full-time modern language teacher, her 39-year-old husband Nick was a tree surgeon, plus children Tom who was nine and Esther four when they left home. Although they experienced a few problems on returning to the 'real world' in southern England, these have not cancelled out the thrills and benefits of a year away, all on a strict family budget of £42 a day. Their story is told in more detail on their website www.thewhitlocks.org.uk.**

*The idea of travelling as a family came up, the opportunity arose, and it seemed to be a 'now-or-never' situation. Our aim was, of course, to see the world, and also to give our children the opportunity to experience Life, in a way that they cannot at home. We decided to live the dream, to exchange armchair for rucksack, and security for adventure!*

*Although my headteacher offered to keep my job open for me while I took a year's sabbatical, at the time I was feeling the need for a clean break, and opted to resign. We decided to go for one year, taking a full year out of teaching for me and a single full year out of school for the children. Once we had designed the route we wished to take, we divided the time fairly arbitrarily between the four continents we planned to visit. We booked the main flights beforehand, and treated each continent as a clean slate, arriving on our planned date, with our only constraint being the date and time of the onward flight at our overland destination.*

*The whole trip in fact fitted into our £25,000 overall budget, with the flights costing about £8000. It is so hard to choose a single highlight, as our experiences were so diverse. Some that come to mind are:*

- *The Wwoof farm we visited in Hungary where we spent one week on a goat farm in a remote area picking fruit, helping in the kitchen, looking after the herd of goats (which our ten-year old took to) and staying in an idyllic old farmhouse.*
- *Matema beach at the northern tip of Lake Nyasa/Malawi in Tanzania which turned out to be one of the most inaccessible places we reached, and our experiences with the people there were some of the most beautiful memories we brought home.*
- *Christmas on Mount Mulanje, Malawi, hiking for three days through beautiful, unspoilt countryside with a guide and porter.*
- *Our stay with the Cocama community in the jungle near Iquitos, Peru.*

*... and many, many more!!*

*Of course there were low points too like the night we spent at Keleti railway station in Budapest, having all been struck down with a severe tummy bug, to the point where we were unable to move and find accommodation, having arrived late at night. Even worse was the boat journey across Lake Malawi. We had been given every reason to believe that a ferry was in operation. However this turned out not to be true and, stranded in the unimaginably remote village on Mbamba Bay on the Tanzanian lake shore, we were left with very few options for continuing. We ended up accepting passage on a small cargo boat, which was unsuitable. This was probably the only time I seriously feared for our lives. I didn't include a detailed account on the online journal, as I honestly couldn't face reliving the experience to write one.*

*There were many surprises as to our differing reactions to experiences. Perhaps the biggest surprise was that, with all the thought we'd given to helping the children to adjust, they managed the upheaval in some ways far more effectively than we were able to! Coming home has not been easy at all which we were totally unprepared for! After a year of moving on every few days, of spending 24 hours a day together, of relying on each other for everything and of the biggest stress of each day being where the next meal/bed would come from, 'normality' was rather a distant memory.*

*For all of us, the feeling that we overcame difficulties and setbacks as a family to do something that some people at home thought impossible or impractical has been amazing. Our individual self-esteem, the children's problem-solving skills and self-belief, and a general bond between us of shared experience outside the norm have all been significant rewards and benefits. I think this is all the greater because we did our trip without the continued help or support of any outside agency. Of course, this also allowed us massive flexibility, opting in and out of different tours, activities and excursions as it suited us.*

*I'd say the main drawback of doing a trip in this way is the immense pressure it puts on relationships of individuals within the family. For us, getting a babysitter was only very rarely a possibility, due to the nature of our trip. We were often staying in one room, very often with less than four beds, and getting 'space' was a very real issue on a day to day basis. I think I speak for all of us when I say that we're genuinely proud of the fact that we, as individuals and as a family, survived and grew as a result.*

## Marjorie Harris

**Marjorie Harris was headteacher of an independent girls' school in Surrey when she decided it was time to call it a day (just prior to yet another inspection). She is now back at home, working part-time (as a school inspector).**

*I went to an open day of Teaching & Projects Abroad with my son who was deciding which project to do for his gap year, and began to consider the opportunities available for myself. I had two or three friends who were seriously ill and had not taken the opportunity to do anything other than work, and I decided not to do that! My family thought it was a great idea and encouraged me. My friends too thought that I had the right experience and outlook on life to benefit and be able to make a difference. My colleagues at school wanted me to take a sabbatical but I resigned.*

*Each break was for three months. On the first break I went for one month to Peru to train teachers and then to work in an orphanage in Bolivia. On the second break I went just to one location, an orphanage in Argentina. I did a course of Spanish before I went and was very glad I did although the organisation did not stipulate that it was a requirement. The cost of a three-month trip was £2,200 including 60 hours Spanish tuition plus £660 for the return flight.*

*The highlight was when we took a busload of the children to swim in a local pool, as they had never been before. The low point was when the director of the project was sacked and the other volunteers were not interested in continuing to work, so I had to carry on single-handed to achieve what I had gone to do. The event in Argentina that lingers with me still is the biscuit making. The children just loved cooking and icing the biscuits and preparing the fizzy drinks. We then took some to the special needs children in their house and the look of pleasure on their faces of sharing something with others was just magical. A new experience for everyone and so easy to organise!*

*These experiences were certainly very good for personal development. It is good to be on your own and have to do things for yourself and get along with strangers. The reward for me is that I have lots of new friends both young and old across the world and in this country. The children in the orphanage gave huge rewards by the end of the time I was there. Such a good thing to do to get to really know another culture and tolerate differences. The drawback is that you have to be prepared to live without luxury and tolerate poor organisation and some possible corruption. Be adaptable and be prepared to wait for things to happen. A willingness to adapt and contribute to any work going on that needs to be done will enable a volunteer to get the most out of the experience.*

## Sylvia Wright

**Sylvia Wright was 32 when she left Glasgow in September 2005 to join a series of volunteer projects in various countries through the Involvement Volunteers Association based in Australia. Part-way through her ten-month gap year, she wrote from New Zealand where she was working with adults with disabilities:**

*I always wanted to go travelling, however, I did not have the money or the confidence to do it ten years ago. I was too busy trying to get myself through university and then into a job and then buying a property. Then when most of my finances were pretty much in good order, I thought 'time to go'. I did try to negotiate a sabbatical with the local authority which employed me as a community worker, but it seems the wheels of bureaucracy were not in favour of supporting employees in this way. To finance my travels I took out a low interest loan and rented out my flat, plus took my credit card for emergencies.*

*I decided to divide up the time by deciding the countries I wanted to visit. As I had been thinking for a couple of years about going I had been looking into volunteer organisations all over the world and assessing the support they could give. I chose my agency and set up a programme of volunteer placements with them for all of the countries I wanted to go to. I liked IVI's website and the range of countries in which they have affiliated projects. I had to pay some fees to IVI for admin and placement but felt these were justified and cheaper than many.*

*Some placements required specialised skills or knowledge while others required none whatsoever - just a willingness to work and be part of a team - and that is pretty much the placements I chose! I have been to five countries so far – India, Nepal, Thailand, Australia and New Zealand. I have still to go to South Africa, Namibia, Botswana and Zambia before I return home. I especially enjoyed teaching English to Burmese children in the north of Thailand, and was very sad to leave those children. They were an inspiration to me. I have also enjoyed working with dolphins on the west coast of Australia, and learning about Ayurveda medicine and yoga in India. I have loved all of it, mainly the meeting of new friends and the things I have learned about other people, cultures, life and about myself.*

*I did not really have many expectations, I just wanted to see and feel and taste and participate in other lives and other cultures. Some have impressed me more than I ever expected they would. I must admit though that I did not realise full-time volunteering would be so full on. Some placements squeeze you for all you are worth! A good and a bad thing!*

*With hindsight, I think I would have organised fewer placements in advance, and more on my own. For the price of a phone call, I organised one in Australia working with Aboriginal young people (I am a youth worker after all) which included free room and board. I feel like I had a bit of a taster session with all of my countries, but sometimes it was a bit too rushed and a bit too organised. It would have been nice to stay in the same place a little bit longer at times and not be so tied to moving on at definite times.*

*The rewards of my experience are numerous. Mainly I have made so many new and wonderful friends, my confidence has increased, I have inspired other people, I feel part of a global community and see how small the world actually is, how alike we all actually are and how simple it really is to travel. People will always point you in the right direction. All you need is a map, a smile, a pair of jeans, a waterproof jacket, pair of shorts, couple of changes of underwear, some anti-malaria tablets, sandals and a pair of good walking shoes. Then off you go! Remember it's about having fun, and take time to watch the sunsets.*